EDUCATIONAL MEDIA AND TECHNOLOGY YEARBOOK

DONALD P. ELY and BARBARA B. MINOR,
Editors

EDUCATIONAL MEDIA AND TECHNOLOGY YEARBOOK

1993

VOLUME 19

Published in Cooperation with the
ERIC® Clearinghouse on Information & Technology
and the
Association for Educational Communications
and Technology

1993

Libraries Unlimited, Inc. • Englewood, Colorado

LIBRARIES UNLIMITED, INC.
P.O. Box 6633
Englewood, CO 80155-6633

Library of Congress Cataloging-in-Publication Data

Suggested Cataloging:

Educational media and technology yearbook,
    1993 volume 19 / Donald P. Ely and Barbara B. Minor, editors.—
Englewood, Colo.: Libraries Unlimited, 1993.
    xii, 369 p. 17x25 cm.
    Includes bibliographical references and index.
    ISBN 1-56308-153-9
    ISSN 8755-2094
    Published in cooperation with the ERIC Clearinghouse on Information
& Technology and the Association for Educational Communications and
Technology.
    1. Educational technology—yearbooks.   2. Instructional materials
centers—yearbooks.   I. ERIC Clearinghouse on Information & Technology.
II. Association for Educational Communications and Technology.
III. Ely, Donald P.   IV. Minor, Barbara B.
LB 1028.3.E372   1993   370.778

Contents

Part One
TRENDS AND ISSUES

Part Two
THE PROFESSION

The Year in Review

Part Three
CURRENT DEVELOPMENTS

Part Four
LEADERSHIP PROFILE

Part Five
THE YEAR IN REVIEW

Part Six
ORGANIZATIONS AND ASSOCIATIONS IN NORTH AMERICA

Part Seven
GRADUATE PROGRAMS

Part Eight
MEDIAGRAPHY
Nancy R. Preston

Preface:
Of Encyclopedias, Textbooks, Yearbooks,
and Electronic Publishing

My writing and editorial tasks this year have included a wide range of textual formats: encyclopedias, textbooks, and yearbooks. Electronic publishing has crept in to disturb the more familiar formats of printed communication. The often-touted concept of the "paperless" work environment does not seem to be any nearer with the expanded volume of printed information. Yet, a basic question of information-seeking educators remains, "Where do I go to get information about _____?"

THE ENCYCLOPEDIA

This question was paramount in the preparation of the *International Encyclopedia of Educational Technology* (in press). The scope of information in an encyclopedia is comprehensive because people often use it to obtain basic, factual information about specific topics within the field. This means that the definition of the field has to be more or less congruent between the editors and the potential users. It also means that the information is "bare bones," that is, the essential facts surrounding the terms are spelled out in sufficient detail that introductory questions are answered and references are provided to go deeper into the topic. The encyclopedia and dictionary (or glossary) are the fundamental tools of the serious information-seeker. Encyclopedia entries help the user to get started.

THE TEXTBOOK

The textbook is a source for more detailed information. It goes beyond the encyclopedia or dictionary by providing a synthesis of existing knowledge, usually from a variety of sources and in detail. It usually draws on conventional knowledge, research findings, examples of practice, and graphic illustrations. It is a state-of-the-art description of what is known and generally accepted in a field at that time. It is usually dated, though, because the time between writing and publication is so long that cutting-edge developments have occurred since the manuscript was submitted for publication. It is considered to be an overview of a body of knowledge or sometimes an area of specialization. Its most frequent use is within a course of study and it is often thought to be the "content" of the course.

THE YEARBOOK

The yearbook has a different function than the encyclopedia or textbook. It is a chronicle of current events. It describes the "hot" topics of the time. It is a reference of current, dependable information that usually cannot be found elsewhere or is difficult to locate. The yearbook serves as documentation of a field's growth and development over the years. It should be possible to trace a topic over time. A yearbook such as the *Educational Media and Technology Yearbook* follows a theme from year to year, rather than introducing a new theme each year. Journals do provide some of the same type of information, but they are usually more random than organized. Each issue is often thematic. Some journals include most manuscripts that are submitted, with no particular attempt to organize them.

This 1993 *EMTY* picks up the themes of last year: trends and issues in the "futures" article by Howard Sullivan and colleagues and the state-of-the-profession in the articles about AECT, the new doctoral program at Northwestern University, and the salary study by Hutchinson and Rankin. As usual, the bulk of the substantive part of the book focuses on current developments in the field: theory, hardware, software, dissemination, applications of technology, organizations, and new delivery systems. There is just one leadership profile this year: Dr. Harry A. Johnson, the 1993 AECT Distinguished Service Award recipient.

As usual, the up-to-date references about educational media and technology organizations and associations in North America, graduate programs in the field, and the mediagraphy are included. Currency and accuracy are important here. All organizations are contacted each year to obtain updates for each listing. There is no other place where all this information is brought together in one source.

ELECTRONIC PUBLISHING?

Will encyclopedias, textbooks, and yearbooks continue to be published, as electronic publishing becomes more accessible? We know of dozens of online journals and desktop publications that are available electronically. Will this be one more source? Will this source replace or add to the publications already available? Will this source permit more selective choices of what individuals want to read? Will it be more current than yearbooks? These questions will be addressed in the years to come. *EMTY* will continue to be available, but its format may change or it may offer alternative formats to provide access to the same information. Stay tuned.

We hope that the *Educational Media and Technology Yearbook 1993* finds its place alongside your educational technology encyclopedia, glossaries, textbooks, and journals. It fulfills a unique function.

Donald P. Ely

Contributors to the
Educational Media and Technology Yearbook 1993

Deborah Y. Bauder, Learning Center Director
SUNY Institute of Technology at Utica/Rome
PO Box 3050
Utica, NY 13504-3050

David Carr, Dean of Social Sciences
Stockton State College
Jimmie Leeds Road
Pomona, NJ 08240-9988

Carrie Costamagna, Market Development
    Manager
AUTODESK, INC.
2320 Marinship Way
Sausalito, CA 94963

Dr. John Cradler, Director
Educational Technology
Far West Laboratory for Educational Research
    and Development
730 Harrison Street
San Francisco, CA 94107-1242

Michael B. Eisenberg, Professor
School of Information Studies and Director
ERIC Clearinghouse on Information & Technology
4-194 Center for Science and Technology
Syracuse University
Syracuse, NY 13244-4100

John Evans, Professor of Education and the
    Learning Sciences
Northwestern University
1890 Maple Avenue
Evanston, IL 60201

Jinny Goldstein, Vice President
Education Project Development
Public Broadcasting System
1320 Braddock Place
Alexandria, VA 22314

Barry Harper
Faculty of Education
University of Wollongong, PO Box 1144
Wollongong, NSW 2500, Australia

Dr. John C. Hedberg, Associate Professor in
    Information Technology in Education
Faculty of Education
University of Wollongong, PO Box 1144
Wollongong, NSW 2500, Australia

Andres Henriquez
Center for Technology in Education
Bank Street College of Education
610 West 112th Street
New York, NY 10025

Margaret Honey, Associate Director
Center for Technology in Education
Bank Street College of Education
610 West 112th Street
New York, NY 10025

Dr. Joseph A. Hutchinson, Associate
    Director
Division of Instructional Support and
    Development
118 Himes Hall
Louisiana State University
Baton Rouge, LA 70803-3504

Ann R. Igoe
Arizona State University
College of Education
Tempe, AZ 85287

David H. Jonassen
Instructional Technology Program
School of Education
University of Colorado at Denver
Denver, CO 80204

Elizabeth E. Jones
Arizona State University
College of Education
Tempe, AZ 85287

Larry Kitchens, Director
Center for Instructional Services
Texas Christian University
Fort Worth, TX 76129

James D. Klein
Arizona State University
College of Education
Tempe, AZ 85287

Mary Harley Kruter, Manager of the PBS Math
    Service
Education Product Development
Public Broadcasting System
1320 Braddock Place
Alexandria, VA 22314

Rose M. Marra
AT&T, Technical Staff
11900 North Pecos
Denver, CO 80234

Suzanne McNamara
Faculty of Education
Monash University
Wellington Road
Clayton, Victoria 3168, Australia

Dr. Roy D. Pea, Chair
Learning Sciences Ph.D. Program
Institute for Learning Sciences
Northwestern University
1890 Maple Avenue
Evanston, IL 60201

Mary Planow, Assistant Professor of Computer
    Science
SUNY Institute of Technology at
    Utica/Rome
PO Box 3050
Utica, NY 13504-3050

Nancy R. Preston, Assistant Director
ERIC Clearinghouse on Information & Technology
4-194 Center for Science & Technology
Syracuse University
Syracuse, NY 13244-4100

James Purcell, Manager
Education Department
AUTODESK, INC.
2320 Marinship Way
Sausalito, CA 94963

Dr. Pauline M. Rankin, Director
Division of Instructional Support and
    Development

118 Himes Hall
Louisiana State University
Baton Rouge, LA 70803-3504

Jim Ritts
President of Network Affairs
Whittle Educational Network
333 Main Street
Knoxville, TN 37902-1807

Ron Sarner, Professor of Computer Science
SUNY Institute of Technology at
    Utica/Rome
PO Box 3050
Utica, NY 13504-3050

Wilhelmina C. Savenye
Arizona State University
College of Education
Tempe, AZ 85287

Dr. Howard J. Sullivan
Arizona State University
College of Education
Tempe, AZ 85287

Don Sutton, Vice President and Managing
    Director
Mind Extension University
9697 East Mineral Avenue
PO Box 3309
Englewood, CO 80155-3309

Roy Tennant, Public Service Automated
    Systems Coordinator
The Library
University of California, Berkeley
Berkeley, CA 94720

Vykuntapathi Thota, Director
University Center for Instructional Media and
    Technology
Virginia State University
Petersburg, VA 23803

Barry Willis, Statewide Director of Distance
    Education
University of Alaska
3900 University Lake Drive
Anchorage, AK 99508

Part One
Trends and Issues

Introduction

At the entrance to the National Archives on Pennsylvania Avenue in Washington, D.C., is a stone block with the phrase "What is past is prologue" chiseled on the surface. If we take these words as a theme for this section of the *Yearbook*, we could look back to the last edition (1992) and discover "Trends in Educational Technology" as the opening chapter. There is some logic in tracing the trends to determine indicators of the future of the field. Sullivan, Igoe, Klein, Jones, and Savenye have performed that service for us.

However, trends look backward over time. It is difficult to determine a trend unless there are baseline data collected over time. Trends are data-based analyses that tell where we have been. They do not necessarily predict the future, nor are they intended to do so. There is a temptation to "ride the curve" from the past, through the present, and to the future. Usually such extrapolations of the future conclude that there will be more of the same.

When individuals are asked about future predictions, the baseline is usually the present with projections into the future. Sullivan et al. asked informed professionals where they thought the field was heading. This crystal ball-gazing exercise blended some observations of the past with current developments to yield perceptions of future directions for the field. In this case, the data are largely in the heads of the individuals and are based on their own experiences. The results come from a large number of respondents who agree (or disagree) with each other.

Charles Wilson, the former chief executive of General Motors, once said, "Of course I'm interested in the future; that's where I am going to spend the rest of my life." Professionals in educational media and technology will be spending the rest of their lives in a future that promises to be substantially different than the past. This chapter serves to give us a glimpse of that future as perceived by 268 professionals who were asked to think ahead. Do they go too far? Are they overly conservative? Only time will tell as trends are analyzed early in the next century.

Educational Technology 2010
A Look Ahead*

Howard J. Sullivan
Ann R. Igoe
James D. Klein
Elizabeth E. Jones
Wilhelmina C. Savenye
Division of Psychology in Education
Arizona State University

INTRODUCTION

This study was conducted to determine the opinions of a broad-based sample of educational technology professionals and students about the future of our field. A nationwide sample of 268 university personnel (faculty members, doctoral students, master's students) and trainers completed a 30-item Likert-type survey covering six topic areas: Educational Technology and Learning Theory, Instructional Design Models, Technology and Individualized Instruction, Advances in Technology, Educational Technology and Schools, and Employment and Job Opportunities. The overall results reveal that educational technologists have a positive outlook toward the future of our field. Opinions were most positive in the areas of Educational Technology and Learning Theory, Employment and Job Opportunities, and Technology and Individualized Instruction, and were least positive in the Advances in Technology area. There were numerous significant differences of opinion on individual items across the four respondent groups, with the greatest number of differences occurring between faculty members and master's students.

PERSPECTIVES ON THE FUTURE

Suppose that a favorite colleague of yours were to call you and ask you to give a talk to the faculty and graduate students at his university about the future of educational technology. Without much thought, you would accept. Right?

But shortly after you hang up, reality sets in as you think about what you've just done. "The future of educational technology? How can I talk about that for 45 minutes?"

That was the problem recently faced by the senior author of this article. I'd made a commitment to speak, but I quickly realized that I had no idea what I could talk about.

Soon it occurred to me that the literature in our field could help me out. Just check what the authors in our leading journals are saying about the future and talk about that.

*This article is reprinted in modified form with permission of the Association for Educational Communications and Technology (AECT) from an article titled "Perspectives on the Future of Technology" published in *Educational Technology Research and Development* 41:2, 97-110 (1993).

I tried that approach, but it didn't work. Only a few articles proved to be very relevant for my purpose, and these articles did not provide broad coverage of the field. Even worse, I found that I didn't agree with many of the statements in the articles. Some of the predictions and assumptions about the future just didn't ring true for me.

"What do other people in our field think about these ideas?" I wondered. I decided to try to find the answer to this question by asking the faculty and graduate students at my own university and subsequently at the university where I had agreed to speak. Fortuitously, an opinion survey plus the ensuing discussion could easily fill up the 45 minutes for my talk there.

It didn't stop there, however. As I developed the survey, some of my co-workers and I got excited about the idea of a more comprehensive study. We decided to conduct a national survey, using the data from the initial two universities as pilot information. This article reports the results of our investigation.

Information about the future of educational technology is, of course, important for what we do today. It can help us determine the jobs for which we should train people, the system components and techniques for use in training settings, university curricula and instructional methods in educational technology, and the focus of our research.

Educational technology is a new discipline. We don't have a scientific basis for predicting its future well. The opinions of professionals in our field may be our best source of information about its future. However, the existing literature does not provide a comprehensive and unbiased information base. Most publications related to the future of educational technology deal primarily with only one or two areas in the field, and collectively they do not provide broad coverage of it. Moreover, these publications typically reflect the opinions of only a single author or a small group of co-authors. These individuals are often experts in their particular areas, but it is not uncommon for their expertise to be accompanied by a bias toward their own area and its importance in the broader field.

The present study was conducted to determine the opinions of a broad-based sample of educational technology professionals and students about the future of our field. Responses to the opinion survey used in the study yielded a measure of opinions across all respondents and a comparison of the opinions of university faculty members, doctoral students, master's students, and personnel employed in training positions.

A comprehensive sample for the study was obtained by surveying educational technology faculty and graduate students at 10 universities and individuals employed as training managers, trainers, and instructional designers at corporations and other agencies nationwide. The 10 universities were selected because their educational technology programs are well known and because the universities provide a geographic balance nationally. Training personnel were selected from individuals known personally by the investigators and from those recommended by other trainers and by faculty at other universities.

The opinion survey used in the study covered six topic areas derived from an analysis of recent literature in educational technology. Collectively, the six areas and their accompanying items in the opinion survey provide broad general coverage of the field of educational technology. The six topic areas, accompanied by brief descriptions of their content and by references that were useful in deriving each area and/or formulating survey items for it, are listed here:

- *Educational Technology and Learning Theory*. The influence of learning theory and cognitive psychology on educational technology and the influence of educational technology on learning theory (Ely 1990; Gagne 1986; Hannafin and Reiber 1989; Winn 1989).

- *Instructional Design Models*. The importance of improved instructional design models and the characteristics that will improve such models (Clark 1989; Kerr 1989; Merrill, Li, and Jones 1990).

- *Technology and Individualized Instruction.* The influence of computer-based instruction on individualization of instruction and the responsiveness of instructional systems to individual learners (Hannafin 1992; Jonassen 1991; Kinzie 1990; Ross and Morrison 1989).

- *Advances in Technology.* The degree to which computers and technology will assume the roles of teachers in delivering instruction and of instructional designers in designing it (Butterfield and Nelson 1989; Ely 1990; Li and Merrill 1991; Richards 1989).

- *Educational Technology and Schools.* The role of educational technology in teacher education, school reform and restructuring, and the design and delivery of classroom instruction (Branson 1990; Kerr 1989; Reigeluth 1989; Reiser and Salisbury 1991).

- *Employment and Job Opportunities.* The need for personnel in educational technology, the major growth area for employment, and the training emphases for graduate programs (Bratton 1988; Reiser 1988; Schwen 1988).

METHOD

Sample

The final sample consisted of 268 respondents: 53 university faculty members, 85 doctoral students, 70 master's students, and 60 trainers. The return rate from trainers was 60 percent. The method of distributing and collecting the survey at each university—through a faculty contact person at the university—precluded determination of an overall return rate for university personnel.

The 10 universities participating in the study were Arizona State, Florida State, Georgia, Indiana, Memphis State, Minnesota, Penn State, San Diego State, Syracuse, and Utah State. The majority of the trainers were employed by large international corporations, including American Express, Arthur Andersen, IBM, Intel, and Motorola.

Survey Measure

The 30-item survey of opinions on the future of educational technology was constructed to cover the six topic areas with five items per area. The survey consisted of five-choice Likert-type items with response choices ranging from strongly agree (scored as 1) to strongly disagree (scored as 5). Items were randomly distributed throughout the survey rather than being formatted into the six topic areas. Respondents were directed to consider the reference period for the "future" to be the next two decades. All 30 survey items are included by topic area in Tables 2 through 7 in the results section.

The pilot version of the survey consisted of statements taken verbatim or nearly verbatim from journal articles, mostly from *Educational Technology Research and Development* (*ETR&D*), and that dealt directly with the future or had clear implications for it. This version was administered to a total of approximately 80 faculty members and graduate students at Arizona State University and Florida State University. Data and suggestions from these respondents were then used to revise the survey into the final version.

The revisions for the final version of the survey changed it into a broader-based measure that focused more on respondents' opinions about the future of educational technology and less on their agreement or disagreement with statements in the literature per se. However, the final version retained a strong basis in the literature because most of the items were initially taken directly from statements in it or were derived by modifying such statements.

Procedures

One faculty member at each of the 10 universities agreed to serve as a contact person to receive, distribute, collect, and return the copies of the survey at his or her university. The surveys and a set of directions were sent directly to each contact person, who subsequently returned the surveys in a single packet after they were completed.

A total of 100 surveys were distributed to trainers. Most were sent individually, although multiple copies were sent to a few training personnel who had previously agreed to enlist the cooperation of other trainers at their workplace. Trainers returned their completed surveys individually in stamped return envelopes provided by the researchers.

Data Analysis

Mean scores were computed for faculty, doctoral students, master's students, trainers, and all respondents combined for each of the 30 survey items and each of the six topic areas. MANOVA was used to test for significant differences between the four respondent groups on the individual items within each topic area. The acceptable significance level was set at $p < .01$ because of the large overall number of comparisons. A Scheffé test was also used to test for significant differences between universities on each item.

RESULTS

The results are reported here across topic areas, within each topic area, for individual items with the highest and lowest levels of overall subject agreement, and by university.

Mean Scores by Topic Area and Respondent Group

Table 1 shows the mean scores, or levels of agreement, for each of the six topic areas and four respondent groups. The highest level of agreement for a topic area was with the statements in the Educational Technology and Learning Theory area, with an overall mean of 2.26. Two other areas—Employment and Job Opportunities, and Technology and Individualized Instruction— were close behind with mean scores of 2.29. The lowest level of agreement was for statements in the Advances in Technology area, which had an overall mean of 3.01. Mean scores by respondent group ranged from 2.34 for master's students, the highest level of agreement among the four groups, to 2.62 for faculty. (A score of 2.00 indicates agreement with a statement and a score of 3.00 indicates neutrality or no opinion on the statement.)

Mean Scores Within Topic Areas

This section reports the level of agreement with each individual item in each of the six topic areas. The topic areas are reported in the order of their overall mean scores from high agreement to low agreement.

Educational Technology and Learning Theory. The mean scores for Educational Technology and Learning Theory are shown in Table 2. The highest level of agreement (overall mean = 1.97) was for the statement "Advances in learning theory will have an important influence on practices in educational technology." Respondents also showed general agreement toward educational technology relying more on the field of human learning ($M = 2.15$), instructional design models based on

Table 1

Mean Scores by Topic Area and Respondent Group

Topic Area	Faculty	Doctoral	Master's	Trainers	Overall
N's	53	85	70	60	268
Ed. Tech. and Learning Theory	2.57	2.04	2.14	2.28	2.26
Employment and Job Opportunities	2.26	2.37	2.26	2.25	2.29
Technology and Individualized Instruction	2.52	2.29	2.14	2.22	2.29
Educational Technology and Schools	2.53	2.60	2.32	2.21	2.42
Instructional Design Models	2.69	2.45	2.38	2.35	2.47
Advances in Technology	3.12	3.12	2.80	2.99	3.01
TOTALS	2.62	2.48	2.34	2.38	2.45

Note: Scores are based on 1 = Strongly Agree to 5 = Strongly Disagree

cognitive psychology yielding better long-term learning than those based on behavioral psychology ($\underline{M}$ = 2.24), and research in educational technology contributing to the development of learning theory ($\underline{M}$ = 2.24).

Table 2 reveals a consistent pattern for doctoral students (overall $\underline{M}$ = 2.04) and master's students ($\underline{M}$ = 2.14) to show the strongest agreement with the individual statements and for faculty members to show the weakest agreement ($\underline{M}$ = 2.57). MANOVA at $\underline{p}$ <.01 followed by Scheffé tests on the significant individual items revealed significant differences between faculty members and both doctoral and master's students on three of the five items. Both doctoral students and master's students had significantly stronger agreement than faculty regarding the influence of advances on learning theory on educational technology, the long-term learning benefits of cognitive design models over behavioral design models, and the role of educational technology research in the development of learning theory. The scores of trainers, which consistently were near the overall mean for the individual items in this topic area, did not differ significantly from those of the other three respondent groups.

Employment and Job Opportunities. Table 3 shows the mean scores for Employment and Job Opportunities. Respondents showed strong agreement (overall $\underline{M}$ = 1.81) with the statement "There will be an increased need for personnel in educational technology." There also was general agreement with statements that training will be the major growth area for employment in our field ($\underline{M}$ = 2.02), that educational technology graduates should be more skilled in instructional design and development than in computers ($\underline{M}$ = 2.20), and that doctoral programs in our field should have a strong focus on preparing good researchers ($\underline{M}$ = 2.20). Respondents showed mild disagreement ($\underline{M}$ = 3.25) with the idea that graduate programs should focus more on preparing students for work in business and industry than in schools and universities.

MANOVA followed by Scheffé tests yielded significant differences between groups on two of the five Employment and Job Opportunities items. Faculty ($\underline{M}$ = 1.77) agreed significantly more strongly than master's students ($\underline{M}$ = 2.37) and trainers ($\underline{M}$ = 2.58) that doctoral programs should have a strong focus on preparing good researchers, and doctoral students ($\underline{M}$ = 2.05) agreed more with this same item than trainers. Trainers, on the other hand, agreed more strongly ($\underline{M}$ = 2.47) than each of the other three groups that graduate programs should focus more on preparing students for work in business and industry than in schools and universities.

Technology and Individualized Instruction. Table 4 shows the mean scores for the Technology and Individualized Instruction area. Respondents showed relatively high overall agreement in this area with statements "Computer-based instruction will result in much greater individualization of instruction" ($\underline{M}$ = 2.06) and "Computer-delivered instruction will benefit individual students by enabling them to manage their own learning to a greater extent" ($\underline{M}$ = 2.08). Master's students ($\underline{M}$ = 1.81) had significantly greater agreement than faculty ($\underline{M}$ = 2.31) with the statement that CBI will result in much greater individualization. Both master's students ($\underline{M}$ = 2.17) and doctoral students ($\underline{M}$ = 2.35) agreed more strongly than faculty ($\underline{M}$ = 2.90) that educational technologists should be as concerned about increasing individualization of instruction as about increasing learner achievement.

Educational Technology and Schools. The mean agreement scores for Educational Technology and Schools are shown in Table 5. The highest overall agreement was with "Educational Technology will play an increasing role in teacher education programs" ($\underline{M}$ = 1.96) and with "Educational Technology will play a major role in restructuring the schools" ($\underline{M}$ = 2.01). The lowest agreement, but still slightly above the "neutral or no opinion" level ($\underline{M}$ = 2.92), was with the statement "By the year 2010, more instruction in the schools will be delivered by computers and other media than by textbooks and teachers."

(Text continues on page 12.)

Table 2

Educational Technology and Learning Theory: Mean Scores

• Item Number		Faculty	Doctoral	Master's	Trainers	Overall
	N's	53	85	70	60	268
9 a	Advances in learning theory will have an important influence on practices in educational technology.	2.36	1.84	1.83	2.00	1.97
13	Educational technology will rely more on the field of human learning than it does now.	2.40	2.05	2.07	2.18	2.15
29 b	Instructional design models based on cognitive psychology will yield better long-term learning than models based on behavioral psychology.	2.69	1.96	2.15	2.33	2.24
24 c	Research in educational technology will play an increasing role in the development of learning theory.	2.70	2.06	2.07	2.32	2.24
18	Research in educational technology should focus more on variables related to cognitive processing and less on achievement per se.	2.71	2.29	2.59	2.58	2.52
TOTALS		2.57	2.04	2.14	2.28	2.26

• The item number column shows the number of the item on the 30-item survey. A letter after the number denotes a statistically significant difference, which is described beneath the table for that item.

a Faculty are significantly different than doctoral and master's students.
b Faculty are significantly different than doctoral and master's students.
c Faculty are significantly different than doctoral and master's students.

Table 3

Employment and Job Opportunities

Item Number		Faculty	Doctoral	Master's	Trainers	Overall
	N's	53	85	70	60	268
19	There will be an increased need for personnel in educational technology during the next two decades.	1.83	1.90	1.72	1.75	1.81
2	The major growth area for employment of educational technologists will be in the training field.	2.06	2.02	1.91	2.08	2.02
27	Graduates of educational technology programs should be more skilled in the design and development of instructional programs than in the computer area.	2.00	2.25	2.15	2.35	2.20
23 a	Doctoral programs in educational technology should have a strong focus on preparing good researchers.	1.77	2.05	2.37	2.58	2.20
12 b	Graduate programs in educational technology should focus more on preparing students for work in business and industry than in schools and universities.	3.64	3.61	3.17	2.47	3.25
	TOTALS	2.26	2.37	2.26	2.25	2.29

a   Master's students are significantly different than faculty; trainers are significantly different than faculty and doctoral students.

b   Trainers are significantly different than faculty, doctoral and master's students.

Table 4

Technology and Individualized Instruction

Item Number			Faculty	Doctoral	Master's	Trainers	Overall
		N's	53	85	70	60	268
3	a	Computer-based instructional programs will result in much greater individualization of instruction than we presently have.	2.31	2.18	1.81	1.95	2.06
30		Computer-delivered instruction will benefit individual students by enabling them to manage their own learning to a greater extent.	2.28	2.16	1.97	1.93	2.08
10		Instructional systems in the schools will be designed to be less group-based and more responsive to individual learners and learning styles.	2.60	2.26	2.29	2.32	2.35
15	b	Educational technologists should be as concerned about increasing individualization of instruction (learner control over instruction, self-selected objectives and strategies, match of instruction to learner characteristics, etc.) as about increasing learner achievement.	2.90	2.35	2.17	2.50	2.45
25		Systematic instructional programs in education and training will involve individual learners more in selecting their own instructional objectives.	2.51	2.51	2.46	2.40	2.47
		TOTALS	2.52	2.29	2.14	2.22	2.29

a Faculty are significantly different than master's students.
b Faculty are significantly different than doctoral and master's students.

Table 5

Educational Technology and Schools

Item Number		Faculty	Doctoral	Master's	Trainers	Overall
N's		53	85	70	60	268
22	Educational technology will play an increasing role in teacher education programs.	2.15	1.93	1.90	1.90	1.96
1	Educational technology will play a major role in the reform and restructuring of the schools.	2.06	2.11	1.97	1.88	2.01
7 a	The field of educational technology should make a strong effort to develop alternatives to the teacher-based model of public education.	2.40	2.85	2.43	1.95	2.45
17	Teachers will think of educational technology more as educational machines and software than as the systematic design of instruction.	2.68	2.99	2.68	2.75	2.79
26 b	By the year 2010, more instruction in the schools will be delivered by computers and other media than by textbooks and teachers.	3.36	3.12	2.62	2.59	2.92
	TOTALS	2.53	2.60	2.32	2.21	2.42

a Doctoral students are significantly different than trainers.
b Faculty and doctoral students are significantly different than master's students and trainers.

Significant differences occurred on two items in the Educational Technology and Schools area. Trainers ($\underline{M}$ = 1.95) showed significantly greater agreement than doctoral students ($\underline{M}$ = 2.85) with the statement "The field of educational technology should make a strong effort to develop alternatives to the teacher-based model of public education." Both trainers ($\underline{M}$ = 2.59) and master's students ($\underline{M}$ = 2.62) had significantly greater agreement than faculty ($\underline{M}$ = 3.36) and doctoral students ($\underline{M}$ = 3.12) with the idea that by the year 2010, more school instruction will be delivered by computers and other media than by textbooks and teachers.

Instructional Design Models. Table 6 shows the mean agreement levels for the Instructional Design Models area. Strongest overall agreement in this area was with the statement "Improving existing models of instructional design is an important goal for educational technology" ($\underline{M}$ = 2.07). Next strongest was with the idea that instructional design models can be improved more by increasing learners' personal control over instruction than by maintaining or increasing the instructional program's control over instruction ($\underline{M}$ = 2.22). Lowest overall agreement was with the statement that "Models of instructional design should focus at least as much on automated development of instructional programs by computer as on development of programs by instructional designers" ($\underline{M}$ = 3.11).

Significant differences between respondent groups were also obtained on two items in the Instructional Design Models area. Trainers ($\underline{M}$ = 2.00) agreed significantly more strongly than faculty members ($\underline{M}$ = 2.60) that increasing learners' personal control over instruction can yield greater improvement in design models than increasing the instructional program's control. Master's students ($\underline{M}$ = 2.87) agreed more strongly than faculty ($\underline{M}$ = 3.40) that design models should focus as much on computer-based automated development of instructional programs as on development by instructional designers.

Advances in Technology. Mean scores of the final topic area, Advances in Technology, are shown in Table 7. Respondents did not show strong general agreement with any of the five items in this area, with the highest overall mean at 2.67. Mean scores were below 3.00 for three of the five items: that technology-as-hardware will have a greater influence in education and training than technology as instructional systems design ($\underline{M}$ = 3.04); that the role of instructional designers will shift from deigning instruction to creating systems that design it ($\underline{M}$ = 3.16); and that expert systems will design effective instructional sequences or programs with minimal human input ($\underline{M}$ = 3.40). A significant difference between groups was obtained only on this final item, with master's students ($\underline{M}$ = 3.01) showing stronger agreement than either doctoral students ($\underline{M}$ = 3.51) or faculty members ($\underline{M}$ = 3.64).

Items with Highest and Lowest Agreement

Table 8 shows 5 items from the 30-item survey with the highest overall agreement from the 268 respondents and the 5 items with the lowest overall agreement. The table reveals that respondents showed the strongest agreement ($\underline{M}$ = 1.81) with the statement "There will be an increased need for personnel in educational technology in the next two decades" and the strongest disagreement ($\underline{M}$ = 3.40) with "Expert systems will design effective instructional sequences or programs with minimal human input." The mean agreement level ranged from 1.81 to 2.02 for the five highest-agreement items and from 3.04 to 3.40 for the five lowest-agreement items. Four of the five lowest-ranking items dealt with technology-as-hardware or with the use of computer or systems applications to design and develop instruction.

(Text continues on page 16.)

Table 6

Instructional Design Models

Item Number		Faculty 53	Doctoral 85	Master's 70	Trainers 60	Overall 268
	N's					
14	Improving existing models of instructional design is an important goal for educational technology.	2.21	1.93	2.07	2.15	2.07
8 a	Instructional design models can be improved more by incorporating steps that increase learners' personal control over instruction than steps that maintain or increase the instructional program's control over instruction.	2.60	2.21	2.13	2.00	2.22
20	Improved models of instructional design are likely to be more prescriptive (that is, provide more detailed guidance to designers) than our existing ones.	2.40	2.36	2.30	2.08	2.29
4	Improved models of instructional design will enable educational technologists to automate (by computer) much of the development of instructional programs.	2.85	2.52	2.53	2.56	2.60
28 b	Models of instructional design should focus at least as much on automated development of instructional programs by computer as on development of programs by instructional designers.	3.40	3.25	2.87	2.95	3.11
	TOTALS	2.69	2.45	2.38	2.35	2.47

a Faculty are significantly different than trainers.
b Faculty are significantly different than master's students.

Table 7

Advances in Technology

Item Number		Faculty	Doctoral	Master's	Trainers	Overall
	N's	53	85	70	60	268
21	Advances in the field of technology will enable the schools to deliver instruction effectively with much less direct involvement from the teacher.	2.57	2.89	2.46	2.70	2.67
16	Computer-delivered instruction will become capable of carrying out many of the human aspects of instruction.	2.94	2.87	2.54	2.73	2.77
5	Technology-as-hardware (i.e., computers, video cameras, etc.) will have a greater influence on education and training than technology as instructional systems design.	3.11	3.09	2.97	2.98	3.04
6	The role of instructional designers will shift from designing instruction to creating systems that design instruction.	3.32	3.24	3.01	3.07	3.16
11 a	Expert systems will design effective instructional sequences or programs with minimal human input.	3.64	3.51	3.01	3.48	3.40
	TOTALS	3.12	3.12	2.80	2.99	3.01

a   Faculty and doctoral students are significantly different than master's students.

Table 8

Items with Highest and Lowest Agreement

Rank	Item Statement	Mean
Highest Agreement		
1	There will be an increased need for personnel in educational technology during the next two decades.	1.81
2	Educational technology will play an increasing role in teacher education.	1.96
3	Advances in learning theory will have an important influence on practices in educational technology.	1.97
4	Educational technology will play a major role in the reform and restructuring of the schools.	2.01
5	The major growth area for employment of educational technologists will be in the training field.	2.02
Lowest Agreement		
26	Technology-as-hardware (i.e., computers, video cameras, etc.) will have a greater influence on education and training than technology as instructional systems design.	3.04
27	Models of instructional design should focus at least as much on automated development of instructional programs by computer as on development of programs by instructional designers.	3.11
28	The role of instructional designers will shift from designing instruction to creating systems that design instruction.	3.16
29	Graduate programs in educational technology should focus more on preparing students for work in business and industry than in schools and universities.	3.25
30	Expert systems will design effective instructional sequences or programs with minimal human input.	3.40

Mean Scores by Topic Area and University

Table 9 shows the mean scores by topic area for each of the 10 universities that participated in the study. The highest level of overall agreement across all areas was from San Diego State ($\underline{M} = 2.25$), followed by Georgia ($\underline{M} = 2.33$) and Penn State ($\underline{M} = 2.35$). The lowest agreement levels were from Arizona State and Memphis State, both with mean scores of 2.72.

MANOVA at $\underline{p} < .01$ followed by Scheffé tests revealed that significant differences between universities occurred on only 2 of the 30 items. Respondents from Georgia ($\underline{M} = 2.00$) showed significantly stronger agreement than those from Arizona State ($\underline{M} = 3.04$) with the statement "Educational technologists should be as concerned about increasing individualization of instruction as about increasing learner achievement." Respondents from Syracuse ($\underline{M} = 1.80$) agreed significantly more strongly than those from Arizona State ($\underline{M} = 3.00$) with the statement "Instructional design models can be improved more by incorporating steps that increase learners' personal control over instruction than steps that maintain or increase the instructional program's control over instruction."

DISCUSSION

It is apparent from this study that educational technologists have positive opinions abut the future of their field. They agreed most strongly of all with the idea that the need for personnel in their field will increase over the next two decades. They felt that educational technology will play important roles in teacher education and in the reform and restructuring of the schools. They also were optimistic that computer-based systems will result in more individualization of instruction and in greater learning benefits to individual students.

Distinct patterns of opinions occurred within each of the six topic areas. Responses in the Educational Technology and Learning Theory area revealed relatively strong opinions that advances in learning theory will influence educational technology and that research in educational technology will influence the development of learning theory. The statement "Advances in learning theory will have an important influence on practices in educational technology" had the third highest overall agreement among all 30 items on the survey. Faculty showed much less agreement than master's and doctoral students with statements about the increasing role of learning theory in educational technology. The higher agreement by graduate students may be due in part to a trend toward emphasizing learning theory and learning research more in educational technology graduate programs today than during earlier times when faculty members were in graduate school. The lower faculty agreement is also consistent with responses of faculty members to many other survey items dealing with changes in our field.

Overall opinions were very positive in the Employment and Job Opportunities area, with the exception of responses to the statement that graduate programs should focus more on preparing students for work in business and industry than in schools and universities. The highest overall agreement for any item, which indicated an increased need for personnel in educational technology, was from this topic area. Curiously, all four groups of respondents agreed quite strongly that our major growth area for employment will be in the training area, yet three of the four groups (trainers were the only exception) disagreed that graduate programs should focus more on preparing students for work in business and industry than in schools and universities. It seems more reasonable to conclude—as only the trainers did—that if training is to be our major growth area, it should receive relatively greater emphasis in our graduate programs. Faculty agreed especially strongly that doctoral programs should prepare good researchers, whereas trainers showed significantly lower agreement with this idea than faculty members and doctoral students.

Table 9

Mean Scores by Topic Area and University

Topic Area	Minn.	ASU	FSU	Memphis	Georgia	San Diego	Indiana	Syracuse	Utah St.	Penn St.	Overall
N's	14	25	15	8	33	26	16	25	17	29	208
Ed. Tech. and Learning Theory	2.18	2.24	2.58	1.93	2.17	2.03	2.45	2.23	2.52	1.95	2.23
Employment and Job Opportunities	2.29	2.33	2.26	2.15	2.32	2.13	2.26	2.51	2.33	2.34	2.29
Technology and Individualized Instruction	2.20	2.72	2.47	2.85	2.01	2.11	2.09	2.25	2.68	2.17	2.36
Educational Technology and Schools	2.47	2.74	2.53	2.93	2.44	2.29	2.40	2.58	2.62	2.24	2.52
Instructional Design Models	2.50	2.92	2.66	2.85	2.33	2.26	2.56	2.50	2.31	2.35	2.52
Advances in Technology	3.10	3.35	3.05	3.63	2.72	2.70	2.96	3.09	3.00	3.04	3.06
TOTALS	2.46	2.72	2.59	2.72	2.33	2.25	2.45	2.53	2.58	2.35	2.50

Opinions were also quite positive in the Technology and Individualized Instruction area. The sixth-ranking and eighth-ranking statements overall indicated agreement that CBI programs will result in greater individualization of instruction and will benefit individual students by enabling them to manage their own learning to a greater extent. The popularity of individualized instruction in our field can be seen in the general agreement ($\underline{M}$ = 2.45) that educational technologists should be as concerned about increasing individualization of instruction as about increasing learner achievement. Agreement on this item appears to ascribe at least equal importance to a means of instruction (individualized instruction) as to the end of producing greater student achievement, a notion that seems somewhat antithetical to common beliefs about the goals of education and educational technology. Faculty were relatively neutral ($\underline{M}$ = 2.90) on this item, whereas doctoral and master's students had significantly stronger agreement on it.

Responses in the Educational Technology and Schools area revealed optimism about the influence of our field on education generally. The second-ranking and fourth-ranking items overall indicated agreement that educational technology will play an increasing role in teacher education programs and a major role in school reform and restructuring. Overall, respondents were relatively neutral ($\underline{M}$ = 2.92) about whether more instruction will be delivered by computers and other media or by textbooks and teachers in the year 2010, but trainers and master's students were much more positive than faculty and doctoral students about greater use of the computer-and-media delivery mode.

In the Instructional Design Models area, respondents agreed that improvement of existing instructional design models is an important goal of our field and that design models can be improved more by increasing learner control over instruction than by increasing program control. Trainers agreed significantly more strongly than faculty with the learner control item. This difference of opinion may be partly due to the fact that faculty typically instruct relatively large classes (many of whom may be preparing for classroom instruction themselves), whereas many trainers work in settings in which small-group and individual instruction and training of adults, often by computer, are the norm. Thus, personal control by individual learners may often be more feasible in the training setting than in regular classroom instruction.

The relatively low overall score in the Advances in Technology area ($\underline{M}$ = 3.01) indicates generally neutral opinions abut the influence of technology on the roles of human beings in designing and delivering instruction. However, members of our field appear to believe that computers and technology will take over more of the functions of teachers in delivering instruction than those of instructional designers in designing it. Respondents showed moderate agreement with items indicating less teacher involvement—i.e., that advances in technology will enable schools to deliver effective instruction with less teacher involvement ($\underline{M}$ = 2.67) and that computer-delivered instruction will be capable of carrying out many human aspects of instruction ($\underline{M}$ = 2.77). In contrast, they moderately disagreed with items that indicated possible reductions of their own involvement in the direct design of instruction—that instructional designers will shift from designing instruction to creating systems that design it ($\underline{M}$ = 3.16) and that expert systems will design effective instructional programs with minimal human input ($\underline{M}$ = 3.40). Respondents' confidence about the future roles of instructional designers may be another manifestation of their positive opinions about employment opportunities and job growth in our field.

Perhaps the most striking data were the differences in opinions across the four respondent groups. Significant differences between groups occurred on 12 of the 30 items—40 percent of the total number. Faculty members had the lowest level of agreement (i.e., the highest mean score) of the four groups on 22 of the 30 items and differed significantly from at least one other group on 11 of the 12 items on which significant differences occurred. Master's students differed significantly from one or more groups on 10 items; doctoral students on 8 items; and trainers on 5 items. The greatest number of significant differences between any pair of groups was eight between faculty members and master's students, followed by four each between faculty and doctoral students and between faculty and trainers.

Our first thought when we found that faculty had the lowest overall level of agreement of the four groups and the greatest number of significant differences of opinion was, "Of course, faculty always have different opinions from everyone else. They probably even had greater differences of opinion among themselves than any other group." Analysis of the mean standard deviations of each group quickly dispelled this notion, however. The four standard deviations were within .04 of one another.

Consideration of the response patterns of the four groups yields comparative portraits for each group. Faculty are relatively skeptical. They had the lowest mean agreement score on the complete survey, the lowest agreement on more than 70 percent of the individual items, and the greatest number of significant differences of opinion with other groups. They had significantly lower agreement than one or more of the other groups with positive statements about the future promise of cognitive psychology in instructional design, advances in learning theory, computer-based instruction, automated instructional development, and the role of expert systems in instructional design.

Master's students contrasted the most with faculty, in that they were most accepting of positive statements about the future. Master's students had the highest agreement level on the complete survey and the highest agreement on 12 of the 30 items. Furthermore, they did not have the lowest agreement score on any of the 30 items. They had significantly different opinions from faculty members on more than one-fourth of all survey items. Master's students were more positive than faculty about the influence of learning theory on educational technology and the influence of educational technology on learning theory, individualization of instruction through CBI, delivery of more instruction by computers and media, and advances in technology.

Doctoral students typically held more intermediate positions than faculty members and master's students. Their overall mean of 2.48 fell directly between the means of 2.62 for faculty and 2.34 for master's students, and their mean scores on individual items were between those of faculty and master's students on more than half of the 30 items. Doctoral students' overall mean for the Educational Technology and Learning Theory area (M = 2.04) was the most positive for any respondent group on any topic area, indicating that they were especially positive about the role of learning theory in educational technology. Their opinions were relatively negative in the Advances in Technology area and toward statements in the Educational Technology and Schools area that implied a diminished role for teachers.

Trainers' responses reflected several different opinions from university personnel about graduate programs in educational technology and about technology and the schools. Trainers had the lowest agreement, significantly different from faculty and doctoral students, that educational technology doctoral programs should have a strong focus on preparing good researchers. Understandably, they had the highest agreement, significantly higher than each of the other three groups, that graduate programs should focus more on preparing students for work in business and industry than in schools and universities. They also had relatively strong opinions that the educational technology field should work to develop alternatives to the teacher-based model of education and that more future instruction in the schools will be delivered by computers and other media than by teachers and textbooks. On these latter two items, their opinions appear to be more supportive than those of faculty and doctoral students toward an instructional approach in the schools that is more technology-based and less teacher-based.

What causes the pattern of less agreement with statements about the future as respondents' university level increases from master's students to doctoral students to faculty members? The present authors have two possible explanations. The three faculty members among us confidently propose that the greater education and experience levels of faculty give us more insight into the realities of the field, and that graduate students gradually become more realistic as their education and experience increase. The two irreverent graduate-student authors, on the other hand, argue that faculty experience a progressive tightening or constricting of the mind from overexposure to academia that makes them less open and enthusiastic toward new ideas and developments in the real world. Following a hallowed tradition in our field, we have named these two theories "realism" and "constrictivism" to encourage further research into their validity.

In contrast to the four groups representing different education and employment levels, respondents across the 10 universities had remarkably few significant differences of opinion. This finding suggests that opinions vary more by education and employment levels than they do across universities, but we hesitate to draw that conclusion definitively. Table 9 reveals considerable variation in mean scores across universities in several topic areas. Of course, differences of similar and greater magnitude occurred on many of the individual items. However, the number of subjects was small for several universities and there was considerable variation in numbers of subjects across universities. In general, then, even though the between-university differences in mean item scores often were greater than between-education/employment group scores, the university differences were not statistically significant because of the larger number of groups (i.e., universities) and the smaller number of subjects in each group.

This study revealed that educational technologists are optimistic about the future of our field over the next two decades. Although opinions varied considerably across respondent groups on particular topics, the overall opinions were positive for each of the four education/employment levels and each of the 10 universities that participated in the study. We hope that future developments will validate this positive outlook and will produce growth in our profession and in its impact on society.

REFERENCES

Branson, R. K. (1990). Issues in the design of schooling: Changing the paradigm. *Educational Technology*, 30(4), 7-10.

Bratton, B. (1988). Roles for educational technologists by the year 2000. *Journal of Instructional Development*, 11(3), 7-9.

Butterfield, E. C., and Nelson, G. D. (1989). Theory and practice of teaching for transfer. *Educational Technology Research and Development*, 37(3), 5-38.

Clark, R. E. (1989). Current progress and future directions for research in instructional technology. *Educational Technology Research and Development*, 37(1), 57-66.

Ely, D. P. (1990). Trends and issues in educational technology. In *Educational Media and Technology Yearbook* vol. 16, ed. B. Branyan-Broadbent and R. K. Woods (Englewood, CO: Libraries Unlimited), 5-30.

Gagné, R. M. (1986). Instructional technology: The research field. *Journal of Instructional Development*, 8(3), 7-14.

Hannafin, M. J. (1992). Emerging technologies, ISD, and learning environments: Critical perspectives. *Educational Technology Research and Development*, 40(1), 49-64.

Hannafin, M. J., and Reiber, L. P. (1989). Psychological foundations of instructional design for emerging computer-based instructional technologies. *Educational Technology Research and Development*, 37(2), 91-101.

Jonassen, D. H. (1991). Objectivism vs. constructivism: Do we need a new philosophical paradigm? *Educational Technology Research and Development*, 39(3), 5-14.

Kerr, S. T. (1989). Technology, teachers, and the search for school reform. *Educational Technology Research and Development*, 37(4), 5-17.

Kinzie, M. B. (1990). Requirements and benefits of effective interactive instruction: Learner control, self-regulation, and continuing motivation. *Educational Technology Research and Development*, 38(1), 5-21.

Li, Z., and Merrill, M. D. (1991). ID expert 2.0: Design theory and process. *Educational Technology Research and Development*, 39(2), 53-69.

Merrill, M. D., Li, Z., and Jones, M. K. (1990). Second generation instructional design (ID2). *Educational Technology*, 30(2), 7-14.

Reigeluth, C. M. (1989). Educational technology at the crossroads: New mindsets and new directions. *Educational Technology Research and Development*, 37(1), 67-80.

Reiser, R. A. (1988). Instructional designers in public schools and higher education: Predictions for the year 2001. *Journal of Instructional Development*, 11(3), 3-6.

Reiser, R. A., and Salisbury, D. F. (1991). Instructional technology and public education: The next decade. In *Instructional Technology: Past, Present and Future*, ed. G. J. Anglin (Englewood, CO: Libraries Unlimited), 227-35.

Richards, B. F. (1989). Should instructional designers design instructional systems? *Educational Technology Research and Development*, 37(3), 63-71.

Ross, S. M., and Morrison, G. R. (1989). In search of a happy medium in instructional technology research: Issues concerning external validity, media replications, and learner control. *Educational Technology Research and Development*, 37(1), 19-33.

Schwen, T. M. (1988). An organizational analysis of the future of educational technology. *Journal of Instructional Technology*, 11(3), 21-27.

Winn, W. (1989). Toward a rationale and theoretical basis for educational technology. *Educational Technology Research and Development*, 37(1), 35-46.

Part Two
The Profession

Introduction

One of the purposes of the *Yearbook* is to present an annual report on the state of the profession. Each year there are articles and studies that speak to new developments related to such topics as professional education, salaries, certification, and continuing education. This year, a professional association, a new academic program, and salaries are featured.

Associations are indicators of professional status and growth, and Kitchens describes significant developments in the Association for Educational Communications and Technology, one of the seven major associations featured in part five, "The Year in Review."

A new program in the field at the doctoral level is especially worthy of mention in the *Yearbook* at a time when reductions in higher education are more common than additions. This year there are two: Pea describes a doctoral training program in the learning sciences at Northwestern University in the second article, and Sutton provides information on a distance education course in educational technology leadership that is being offered jointly by Mind Extension University and George Washington University in the third article.

In the fourth article, Hutchinson and Rankin report the results of salary surveys conducted in 1984, 1987, 1989, and 1992. They also make long-term observations on compensation based on information requested via the survey questionnaires, and provide comparative employment profiles.

It is the intention of the editors to continue this section in each *Yearbook* as an important component of an annual status report to the profession.

—THE YEAR IN REVIEW—

AECT
Association for Educational Communications and Technology
State-of-the-Association 1993

Larry Kitchens
Director, Center for Instructional Services
Texas Christian University

During the past year, the Association for Educational Communications and Technology has experienced growth and a renewed sense of optimism for the future. The purpose of this report is to highlight some of the activities and accomplishments of AECT over the past year.

STRATEGIC PLANNING/VISION 2000

AECT, over the past couple of years, has been involved in serious discussions regarding the directions AECT should be taking and whether AECT is making progress in getting where it should be. The AECT Board of Directors has taken the time to look first at the process of strategic planning and is now directly involved in that activity. Initial efforts among members of the Board have resulted in identification of several key elements that they deem essential for AECT to consider in establishing clear and concise directions for the future. These efforts have resulted in the development of the concept of "VISION 2000."

Working with the leadership of AECT, the Board of Directors developed a plan for an internal and external audit of AECT to assist in the development of VISION 2000. The purpose of these audits is not only to examine the current mission, program, and structure of the association, but also to provide the opportunity for individuals within AECT to determine what we should become and how we should get there. A special task force administered a questionnaire during the national convention in New Orleans, to seek input as to what individual members thought AECT should be like in the year 2000. Additionally, the Executive Director and the national office staff have also been asked to develop their concept of what AECT should be like.

One other aspect of the audit process yet to be addressed by the Board of Directors is that of seeking an individual or individuals to perform an external audit of the association in terms of how we are viewed from the outside.

A special strategic planning task force, chaired by a member of the Board of Directors, will undertake to synthesize all this information and develop a strategic plan for AECT. The timeline for the development and submission of this plan to the membership and to the Board of Directors is anticipated to be by the 1993 Summer Leadership Development Conference. It is hoped that ratification of VISION 2000 can occur prior to the 1994 convention in Nashville.

As a result of these efforts, it is anticipated that a strategic plan will provide for an organization that will be capable of meeting the needs not only of its members but also of the profession. It will be a plan that will permit us to take those steps necessary to truly have an influence upon the teaching/learning process in our educational systems.

InCITE '94

Starting in 1994, AECT will no longer be part of INFOCOMM. Instead, in its place will be a new trade show managed by AECT called InCITE. Much work has already been done to make InCITE as exciting and beneficial as INFOCOMM has been in the past. Several major companies have already agreed to exhibit in Nashville, with several indicating they will want a larger space for exhibits than they had in New Orleans. Because of the opportunity to manage our own trade show and convention for the first time in several years, AECT will be able to accomplish many of the activities that have been suggested by members over the years.

PARTNERSHIPS

Last year, AECT indicated that it would be seeking "strategic alliances" with other professional organizations. Beginning with InCITE '94, the International Society for Technology in Education (ISTE) and the Association for the Development of Computer-based Instructional Systems (ADCIS) will meet with AECT and InCITE for the first time. These partnerships will benefit everyone involved by assuring a strong trade show and a diverse convention program in 1994. Such alliances will make for a stronger voice in educational technology.

ACTIVITIES

This past year, AECT has been actively involved in several activities promoting the profession and educational communications and technology. Examples of some of these activities are:

- A letter from the AECT president was sent to the Honorable Albert Gore in support of legislation for a National Research and Education Network (NREN).

- A letter from the AECT president was sent to every chief state school officer stating AECT's support for school library media programs in public schools and that AECT strongly supported the certification recommendations for school library media personnel reflected in *Information Power*, a joint publication of AECT and the American Association of School Librarians (AASL).

- A task force was established to work with AASL in the revision and update of *Information Power*.

- AECT endorsed the Youth Services Omnibus Bill, which received the highest priority at the White House Conference on Libraries and Information Services, and a portion of which will fund technology projects.

- AECT appointed four representatives to serve on a joint AECT/Association for College and Research Libraries (ACRL) Task Force for purposes of drafting an update on guidelines.

- AECT agreed to be a participant on the National Board of Professional Teaching Standards as it considers the issues involved in and recommendations for high and rigorous standards for the teaching profession.

- The Board of Directors endorsed the concept of AECT taking the lead in hosting an "Educational Technology Summit." The purpose of this endeavor would be for professional organizations involved in educational communications and technology to gather in one place to discuss common issues. By working together, we could speak with a stronger voice and have the desired impact upon the teaching/learning enterprise.

INTERNAL

Through the efforts of the Board of Directors, the leadership of AECT, and the staff of the national office, AECT has maintained its fiscal integrity this past year. At the same time, AECT has stabilized its membership base and is now in a period of growth.

Communications within a volunteer-based organization are always a concern. This past year has seen a marked effort to increase the level of communications within the association. In addition to numerous letters to and phone calls with the leadership of the association, several audio teleconference calls were held during the year. Every division, committee, task force, region, and affiliate was asked to submit written and end-of-the-year reports, and most of them complied with the request.

No one person can lay claim to the success and achievement that AECT has enjoyed this past year. It is because many individuals have worked hard and have worked together that AECT was able to accomplish everything it has accomplished this past year. Indeed, it is by working together that our dreams and our "visions" will inevitably come to pass.

Current Developments in Educational Technology Programs
Doctoral Training in the Learning Sciences at Northwestern University

Roy D. Pea*
Chair, Learning Sciences Ph.D. Program
Northwestern University

John Evans
Professor of Education and the Learning Sciences
Northwestern University

At a time when fresh approaches to the critical problems in education are desperately needed, future educators and researchers in the field of education must equip themselves to confront the challenges of educational reform creatively. Northwestern University is addressing these challenges through its new doctoral program in the Learning Sciences. Launched in 1991 and administered through Northwestern's School of Education and Social Policy, the interdisciplinary Learning Sciences program will prepare future leaders to advance innovative approaches to examining and addressing the practices of learning and teaching, broadly conceived. Problems of learning underlie issues of education, training, and lifelong contributions to society. The research-informed use of technology in education is critical as technology has come to play an ever more prevalent role in work, science, government, and human activities broadly considered. The integration of computing, telecommunications, and media-rich information technologies will come to play central roles in the processes of learning and teaching. These vital concerns demand attention from the most rigorous research and theory available, which will contribute the understanding necessary to advance both the practice and sciences of learning. The Learning Sciences program is devoted to this agenda.

The goal of the Learning Sciences Ph.D. program is to advance the research and development of innovative learning environments (including small-group learning and network-supported, remote collaboration), human cognition as it relates to the processes of learning and teaching, and multimedia computing and telecommunications technologies that may effectively support these processes. With advances in networking and models of collaborative learning, even learners from underserved populations and those in remote areas would have the opportunity to experience the most advanced approaches to teaching and learning and could gain access to information and resources that were previously unavailable to them. Research in the Learning Sciences is aimed at creating environments that offer all students a rich variety of opportunities for learning to think more effectively and more creatively.

Northwestern has assembled a distinguished initial faculty of 20 members from diverse departments, including computer science, education, psychology, and philosophy, with two new faculty members to be added during the 1993-94 academic year. Northwestern's Learning Sciences faculty have provided leadership in the cognitive sciences, artificial intelligence, and

*I would like to thank Celia Duroe for assistance in the preparation of this chapter.

research on learning and education, and contribute a diversity of theoretical and methodological perspectives to considerations of these problems, including but not limited to work in anthropology, artificial intelligence, cognitive and developmental psychology, computer science, educational research, linguistics, philosophy, and fields that develop strategies for promoting understanding and appropriate use of complex subject matter knowledge. The unique co-location of practitioners in these distinct disciplines brings a rich interdisciplinary perspective to the Learning Sciences Ph.D. program.

An active environment of research programs, supported by well-equipped facilities, promises rich opportunities for student participation in frontier investigations of learning in schools, workplaces, and other settings. Strategic alliances with corporate funders such as Andersen Consulting and Ameritech ensure attention to real problems of learning-at-work, while research activities with local schools and educational systems provide collaborations that may affect restructuring and offer models for constructive change. These resources are directed at understanding, effecting, and, importantly, replicating in educational activities the conditions that give rise to successful learning.

The design and use of technologies play a special role in Learning Sciences inquiries. Multimedia computing and telecommunications are increasingly prevalent in society, in the world of work, and in schools, as new tools for enhancing workplace activities and educational practices. Computer tools have also served as new instruments for investigative research on cognition, learning, and social interaction. Integrations of computing and video provide tools for deeper analyses of learning and teaching situations, and designs for novel architectures of learning, teaching, and assessment tools. Research and theory in the Learning Sciences Program pay both constructive and critical attention to these issues, by integrating three areas of specialization in its core coursework and methodological foundations:

Environments—Deepening understanding of the social, contextual, and cultural dynamics of learning in situations ranging from classrooms to out-of-school settings.

Cognition—Articulating scientific models of the structures and processes of learning and teaching of organized knowledge, skills, and understanding.

Architectures—Theory-guided design, construction, and use of multimedia computing and telecommunications technologies for supporting learning and teaching processes.

CURRENT STUDENTS

In 1992-93, there were 11 Learning Sciences Ph.D. students, with an expected enrollment of 20 in 1993-94 and 30 in 1994-95. Students, who have come from as far away as Canada, England, Israel, Korea, Singapore, and Yugoslavia to take part in the Learning Sciences program, have diverse backgrounds in such disciplines as comparative literature and music, as well as computer science, electrical engineering, psychology, and education. Graduate students in the Learning Sciences program range in age from 25 to 35 and approximately half of them have already acquired a master's degree before entering the program. An affiliated Ph.D. program in Computer Science through Northwestern's School of Engineering enrolled 43 students in 1992-93, and many of these students participate in the Learning Sciences course offerings and in the training activities of the affiliated Institute for the Learning Sciences (described later).

BACKGROUND

Research during the last two decades has led to a foundational shift in the disciplines and quality of research and theory contributing to the sciences of learning and teaching processes.

Influential interdisciplinary work in the cognitive sciences has taken problems of learning as its core topic. Research in the Learning Sciences is aimed at understanding and creating environments and educational strategies that offer learners from *all* cultural backgrounds a variety of opportunities for learning to think and act effectively, both within and outside of formal learning settings, and throughout the life span. Fundamental advances have occurred for such topics as the scientific understanding of the nature of expertise, culture-cognition relationships, constraints on learning, the social construction of knowledge, conceptual development, text comprehension, community and family influences on learning, relations between in-school and out-of-school learning, and the interactive and processing characteristics of successful learning conditions. National centers for research on aspects of these problems have been formed, programs and priorities of research funding in government agencies and private foundations have come to represent these concerns, and new scientific journals and societies have been established. National organizations of educational practitioners for diverse fields of study, such as science, mathematics, and reading, now routinely call for the practice of instruction, materials development, and teacher education to be more deeply informed by these new scientific understandings.

There has been a slow emergence of graduate training programs and departments that systematically reflect these developments. Although a significant number of cognitive science programs have appeared, few institutions have defined initiatives that systematically build on these scientific achievements to improve learning and education. Northwestern has created the Learning Sciences Ph.D. Program to contribute specifically to research and the training of professionals qualified to advance the scientific and humanistic understanding and practice of learning and teaching, broadly conceived. The training experience must contribute to the development of professionals ready to creatively define and respond to new issues that emerge in the changing conditions of learning in an increasingly global economy, in a multicultural society, and amidst a world of rapidly evolving patterns of work and life. Program graduates would be sought out for their capabilities to formulate and empirically address seminal questions; to engage in critical thinking, research, and development; and to provide leadership both within and at the crossroads of the cognate fields of the Learning Sciences.

FACULTY RESOURCES AND AFFILIATIONS

Reflecting the interdisciplinary nature of the sciences of learning, program faculty are drawn from several departments and schools of Northwestern, including the School of Education and Social Policy, the Department of Electrical Engineering and Computer Science, and the Department of Psychology. Two new faculty appointments in 1993-94 will further enhance the contributions of these departments and schools in the "Environments" specialization described later.

The Learning Sciences Program is affiliated with The Institute for the Learning Sciences, an interdisciplinary center devoted to basic and applied research in artificial intelligence, cognitive science, education, and educational software and related activities. The Institute was formed in September 1989, with founding support from Andersen Consulting, and is directed by Professor Roger C. Schank. It is a lively intellectual community of more than 180 scholars and scientists, corporate representatives, and professional programmers who collaborate to advance the research and development of the past 20 years of research in artificial intelligence through its refocusing on the educational needs of schools and corporations. Key research areas include scientific problems of language, thought, and memory; the construction of computer programs that reason, learn, conduct conversations, display characteristics of human memory, plan, and contain realistic models of the world; the understanding of how children learn language, learn to think, plan, and reason; education, especially the development of effective teaching-learning methods from a plurality of cultural and social contexts; subject matter learning, especially in situations presenting intellectual difficulties, such as reading comprehension, and reasoning in mathematics, science, and with technology; augmentation of intelligent activity with cognitive technologies; computer vision; models of emotion, human problem solving and decision making; and qualitative reasoning about physical systems. Research activities are supported by a state-of-the-art, networked computing infrastructure and an unusual commitment to building technologies and supporting activities that function effectively in the complexities of human learning environments.

Learning Sciences faculty are actively involved in the publishing world as well, as founders and editors of journals such as *Cognition, Cognition and Emotion, Cognition and Instruction, Cognitive Science, Computational Intelligence, Discourse Processes, Interactive Learning Environments, Instructional Science, Journal of the Learning Sciences, Journal of Metaphor and Symbolic Activity*, and *Machine Learning*; as regular contributors to disciplinary journals in their respective fields; and as book authors and book series editors with distinguished international presses.

Following is a listing of Learning Sciences faculty and their areas of specialization:

Professors

- Allan Collins
  Ph.D. University of Michigan, 1970
  Professor of Education
  Theories of knowledge in teaching and learning; assessment; technologically based school reform.

- Karen C. Fuson
  Ph.D. University of Chicago, 1972
  Professor of Education
  Mathematics and learning; cognitive development.

- Dedre Gentner
  Ph.D. University of California at San Diego, 1974
  Professor of Psychology
  Learning, reasoning, and conceptual change in adults and children, especially processes of similarity, metaphor, and analogy; mental models; acquisition of meaning.

- Douglas L. Medin
  Ph.D. University of South Dakota, 1968
  Professor of Psychology
  Theories of learning, memory, and induction; concept and classification learning; medical problem solving; comparative psychology.

- Andrew Ortony
  Ph.D. University of London, 1972
  Professor of Education and Psychology
  Knowledge representation and language comprehension; models of cognition, motivation, and emotion.

- Roy D. Pea
  D.Phil. University of Oxford, 1978
  John Evans Professor of Education and the Learning Sciences
  (Learning Sciences Program Founder and Coordinator, 1991-1993)
  Learning-teaching processes and environments in science, mathematics, and technology; sociocultural foundations of complex learning; cognitive and conceptual development; multimedia learning and communication.

- Roger C. Schank
  Ph.D. University of Texas, 1969
  John Evans Professor of Electrical Engineering & Computer Science and Professor of Psychology and Education
  Theories of learning, understanding, teaching, and creativity; applications of artificial intelligence to education, memory processing, natural language understanding, and case-based reasoning.

Associate Professors

- Kenneth D. Forbus
  Ph.D. Massachusetts Institute of Technology, 1984
  Associate Professor of Computer Science
  Qualitative physics; cognitive simulation of analogy; inference systems.

- Brian J. Reiser
  Ph.D. Yale University, 1983
  Associate Professor of Education
  (Learning Sciences Program Coordinator, starting in 1993)
  Cognitive science; problem solving; intelligent tutoring systems.

- Christopher K. Riesbeck
  Ph.D. Stanford University, 1974
  Associate Professor of Computer Science
  Natural language analyzers; case-based reasoners; intelligent interfaces for training and tutoring.

- Sandra Waxman
  Ph.D. University of Pennsylvania, 1985
  Associate Professor of Psychology
  Issues of language and conceptual development from infancy through early childhood.

Assistant Professors

- Ray Bareiss
  Ph.D. University of Texas, 1988
  Assistant Professor (Research) of the Institute for the Learning Sciences
  Case-based reasoning; intelligent tutoring systems; multimedia computing; automated knowledge acquisition.

- Richard Beckwith
  Ph.D. Columbia University, 1988
  Assistant Professor (Research) of the Institute for the Learning Sciences
  Developmental and educational psychology.

- Lawrence Birnbaum
  Ph.D. Yale University, 1986
  Assistant Professor of Computer Science
  Natural language understanding; opportunistic planning; machine learning.

- Gregg Collins
  Ph.D. Yale University, 1987
  Assistant Professor of Computer Science
  Machine learning, especially planning and problem solving.

- Jeremiah M. Faries
  Ph.D. Princeton University, 1991
  Assistant Professor of Psychology and Education
  Memory organization and retrieval; analogy; problem solving; mental imagery; language comprehension; metaphor.

- Richard G. Feifer
  Ph.D. University of California at Los Angeles, 1989
  Assistant Professor (Research) of the Institute for the Learning Sciences
  Human and computer-based learning environments.

- Alex Kass
  Ph.D. Yale University, 1990
  Assistant Professor (Research) of the Institute for the Learning Sciences
  Case-based reasoning; story understanding; machine learning; models of creativity; computer-based education.

- Edward Wisniewski
  Ph.D. Brown University, 1989
  Assistant Professor of Psychology
  Cognitive science, conceptual combinations, and category learning.

Faculty Affiliates

- Michael Garet
  Ph.D. Massachusetts Institute of Technology, 1979
  Associate Professor of Education.

- Carol D. Lee
  Ph.D. University of Chicago, 1991
  Assistant Professor of Education.

- Stephen E. Toulmin
  Ph.D. University of Cambridge, 1948
  Avalon Foundation Professor of the Humanities and Professor of Philosophy.

- David E. Wiley
  Ph.D. University of Wisconsin, 1964
  Professor of Education.

CAREERS IN THE LEARNING SCIENCES

Graduates will be prepared to assume significant roles in advancing the understanding and practice of learning and teaching. Their work settings would include university research and teaching (such as in social science, computer science, or education departments); business, industry, or school system-based careers studying, designing, and/or implementing learning environments, broadly conceived to include learning materials, technologies (such as industrial training and educational software systems), and activities in their organizational contexts. Students of Learning Sciences faculty have often gone on to leadership positions in university faculties and industry.

THE Ph.D. PROGRAM IN THE LEARNING SCIENCES

The course of studies for the Learning Sciences Ph.D. reflects the philosophy that learning is both an *active* and a *reflective* process, requiring a breadth of experience in diverse research settings. Students' work in developing facility with theory and methods in the Learning Sciences is firmly rooted in laboratory work, as well as field experiences and studies of learning and education in nonlaboratory settings. Foundational coursework and seminars are integrated with local and Chicago-area apprenticeships in research projects, and increasingly, independent research guided by faculty mentors. The fact that the program's faculty is diverse, both in its disciplinary background and its ideology, strengthens its purpose as a premier intellectual forum. Lively debates in regular colloquia contribute to this environment.

SPECIALIZATIONS OF THE LEARNING SCIENCES PROGRAM

Learning Sciences graduate students follow a core curriculum for approximately the first two years, as described later. Additional courses taken are based on consultation between the advisor and student. The remainder of the graduate training is dedicated to research under the direction of the Learning Sciences program faculty.

Corresponding to the breadth of faculty interests, three flexible tracks of specialization beyond the core are available for doctoral students. They focus on different levels of analysis: *Environments*, *Cognition*, and *Architectures*. The differences are primarily of relative emphasis— on either issues in teaching-learning environments (broadly construed to include sociocultural dynamics and cognitive aspects of learning), or computational and technological issues in building teaching-learning systems—and in the probable career paths of those pursuing these options. These specializations are also components of the core curriculum.

Those electing *Environments* will devote more of their training to rigorous study of theory, methods, and research for understanding cognitive, cultural, and social issues in the practices in which teaching-learning processes and technology use are embedded. Topics include small-group and network-supported collaborative learning, classroom discourse practices, cultural contexts of learning, social construction of subject matter understanding, and learning environments collaboratively designed with learners and teachers. Learning environments may but do not necessarily include the use of computational systems for learning and teaching. Methods include ethnographic study, discourse analysis, clinical interviews, protocol analysis, experimental design, and surveys. Such research often utilizes video recordings of learning-teaching interactions in settings such as schools and classrooms.

Those electing *Cognition* will devote more of their training to rigorous study of theory, methods, and research for understanding cognitive aspects of learning, especially for complex subject matter domains (e.g., mathematics, physics, technology). Topics include adaptive knowledge structures and processes; experience-based mechanisms of learning and development; mental models; individual differences in aptitudes and learning strategies, including those affected by ethnicity, social class, and gender; novice-expert differences in categorization and problem-solving processes; skill acquisition; belief systems and conceptual change; explanation and understanding; transfer of learning; and the related cultural and social factors embedded in these psychological processes. Methods include analysis of think-aloud protocols, building computer models of reasoning and learning, clinical interviews, and experimental psychological techniques.

Those electing *Architectures* will devote more of their training to rigorous study of basic and applied science issues concerning the design and development of effective computational and multimedia architectures for learning and teaching. Topics include architectures for guided discovery, incidental learning, collaborative learning, case-based tutors and coaches, intelligent tutoring systems, and designs for student-initiated, question-driven learning. Methods include artificial intelligence programming and theory, instructional design methods, and theory and research concerning learning-teaching processes from both cognitive and social science perspectives.

THE LEARNING SCIENCES CURRICULUM

An integrated body of coursework and apprenticing activities is designed for all students, regardless of specialization, so as to create a collegial learning culture in which faculty and students alike contribute to cultivating critical questions and shaping the programmatic directions of the interdisciplinary learning sciences. The training activities beyond seminars and lecture courses focus on learning-by-doing, in terms of apprenticeships in which students participate in ongoing research and development projects with program faculty. In this way, students come to understand, for future replication in their careers, the entire process of science and practice within the learning sciences, e.g., from planning and conducting research and analyzing results; to designing, building, and implementing new learning environments for real settings; to publication and dissemination efforts.

The core curriculum consists of seven quarter courses, three methods courses, three additional courses on Advanced Topics in the Learning Sciences selected in consultation with the student's advisor, and a number of additional lecture courses, seminars, research courses, and apprenticeship activities defined in consultation with the student's advisor from courses offered in the School of Education and Social Policy, the Department of Psychology, the Department of Electrical Engineering and Computer Science, and other units in the University. Students are normally expected to complete the first seven courses and the three methods courses in the first two years.

Core Courses in Learning Sciences

The seven quarter courses, to be taken by all Learning Sciences students, include:

- The first quarter *Learning Sciences Proseminar*, taught by Learning Sciences faculty. The aim here is to introduce the fundamental concepts, methods, and theories that constitute the learning sciences, as realized through the research of our faculty. Student teams analyze the work of a given faculty member each week and present synthetic discussions with that faculty member present for questions and discussion. The concepts, methods, and theories are likely to be drawn from the contributions of such fields as artificial intelligence, cognitive science, cognitive and developmental psychology, cognitive and cultural anthropology, education, epistemology, humanities, linguistics, organizational science, and subject matter disciplines.

- Two courses in *Learning Environments*: One course focuses on design of learning environments (including instructional materials and design of activities), effective learning conditions in nonschool settings, and the assessment of learning environments. One course critically examines the philosophical and historical foundations of educational technology. Together, these courses cover research on naturalistic and designed learning environments, different educational philosophies and examples of their embodiments in educational technology and learning environment design, and examples from different methodological perspectives of the systematic study of learning-teaching processes and outcomes resulting from learning environments.

- Two courses in *Cognition*: One is an introductory course on cognitive science models of learning and problem solving, providing interdisciplinary treatment of key research and theory. The second course may be selected from a list of courses on cognitive development and learning.

- Two courses in *Artificial Intelligence*: These courses examine theoretical issues relating to human and machine intelligence and the practical issues of implementing aspects of intelligence on machines. Some central issues include: methods of representing complex knowledge, the organization and access of large yet flexible memory systems, modifying knowledge based on experience (learning), planning and problem solving, inferential reasoning, and language processing.

Because students may have previously completed coursework meeting any of these requirements, a review determines whether students may, with faculty advisement, replace one of these courses with more advanced coursework.

Methods Courses

All students are also required to take three methods courses, with one or more additional methods courses recommended, depending on the student's area of specialization. One course is centered on artificial intelligence programming and system design. A second course provides rigorous experience and theory in observational methods and techniques for studying human activity, emphasizing observational fieldwork on learning environments, and including study of learning in situ. A third course is on statistics and experimental design.

Advanced Topics Courses

At least three additional courses on Advanced Topics in the Learning Sciences are to be drawn from other offerings arranged with faculty advisement.

Research Apprenticeships

All Learning Science students apprentice to a variety of research laboratories and activities during their training. Students typically spend a total of three quarters participating in several different faculty-directed research activities during their first four quarters of study, at least one of which is outside their area of specialization.

Subsequent research requirements differ for the three concentrations. *Environments* students pursue field-based observation, design, and implementation research on learning environments; *Cognition* students focus on empirical studies of learning; *Architectures* students devote their efforts to designing and building computational systems. Students are expected to examine a plurality of cultural and social contexts during their training.

After the first year, doctoral students participate in a research activity in which they are assigned to work with one or more faculty members on a research project. Specific activities are tailored to the student's interests in consultation with the faculty advisor.

Other Requirements for the Degree of Doctor of Philosophy

- Student progress is reviewed annually by program faculty. Progress reports based on this review determine a student's eligibility to form a preliminary advisory committee and to take the preliminary examination.

- A written preliminary comprehensive examination in the Learning Sciences is required. This exam is constructed and revised on a regular basis by a representative Learning Sciences faculty group. The comprehensive exam includes two parts: a common set of questions covering the core topics for all students, and a divergent set of questions depending on the subsequent area of student specialization beyond the core.

- All doctoral students are required to complete a major, publication-quality predissertation paper reporting research conducted under the supervision of a Learning Sciences faculty member. This paper is prerequisite to admission to candidacy and is viewed as an apprenticeship experience rather than as independent research.

- The student must also pass an oral qualifying examination, in which the proposed dissertation topic is presented, and its significance to the development of knowledge in the learning sciences is discussed, as well as proposed research methodology and preliminary results.

- Advancement to candidacy is expected by the end of the third year of graduate study.

- A dissertation demonstrating original and significant research is required of each candidate, which is defended in the final oral examination.

SUMMARY

The pursuit of a Ph.D. in the Learning Sciences will provide students with a deep and action-oriented understanding of the dynamics of learning environments; the nature of the cognitive processes involved in learning and teaching; and how to design, construct, and use technology to support the learning and teaching processes. The program offers coursework tailored to the individual's needs and interests. The seven required core courses that introduce the student to the fundamentals of the learning sciences draw upon relevant concepts, methods, and theories from an array of fields and subject matter, including education, psychology, and computer science. Subsequent to the foundational courses, the student will typically focus on one of the three areas of specialization that he or she has experienced through the core curriculum: Environments, Cognition, or Architectures. Included in the course of study are methods courses and apprenticeships that provide hands-on experience in both laboratory and Chicago-area classroom settings. Upon completion of the program, graduates are ready to advance the understanding and practice of learning and teaching by assuming leadership roles in universities, school systems, industry, and in the broader society.

APPLICATION AND ADMISSIONS

For financial aid considerations, we hope to have all applications in hand by January 15 of each year, although applications received later than February 1 may be considered. Admission to the Learning Sciences program is highly selective. Learning Sciences students are eligible for multiyear funding, including summer support, which is competitively awarded.

For further information on the Learning Sciences Ph.D. Program, or to request a listing of technical reports published by The Institute for the Learning Sciences, please contact: Ms. Tina Turnbull, Graduate Program Coordinator, The Institute for the Learning Sciences, 1890 Maple Avenue, Evanston, Illinois 60201, U.S.A. 708-467-1332; electronic mail: tina@ils.nwu.edu; fax: 708-491-5258.

Master's Program in Educational Technology Leadership
Offered by The George Washington University and Mind Extension University

Don Sutton
Vice President and Managing Director
Mind Extension University: The Education Network

Recognizing that there is a growing need for qualified and experienced professionals to lead the way for the effective and innovative use of computer and communications technologies at all educational levels, The George Washington University School of Education and Human Development (SEHD) and Mind Extension University (ME/U): The Education Network has teamed up to offer a Master of Arts in Education and Human Development, with a major in Educational Technology Leadership. Through their unique partnership, ME/U and SEHD make the 36-hour degree program available via cable television, satellite, and/or videotape to students across North America and other locations. Because coursework is completed at home or at a school site by watching classes on television, reading, and communicating through a computer and telephone, the degree program is an ideal option for people who otherwise could not return to school: full-time workers without the time to attend a traditional university, persons living in areas without a college or university, parents who cannot afford to hire a babysitter so they can return to the classroom, and the physically disabled.

The Educational Technology Leadership program, leading to a Master of Arts in Education and Human Development, was designed by Dr. William Lynch of The George Washington University School of Education and Human Development, which also awards the degree. All courses originate at The George Washington University and are taught by its nationally recognized faculty. The program is specifically designed for persons entering or advancing in careers at schools, higher education institutions, museums, alternative educational settings, human service agencies, or other arenas in which information systems delivery technologies are used. The program provides students with opportunities to develop the knowledge, understanding, and skills necessary to become leaders in the dynamic world of instructional technology.

THE DEGREE PROGRAM

Curriculum

Required Courses:

EDUC230 Managing Computer Applications (3)

EDUC231 Educational Hardware Systems (3)

EDUC232 Applying Educational Media and Technology (3)

EDUC234 Computers in Education and Human Development (3)

EDUC235 Design and Implementation of Educational Software (3)

EDUC268 Power, Leadership, and Education (3)

EDUC271 Policy-Making for Public Education (3)

EDUC295 Quantitative Research Methods II (3)

Electives:

EDUC220a Media Services Management (3)

EDUC220b Introduction to Interactive Multimedia (3)

EDUC220c Telecommunications in Education (3)

EDUC220d Developing Interactive Media (3)

Course Descriptions

EDUC230 *Managing Computer Applications.* For managers and prospective managers in education and human services who are concerned with the automation of their operations. Basic principles needed to design, implement, and manage an information system.

EDUC231 *Educational Hardware Systems.* An exploration of the design and implementation of educational hardware systems, including computers, videodiscs, networks, film technology, video systems, and ITV for educational use.

EDUC232 *Applying Educational Media and Technology.* An introductory course in the theory and practice of educational technology for persons using technology in settings in which effective communication, information sharing, and learning are important. Key characteristics of different media are surveyed, principles of application are presented, and issues concerning their appropriate use are discussed.

EDUC234 *Computers in Education and Human Development.* The research and practice surrounding the use of computers in educational and training settings. Students will acquire the practical knowledge necessary for the development and evaluation of computer-related curricula through the study of current software applications and programming environments.

EDUC235 *Design and Implementation of Educational Software.* Theory and practices of creating educational software. Students will examine the psychological foundations of learning as applied to the use of electronic technology in education and a variety of authoring/programming tools. Students also will examine the process of software design and implementation.

EDUC268 *Power, Leadership, and Education.* The nature of power, leadership, and education; the relationship of power to leadership; the essential nature of education in the exercise of power and leadership in a democratic setting.

EDUC271 *Policy-Making for Public Education.* The nature of educational policy: the role of single-interest groups, the courts, legislative bodies, administrative bureaucracies, and professionals in establishing parameters and allocating resources. Analysis of specific techniques of policy formation.

EDUC295 *Quantitative Research Methods II.* Required of all candidates for master's degrees in education. Analysis of scientific approaches to problems in education; evaluation of research techniques. Prerequisite: EDUC 112, 212, or equivalent.

EDUC212 *Quantitative Research Methods I*. Introduction to Survey and Measurements and Research is a prerequisite to EDUC295. This course (EDUC212) is not required of students who have completed an equivalent course in educational tests and measurement techniques and evaluation. Emphasis is on application and interpretation of data-gathering techniques and descriptive statistics.

EDUC220a *Media Services Management*. This course addresses the acute need of educational organizations to prepare individuals who can facilitate the integration of various information resources into educational situations. It prepares individuals to manage the media programs, personnel, budgets, and public relations necessary for effective media services. The course also prepares individuals to participate in designing media-related instruction and media facilities.

EDUC220b *Introduction to Interactive Multimedia*. This course surveys the fundamentals of interactive multimedia hardware systems, software applications, and industry trends. Taking examples from a variety of education, training, and information sources, students will have the opportunity to experience and evaluate the potential of interactive multimedia.

EDUC220c *Telecommunications in Education*. This course presents the history, current application, and future use of telecommunication technologies in educational contexts. Students will gain a practical understanding of the use and implications of communications systems such as telephone lines and networks, cellular systems, radio and television transmission and reception, cable television, fiber optics, satellites, and the electronic devices that make use of them.

EDUC220d *Developing Interactive Media*. This course examines approaches to developing interactive multimedia. Phases in the process that are specifically addressed include project analysis, design, development, production, authoring, and validation. Students will review examples of existing applications and apply their acquired knowledge in the design of an original project.

EARNING A DEGREE FROM THE GEORGE WASHINGTON UNIVERSITY THROUGH MIND EXTENSION UNIVERSITY

Mind Extension University (ME/U): The Education Network functions as the distributor and co-administrator of the Educational Technology Leadership degree program. The George Washington University exclusively admits, evaluates, and awards degrees to students participating in the program.

Enrollment

Students interested in the Educational Technology Leadership program of The George Washington University work directly with ME/U or GWU to enroll. Student advisors at the ME/U Education Center, 1-800-777-MIND, handle inquiries about the program, send out enrollment forms and applications, process book orders, and set up students on an electronic bulletin board system. Student advisors are available Monday through Friday from 4 a.m. to 8 p.m. ET.

Applicants are solely responsible for compiling their own credentials packages, which include the completed application, an official transcript from all graduate and undergraduate institutions where academic work was completed, and two letters of recommendation, one from an academic source and one from a professional source. Applicants must submit scores from the Graduate Record Exam or the Miller Analogies Test and all other materials directly to GWU's School of Education and Human Development.

International students need to submit certified English translations of academic records for coursework that corresponds or is equivalent to the bachelor's degree in the United States, and a Financial Certificate, which is required of any applicant who plans to enter the United States to study at GWU and whose visa status is either (F) or exchange visitor (J). International applicants must also submit scores of at least 600 on the Test of English as a Foreign Language.

Course Materials

All course materials, such as syllabi and handouts, are sent directly to students. Textbooks are available through ME/U's own "bookstore" and are sent to students. ME/U also makes available videotapes of missed classes. Students are encouraged to order taped classes within 24 hours of the original airing to minimize delay in coursework.

Tuning In

The M.A. program offered through ME/U involves a wide variety of communications mechanisms between students and classrooms. The primary technology employed is video.

ME/U is available in hundreds of communities across the United States via cable television. Home satellite dish users can also participate in the program by tuning into Galaxy III, transponder 11. If neither of these options is available, students also have the option of purchasing videotapes of the classes from ME/U.

Portions of the classes are audio interactive. Students call a toll-free number to speak to instructors and guests and to interact with on-campus students while class is in session.

Another significant communications component of the M.A. program is an electronic bulletin board system. The bulletin board system offers electronic mail and document transfer options. Students might use the system to work jointly on a class project. Or, the system could be used for the study of a computer language, enabling students and instructors to send the programs back and forth. Course instructors make their own decisions on utilization of the bulletin board system.

Participation in the bulletin board system requires students to have access to a computer and modem. A user fee paid to ME/U allows access.

Exams

Because exams in the M.A. program tend to be open-book and without rigid time limits, proctors usually are not necessary. Any exceptions are addressed on a case-by-case basis.

Cost

Earning a degree through ME/U offers students not only flexibility and convenience, but also possibly significant cost savings. Students are not faced with having to quit their jobs to earn the degree, or move so they can attend classes on campus. Also, students do not have expenses associated with housing, parking, babysitting, or other things that can add up during the course of a semester.

Fees payable to ME/U include:

Tuition:	$594 per 3-credit course
One-time registration fee:	$25
Electronic Bulletin Board:	$45 per course

Fees payable to The George Washington University include:

Nonrefundable application fee:	$45 (one time only)
Transcript fee:	$3 (one time only)
Graduation fee:	$78 (one time only)

All fees and book purchases are nonrefundable. Tuition, however, is refundable, based on the following schedule:

Prior to first class cablecast: 100 percent

After the first class cablecast but before the third: 80 percent

After the third cablecast but before the fifth: 50 percent

After the fifth cablecast: None

Scholarships and Financial Aid

Financial aid information is available from the Office of Student Financial Assistance, The George Washington University, Washington, DC 20052. Also, some cable systems that carry ME/U offer local scholarships.

ABOUT ME/U

Mind Extension University (ME/U): The Education Network is one of the fastest growing basic cable television networks in the United States. By November 1992, five years after first going on the air, the Englewood, Colorado-based network was available to 21 million households in nearly 7,000 communities around the United States. Additionally, ME/U has students in Germany, Venezuela, London, Egypt, and other countries.

A subsidiary of Jones Education Networks Inc., ME/U was founded by Glenn R. Jones, CEO of Jones Spacelink, Ltd., and Jones Intercable, Inc., and author of the book *Make All America a School.*

Degree Programs

The George Washington University's M.A. is just one of several degree programs offered by Mind Extension University.

In 1989 the network began offering a Master's of Business Administration from Colorado State University. This was ME/U's first degree program and the first four graduates received their diplomas in May 1992.

ME/U also offers a Master's of Library Science from the University of Arizona. Although most coursework is completed by video, the M.L.S. program does require 12 hours of on-campus work.

For undergraduate students, ME/U offers a Bachelor's Completion Degree in Management from the University of Maryland University College and a Bachelor's Completion

Degree in Social Science from Washington State University. The programs are for students who need to finish the final two years of their bachelor's degree.

Each semester the network also airs for-credit, graduate and undergraduate General Studies courses from a variety of universities. Course offerings include Introduction to Art from Oklahoma State University and Introduction to Computer Science from the New Jersey Institute of Technology.

In all, Mind Extension University is affiliated with 25 accredited universities around the United States.

High School Programming

In addition to college and graduate-level courses, the network offers live, interactive high school classes produced by the nationally acclaimed TI-IN Network, San Antonio, Texas. Classes include Japanese, German, Spanish, Sign Language, Marine Biology, and Anatomy.

Personal and Professional Development

To round out its educational programming format, ME/U offers a wide variety of personal and professional development courses for lifelong learners of all ages and education levels. Such classes include foreign languages, GED preparation courses, continuing education for teachers, and seminars for professionals.

The network also is a partner with the U.S. Library of Congress on the Global Library Project. The project produces ME/U programs that focus on the treasures found in libraries around the world.

ABOUT THE GEORGE WASHINGTON UNIVERSITY

The George Washington University had its beginning in 1821 as The Columbian College in the District of Columbia. The name of the institution was changed in 1873 to Columbian University and in 1940 to The George Washington University. The debt of the University to George Washington, whose name it bears, is an intangible one.

George Washington, as president and as private citizen, had urgently insisted upon the establishment of a national university in the federal city. There he hoped that, while being instructed in the arts and sciences, students from all parts of the country would acquire the habits of good citizenship, throwing off local prejudices and gaining firsthand a knowledge of the practice, as well as the theory, of republican government. To further the materialization of his hopes, Washington left a bequest of 50 shares of the Potomac Company "towards the endowment of a University to be established within the limits of the District of Columbia, under the auspices of the Central Government, if that government should incline to extend a fostering hand towards it." The Congress never extended a "fostering hand." The Potomac Company passed out of existence, and Washington's bequest became worthless.

Fully conscious of Washington's hopes, but motivated primarily by a great missionary urge and the need for a learned clergy, a group of dedicated ministers and laymen sponsored a movement for the establishment of a college in the District of Columbia. They raised funds for the purchase of a site and petitioned Congress for a charter. After much delay and amendment, Congress granted a charter, which was approved by President Monroe on February 9, 1821. To safeguard the College's nonsectarian character, it provided "That persons of every religious denomination shall be capable of being elected Trustees; nor shall any person, either as President, Professor, Tutor, or pupil, be refused admittance into said College, or denied any of the privileges, immunities, or advantages thereof, for or on account of his sentiments in matters of religion."

During the entire time when the institution was known as Columbian College, its activities were centered on College Hill, a tract of 46 acres between the present 14th and 15th streets extending north from Florida Avenue to somewhat beyond Columbia Road. The Medical School was located downtown. For the better part of the Columbian University period, the buildings of the University were situated along H Street between 13th and 15th streets.

During the last half-century, the University's campus has been developed in that section of the old First Ward familiarly known as Foggy Bottom, between 19th and 24th streets, south of Pennsylvania Avenue. This area has many reminders of the historic interest to the University.

Purpose and Objectives

The purpose of The George Washington University was to realize "the aspirations of Washington, Jefferson and Madison, for the erection of a university at the seat of the Federal Government." Over the years it has been the aim to develop the University ideal in the nation's capital with a view toward meeting the changing needs of society while continuing to pursue the traditional principles of learning and research.

The University recognizes its special opportunities in and obligations to one of the principal capitals of the world. It is a primary objective of the University to utilize its location in the nation's capital in continuing the development of a great nationally and internationally oriented university.

Comparative Employment Profiles

Joseph A. Hutchinson
Associate Director

Pauline M. Rankin
Director
Division of Instructional Support and Development
Louisiana State University

INTRODUCTION

People work for a variety of reasons, but one of the primary incentives is a monetary one. Although salary alone does not provide an adequate measure of job performance, self-worth, or professional growth, it is closely associated with all three. Small wonder that salary information has universal appeal!

The authors published salary survey results in 1984, 1987, 1989, and 1992. Information requested via the survey questionnaires has remained constant; therefore, some long-term observations are possible regarding compensation.

METHODOLOGY

Questionnaires were mailed to members of the Association for Educational Communications and Technology (AECT). Items on the survey instrument examined the following employment factors:

- Primary work setting

- Job classification

- Minimum education required for employment

- Education achieved

- Length of employment in the field

- Length of employment in present position

- Annual income

- Number of months employed per year

- Primary source of funding

- Demographic information (age, gender, ethnicity, location).

In the first study, the authors used a random sample of 15 percent of the AECT membership. In each of the three subsequent surveys, the authors sampled 20 percent of the membership; those samples were stratified by work setting. Figure 1 indicates the number and percentage of usable questionnaires that were returned.

	USABLE RETURNS	% OF MAILOUTS
1983	474	60.0
1986	440	57.0
1989	392	59.6
1991	422	54.5

Fig. 1. Survey Returns

FINDINGS

Work Setting

Two employment settings have consistently remained the most frequently reported: College/University and School District. Figure 2 on page 46 indicates the percentage of respondents for each work setting used by AECT.

Job Titles

Although the job categories were redefined by AECT, those most frequently reported were Audiovisual Specialist, Media Director, and Teacher/Professor. Figure 3 on page 47 provides the primary job titles of respondents.

Education

In most cases, the level of education achieved by respondents equalled or exceeded requirements for their positions. In the most recent survey, college degrees were required for 97 percent of the jobs reported, whereas 74 percent of the jobs called for graduate degrees; more than 93 percent of the respondents held graduate degrees (57.0 percent masters and 36.1 percent doctorates). This pattern has been consistent throughout the four studies conducted by the authors.

Length of Employment

The percentage of members reporting employment in the field for 10 years or less has declined overall during the decade (37 percent to 31 percent), while those employed 21 to 30 years have increased from 17 percent to almost 25 percent (Figure 4 on page 48). In each survey, approximately two-thirds of the respondents indicated that they had been in their present positions for 10 years or less.

(Text continues on page 48.)

	1983	1986	1989	1991
Business/Industry	7.0%	5.7%	6.6%	5.7%
College/University	41.8%	42.1%	41.6%	43.6%
Elementary School	3.8%	3.4%	2.8%	4.0%
Government Agency	*	*	1.3%	1.4%
Jr./Comm.Coll./Tech.Inst.	9.6%	8.0%	8.6%	8.5%
Military	0.6%	0.7%	1.0%	0.7%
Nonprofit Organization	2.6%	0.2%	3.3%	1.9%
Other	8.1%	5.7%	3.0%	4.7%
Public Library	*	*	0.5%	0.2%
Regional Media/Ed. Serv. Ctr.	4.3%	5.5%	6.6%	6.6%
School District	12.3%	16.6%	13.7%	14.5%
Secondary School	9.1%	9.1%	9.6%	7.3%
State Dept. of Education	0.9%	3.0%	1.3%	0.7%

* Not used by AECT at time of survey

Fig. 2. Distribution of AECT Members by Work Setting

	1983	1986	1989	1991
AV Specialist/Media Director	*	*	*	19.9%
Audiovisual Specialist	14.6%	10.5%	7.4%	*
Curricula/Instructional Developer	9.4%	7.1%	4.8%	4.1%
Educational Computing Specialist	5.8%	2.1%	2.0%	*
Library/Information Specialist	10.6%	9.6%	9.4%	11.3%
Media Director (Print & Nonprt)	*	*	*	21.6%
Media Director/Administrator	25.0%	40.9%	36.2%	*
Other	*	*	1.0%	6.7%
Other Educational Administrator	5.0%	7.3%	12.0%	7.7%
Researcher/Consultant	7.1%	2.3%	1.8%	2.6%
Sales/Promotional Representative	*	*	0.8%	1.4%
Staff Mbr. Gov. Agency/Project	*	*	0.8%	1.0%
TV Spec/Producer/Director	8.1%	2.7%	3.8%	2.4%
Tch/Prof-media responsibilities	*	*	6.4%	6.7%
Tch/Prof-no media responsibilities	*	*	12.2%	12.5%
Teacher/Professor	14.5%	17.7%	*	*
Training Director	*	*	1.3%	2.2%

* Not used by AECT at time of survey

Fig. 3. Distribution of AECT Members by Job Title

	< or = 10	11-20	21-30	> 30
1983	37.0 %	44.0 %	16.0 %	3.0 %
1986	34.6 %	45.7 %	18.0 %	1.7 %
1989	29.3 %	45.9 %	21.5 %	3.3 %
1991	31.0 %	41.3 %	24.8 %	2.9 %

Fig. 4. Number of Years Employed

General

The average age of survey respondents continues to increase slowly, 46.4 years in the 1991 study. The minimum reported age of 24 remains fairly constant compared to earlier surveys, but the maximum age of 73 has declined by four years since the 1983 study. Most of the respondents were employed on a 12-month basis (Figure 5).

The percentage of salaries funded by governmental appropriations has increased during the four studies, while the percentage of salaries funded by generated revenue has decreased (Figure 6).

As in previous studies, most of the 1991 survey respondents were Caucasian (93.3 percent). The other participants were Hispanic (2.8 percent), African-American (1.8 percent), Asian/Pacific Islander (1.6 percent), and Native American (0.5 percent).

Gender

Survey results indicate an increase in the proportion of females among educational technologists from 1986 to 1991. Six years ago, males outnumbered females almost two to one. Women presently comprise 43.1 percent of the membership. In 1991, the average female respondent earned $41,311 during an 11-month period, was 45.3 years of age, had 14.2 years of experience in the field, and had been 8.5 years in her current position. Figures for the average male respondent were higher in all categories: a salary of $47,873 for 11.3 months, age of 47.1 years, experience of 16.8 years in the field, and 9.7 years in his current position. In the 1991 study, 38.0 percent of the male respondents held doctoral degrees, compared with 33.3 percent of the females.

Compensation

The primary objective for surveying AECT members over much of the past decade has been to obtain comparative salary data that could be analyzed in terms of employment variables and national economic trends. A long-term examination of compensation must consider the relative value of the dollar during the same period.

	12 MONTHS	11 MONTHS	10 MONTHS	9 MONTHS	OTHER
1983	63.0 %	*	*	20.0 %	16.0 %
1986	59.3 %	*	*	21.6 %	19.1 %
1989	61.8 %	5.6 %	10.4 %	18.1 %	4.1 %
1991	62.0 %	6.7 %	16.0 %	12.2 %	3.1 %

* Did not appear on survey form.

Fig. 5. Number of Months Employed Per Year

	GOVERNMENTAL APPROPRIATION	GENERATED REVENUE (PROFIT, TUITION, ETC.)	OTHER
1983	63.0 %	31.0 %	6.0 %
1986	64.6 %	27.1 %	8.3 %
1989	68.5 %	22.8 %	8.7 %
1991	74.4 %	16.2 %	9.4 %

Fig. 6. Source of Funding

Salary levels reported during the initial (1983) survey were used as a base from which adjustments for economic fluctuations were made to subsequent survey findings. All computations were made on the basis of the Consumer Price Index (CPI) values issued for the year and month in which each of the respective surveys was conducted. The Consumer Price Index is issued monthly by the U.S. Department of Labor, Bureau of Labor Statistics. The values used by the authors reflect the number of months between surveys, *not* annual inflation rates. Figure 7 on page 50 provides information on the average salary of AECT members as a whole.

Unadjusted salary averages increased significantly, from $29,672 to $44,990, between 1983 and 1991. However, a different pattern emerged when adjustments were made for the effect of inflation. A modest gain of 6.6 percent was experienced between 1983 and 1986. The 1989 CPI adjusted average was a marginal 1.6 percent above the 1986 reported salary. Between 1989 and 1991, the cumulative inflation rate of 15.3 percent exceeded the average salary growth by 5.5 percent, resulting in a net loss in purchasing power. This general pattern emerged repeatedly when the data were examined in terms of variables such as education, work setting, and geographic location.

Figure 8 on page 50 provides information on salaries as a function of the education attained by survey respondents. During the first period of comparison (1983-1986), all categories experienced economic growth. Only graduate degrees held their own against inflation during the second period. All lost in the final period. The master's degree posted the best long-term record and was the only category that provided a composite gain.

1983 Avg.	1986 Avg.	Adj. '86 Average -8.9%	'83-'86 Gain/Loss	1989 Avg.	Adj. '89 Average -12.5%	'86-'89 Gain/Loss	1991 Avg.	Adj. '91 Average -15.3%	'89-'91 Gain/Loss
$29,672	$34,736	$31,644	$1,972 6.6%	$40,316	$35,277	$541 1.6%	$44,990	$38,107	($2,209) -5.5%

Fig. 7. Average Salaries of AECT Members: 1983-91

	1983 Avg.	1986 Avg.	Adj. '86 Average -8.9%	'83-'86 Gain/Loss	1989 Avg.	Adj. '89 Average -12.5%	'86-'89 Gain/Loss	1991 Avg.	Adj. '91 Average -15.3%	'89-'91 Gain/Loss
A/T	$24,333	$27,800	$25,326	$993 4.1%	$30,800	$26,950	($850) -3.1%	$34,000	$28,798	($2,002) -6.5%
Bach.	$25,041	$30,217	$27,528	$2,487 9.9%	$29,466	$25,799	($4,418) -14.6%	$32,333	$27,386	($2,099) -7.1%
Mast.	$28,054	$32,415	$29,530	$1,476 5.3%	$38,765	$33,919	$1,504 4.6%	$43,428	$36,784	($1,981) -5.1%
Doct.	$34,378	$39,496	$35,981	$1,603 4.7%	$45,894	$40,157	$661 1.7%	$49,816	$42,194	($3,700) -8.1%

Fig. 8. Comparison of Salaries by Education

An analysis of salaries by AECT membership regions resulted in the values displayed in Figure 9 on page 52. Region 1 was the only area experiencing gains during each of the survey periods. Most of the regions gained during all but the 1989-1991 period.

Salary comparisons were also made in terms of the work setting in which respondents indicated employment (Figure 10 on page 53). Two categories, Governmental Agency and Public Library, were created by AECT between the 1986 and 1989 studies. Therefore, comparisons for them could only be made between the last two surveys.

Wide fluctuations in the salary levels of some work settings can generally be attributed to sampling, or the fact that they include relatively small numbers of AECT members, rather than to actual economic gains or losses (refer to Figure 2 for work settings containing less than 10 percent of the association's membership).

Changes in the job categories used by AECT made it possible to provide long-term comparisons for only five titles: Curricula/Instructional Developer, Library/Information Specialist, Other Educational Administrator, Researcher/Consultant, and TV Specialist/Producer/Director. However, as Figure 11 on page 54 shows, comparisons can be made between at least two surveys for all job classes.

REFERENCES

Hutchinson, J. A., and Rankin, P. M. (1984, April). Survey of salaries, education, and funding in instructional technology. *Instructional Innovator*, 29(4), 14-35.

Hutchinson, J. A., and Rankin, P. M. (1987). Employment profiles and compensation for educational technologists, 1983-1986. In *Educational Media and Technology Yearbook* vol. 13 (Littleton, CO: Libraries Unlimited), 100-112.

Hutchinson, J. A., and Rankin, P. M. (1989, September). 1989 AECT member salary survey. *Tech Trends*, 34(4), 10-15.

Hutchinson, J. A., and Rankin, P. M. (1992). Factors influencing salaries for educational technologists. *Tech Trends*, 37(3), 15-18.

	1983 Avg.	1986 Avg.	Adj. '86 Average -8.9%	'83-'86 Gain/Loss		1989 Avg.	Adj. '89 Average -12.5%	'86-'89 Gain/Loss		1991 Avg.	Adj. '91 Average -15.3%	'89-'91 Gain/Loss	
1	$24,453	$33,187	$30,233	$5,780	23.6%	$40,519	$35,454	$2,267	6.8%	$48,833	$41,362	$843	2.1%
2	$28,538	$34,491	$31,421	$2,883	10.1%	$42,855	$37,498	$3,007	8.7%	$47,643	$40,354	($2,501)	-5.8%
3	$26,728	$33,571	$30,583	$3,855	14.4%	$40,186	$35,163	$1,592	4.7%	$46,919	$39,740	($446)	-1.1%
4	$24,577	$32,357	$29,477	$4,900	19.9%	$32,750	$28,656	($3,701)	-11.4%	$37,692	$31,925	($825)	-2.5%
5	$31,094	$34,578	$31,501	$407	1.3%	$40,458	$35,401	$823	2.4%	$46,706	$39,560	($898)	-2.2%
6	$32,580	$34,791	$31,695	($885)	-2.7%	$41,643	$36,438	$1,647	4.7%	$46,523	$39,405	($2,238)	-5.4%
7	$28,111	$34,508	$31,437	$3,326	11.8%	$36,844	$32,239	($2,270)	-6.6%	$40,327	$34,157	($2,687)	-7.3%
8	$28,028	$30,724	$27,990	($38)	-0.1%	$39,400	$34,475	$3,751	12.2%	$41,333	$35,009	($4,391)	-11.1%
9	$31,498	$38,866	$35,407	$3,909	12.4%	$44,558	$38,988	$122	0.3%	$49,455	$41,888	($2,670)	-6.0%

Fig. 9. Comparison of Salaries by AECT Region

	1983 Avg.	1986 Avg.	Adj. '86 Average -8.9%	'83-'86 Gain/Loss	1989 Avg.	Adj. '89 Average -12.5%	'86-'89 Gain/Loss	1991 Avg.	Adj. '91 Average -15.3%	'89-'91 Gain/Loss
Business/Industry	$34,635	$36,520	$33,270	($1,365) -3.9%	$45,923	$40,183	$3,663 10.0%	$48,167	$40,797	($5,126) -11.2%
College/University	$29,455	$33,281	$30,319	$864 2.9%	$39,244	$34,339	$1,058 3.2%	$42,546	$36,036	($3,208) -8.2%
Elementary School	$24,666	$27,933	$25,447	$781 3.2%	$33,273	$29,114	$1,181 4.2%	$41,094	$34,807	$1,534 4.6%
Government Agency	*	*	*	* *	$48,800	*	* *	$48,333	$40,938	($7,862) -16.1%
Comm.Coll Tech. Inst.	$29,488	$33,971	$30,948	$1,460 4.9%	$37,294	$32,632	($1,339) -3.9%	$45,278	$38,350	$1,056 2.8%
Military	$34,332	$39,666	$36,136	$1,804 5.3%	$29,000	$25,375	($14,291) -36.0%	$34,000	$28,798	($202) -0.7%
Nonprofit Org.	$27,332	$33,000	$30,063	$2,731 10.0%	$44,769	$39,173	$6,173 18.7%	$41,500	$35,151	($9,619) -21.5%
Other	$28,221	$39,960	$36,404	$8,183 29.0%	$41,333	$36,166	($3,794) -9.5%	$44,200	$37,437	($3,896) -9.4%
Public Library	*	*	*	* *	$50,000	*	* *	$50,000	$42,350	($7,650) -15.3%
Reg.Media Ed.Serv.Ct.	$31,899	$40,500	$36,896	$4,997 15.7%	$43,462	$38,029	($2,471) -6.1%	$53,500	$45,315	$1,853 4.3%
School Dist.	$31,982	$37,054	$33,756	$1,774 5.5%	$43,556	$38,112	$1,058 2.9%	$51,311	$43,460	($96) -0.2%
Secondary School	$26,208	$31,800	$28,970	$2,762 10.5%	$37,459	$32,777	$977 3.1%	$39,548	$33,497	($3,962) -10.6%
State Dept. of Ed.	$32,999	$37,000	$33,707	$708 2.1%	$34,800	$30,450	($6,550) -17.7%	$52,667	$44,609	$9,809 28.2%

* Not used by AECT at time of survey

Fig. 10. Comparison of Salaries by Work Setting

Job	1983 Avg.	1986 Avg.	Adj.86 Average -8.9%	'83-'86 Gain/Loss		1989 Avg.	Adj.'89 Average -12.5%	'86-'89 Gain/Loss		1991 Avg.	Adj.'91 Average -15.3%	'89-'91 Gain/Loss	
AV Spec/Media Dir.	*	*	*	*	*	*	*	*	*	$40,262	*	*	*
AV Spec.	$24,346	$27,434	$24,992	$646	2.7%	$28,929	$25,313	($2,121)	-7.7%	*	*	*	*
Curr/Inst.Developer	$30,148	$35,516	$32,355	$2,207	7.3%	$35,579	$31,132	($4,384)	-12.3%	$41,889	$35,480	($399)	-0.3%
Ed.Computing Spec.	$28,500	$27,000	$24,597	($3,903)	-13.7%	$33,500	$29,313	$2,313	8.6%	*	*	*	*
Library/Info Spec.	$23,983	$30,761	$28,023	$4,040	16.8%	$38,324	$33,534	$2,773	9.0%	$37,545	$31,801	($6,523)	-17.0%
Media Dir. (Print/nonprt)	*	*	* -	*	*	*	*	*	*	$50,330	*	*	*
Media Dir./Admin.	$31,119	$37,822	$34,456	$3,337	10.7%	$41,937	$36,695	($1,127)	-3.0%	*	*	*	*
Other	*	*	*	*	*	$37,000	*	*	*	$44,345	$37,560	$560	1.5%
Other Ed.Administrator	$36,666	$41,687	$37,977	$1,311	3.6%	$43,333	$37,916	($3,771)	-9.0%	$53,188	$45,050	$1,717	4.0%
Researcher/Consult.	$30,500	$37,100	$33,798	$3,298	10.8%	$40,143	$35,125	($1,975)	-5.3%	$42,909	$36,344	($3,799)	-9.5%
Sales/Promo Rep	*	*	*	*	*	$27,333	*	*	*	$48,333	$40,938	$13,605	49.8%
Mbr. Gov. Agency/Proj	*	*	*	*	*	$43,333	*	*	*	$50,000	$42,350	($983)	-2.3%
TV Spec/Producer/Dir.	$30,476	$32,166	$29,303	($1,173)	-3.8%	$38,000	$33,250	$1,084	3.4%	$44,000	$37,268	($732)	-1.9%
Tch-media resp.	*	*	*	*	*	$36,880	*	*	*	$43,000	$36,421	($459)	-1.2%
Tch-no media resp.	*	*	*	*	*	$42,167	*	*	*	$46,615	$39,483	($2,684)	-6.4%
Teacher/Professor	$30,923	$31,884	$29,046	($1,877)	-6.1%	*	*	*	*	*	*	*	*
Training Director	*	*	*	*	*	$59,000	*	*	*	$49,111	$41,597	($17,403)	-29.5%

* Not used by AECT at time of survey

Fig. 11. Comparison of Salaries by Job

Part Three
Current Developments

Introduction

One obligation of an annual review such as the *Educational Media and Technology Yearbook* is to present up-to-date information on new developments in the field. This book represents a growing field with new products, innovative ideas, and exciting new applications of media and technology to the processes of teaching and learning. This section offers a smorgasbord of information that should be useful to every educational media and technology professional. Although it would be impossible to capture all of the new developments, there is some order and rationale for the articles presented here.

The categories used in the design of this part facilitated the solicitation of the specific articles presented here. It is the intention of the editors to continue these categories in future editions of the *Yearbook* so that there will be a regular chronicle of developments in the field over the years. There has not been any such documentation, except for what appears on a random basis in professional journals. The categories and the authors for each article represented in this edition are

Research	Rose M. Marra and David H. Jonassen
Information Technology	James Purcell and Carrie Costamagna
	Deborah Y. Bauder, Mary Planow, Ron Sarner, and David Carr
Networking	John Cradler
	Roy Tennant
	Michael B. Eisenberg
Telecommunications	Margaret Honey and Andres Henriquez
	John C. Hedberg, Barry Harper, and Suzanne McNamara
	Jinny Goldstein and Mary Harley Kruter
	Jim Ritts
	Barry Willis

Individuals may read articles in this part selectively. Each article is self-contained; there is no overall theme. Each article offers state-of-the-art information that speaks to contemporary issues and each author is a specialist in his or her respective area.

Whither Constructivism

Rose M. Marra
AT&T

David H. Jonassen
University of Colorado at Denver

The philosophical perspective of *constructivism*, and the paradigm shift for instructional design that it may imply, continue to be widely discussed topics in our field. Literature on constructivism has primarily contrasted the constructivist and objectivist paradigms (Jonassen 1991; Duffy and Jonassen 1992). The implications of constructivism and existing and potential results from these applications are the focus of this paper.

In this paper, we begin with an overview of the current literature on constructivism, the theoretical foundations of constructivism and how they compare with objectivism, and a look at constructivistic principles. As is often the case, it is difficult to apply theory in practice. So, next we address specific differences between constructivism and objectivism at the implementation level, as well as analysis of applications and the strategies used to implement constructivistic principles, with specific foci on implementing constructivism in instructional design and in the classroom.

THEORETICAL FOUNDATIONS OF OBJECTIVISM AND CONSTRUCTIVISM

This section provides an overview of the theoretical foundations of objectivism and constructivism. This includes a discussion of the paradigms' basic assumptions, strengths, and weaknesses, and then a look at constructivistic principles. These comparisons will be the basis for the application analysis performed in subsequent sections.

Objectivism

Objectivism has its roots in *realism* and *essentialism* (Lakoff 1987). Realists believe in the existence of the real world, which is external to humans and therefore independent of any human experience. This belief bases itself on the existence of reliable knowledge about the world. As humans, we strive to gain this knowledge. What is epistemologically important to this position is that it assumes that we all gain the same understanding. Essentialism holds that among the characteristics of this stable knowledge is the existence of essential properties in things. Objectivism and its advocates therefore seek to analyze entities in the world to isolate those properties. Learning then is a process of remembering and applying those properties.

The important metaphysical position that objectivism takes (see Table 1; Jonassen 1991) is that the world is real, it is structured, and that structure can be modeled for the learner. The purpose of the mind is to "mirror" that reality and its structure. It does so by thought processes that manipulate abstract symbols (primarily language) that represent that reality. The meaning that is produced by the thought processes is external to the understander; it is determined by the structure of the real world.

Table 1

Comparison of objectivist and constructivist perspectives (Jonassen 1991). Reprinted with permission of the Association for Educational Communications and Technology.

	Objectivist	*Constructivist*
Reality (real world)	External to the knower	Determined by the knower
	Structure determined by entities, properties, and relations	Product of mind Symbolic procedures construct reality
	Structure can be modeled	Structure relies on experiences and interpretations
Mind	Processor of symbols	Builder of symbols
	Mirror of nature	Perceiver/interpreter of nature
	Abstract machine for manipulating symbols	Conceptual system for constructing reality
Thought	Disembodied: independent of human experience	Embodied: grows out of bodily experience
	Governed by external reality	Grounded in perception/construction
	Reflects external reality	Grows out of physical and social experience
	Manipulates abstract symbols	Imaginative: enables abstract thought
	Represents (mirrors) reality	More than representation (mirror) of reality
	Atomistic: decomposable into "building blocks"	Gestalt properties
	Algorithmic	Relies on ecological structure of conceptual system
	Classification	Building cognitive models
	What machines do	More than machines are capable of
Meaning	Corresponds to entities and categories in the world	Does not rely on correspondence to world
	Independent of the understanding of any organism	Dependent upon understanding
	External to the understander	Determined by understander
Symbols	Represent reality	Tools for constructing reality
	Internal representations of external reality ("building blocks")	Representations of internal reality

In objectivism, the role of education is to help students learn about the real world. Students are not encouraged to make their own interpretations of what they perceive; however, the objectivist view does acknowledge that people may have different understandings based on differing experiences. Indeed, because of prior experience, it is unlikely that two people will have identical understandings. The impact of prior experience and human interpretation is seen as leading to partial understandings and biased understandings. It is the role of the teacher or the instruction to interpret events for learners in order to attenuate the impact of a learner's prior experience on learning. For objectivists, learning takes place as a continuum from novice to expert.

Although behaviorism is certainly based on an objectivist tradition, it is not the only objectivist class of theories and ID models. An objectivist epistemology also underlies much of information-processing-based cognitive psychology (Bednar, Cunningham, Duffy, and Perry 1991; Bruner 1990). Even though this family of models posits a greater role for the mind in learning than traditional behaviorist theory, it still espouses the view that there exists an objective reality external to the learner that the learner is to internalize. ID models such as Dick and Carey's (1985) and Gagné and Briggs's Events of Instruction (Aronson and Briggs 1983) have their roots in this objectivist tradition. Both of these models focus on defining learning objectives based on an externally defined reality, and then address means for learners to achieve these objectives.

Objectivism has several strengths, one being its ability to deal with novice learning situations. This is not to say that constructivism cannot be applied to novice learning (Cunningham 1991; Fosnot 1989), but the well-structured learning environments normally fostered by objectivist models of instruction can be helpful for some novices. Wilson (1991) tells of a class's sense of "relief" that occurred when a very open-minded teacher enforced a seating chart on unruly learners, or when Wilson himself gave a drill program for learning the basic math facts to his youngest son. In both of these cases, the instructors normally used constructivistic methods; however, these objectivist-based strategies proved useful in these novice-learning situations.

Objectivism has also provided a common language for instructional design. Critics may—and perhaps validly so—point out that this starting place oversimplifies the learning process and provides a language that is not completely representative of learning, but others recognize as an advantage the objectivist view as a way to at least *begin* to think about instructional models and theories. Fundamental IST processes, such as task analysis, behavioral objectives, criterion-referenced evaluation, and mathemagenic strategies all reflect a behavioristic tradition. These should probably not be construed as universal solutions to all learning situations, but they remain useful models of instruction.

As designers and theorists have examined and applied objectivism, weaknesses have been revealed. Critics claim that the objectivist traditions do little to deal with individual learner differences. All learners are treated as a single, like-minded group of passive objects whose purpose is to come as close as possible to ingesting the presented knowledge and store it away with as little variation as possible from an externally defined reality.

There is also a certain arrogance, critics claim, to the objectivist's long-standing presumption that instruction can externally control what individuals learn. At best, teachers and designers guide learning, but to maximize individual learning, we may have to yield some control purposely, and instead prepare learners to regulate their own learning by providing supportive rather than intervening learning environments.

Constructivism

Constructivism, in contrast, claims that reality is more in the mind of the knower, that the knower constructs a reality or at least interprets it based upon his or her apperceptions. The emphasis in objectivism is on the *object* or product of our knowing, whereas constructivism is concerned with the process of how we *construct* knowledge. How we construct knowledge is a function of one's prior experiences, mental structures, and beliefs that are used to interpret objects and events. Constructivism does not obviate the existence of an external reality. It merely claims that we construct our own reality through interpreting experiences in the world. Critics claim that constructivism is *solipsistic*, that is, the mind can only know its own interpretations, that reality is completely individualistic. Constructivists believe that we are clearly able to comprehend a variety of interpretations and use those in arriving at our own interpretation (Jonassen 1991).

Constructivism begins with fundamentally different assumptions than objectivism (see Table 1). Like many other beliefs, constructivism has varying interpretations. Radical constructivists (Goodman 1984; von Glasersfeld 1984; Watzlawick 1984) believe that there is no external real world other than what our minds create. Our personal world is created by our mind, and that creation defines our own realities, and furthermore those realities cannot be shared in any objective way. Rather, the real world is a product of some mind that constructs the world. A less radical form of constructivism holds that the mind is instrumental and essential in interpreting events, objects, and perspectives on the real world, and that those interpretations comprise a knowledge base that is personal and individualistic. The mind filters input from the world in making those interpretations. Note that in both of these perspectives of constructivism, the mind takes on an essential role in interpreting the world, versus the less prominent role of the mind in the objectivist conceptions.

The important epistemological assumption of constructivism is that meaning is a function of how the individual creates meaning from his or her experiences. We all conceive of the external reality somewhat differently, based upon our unique set of experiences with the world and our beliefs about them. Constructivist models of instruction strive to create environments where learners actively participate in the environment in ways that are intended to help them construct their own knowledge. This is not "active" in the sense of the objectivist model, where a learner is to actively listen and then mirror the *one* correct view of reality, but rather "active" in that the learner must participate and interact with the surrounding environment in order to create his or her own view of the subject. Active learning (Cognition and Technology Group at Vanderbilt 1992) can combat the occurrence of so-called inert knowledge. If learners actively build their own schematic links to the new learning, they have more ownership in those links and those links are less likely to degenerate over time.

For example, cognitive flexibility theory is implemented in a computer-based environment called *Kane* (Spiro and Jehng 1990). The purpose of *Kane* is to help film students critique the motivating forces for the central character in the movie *Citizen Kane*. There are various views on what drove Kane to act in the way he did; the program aids students in constructing example-based arguments for various perspectives, rather than reiterating a particular, accepted view of Kane.

No theory is without its critics, and constructivism is no exception. Advocates of constructivism claim that self-generated knowledge, when combined with learner control of instruction, increases the likelihood of far transfer of learning. Critics claim that when learners are given more opportunity to construct their own, that knowledge is more likely to be erroneous (Cognition and Technology Group at Vanderbilt 1992). Although the possibility of erroneous knowledge exists in objectivist learning as well, it is more likely to occur in the more learner-controlled constructivistic environments. Note that a radical constructivist would challenge the idea that a learner's own knowledge could be erroneous—if one builds one's own view, it cannot be erroneous. The challenge for constructivists then becomes how to correct those errors, given that the learner is in control. Though such erroneous knowledge might be caught during evaluation, it would be more effective to detect errors earlier in the instructional process. The earlier the knowledge is detected, the less entrenched or strengthened are the erroneous constructs. This implies a need for improved methods of monitoring and diagramming the constructs being developed by the learner while they are being constructed. (Note, however, that understanding how to do evaluation in a constructivist environment is not a straightforward question, and has been widely discussed in constructivistic literature [Jonassen 1992b; Perkins 1991].)

Perhaps the most consistent criticism of constructivism is that it must necessarily result in academic chaos. If all learners construct their own meaning from information, how can we share enough knowledge to even communicate? (Not that we always do such a good job even when we assume we are dealing with an externally defined reality.) Nonetheless, we do come to share the same meaning (or at least close enough to the same) for objects, events, and ideas through a process of social negotiation of meaning. That is, most of us have socially agreed on the interpretations of the meaning and purpose of traffic lights. Although individual differences still exist (in the latter case, resulting in a socially negotiated form of punishment), we clearly share enough meaning to enable us to communicate with each other (see also Cunningham 1991).

Summary

Each paradigm has an underlying conceptualization of what it means to learn, to understand, and to instruct. For purposes of differentiating these paradigms and their assumptions, objectivism and constructivism are often described as polar extremes on a continuum. Most practitioners, however, assume positions that fall nearer the middle of the continuum (Jonassen 1991).

objectivism - - - - - - - - - -•- - - - - - - - - - - - - - - - - - constructivism
externally "mediated" reality   internally "mediated" reality

Neither perspective, despite the zealousness of its proponents, necessarily tells the whole story or provides the correct solutions to any or all learning problems. They each provide beliefs that are converted to recommendations about how instruction ought to support learning. Both objectivist and constructivist instructional models will result in some learning. Constructivism, the primary topic of this paper, provides recommendations that are described in the next section.

ANALYSIS OF CONSTRUCTIVIST PRINCIPLES AS APPLIED TO INSTRUCTION

In this section of the paper we examine some of the instructional implications of constructivism. Although the constructivist literature is quite rich at the philosophical level (see *Educational Technology*, May 1991 issue), practitioners and theorists alike desire more discussion at the application level (Jonassen 1992b; Rieber 1992; Fosnot 1989). For example, Duffy and Jonassen (1992) recommend that instruction should be *situated* and that cognitive activities should be *authentic*. The challenge is to determine what those concepts mean at an application level and how to implement them. In this section, we begin by describing constructivist recommendations for instruction. Later, we analyze the use of constructivistic principles in several instructional implementations.

Why look at implementations when one is discussing theories? Implementations reflect an underlying conceptualization of what the designer feels it means to learn, to understand, and to instruct. Carroll and Campbell (1988) argue that the things we build (computer interfaces in their case) provide a rich basis for studying and understanding the theory that underlies our design. That is, our theory of learning is implicit in our design, and hence one can come to a reasonable understanding of our beliefs about learning from an analysis of that design and subsequent implementation. Though instructional designers typically may not have the time or support to explicitly apply a theory of learning during a design or development task, the theory is nonetheless an implicit and integral part of the instruction that results.

Constructivism's Principles

Proponents of constructivism maintain that purposeful learning may be supported by constructivistic learning environments that exhibit these principles and that have been developed from the assumptions outlined previously. Each of the following constructivist principles is discussed with an emphasis on how it affects instructional implementations. The following section, which focuses on specific application examples, addresses how these principles may be carried out.

Focus on knowledge construction, not reconstruction. Constructivism is concerned with holistic learning that focuses on a *domain* of knowledge as opposed to limiting itself to particular skills within that domain (Spiro, Feltovich, Jacobson, and Coulson 1992). This holistic view includes not only a more complete view of the topic being taught (for instance, math taught in the context of being used to calculate the amount of lumber available in a particular tree), but also a more complete view of the learner. What are the learner's goals? How motivated is the learner to go beyond a simple mirroring of the knowledge presented?

The *ScienceVision* application (Tobin and Dawson 1992), which describes itself as a constructivistic application and focuses on math and science learning, illustrates this holistic aspect of constructivism when it actually states that one of its goals is to increase learner confidence.

Similarly, Cunningham (1991) argues that it is not the goal of instruction to teach individuals to know specific things, but rather to show them how to construct interpretations of those things. He takes a tools approach to learning whereby the tools instructors provide or, alternatively, that are collaboratively developed, are the means by which learners construct their interpretations.

Promote context-dependent knowledge construction. Knowledge that is taken out of context during instruction is not authentic and does not have as much meaning to the learner. If you decontextualize teaching by teaching abstract symbols and then ask learners to manipulate those symbols, then what was supposedly learned has less meaning. This is the basis for the cognitive apprenticeship model (Collins, Brown, and Newman 1988), wherein learning takes place in as close to the actual context as is possible. For instance, in the analysis of *Kane* (described earlier), students construct arguments for what motivates the character Kane by putting together actual segments of the movie. Although a verbal treatment of the same topic would be feasible, the film snips have the potential for creating a more convincing argument (because the actual film is referenced) while still requiring the learner to discriminate between those items that support the position and those that do not.

Provide multiple representations of reality. Spiro and colleagues (1992) maintain that teaching must not remove the complexity that is natural to so many ideas in the world, but must rather be carried out within that complexity. Complexity, they claim, results from the multiple viewpoints that provide interpretations or advice on any topic. For instance, in the philosophical discussion earlier, the interpretation that you, the reader, ultimately construct results from considering each of the perspectives and accepting, adapting, or rejecting parts of each. Focusing on a narrowed, boiled-down version of a concept can result in a limited and perhaps misleading understanding of that concept. This often happens when a metaphor is used to explain a complex phenomenon. Using metaphors is certainly not a bad or ineffective instructional strategy, but one must guard against the possible oversimplification that may result. An alternative might be to use a family of metaphors to describe different aspects of the concept. Spiro helps learners appreciate the complexity of a domain through representing multiple perspectives and points of view on the topic under consideration. Learners achieve a more complete view of the knowledge by "criss-crossing the information landscape" represented by these multiple representations.

Provide real-world, case-based learning environments. Constructivists believe that meaning is indexed by experience or context. Therefore, case-based instruction is recommended as an alternative to abstract, rule-based learning methods. In rule-based systems, knowledge is presented as being static and simply defined. Jonassen, Mayes, and McAleese (1993) indicate that the most meaningful learning—learning where the most transfer takes place—is case-based and involves meaningful real-world tasks. Resnick (1987) argues in a similar fashion that one of the reasons school learning is so often not useful is that it is too removed from the real world and does not often provide the case-based situations promoted by constructivism. So, for instance, a learner might learn the steps for deriving the equation for a line, but may not understand *why* these steps work. A case-based approach might coach learners through a series of exercises regarding lines in the Cartesian system and help them to derive a method for describing a line via an equation. Case-based instruction allows a richer set of principles to be conveyed and avoids the problem of oversimplification.

Collins's cognitive apprenticeship model (1991) also provides real-world, case-based experiences. The model uses "situated learning," where students learn the conditions for applying knowledge in situations that promote creativity and invention. Thus the knowledge and content are structured by their appropriate uses. Apprenticeship uses different pedagogical tools than traditional instruction, such as modeling processes in the world, and, of course, modeling expert performance. Modeling allows the student to see expert solutions to student-generated problems and makes visible the parts of a process not normally seen. This enables the student to integrate what happens with why it happens.

Support reflective practice. Much of current instructional design is based on the presumption that we can give individuals plans of action, and success is simply a matter of following the plans. Suchman (1987) argues that plans are simply projective or retrospective accounts of action. An individual may enter a situation with a plan, but the critical aspect of performance is the ability to respond to the situational constraints—to be able to construct new plans based on the changing demands and constraints of the situation. In this view, then, plans (the principles, rules, and procedures we teach) are "part of the subject matter of purposeful action, not something to be improved upon or transformed into axiomatic theories of action." Instruction, according to constructivists, should not focus on transmitting plans to the learner but rather on developing the skills of the learner to construct (and reconstruct) plans in response to situational demands and opportunities (Duffy and Jonassen 1992).

Support collaboration, not competition. Collaboration is being encouraged in constructivist learning environments. In their work on *intentional learning*, Bereiter and Scardamalia (1989) describe the benefits of collaboration among learners while working through learning problems. The *Jasper Woodbury* series from the Cognition and Technology Group at Vanderbilt (1992) also draws on collaboration as a principle, basing the argument on the position that collaboration and cooperative learning increases the chances for students to generate their own knowledge. In these environments students have more opportunity to pose questions to one another and develop their own explanations for ideas and theories.

Focus control in the learner level. Many of the preceding principles imply this one: If learners are active, learning in context, collaborating with other learners and the instructor, and generating their own knowledge, then they are necessarily more in control of their learning process than if they were passively listening to an instructor-controlled lecture. Learner control may be implied by these other constructivist principles, but it is worth mentioning again because transferring control from the instructor to the learner represents a major change in instructional practice and a necessary condition for achieving many of the principles already described. For example, if individual learners are controlled in their analysis of the multiple perspectives presented in a cognitive flexibility application like *Kane*, they may not have the opportunity to generate their own views about these perspectives. Although it may be necessary to scaffold and model how to actually do this criss-crossing, fading must occur for the full benefits of the strategy to be realized.

ANALYSIS OF CONSTRUCTIVIST LEARNING APPLICATIONS

The continuum in Figure 1 (Jonassen and Mann, in press) illustrates the transition from objectivist to constructivist applications of learning technologies. The learning technologies range from programmed instruction to intellectual tool kits. The earliest (and some claim the first true) technology of instruction, programmed instruction, led an objectivist series of technology applications including computer-assisted instruction and, to a lesser degree, computer-based learning. The latter included simulations, which may be objectivist or constructivist in nature. Constructivist learning environments include complex content, such as cognitive flexibility theory (described later), generative learning environments that facilitate the use of cognitive learning strategies, and knowledge construction environments, such as computer-supported intentional learning environments (described later). Intellectual tool kits describe an emerging class of technologies that may be embedded in other technologies and that distribute appropriate cognitive functions to the computer.

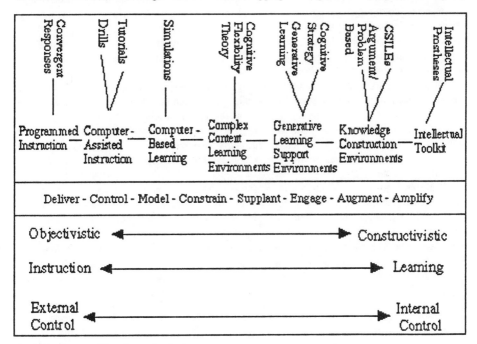

Fig. 1. Continuum of learning technologies.

The purpose or functions of these technologies have evolved as well, from delivery of instruction and modeling and controlling learning through instructional processes. Early technologies were objectivist in nature. They assumed a model of reality that was mapped onto the learner through mathemagenic control of the learning activities. That is, the instruction drove learning, so learners had little ownership of the learning process. Newer, constructivist environments are intended to constrain the learner's options through multiple representations of realities, to supplant some of the required thinking, and always to engage the learner in authentic, meaningful learning tasks. They are learner controlled, and they focus on learning activities that are controlled by the learner rather than the instructional engine. Newer environments and (we believe) future learning environments will increasingly augment and even amplify the learning potential of learners by applying the computational power of the computer to eliminate the drudgery of learning and amplify the capacities of learners.

Although each of these applications and their representative technologies continue to make their contributions to instructional technology, the point of this graphic is to illustrate the trends in learning theory and instructional design. Clearly, a discernible trend exists from applications that simply use technology to aid the student in faithfully reproducing and mirroring the knowledge presented, as represented in traditional drill and practice software, to applications that use the technology to help students build, create, and integrate new knowledge with their existing structures. The objectivist applications tend to be more parts-oriented, whereas the constructivistic ones address knowledge in a more holistic fashion. The instructional implications of both paradigms are contrasted in Table 2. Before examining Table 2, we should point out that there are risks in attempting to describe implementation-level assumptions for constructivism. As Scardamalia and Bereiter (1991) argue, constructivism does not offer many specific guidelines for instruction, and perhaps it is in the very nature of constructivism that it cannot be defined in a precise way at the implementation level. After all, constructivism does recommend personally constructing knowledge bases. Does this not then translate to developing, as designers, our own view of what instruction entails, given the context of a situation at hand? Perhaps that is the case, but nonetheless, there is value in looking at what characteristics might apply to a constructivistic application. Table 2 addresses assumptions at both the design and implementation levels.

Learning, instruction, and assessment activities are not implicitly constructivist or objectivist. For example, strategies such as embedded learning and authentic tasks clearly support meaning construction; however, they can also be used as objectivist strategies. The context in which strategies are used determines, for the most part, whether a strategy is constructivist or objectivist. So strategies that have been traditionally used in the past in an objectivistic fashion at both the design and implementation levels, could possibly be used in a constructivistic way, given the proper context.

Take as an example objective setting, a strategy that by its very name seems objectivistic and, if done in the traditional way of defining exactly what the learner is to accomplish, under what conditions, and at what performance level, is certainly an objectivistic strategy. However, the Cognition and Technology Group at Vanderbilt (1992) provides an example of using objectives in a constructivistic manner with their *Jasper Woodbury* learning environment. *Jasper*, as applied to math, does have an objective. It is not that students be able to do specific sorts of computational math in an *isolated* setting, but is at a higher, perhaps more vague level:

> helping students—all learners—learn to become independent thinkers and learners rather than simply become able to perform basic computations and retrieve simple knowledge facts. (p. 66)

Students must learn to find the computational problem themselves from the surrounding context, so a strategy normally used in an objectivist manner becomes constructivist.

Table 2

Constructivist and objectivist conceptions of learning, instruction, and assessment.

	Constructivist	*Objectivist*
Analysis	Big picture, holistic	Parts-oriented, reductionist
	Occurs in context of problem	Isolated from problem context
Design	Creates plan for knowledge construction	Creates single knowledge representation
	Design in learner control	Designs in instructor control
	Dynamic sequencing	Reductionism-based sequencing
	Tool-oriented	Presentation-centered
Implementation	Distributed control	Centralized control
	Distributed activities	Centralized activities
	Presents multiple perspectives	Presents single correct perspective
	Includes complexity	Simplifies complexity
	Negotiates objectives	Receives objectives
	Integrates across disciplines	Compartmentalizes knowledge
Learner Role	Active	Passive
	Problem definer and solver	Problem receiver and solver
	Controls learning activities	Controlled by learning activities
	Errors are part of learning	Error-free learning sought
	Co-teacher role	Strictly learner
	Collaborative/cooperative	Solitary
	Constructs own world view	Receives a world view
Strategies/ Learning Activities	Authentic, in context activities	Isolated, nonauthentic activities
	Generative learning	Preconstructed learning
	Focus on process and reasoning	Focus on specific content
	Erroneous knowledge generation possible	Errors less likely
	Question generation	Question answerers
Assessment	Dynamic; formed to each learner	Static; same for all learners
	Based on learner's own world view	based on a single world view based on external reality
	Looks for evidence of constructed knowledge	Looks for evidence of an externally defined reality
	Individual learner-based	External to the learner
	Embedded in instruction	Follows instruction

ANALYZING CONSTRUCTIVIST LEARNING APPLICATIONS

The following section examines constructivistic applications for the ways in which they implement the principles discussed earlier. For each application, we describe how the application functions and how learners interact with it, its theoretical foundations as presented by its creators, constructivist principles as applied at the application level, and any issues associated with the application.

The two applications chosen for analysis, the *Jasper Woodbury* series from the Cognition and Technology Group at Vanderbilt (1992) and the *Minimal Manual* (Carroll 1991; Lazonder and van der Meij 1992), are quite different in nature. Though they both potentially implement some subset of the constructivist principles discussed earlier, they are delivered in very different fashions and most probably would be used by different audiences. These differences, as well as their similarities, will become evident in the following discussions.

Jasper Woodbury

The *Jasper Woodbury* series (Cognition and Technology Group at Vanderbilt 1992) is a learning environment designed to offer "generative and cooperative learning activities" in the math and science disciplines. The environment is designed to be an alternative to traditional methods of math and science instruction. The Vanderbilt Group describes *Jasper* as an instructional design approach called "anchored instruction" (Cognition and Technology Group at Vanderbilt 1992). *Anchored instruction* means that learning is situated, or anchored, in engaging, problem-solving-oriented environments that encourage student exploration. This type of environment instructs not only on the "whats" of learning, but also the metaknowledge of "how" and "why" to apply the knowledge.

The *Jasper Woodbury* problem-solving series is a set of video-based adventures designed to provide a realistic basis for problem solving and reasoning in the math and science disciplines. A sample of a *Jasper* adventure is described by Vanderbilt Group (1992). In one adventure, "Rescue at Boone's Meadow," the learner watches as the stage is set for rescuing an injured eagle that Jasper discovers while in a remote location on a fishing trip. Earlier in the video, learners have been exposed to the fuel requirements of an ultralight aircraft. Learners are confronted with the problem of what is the quickest way to get to the remote location and rescue the injured eagle. All the data necessary to solve the problem have been presented in the video story. Students are then asked to collect the necessary data from the video to determine the problem solution. Additionally, the adventures come in pairs designed to reinforce transferring core skills (perhaps applying some sort of calculation) from one adventure scenario to another. This sort of problem solving is an alternative to the often-seen math tests full of nonauthentic questions.

The way *Jasper* is designed offers several ways of using the series in a classroom environment. The descriptions here begin with the most complex model and the one that most completely exercises *Jasper*'s learning functionality.

- The *guided generation* model, more than the other models, emphasizes the importance of generative activities and implements the math learning in the most complex learning environment. Students using this model are required to take the problem stated in the *Jasper* video and then generate their own subgoals and problems that will lead them to the total solution. Although this model poses the most "hands-off" role for the teacher, there is an integral teacher role. The teacher in this model operates as a facilitator to the learning process; the word Vanderbilt Group uses is that the teacher "scaffolds" the learning, but does not by any means structure the problem-solving process. An example of when the teacher might "scaffold" occurs if learners don't know yet how to multiply decimals. The teacher could propose the alternative of thinking of 1.5 hours as 60 minutes and 30 minutes, so that students can deal with these whole-number calculations and then put the results back together.

- The *structured problem-solving* model focuses on the need to minimize student generation of erroneous knowledge during the learning process. The character *Jasper* is not used as fully as in the model just described, but he might be used in parallel to teach some of the basic computational skills needed to solve the problem. Additionally, in an effort to avoid errors and confusion during the problem-solving period, *Jasper* is used with a series of worksheets to guide, mold, and scaffold the necessary thinking and subgoals for solving the overall problem. Thus, the students experience a guided problem-solving environment rather than one in which all steps are learner-controlled.

- The *direct instruction* model is the least generative of the three models. This model uses the *Jasper* series simply as a place to practice the component skills of math and science that they have previously learned in more traditional component, parts-based lessons. Although students still may enjoy the engaging nature of the *Jasper* videos, this model affords few of the generative problem-solving skills that *Jasper* is capable of. *Jasper* is based on the underlying principle that instructional goals for math and science should not be established based on what questions are askable on a test (which tend to focus on component skills and are typically of a reductionist nature), but rather these components should be used in the context of an authentic, real-world-based instructional experience, as opposed to the normally isolated experiences used in a test environment.

The *Jasper* series illustrates the use of cooperative learning and learner-generated information. These characteristics and others were proposed as implementation recommendations by the NCTM Commission on Standards for School Mathematics (1989). They proposed that learning be complex and open-ended, and that it involve problem solving and reasoning and connect the instructional material to the real world.

The degree to which constructivism is evidenced in this application depends on which implementation model is used; however, the very fact that *Jasper* is flexible enough to be used in a variety of ways makes it more constructivist than if it were useful in only a single way. Because of this flexibility, *Jasper* takes on the character of a tool, as opposed to a single instructional device. Many of the theoretical foundations described in the preceding paragraphs are of a constructive nature. In addition, the Vanderbilt Group directly states that the set of learning assumptions that they apply to *Jasper* "are consistent with a class of theories called constructive theories." *Jasper* illustrates several of the aforementioned constructivist attributes. The emphasis on generative learning is a way of supporting the constructivist principle of context-specific knowledge construction. As students are required to generate subgoals for solving the overall problem, they are generating their own knowledge in the context of that problem. All of *Jasper* employs so-called authentic tasks. In *Jasper* the student is immersed in a problem situation that could actually happen and is of interest to the student. Finally, the fact that students tend to do better in solving *Jasper* problems in groups, rather than individually, supports the collaborative nature of constructivism. If one assumes that students, being individuals, necessarily have different existing knowledge constructions, and that these existing constructions will influence how they process the video presentation, then a group of students is more likely to be able to identify the necessary information for solving the problem than an individual. In addition, a group of students is more likely to correct each other's mistakes, whereas an individual student has more of a chance to continue down an incorrect path.

Several issues focus on using *Jasper* in the classroom. Certainly, the most important is which implementation model is chosen. The full, generative nature of the environment is not gained unless the structured problem-solving approach is taken. The other models are not without merit, but will not afford learners the opportunity to generate subgoals and guide themselves through solving the problem. This choice, although providing the opportunity for a less than totally constructivist solution, can also be advantageous, as it offers teachers who are reticent to use such a learning environment as structured problem solving a way to at least begin to expose both themselves and the students to such an environment. By positively experiencing this limited implementation, they may in the future be more likely to consider using a more constructivist model. The self-generated information aspect of the program is a two-edged sword; if the generated information is correct, it is more likely to be better remembered. However, if it is incorrect, the error may not be discovered until the incorrect information is as well embedded as one would hope correct information is.

As mentioned previously, *Jasper* promotes group interactions. Vanderbilt Group has found that, in general, students working in groups are more likely to solve *Jasper* than are individuals. The potential limitation of this finding, as for any group activity, is the failure of students to work cooperatively in groups. This can be a challenge to instructors as they attempt to take on a facilitator role while the *Jasper* series is in use.

A final issue for implementing *Jasper* is the very complexity that is also a source of the environment's value. Though complexity allows learners to experience a real-world problem and avoid the results of instructional oversimplification, the same complexity may actually be discouraging if it is too difficult for the student or not properly facilitated by the instructor. Walter Dick (1991) points out the same danger—that designers would have little problem with Bransford's principles except for the problem complexity, which may overwhelm some learners without adequate entry-level skills.

Initial findings with the *Jasper* series verify the hypothesis that using complex problem examples improves students' ability to perform problem identification and formulation, that is, their ability to know when to apply certain problem-solving strategies and how to proceed given any particular problem. Students may be skilled at the subskills necessary to solve a problem but poor at assembling those subskills into solutions (Cognition and Technology Group at Vanderbilt 1992). The Vanderbilt Group (1990) found that fifth-grade students' abilities at problem formulation improved after four or five class sessions using *Jasper*. Additionally, teachers show a great deal of enthusiasm as they see their students get excited about doing math problems.

Minimal Manual

The *minimal manual*, originally proposed by Carroll (1991) and since further explored by Lazonder and van der Meij (1992), is a computer training manual designed to facilitate the quick productivity startup needs of the novice computer user. For instance, a minimal manual might be implemented for word processing software. The minimal manual differs from conventional manuals in (1) its emphasis on making the users productive as soon as possible, (2) its brevity, and (3) its emphasis on developing error recovery skills. Novice learners use the minimal manual to work on their own and *quickly* learn how to perform the functions they are most interested in. It intends to provide a quick sense of learner satisfaction, accomplishment, and control. To effectively implement the minimal manual and accomplish the goal of having the users in control of their own learning (and, additionally, have the manual accommodate the user's needs), the designers must have a thorough knowledge of this target user population.

The minimal manual is based on four "minimalist" principles, which, as will be discussed, are closely related to constructivist principles: (1) action-oriented nature, (2) support of error recognition and recovery, (3) optimal text usage, and (4) modularity.

The *action-oriented* nature of the manual means it is organized so that it is task- or function-oriented, as opposed to being organized around the structure of the software itself (as in a conventional manual). Thus, a software-organized manual might begin with a description of the first menu item, which may have little to do with what the user most often wants to accomplish. In contrast, the minimal manual would be organized by the tasks the user performs, such as how to exit from any screen. To further emphasize productivity and to capitalize on the fact that learners prefer to learn by doing, the minimal manual focuses on procedural rather than conceptual knowledge. In either case, the minimal manual focuses immediately on real tasks that the user desires to perform. Although several strategies follow from the action-oriented nature of the minimal manual, one is particularly worth mentioning—the use and encouragement of learner exploration and problem solving. As in other constructivist applications (such as *Jasper*), the minimal manual recognizes learner exploration as a motivating experience, as well as placing different demands on the learner's processing than simply following an already written-out procedure. During exploration, learners must construct their own model of the program's operation, as opposed to just following along with one already defined. Finally, exploration can be a learner-motivating experience, for if the learners succeed in constructing meaning through the exploration, they may feel more confident of success in further lessons. Note that for exploration to be successful in the context of the minimal manual, or in any other constructivist application, there must exist a feeling of security for the learners. That is, they must feel protected from irreparably harming any part of the system or their work during the exploration process. This user interface design issue is critical to the success of this strategy.

The *error recognition and recovery* principle answers a concern often raised in connection with constructivism. Namely, the learner in a constructivistic environment has more of a chance of constructing erroneous knowledge, and furthermore, may not discover that erroneous knowledge until it has been firmly ingrained in memory. To address a similar concern in a computer environment, the minimal manual is designed to build not only constructive skills, but corrective skills as well. This is accomplished by having on-the-spot error recovery information associated with every procedure in the minimal manual. In addition, *general* corrective information is given so it applies to a large range of situations, not just the one in question.

To address the *optimal text usage* principle, the minimal manual implements the adage that "less is more." The aim of the manual is to give the learners only what they need to know when they need to know it. This is not intended as a conspiracy to withhold information from the learner, but rather to present information in a timely fashion. Thus, explanations are reduced to a minimum, and furthermore are presented "close to the action." Similar to what the constructivists promote (Duffy and Jonassen 1992), background information in the minimal manual is presented when the learner can make the most use of it in a particular application context.

The *modularity* aspect of the minimal manual means that its chapters are self-contained. A further implication is that users may browse through these chapters in nearly any order that pleases them or that matches their learning goals. Conventional manual chapters can be quite long, sometimes up to 100 pages. The minimal manual, in an effort to allow users to avoid getting bogged down in a long chapter, is designed to have short chapters that require on the average 20 minutes to complete (van der Meij 1992).

In controlled experiments comparing a minimal manual for a word processor to a conventional manual, van der Meij's results confirmed those of a previous, if less rigorous, study by Carroll and Campbell (1988). The hypotheses were that subjects using the minimal manual should complete training faster, complete more test items successfully, and make fewer errors. Though the results were not totally conclusive in all these areas, they did overall favor a minimal approach over the conventional manual.

Lazonder and van der Meij (1992) discuss several issues regarding the minimal manual. Van der Meij (1992) points out that, with the minimal manual's procedure-oriented approach, there is the risk of underdeveloping a deeper model of the program. A look at the error types and error data on success of transfer shows that the minimal manual is no worse than the conventional manual, but also no better.

How does the minimal manual implement constructivism in a text-based environment? By implementing a manual where the "user is focal" (van der Meij 1992), the minimal manual mirrors the constructivistic principle of shifting control away from any external source (whether that be a computer training manual or an instructor is not critical) toward the learner. The minimal manual also implements the constructivist principle of implementing "experience-based learning" (van der Meij 1992). As was also seen in *Jasper* (Cognition and Technology Group at Vanderbilt 1992), the minimal manual quickly immerses the learner in real-world-type tasks, as opposed to long conceptual explanations. The minimalist manual is intended for novices; constructivism, on the other hand, is a more general philosophy that applies to many levels of learning. In fact, there is a certain irony in that some constructivist proponents have argued that constructivism is best applied for advanced knowledge acquisition (Jonassen 1992b), although this is a point on which constructivists disagree (Cunningham 1991; Fosnot 1989). The minimal manual itself, with its novice orientation, seems to be a constructivistic implementation, and perhaps another indication that constructivism is not just for advanced knowledge acquisition anymore.

ISSUES FOR IMPLEMENTING CONSTRUCTIVISM IN INSTRUCTIONAL DESIGN

As has been illustrated, constructivist applications increasingly are being implemented. In addition, the early results indicate a positive and enhanced learning experience when compared with objectivistic approaches, especially for transfer of learning. However, these gains are not without added complexities and issues. Some were mentioned earlier, but not thoroughly explored. This section examines the issues surrounding the application and implementation of constructivism, but it follows that any just criticism of implementing constructivism necessarily reflects on the underlying theoretical basis.

How Practical and Feasible Is Constructivism?

The practicality of constructivist implementations relates to the technological requirements of these implementations. For example, the *Jasper Woodbury* series (Cognitive and Technology Group at Vanderbilt 1992), to be used most constructively, requires a videodisc player with a remote control or barcode reader, as well as the *Jasper* videodisc. Although it can be implemented in a more structured way, the constructivist attributes are often lost. Most constructivist implementations are in the form of complex learning environments that require the computational power of more sophisticated computers, which also often require expensive peripheral devices. Considerations of compatibility, both within and between manufacturers, make some environments impossible or difficult to implement. Many of these environments simply will not run on lower-end equipment.

Does Constructivism Require Retraining Instructors and Learners?

The other requirements for implementing constructivist environments, such as *Jasper*, may be more elusive. *Jasper* may, of course, be implemented in the classroom in a fairly structured environment, with the teacher guiding the students through the exercises, but the full benefits of *Jasper*, including generative learning and problem construction, occur when the teacher relinquishes control and allows the students to actively explore the environments. If the teacher must relinquish control, then the students must assume that control and actively pursue solutions to the complex problems posed. The Vanderbilt Group (1992) found that students often would generate only a single solution possibility and continue with that, without considering other possibilities. Instructors often coached the students on considering a full solution set. This was not necessarily surprising, as the students were not accustomed to this type of activity. So in this case, and perhaps with most constructivist environments, the most significant impediment to successful implementation, beyond actually having the technology available, is getting the teachers and learners to assume the required roles, to gain the full benefits of the program—roles that controvert normally expected activities. Cunningham (1991) describes the teacher's new role as follows:

The role of the teacher, under such a view, changes from authority figure who presents knowledge to students, to one of senior partner, or master in a master/apprentice relationship (p. 16).

The Vanderbilt Group (Cognitive and Technology Group at Vanderbilt 1992) points to this changing-role issue as a possible explanation for why some teachers prefer to use the *Jasper Woodbury* series only to support teaching subskills and basics, rather than in the full-blown generative learning scenarios that are possible. How do you convince teachers that they do not need to be in control in the traditional sense to promote a good learning environment?

Tobin and Dawson (1992) suggest that ownership in the actual constructivistic tool is essential for success and teacher buy-in: "From a constructivist perspective, a curriculum designed by outsiders to be implemented by teachers is doomed." They further describe the teacher and student roles:

> The curriculum takes on a different look as teacher and student roles evolve away from learning facts by rote toward providing learners opportunities to make sense of problems, building knowledge on what is already known in an environment where responsibility is given [to] students for their own learning (p. 91).

Tobin and Dawson promote *ScienceVision*, which is a resource for teachers to create their own constructive environments. Similar ideas are expressed by Jonassen and Wang (1993) regarding constructivistic tools—namely, that a great deal of benefit comes from using the tool to create a knowledge base for subsequent use. Even if that knowledge base is not used later on, the constructivistic benefits are still achieved as the participants go through the creation process. So, just as Tobin and Dawson maintain that the teacher must have ownership in the tool being used, Jonassen and Wang maintain it would do no good to hand students a completed knowledge base, because they would not have engaged the constructivistic process where the learning actually occurs.

Regarding the learner's new role, Tobin and Dawson (1992) pointed out that these new learning environments make learners much more responsible for their own learning. This new role is no different from any other thing that a person must learn—if it is something you have never done before, you may not succeed the first few times you attempt it. Likewise, if learners are unaccustomed to being self-directed, in control, and actively filling their own gaps using the tools provided, they may not succeed, even given the best constructivist environment. A considerable body of research has shown that learners do not readily adapt to learner control treatments, making good, strategic decisions about their instruction. They tend to skip important instructional elements. It is clear from the literature (Kinzie 1990) that learners require training and experience in learner control strategies. However, adding even more responsibility to the learning process by requiring learners to decide not only how to study, but also what to study and how to derive meaning from it, may require a revolution in education. Just as students lacked appropriate learning scripts for how to study from hypertext (Jonassen and Wang 1993), thereby precluding more effective use of the technology, students lack scripts for participating actively in generative learning processes.

What Are the Best Applications for Constructivism?

On the surface, this may appear to be a specious question, but it is undeniably better to ask this question and attempt to discern when one should and should not apply a theory rather than to use it in all situations, valid or not, which is perhaps the consistent error in our field. For constructivism, this is nearly the same thing as asking if the critical thinking necessary to all constructivist environments is a realistic and reasonable goal for particular learning situations (Bednar, Cunningham, Duffy, and Perry 1991). Constructivistic learning must be supported by rich contexts, which fact requires that designers and evaluators consider the context in which constructivistic learning should take place (an activity not in evidence in many design models). Otherwise, instructional designers risk falling into the academic pit that is filled with so many other panaceas for learning. Though Cunningham (1991) and others (Fosnot 1989) insist that constructivism is not just for higher-order learning (i.e., all higher-order subskills should be taught via *embedded* techniques as well), Jonassen (1991) argues that "the most realistic model of learning lies somewhere on the continuum between these positions" (of objectivism and constructivism), and that the decision should be based on the instructional context. He suggests, for instance, that the flying public would probably prefer that air traffic controllers *not* construct their own meaning of air traffic regulations (despite the fact that they may understand and believe differently in them). So, what guidelines or heuristics can be provided for when to use constructivism and when not to?

Jonassen, Mayes, and McAleese (1993) believe that constructivistic learning environments, although appropriate for stimulating thinking in younger, novice learners (Fosnot 1989), most reliably support the advanced knowledge acquisition stage of learning. This stage of knowledge acquisition is most consistently required in university courses. Therefore, universities are among the most appropriate venues for implementing constructivistic learning environments.

While that argument may continue to hold true in some circumstances, Fosnot (1989) has successfully implemented constructivist activities with elementary school learning. Additionally, McMahon and O'Neill (1993), with their Bubble Dialog and the entire Piagetian and Vygotskian heritage, maintain that younger, novice learners are probably the most constructivistic learners.

Additional concerns exist regarding when it is best to implement constructivism. Dick (1991) expressed a more local concern about successfully implementing the complexity of constructivism, particularly as implemented in applications like *Jasper* (Cognition and Technology Group at Vanderbilt 1992) and *Kane* (Spiro and Jehng 1990). He points out the danger of learning in reference to the generative learning environment principles Bransford of the Vanderbilt Group (1992) describes for constructivism; Dick claims that designers would have little problem with Bransford's principles except for the problem of complexity, which may overwhelm some learners without adequate entry-level skills. This understanding of the target learner's "entry-level" skills might then be one place to determine whether a constructivist activity, and certainly one such as the generative learning environment of *Jasper*, is appropriate.

How Do You Evaluate Learning from Constructivist Environments?

A rather typical response to evaluation in regard to constructivism is expressed by Cunningham's (1991) character Simplicio in his dialogue on constructivism and objectivism.

> I find myself agreeing with the sentiment of Thorndike that was referred to by Salviati. If constructions exist, they can be measured. If they don't exist, then you are wasting my time (p. 15).

Simplicio's concerns are responded to in a rather unsatisfactory way; Sagredo, another of Cunningham's characters, indicates that he shares the same concerns and unfortunately does not have complete satisfactory answers. Cunningham assumes the constructivist view that any notion of objective evaluation is just that—only a notion—and that if it does exist, it is only in the situations where the context of the knowledge being evaluated is so isolated (e.g., in a school setting) that it is of little relevance.

Evaluation in constructivism requires new skills from instructors. Where objectivists have traditionally evaluated via testing for externally represented and decontextualized knowledge (Jonassen 1991), assessment in a constructivist tradition assumes new aspects. If learning occurs in authentic, real-world scenarios and learners construct their own meanings from such contextual scenarios, it no longer makes sense to test learners in the same decontextualized way as was previously done. Rather, evaluation in the constructivist world will require a more active and less well-defined role for the instructor.

The next few paragraphs provide some general criteria suggested as a starting point for conceiving of evaluation methods from a constructivist perspective. These criteria represent integral components of most definitions of constructivistic learning. For a more complete treatment of this topic, see Jonassen (1992b). Though some of these criteria exist independent of constructivism, many are the direct result of constructivistic tactics. Just as these tactics introduce more flexibility into the classroom, so too do the associated evaluation techniques. If these criteria are to be used successfully, changes similar to those applying to the instruction techniques will be necessary.

Goal-Free Evaluation. When the evaluator is not informed in advance of what the goals are, goal-free evaluation (Scriven 1973) overcomes the biasing of evaluation by the specific project goals. Scriven recommended using needs assessment methods to determine what the goals of education should be. Constructivistic outcomes may be better judged by goal-free evaluation methodologies because predetermined, convergent outcomes are less likely to occur when using constructivistic environments. Knowledge construction, unless it involves a considerable amount of social negotiation, seldom produces equivalent responses from different learners.

Authentic Tasks. If we believe in authentic tasks for constructivistic instruction, then evaluating the outcomes of instruction requires a more flexible conceptualization of the evaluation process. Once again, this flexibility implies a moving away from the knowns of the more static, objectivist, criterion-based evaluation.

Context-Driven Evaluation. Most constructivistic environments assume that instruction should be anchored in some meaningful, real-world context or authentic task. *Authentic tasks* are those that have real-world relevance and utility, that integrate those tasks across the curriculum, that provide appropriate levels of complexity, and that allow students to select appropriate levels of difficulty or involvement. It is important that the criteria that we use to evaluate learners should, to some degree, derive from those used in the real world and that evaluation occur in the context being modeled during instruction. Simplified, decontextualized problems are inappropriate outcomes from constructivistic environments, so they should not be used to measure learning. It is quite simply incongruous to do so. If the instruction is context-dependent, so too should the criteria for evaluating learning be context-dependent. If the tasks are authentic, then evaluators should turn to the real-world environment being modeled in the constructivistic environment to find the most relevant evaluation variables.

Multiple Perspectives. If it is appropriate to present multiple perspectives in learning environments with the expectation that learners will meaningfully accommodate these different perspectives, then it may be equally important to reflect and accept those multiple perspectives in the evaluation process. Though this is troubling to instructors, using a single type of outcome or a single set of criteria for assessing the quality of outcomes is insufficient for assessing constructive learning outcomes. Instructors should, at the very least, consider student constructions from the perspective of an involved participant rather than an "objective" teacher. Another option is to evaluate the outcomes by a panel of reviewers, each with a meaningful perspective from which to evaluate the outcomes and each with reasonable credentials for evaluating the learner. Perhaps the most radical suggestion is to allow learners to evaluate each other. Who can provide a more meaningful perspective on student constructions than those trying to learn?

Socially Constructed (Negotiated) Meaning. If meanings are negotiated, then why not negotiate what terms should be applied to the evaluation? Even if one looks at how objectives and goals are used in the objectivist tradition, one sees that the objectives set determine the evaluation. We propose that objectives be negotiated between learner and instructor in a constructivist setting (yet another way in which the learners are more in control of their own learning), so it necessarily follows that the evaluation methods should also be negotiated.

The proposed methods of evaluation are necessarily very different from the decontextualized, test-oriented methods traditionally used. At this point, one may legitimately ask again whether it is practical to implement constructivism in the classroom, especially given that the differences between constructivism and objectivism do not stop at the instruction level, but carry on through evaluation.

It is important to note that these recommendations, though certainly not supportive of traditional testing methods, emphasize the objectivist belief that the evaluation form should match the instruction. The constructivist position is not so much an anti-test movement as a plea for instruction/evaluation congruity (Cunningham 1991).

CONCLUSIONS

In reality, it may be too early to draw ultimate conclusions regarding how constructivism affects instruction and instructional design, but perhaps that should not be the goal. Rather, it may be more appropriate to continually revisit and revise our perceptions of this paradigm in our field. However, a few observations are worth emphasizing.

It seems clear that constructivism is more than an instructional theory. After all, it defines how individuals view the world and how they define *reality*. Such a view seems to be a philosophy or worldview. If constructivism is a philosophy as much as, or perhaps more than, it is an instructional theory, it does not preclude certain tactics or instructional pieces that have been in an objectivist tradition over the years. Just as we cannot definitely say that the instructional tactic of *generating or posing questions* is necessarily a behaviorist tactic (it depends on the nature of the questions generated or posed and how they are used or rewarded within the instructional context), we cannot necessarily eliminate all techniques traditionally thought of as objectivist. For instance, behavioral objectives (the conceptual foundation of objectivism) can be used in a constructivistic implementation by having the objectives negotiated by the instructor and learner rather than dictated by the instructor for all learners. Wilson (1991) points out that often constructivism is criticized for having too little structure and being too permissive. Some constructivists respond that any sort of instructional strategy imposes a certain degree of order or limitation and therefore must be contrary to constructivism. Wilson also proposes that one cannot look at the strategy in isolation, but must view it in the context of how it is being used. So even if a designer is to adopt constructivism, this does not mean he or she is necessarily abandoning the "old" strategies. It might be easier if that were the case, but, as with other aspects of the field, it is not that clear.

An implication of this question is the feasibility of developing a set of heuristics for knowing when it is best to apply constructivism. Is it realistic to attempt such a set of heuristics (heuristics generally being accepted as more flexible than rules)? Or does one have to examine each instructional situation and make a determination about what paradigm, or combination of paradigms and models, makes the most sense? The danger is that whenever we try to pin down how and when to use a theory, paradigm, or model with heuristics, that knowledge often gets misused at the application level. Are the heuristics themselves not specific enough so that they are open to multiple interpretations? Or is the individual using the heuristics misinterpreting them? If the heuristics are so well defined that they are not likely to be misinterpreted, there are also ramifications. First, is that even possible? If one adopts a constructivistic philosophy, then one must acknowledge that every individual interprets these heuristics. Certainly those interpretations may be socially negotiated and end up resembling one another, but interpretations will nonetheless depend on the individual; thus there is no guarantee, regardless of how well written the heuristics are, that they will not be subject to multiple meanings. Besides, there may actually be some benefits from multiple interpretations that would be missed in more specific definitions. Ultimately, designers and instructors must make their own decisions about what the best choice is, given the instructional context.

REFERENCES AND ADDITIONAL READINGS

Aronson, D. T., and Briggs, L. J. (1983). Contributions of Gagné and Briggs to a prescriptive model of instruction. In *Instructional-design theories and models: An overview of their current status*, ed. C. M. Reigeluth (Hillsdale, NJ: Erlbaum).

Bednar, A. K., Cunningham, D., Duffy, T. M., and Perry, J. D. (1991). Theory into practice: How do we link? In *Instructional technology: Past, present and future*, ed. G. J. Anglin (Englewood, CO: Libraries Unlimited).

Bereiter, C., and Scardamalia, M. (1989). Intentional learning as a goal of instruction. In *Learning and instruction: Essays in honor of Robert Glaser*, ed. L. B. Resnick (Hillsdale, NJ: Erlbaum).

Bruner, J. S. (1990). *Acts of meaning*. Cambridge, MA: Harvard University Press.

Carroll, J. M. (1991). *The Nurnberg Funnel: Designing minimalist instruction for practical computer skill*. Cambridge, MA: MIT Press.

Carroll, J. M., and Campbell, R. L. (1988). *Artifacts as psychological theories: The case of human-computer interaction*. Technical Report RC 13454 (#60225). Yorktown Heights, NJ: IBM Research Division, T. J. Watson Research Center.

Cognition and Technology Group at Vanderbilt. (1990). Anchored instruction and its relationship to situated cognition. *Educational Researcher*, 19(6), 2-10.

Cognition and Technology Group at Vanderbilt. (1992). The Jasper experiment: An exploration of issues in learning and instructional design. *Educational Technology Research and Development*, 40(1), 65-80.

Cognition and Technology Group at Vanderbilt. (1992b). Technology and the design of generative learning environments. In *Constructivism and the technology of instruction: A conversation*, ed. D. H. Jonassen and T. M. Duffy (Hillsdale, NJ: Erlbaum).

Collins, A. (1991). Cognitive apprenticeship and instructional technology. In *Educational values and cognitive instruction: Implications for reform*, ed. L. Idol and B. F. Jones (Hillsdale, NJ: Erlbaum).

Collins, A., Brown, J. S., and Newman, S. E. (1988). Cognitive apprenticeship: Teaching the craft of reading, writing, and mathematics. In *Cognition and instruction: Issues and agendas*, ed. L. B. Resnick (Hillsdale, NJ: Erlbaum).

Cunningham, D. J. (1991). Assessing constructions and constructing assessments: A dialogue. *Educational Technology*, 31(5), 13-17.

Dick, W. (1991). An instructional designer's view of constructivism. *Educational Technology*, 31(5), 41-44.

Dick, W., and Carey, L. (1985). *The systematic design of instruction*. Glenview, IL: Scott, Foresman.

Duffy, T. M., and Jonassen, D. H. (1992). Constructivism: New implications for instructional technology. In *Constructivism and the technology of instruction: A conversation*, ed. D. H. Jonassen and T. M. Duffy (Hillsdale, NJ: Erlbaum).

Fosnot, C. T. (1989). *Inquiring teachers, learners: A constructivist approach for teaching*. New York: Teachers College Press.

Goodman, N. (1984). *Of mind and other matters*. Cambridge, MA: Harvard University Press.

Jonassen, D. H. (1991). Objectivism versus constructivism: Do we need a new philosophical paradigm shift? *Educational Technology Research and Development*, 39(3), 3-14.

Jonassen, D. H. (1992, June). *The past and future of computer based learning: Entailments, problems, and prospects*. Paper presented at the European Conference on Educational Research, University of Twente, Enschede, The Netherlands.

Jonassen, D. H. (1992b). Evaluating constructivistic learning. In *Constructivism and the technology of instruction: A conversation*, ed. D. H. Jonassen and T. M. Duffy (Hillsdale, NJ: Erlbaum).

Jonassen, D. H., Grabinger, R. S., and Harris, N. D. (1991). Analyzing and selecting instructional strategies and tactics. *Performance Improvement Quarterly*, 4(2), 77-97.

Jonassen, D. H., and Mann, E. (in press). Computer-based technologies past, present and future. *Journal of Computer Based Learning*.

Jonassen, D. H., Mayes, T., and McAleese, R. (1993). A manifesto for a constructivist approach to technology in higher education. In *Designing environments for constructive learning*, ed. T. Duffy, J. Lowyck, and D. H. Jonassen (Berlin: Springer-Verlag).

Jonassen, D. H., and Wang, S. (1993). Acquiring structural knowledge from semantically structured hypertext. *Journal of Computer Based Instruction*, 20(1), 1-8.

Kinzie, M. B. (1990). Requirements and benefits of effective interactive instruction: Learner control, self-regulation, and continuing motivation. *Educational Technology Research and Development*, 38(1), 5-21.

Lakoff, G. (1987). *Women, fire, and dangerous things: What categories reveal about the mind*. Chicago: University of Chicago Press.

Lazonder, A. W., and van der Meij, H. (1992). *Towards an operational definition of the minimal manual*. Enschede, The Netherlands: Universiteit Twente (in press).

McMahon, H., and O'Neill, W. (1993). Computer-mediated zones of engagement in learning. In *Designing environments for constructivist learning*, ed. T. M. Duffy, J. Lowyck, and D. H. Jonassen (Hillsdale, NJ: Erlbaum).

Merrill, M. D. (1992). Constructivism and instructional design. In *Constructivism and the technology of instruction: A conversation*, ed. D. H. Jonassen and T. M. Duffy (Hillsdale, NJ: Erlbaum).

National Council of Teachers of Mathematics. (1989). *Curriculum and evaluation standards for school mathematics*. Reston, VA: Author.

Perkins, D. N. (1991). Technology meets constructivism: Do they make a marriage? *Educational Technology*, 31(5), 18-22.

Rand, A. (1966). *Introduction to objectivist epistemology*. New York: New American Library.

Reigeluth, C. (1992). Reflections on the implications of constructivism for educational technology. In *Constructivism and the technology of instruction: A conversation*, ed. D. H. Jonassen and T. M. Duffy (Hillsdale, NJ: Erlbaum).

Resnick, L. (1987). Learning in school and out. *Educational Researcher*, 16, 13-20.

Rieber, L. P. (1992). Computer-based microworlds: A bridge between constructivism and direct instruction. *Educational Technology Research and Development*, 40(1), 93-106.

Scardamalia, M., and Bereiter, C. (1991). Higher levels of agency for children in knowledge building: A challenge for the design of new knowledge media. *Journal of the Learning Sciences*, 1(1), 37-68.

Scriven, M. (1973). Goal free evaluation. In *School evaluation*, ed. E. R. House (Berkeley, CA: McCutchan).

Spiro, R. J., Feltovich, P. J., Jacobson, M. J., and Coulson, R. L. (1991). Cognitive flexibility, constructivism, and hypertext: Random access instruction for advanced knowledge acquisition in ill-structured domains. *Educational Technology*, 31(5), 24-33.

Spiro, R. J., Feltovich, P. J., Jacobson, M. J., and Coulson, R. L. (1992). Cognitive flexibility, constructivism, and hypertext: Random access instruction for advanced knowledge acquisition in ill-structured domains. In *Constructivism and the technology of instruction: A conversation*, ed. D. H. Jonassen and T. M. Duffy (Hillsdale, NJ: Erlbaum), 57-76.

Spiro, R. J., and Jehng, J. C. (1990). Cognitive flexibility and hypertext: Theory and technology for the nonlinear and multidimensional traversal of complex subject matter. In *Cognition, education, and multimedia: Exploring ideas in high technology*, ed. D. Nix and R. J. Spiro (Hillsdale, NJ: Erlbaum).

Suchman, L. A. (1987). *Plans and situated actions*. New York: Cambridge University Press.

Tobin, K. (1990). Social constructivist perspectives on the reform of science education. *Australian Science Teachers Journal*, 36(4), 29-35.

Tobin, K., and Dawson, G. (1992). Constraints to curriculum reform: Teachers and the myths of schooling. *Educational Technology Research and Development*, 40(1), 80-81.

van der Meij, H. (1992). *A critical assessment of the minimalist approach to documentation*. Enschede, The Netherlands: Universiteit Twente (in press).

von Glasersfeld, E. (1984). Radical constructivism. In *The invented reality*, ed. P. Watzlawick (Cambridge, MA: Harvard University Press).

Watzlawick, P. (1984). *The invented reality*. Cambridge, MA: Harvard University Press.

Wilson, B. G. (1991). *Constructivism and instructional design: Some personal reflections*. A paper prepared for a talk given at Brigham Young University, Provo, Utah.

Witt, S. (1992). Context, text, interest: Toward a constructivist semiotic of writing. *Written Communication*, 9(2), 237-308.

Autodesk, Inc.—Helping Students Bring Ideas to Reality*

James Purcell
Manager

Carrie Costamagna
Market Development Manager
Education Department, AUTODESK, INC.

Knowledge and skills are two important assets that graduating students take with them on the job hunt. They have to show employers they have what it takes to get that job done. Because technology is an indispensable part of today's workplace, it must be an indispensable part of students' education. Students must understand technology and use it to uncover solutions and new problems, and to express their ideas.

But when new software tools are introduced to the classroom and lab, they usually come with a high price tag and require costly hardware investments. Only a few can afford to take advantage of the exciting capabilities of the software. When the price does come down, new technology has been introduced that surpasses the capabilities of its predecessors. These changes occur so rapidly that it is difficult for teachers and professors, already busy with other classroom and lab concerns, to keep track of what's new.

Business and industry must step alongside education to help students develop the real-world skills and knowledge students need to succeed in the workplace. That means providing the real-world technology students will encounter on the job and providing the support schools need to integrate the technology into the curriculum.

YOUR IDEAS, OUR SOFTWARE TECHNOLOGY

Autodesk has a long-standing tradition of providing industry and education with leading-edge software technology—at an affordable price—for personal computers (PCs) and desktop workstations, which have steadily become less costly. Autodesk is the world's sixth-largest PC application software company and the world's leading developer of PC-based, computer-aided design (CAD) software. Autodesk software has revolutionized the design process for industry professionals and continues to influence the way people, including educators and students, develop and communicate ideas.

Autodesk's flagship product is AutoCAD, the worldwide education and industry standard for computer-aided design and drafting. AutoCAD software is the favored design automation tool in such fields as engineering, architecture, cartography, landscape architecture, and interior design. AutoCAD is also used in such diverse fields as anthropology, psychology, archaeology, theater, and law, and the more than 1,100 applications created by independent developers allow for such specialized uses as analyzing storm drain systems or creating fashions.

---

*Portions of text are reprinted with permission from *T.H.E. Journal* (October 1992, Autodesk, Inc., Supplement to *T.H.E. Journal*).

Autodesk has recently expanded its family of design automation software products with the acquisition of Micro Engineering Solutions, Inc. As Autodesk's new Mechanical Division, they will develop products and technology, such as the CAD/CAM (computer-aided manufacturing) products AutoSurf™ and AutoMill™, for concurrent engineering. This acquisition will help Autodesk to meet many more of our customers' needs in the areas of sophisticated surfacing, modeling, 2- through 5-axis machining, and interfacing to coordinate measuring machines and prototyping systems.

Autodesk's influence in industry and education goes well beyond CAD/CAM, however. Autodesk's Multimedia software, including Animator Pro™, 3D Studio, and Multimedia Explorer, with their sophisticated visualization, modeling, animation, rendering, and presentation tools, further enhances our value in the classroom. They are the most widely used PC-based animation software packages in the world. The release of HyperChem™, a computer-aided molecular design and analysis software tool, brings design automation to the molecular level. Other new products, such as Instant Artist™, Graphic Impact™, and the Home Series™, as well as new releases of workhorse packages AutoSketch and AutoCAD Simulator™, continue to make sophisticated computer graphics accessible in the workplace, home, and classroom.

Most recently, Autodesk introduced the Cyberspace Developer Kit (CDK), a C++ toolset that provides an object-oriented framework for virtual reality (VR) applications. Unlike software development tools for creating mainstream applications like spreadsheets, the CDK provides capabilities for creating realistic, 3D worlds. The CDK addresses programming issues such as 3D geometry, physical phenomena (assigning objects and environments real physical properties, such as mass and density; applying forces such as gravity, friction, and spring), and an open interface.

SUPPORTING THE INTEGRATION OF TECHNOLOGY INTO THE CLASSROOM

Providing real-world technologies is just one part of the commitment business and industry must make to education to ensure that students are equipped with the necessary skills and knowledge to tackle challenges in their professional lives. Companies should also assist schools with integrating this technology into the classroom or lab.

Autodesk's Education Programs were developed to do just that. Through these programs, Autodesk has introduced countless students, educators, and researchers to Autodesk software. Every year Autodesk inservice teacher training workshops introduce Autodesk software to over 6,000 teachers and professors, and every year one million primary through postsecondary students learn with Autodesk software. But the learning doesn't stop there. Recognizing the importance of adult education in maintaining a skilled work force, Autodesk established the Autodesk Training Center (ATC) network in 1985 to provide technical training to business and industry professionals using Autodesk software. Today there are more than 500 ATC sites worldwide, and in North America alone over 200,000 professionals have been trained at these centers.

Autodesk's efforts and the dedication of many in the education community help make such successes possible. Autodesk continues to develop programs that encourage and support excellence. The programs are wide-ranging, from a learning systems approach to the training of Autodesk customers, to partnership opportunities designed to support the activities of leading educators and institutions.

Education Program Partnerships: Autodesk establishes partnerships with selected educators, schools, and professional associations interested in evaluating new Autodesk software and applying the software to projects and programs that have broad implications for education. These organizations and persons are leaders and innovators in education. K-12 Education

Programs, University and College Partnership Programs, and the Education Grants Program are among the many partnership opportunities available from Autodesk.

Learning Systems Group: The Learning Systems Group (LSG) provides training and learning resources for Autodesk customers. LSG addresses the needs of students of all ages. In addition, LSG works with educators to support the use of Autodesk software in the classroom and to guide the introduction of computer technology into the curriculum. LSG manages a variety of programs and resources, including Autodesk Training Centers, AutoCAD Certification exams, Instructor Development Workshops, CAD Contests, and the Learning Resource Series (curriculum and instructional materials for Autodesk customers).

Autodesk Area Education Representatives (AERs): Autodesk maintains a select and highly qualified group of dealers with extensive educational experience. Supported by Autodesk's Education Sales staff, AERs provide consulting services and technical support to schools, faculty, and students who are using Autodesk software.

MODELS OF SUCCESSFUL INTEGRATION

Autodesk has worked with numerous schools and individuals to guide the successful integration of software technology into the classroom. "Special Day" middle school students in California produce their own talking books by combining poetry, word processing, and animation. They like to write and have learned to write well. Ninth-graders in a Fairfax County high school in northern Virginia learn AutoCAD, then go on to use it to solve professional-level design problems. The curriculum in this school has been restructured to make both math and science integral parts of the technology program.

Tech Prep, a national focus of the U.S. Department of Education, is expected to transform vocational education by supporting not only integration of curriculum, but also strengthening of connections between high school and postsecondary education. Community colleges, such as Moraine Valley in Palos Hills, Illinois, have taken the lead in revving up and restructuring substantial parts of their programs to enable students to experience computer graphics-based modeling, CAD, CAM, and CIM (computer-integrated manufacturing). This experience prepares students not just to cope with holding their own in the work force, but to lead the pack. At the university level, traditionally the segment of the education community slowest to change, Rensselaer Polytechnic Institute is two years into a plan for restructuring the expectations and methods of its teaching staff so that students will be using applications software to solve problems they will soon encounter in the workplace.

Beyond individual school efforts, programs such as the National Science Foundation (NSF)-sponsored Technology Literacy and Principles of Engineering—which started in New York this year and is expanding to 16 states next year—are already training teachers to work with technology, such as AutoCAD, and curriculum content that is closely integrated. For any education reform to have a lasting effect, teacher training must also be continuous and supporting.

Technology must be integrated into the educational process on a much broader scale than these few and rather specific examples if our education system is to adequately serve society and business—and adequately engage and motivate students to learn.

There is the need to teach students how to apply technology appropriately as a learning tool across all areas of the curriculum. Unfortunately, at present this is more easily said than done. Accessibility and affordability, differing user interfaces, and multiple operation systems make the process of integrating computer hardware and software into education more difficult than it should be. The computer industry can and will solve these problems, and progress is being made on a daily basis.

Despite these problems, there have been successes. It has often proved difficult to replicate those successes elsewhere, or to extend them on a broader scale; however, a strategy is emerging by which educational institutions are endeavoring to infuse technology into the learning process. That strategy hinges on the concept of integration.

One of the most obvious ways for integration to occur is to have all varieties of hardware and software work together, without presenting barriers to problem solving. One outstanding example of successful hardware/software integration is in the Bergen County Technical Schools in Hackensack, New Jersey, where students develop prototypes as part of the design process. This high school is ahead of many industries, and the integration of the technology is so complete that the process goes from design to product electronically. Paper drawings as the means of communication between the designer and the manufacturer have been determined to be mostly extraneous.

Curriculum integration will come about more slowly, because of the traditionally compartmentalized structure of schools. Mathematics teachers seem to have forgotten that there are real-world reasons to learn math, while science teachers often teach sciences as if they were foreign languages rather than sets of observations, relevant concepts, and practical problems. Art is seldom seen as a consideration in problem solving. However, in the North Carolina School of Science and Mathematics in Durham, fractal equations have brought a visual dimension to math and have even been transformed into art. In the San Jose Middle School in California's Novato Unified School District, the use of computer animation has allowed science and language arts to come together creatively in an integrated curriculum unit. In both cases, computer graphics technology is the tool, and the students have been put in control of the toolset.

Curricular reform must be driven by feedback from the workplace. Modernizing or bringing the curriculum up to date should be a continuous effort, not one brought about by a crisis or by comparisons with other countries' test scores. Curricular reform does not necessarily mean that the curriculum must change. It can mean that we reorganize, restructure, or simply do better some of the things we are already doing. In Harvard's chemistry department, students can now spend more time discussing molecular structure because computer graphics allow them to visualize the shapes and geometry of molecules, while the dynamic aspects of the software allow the professor to demonstrate changes and reactions quite dramatically.

BRINGING IDEAS TO (VIRTUAL) REALITY

Many new technologies have tremendous possibilities for transforming the education process even further than we might imagine. One popular emerging technology with significant prospects for learning is virtual reality (VR). VR software, such as CDK, will enable students to enter a computer-generated environment known as "cyberspace." To fully experience this virtual space, an individual may don specialized equipment such as eyewear and headphones. Movement in cyberspace can be activated with a variety of devices, including a mouse. More important than the hardware or peripheral devices, however, is the leap forward in man-machine interface that VR represents.

VR signifies the next wave in computer user interfaces, which have evolved from the knobs and dials that controlled ENIAC in the 1950s, through batch cards and keyboards, to the icons and windows of today's mouse-navigated graphical environments. At each stage, the level of interactivity possible between user and machine has increased. Virtual reality takes interactivity into new realms, allowing users to interact with objects—and with each other—in a highly dynamic, social, six-dimensional space.

VR's educational potential is limited only by the imagination. Medical students might "enter" the human nervous system to better understand the complex interaction of nerves, muscles, and body tissues. Students of history could travel to another time and return much less tattered than did George in H. G. Wells's classic, *The Time Machine*. Using the CDK architecture, students at Rensselaer Polytechnic Institute recently toured a virtual world containing architectural structures they had designed. The ability to move about within a full-sized space they had created gave them a perspective of their models not previously possible. With CDK, Rensselaer students experienced firsthand the consequences of their design decision making, and had the opportunity then to refine their designs as part of the learning process. Students of all ages will have the chance to experience, on a highly personal level, the consequences of their critical thinking and judgment.

CONCLUSIONS

While some experts foresee a gradual integration of technology into the classroom, others expect more radical change. In his 1992 book, *School's Out*, Lewis J. Perelman, senior fellow with the Discovery Institute in Washington, D.C., predicts the complete disappearance of the classroom itself. Perelman asserts that new and emerging technologies will replace conventional education with immediate and universal information access that enables "anyone to learn anything, anywhere, anytime."

Others expect the impact of technology on teaching and learning to be less dramatic, if no less significant. Everyone agrees that the integration of technology into education—undertaken with an appreciation for the interdependency of many components and for the need to plan intelligently for continuous change—will result in profound and long-lasting learning opportunities for students of all ages.

Students of today represent our best hope for tomorrow. Schools and business together must serve and support these students well, providing the highest quality of learning possible. Teaching and learning must be highly integrated and closely connected with the needs and demands of society. Areas of the curriculum must be integrated so that the meaning, not just the content, is learned and can be applied. And technology, specifically Autodesk software, is a critical piece of the integration puzzle.

If you would like more information about Autodesk, Autodesk's Education Programs or publications, please write to us at Autodesk, Inc., Education Department, 2320 Marinship Way, Sausalito, CA 94965 or fax your request to 415-491-8337. You may also call directly at 415-491-8240.

REFERENCE

Perelman, L. J. (1992). *School's out!* New York: William Morrow & Co.

California Implements a Plan to Improve Education with the Assistance of Technology

John Cradler

Far West Laboratory for Educational Research and Development

LEGISLATURE MANDATES A STATE TECHNOLOGY PLAN

In 1989, the California legislature determined that it would be necessary to develop a long-range strategic plan for the funding and use of technology in schools. More than $100 million had been allocated for educational technology since 1984 without such a plan; without a plan it was not possible to evaluate the benefits of this investment. It was also believed that a plan could improve statewide coordination of technology, reduce duplication of effort, and establish guidelines for planning, implementing, evaluating, and funding technology in California schools.

Legislation passed to remedy the situation addressed the problem from two perspectives. The measure (A.B. 1470) provided for the establishment of the California Planning Commission for Educational Technology and a comprehensive study of the implementation, use, and impact of technology in California schools. The Commission, which was composed of teachers, administrators, college faculty, and representatives of business and industry, was charged with the development of a Master Plan for Educational Technology.

Conducted by the Far West Laboratory for Educational Research and Development, *The Comprehensive Study of California Educational Technology Programs* evaluates and documents the effectiveness of past and current technology implementation. Data from the study were a major source of input to the Master Plan. Also considered in the development of the Master Plan were the California Department of Education's *Strategic Plan for Information Technology*; plans from other states, including New York, Texas, and Utah; and input from various professional organizations.

With financial and in-kind support from business and the Far West Laboratory, the Planning Commission conducted a two-day Educational Technology Summit, representing the state legislature, education, and business leaders, to address issues and make specific recommendations for the state educational technology plan. The Commission also conducted regional "town meetings" to gather additional input. The plan developed by the Commission would be implemented by education leaders in close collaboration with California's leaders of business and industry.

THE MASTER PLAN FOR EDUCATIONAL TECHNOLOGY

The Master Plan was unveiled by the Planning Commission in April 1992. The vision of the Master Plan is that:

> Technology will enhance students' learning, increase the intellectual productivity of faculty, and contribute to the management efficiency of administrators and staff through the use of instructional and information technologies.

The Commission identified a number of objectives crucial to the future success of education in California and the contribution of technology to that success. Chief among these objectives are: (1) equity of access to technology resources; (2) equity of resources wherever teaching and learning occur; (3) coordination of resources from public and private providers; (4) electronic linking of educational agencies; and (5) coordination of educational technology among the four segments of California public education: K-12 education, California community colleges, the University of California, and the California State University.

The Commission issued the State Master Plan with nine recommendations for action, as follows:

1. *Technology in every learning environment.* Provide access to an array of information with instructional technology devices and instructional resources for every learner, faculty, and staff member in every teaching/learning environment.

2. *Professional development and support.* Provide equity of access to ongoing professional development and support for every information technology user in the teaching/learning process.

3. *Golden State Education Network.* Establish and coordinate a statewide, integrated linking of voice, video, and data networks.

4. *Instructional and information source.* Improve existing and establish new statewide instructional and information resources.

5. *Student data resource.* Establish a statewide student data resource system for educators and administrators.

6. *Management information resource.* Establish a statewide electronic administrative management information resource system.

7. *Education technology coordination.* Establish a state-level intersegmental education council and an industry council to collaboratively implement the Master Plan and to develop future plans.

8. *Master Plan implementation evaluation.* Provide for ongoing evaluation of the extent and impact of the implementation of each recommendation of the Master Plan.

9. *Resources to fully implement the Master Plan.* Develop a substantial and sustained public and private funding mechanism to implement the recommendations of the Master Plan.

IMPLEMENTATION OF THE MASTER PLAN

The Morgan-Farr-Quackenbush Educational Technology Act of 1992 (S.B. 1510) is designed to provide for implementation of most of the recommendations of the State Master Plan and to reauthorize and restructure effective components of the existing educational technology program. Computer Using Educators (CUE), representing more than 10,000 teachers and administrators in California, was the major sponsor of the measure and served to facilitate and garner most of the support needed to pass the bill.

Amendments incorporated into the bill came from organizations and stakeholders, including the California Department of Education, directors of currently funded educational technology programs and projects, the California Teacher's Association, the Association of California School Administrators, the Computer Using Educators, the California Math Council, and others.

MAJOR PROVISIONS OF S.B. 1510

The intent language in the introduction of the bill specified that programs should address the needs of California's non-English-speaking population and encourage involvement of higher education and business in planning and implementation. The bill specified that the students served by the projects and programs in S.B. 1510 should represent the state's population of non-English-speaking students and their parents. Following is a brief summary of the major provisions of the bill:

School-based grants. The provision of School-Based Educational Technology Grants to school districts and county offices of education to develop, adapt, or expand existing technological applications is authorized by the bill. To receive a grant, the school shall develop a Technology Use Plan (TUP) that:

- Addresses the needs of students and teachers

- Is part of existing district and school-level planning

- Supports the local and state curriculum frameworks

- Includes teacher staff development and evaluation.

Research and development grants. R&D grants shall be awarded to school districts and county offices of education for the purpose of supporting innovation by using educational technology. These grants should support general education, English acquisition, non-English-speaking parent education, and the solution of educational problems with a high probability of being adopted or adapted by other schools in a variety of demographic contexts and within existing resources.

Dissemination grants. Educational technology dissemination project grants shall be provided to school districts and county offices of education to identify, disseminate, and install exemplary practices and products. The state would establish a central clearinghouse whereby any teacher can call an 800 number, or access through telecommunications, information about state and local resources to support the effective use of technology in the classroom.

Instructional video. Instructional video services shall be provided on a regional basis to school districts and county offices of education for the purpose of facilitating the use of effective instructional video and television in the classroom.

Statewide telecommunications network and regional staff development. An expert communications task force will be established to develop a phased-in plan for a statewide telecommunications network to serve California's K-12 schools and to connect schools to community agencies and businesses as appropriate.

Regional teacher support. Regional consortia known as the California Technology Project involve business with educators to provide support to schools for the integration of technology and training in the use of the existing telecommunications networks.

Governance. The bill provides for an Educational Council for Technology in Learning (ECTL) that will combine the duties of the previous Educational Technology Committee and the Planning Commission. This 11-member council will consist of one county office of education representative, one administrator, three business representatives, four teachers, one media specialist, and one public member. The ECTL will collaborate with educational institutions, professional educational associations, and businesses to ensure that the recommendations of the California State Master Plan for Educational Technology are considered in implementing educational technology programs.

The bill encourages the formation of an Industry Council for Technology in Learning (ICTL) to provide collaborative business involvement with the ECTL in the implementation of technology in California schools. To facilitate collaboration, four ECTL members will serve on the ICTL as joint members.

Legislation to integrate technology into existing programs. The Master Plan and the FWL study suggested that technology be integrated into existing reform initiatives and programs. The governor signed A.B. 1162, a technology bill that is intended to accomplish this suggestion. This legislation specified the following:

- Each school improvement plan must document consideration of the use of educational technology to achieve instructional improvement objectives.

- The California Department of Education must apply appropriate educational technology in the evaluation of individual pupil performance under the statewide pupil assessment program.

- Educational technology and related hardware are determined to be an allowable purchase in the reconstruction, remodeling, and furnishing and equipping of school buildings.

CURRENT STATUS OF STATE-INITIATED EDUCATIONAL TECHNOLOGY IN CALIFORNIA

S.B. 150 is funding the dissemination of California's 13 Model Technology Schools, which are now serving as demonstration programs to be adapted and modeled by other schools across California. The Far West Laboratory in San Francisco serves as a resource and information dissemination center for these projects and other technology resources. More than 200 schools are now recipients of school-based grants for 1992-93.

Instructional television services are provided by seven agencies associated with public television stations and county offices of education. The California Technology Project manages 14 regional teacher support consortia and is supported by the California State University (CSU) Chancellor's Office. These programs were initiated and recently adapted to meet the new requirements of S.B. 1510.

Business and industry are now in the process of developing plans to establish the ICTL, so that technology in education will receive expanded resource support and involvement with state and local employers. Organizations and businesses, such as the Industry Education Council of California (IECC), IBM, Apple, GTE, Pacific Bell, Macmillan, and CTB-McGraw Hill, with CUE, CSU, the California Department of Education, and others, are now organizing the ICTL. Various education organizations are identifying individuals to nominate to become members of the ECTL. Finally, the California Department of Education and the Educational Council for Technology in Learning (ECTL) will develop specific guidelines for the implementation of S.B. 1510.

ADDITIONAL READINGS

The analysis of the impact of California educational technology regional and local assistance programs. Summary Report. (1991, December 20). San Francisco, CA: Far West Laboratory for Educational Research and Development. ED 348 951.

The California Master Plan for Educational Technology. Submitted to the California Legislature April 22, 1992. (1992, April 22). California State Planning Commission for Educational Technology. ED 348 953.

Cradler, John. (1992). *Comprehensive study of educational technology programs in California authorized from 1984-92. Executive summary.* Sacramento, CA: California State Department of Education. Office of Educational Technology. ED 348 976.

Pursuing the Goals
The New PBS Math Service

Jinny Goldstein
Vice President

Mary Harley Kruter
Manager, PBS Math Service
Education Product Development
Public Broadcasting System

Public television will soon complete a new telecommunications highway for education. With its December 1993 move to Telstar 401, a new state-of-the-art satellite, coupled with the use of advanced digital compression technology, PBS will be able to expand its satellite channel capacity as much as eightfold. In addition, public TV will pioneer the educational use of VSAT—Very Small Aperture Terminal—satellite technology, which will, for the first time, make possible truly interactive *two-way* data, voice, and perhaps even video exchange, giving schools unparalleled access to information and databases.

The PBS Board of Directors is committed to devoting most of public television's new delivery capacity to speeding the country's progress toward its national education goals. Also, recent increases in public TV's federal funds have been earmarked for use in developing new services for the nation's teachers and students.

In the fall of 1989, the President of the United States and the governors of the 50 states framed six national education goals. The goals address

Readiness for school

High school completion

Student achievement and citizenship

Science and mathematics competencies

Adult literacy and lifelong learning

Safe, disciplined, and drug-free schools.

Although public television's new telecommunications highway will ultimately address all six national goals, PBS and its member stations are focusing first on *readiness for school* and on *mathematics*.

THE SITUATION IN MATH

National Education Goal 4 states that "by the year 2000, U.S. students will be first in the world in mathematics and science achievement."

Over and over again this past decade, research has demonstrated that U.S. students, on average, are unable to do the sophisticated problem solving, abstract thinking, and writing that are needed in today's workplace. International comparisons of mathematics achievement have consistently shown U.S. students at or near the bottom among developed nations. There is widespread consensus that unless change takes place at every level of math education, the

American work force will not be able to compete effectively in the 21st century. But how will such change take place?

The mathematics community, under the leadership of the National Council of Teachers of Mathematics (NCTM), has developed new and demanding standards for what students at every grade level need to know to be ready to meet the challenges ahead. NCTM has established specific teaching standards to enable teachers to translate curriculum standards into classroom practices. Over the past four years, the math community has built an impressive national consensus on these standards. There is an emerging, shared vision for mathematics education, accompanied by a strategy for reform, based on the concept of national standards and local implementation.

In our highly decentralized system of education, real change takes place classroom by classroom, school by school—in districts where local leadership has created an environment for change and where teachers understand what is expected of them. The challenge, as stated by Luther Williams, Assistant Director of the National Science Foundation, is to create the support structures teachers and schools need to deliver standards-based mathematics and science education to the nation's youth. (Some 1.2 million teachers currently teach math in the nation's elementary schools, and there are at least 155,000 math teachers at the secondary school level.)

Late in 1991, the National Science Foundation and the Aspen Institute convened a prestigious group of the nation's leading math educators and educational technologists to examine how it might be possible to use technology to support the NCTM standards. The NSF-Aspen group concluded that telecommunications is ideally suited to help mathematics educators meet their goals. Telecommunications has unique capacities, the conference report argues, as a mathematical teaching tool, as a multiplier of expertise, as a lever for change, and as a collaborative tool.

PUBLIC TELEVISION AND EDUCATION

Public television is well positioned to help American schools and teachers harness new technology on behalf of math reform. PBS, along with its member stations, has a distinguished record as a leader in technological innovation, having received Emmy awards for Outstanding Achievement in Engineering for being the first network to distribute its programming via satellite; for inventing and widely offering closed captioning for the hearing-impaired; and for inventing descriptive video services for the blind.

Public TV's network comprises 346 stations, the majority of which are licensed to state and local education agencies or to colleges and universities. Almost all these stations have, on staff, education specialists who have long-standing, productive partnerships with their local schools.

By any measure, public TV's services to America's schools are already immense. Last year these services reached 30 million elementary and secondary school students, more than 1.5 million teachers, and more than 63,000 schools. Two recent studies *commissioned by the cable television industry* show PBS to be the preferred source for classroom programs among teachers.

Public TV is already working to fill critical needs in math education:

- Public TV's programs reinforce math instruction in school and at home—programs like "The Power of Algebra" and "Square One TV."

- Through programs like "Math: Who Needs It?" and "Futures," public TV motivates kids to pursue careers in math and helps parents understand the importance of math skills to their children's future.

- Public TV's live, satellite distance learning courses in math help combat severe teacher shortages and financial austerity. These courses now reach teachers in hundreds of schools in 28 states.

- In projects like the WNET Texaco Teacher Training Institute for Science, Television, and Technology, public television trains thousands of teachers in useful ways to integrate instructional television into classroom lessons.

THE PBS MATH SERVICE

The time is ripe for bold, collaborative action. PBS has a much increased capability to communicate and deliver services, and the mathematics community has a vision, a plan, and a strategy for greatly improving math education that requires advanced communication services. The opportunity to join forces is compelling. The result? PBS and its member stations, with the advice and counsel of math educators across the country, is developing a comprehensive Math Service, taking advantage of new and innovative uses of technology and the knowledge and expertise of the math community.

The PBS Math Service will be the nation's first telecommunications system used to improve the math achievement of young people in America. It will be an umbrella service of video, data, and voice *interactive* resources for teachers, students, and parents, all designed to advance the NCTM curriculum and teaching standards. It will employ telecommunications and computer technologies to connect and enhance exemplary projects in math reform currently under way at many organizations across America—connecting them, in turn, with state reform initiatives, schools, and families. It will also stimulate useful approaches not possible without the emerging technologies and local support personnel of public television stations.

The PBS Math Service will take advantage of public television's leadership position in educational telecommunications. Aside from public television, no telecommunications service—broadcast or cable—is taking a comprehensive approach to education reform. Aside from public television, no broadcast or cable company has either the capacity or the inclination to marshall emergent technologies and commit them to the singular purpose of advancing the new math curriculum and teaching standards. Aside from public television, no broadcast or cable company has the necessary track record or the national professional education partnerships that will enable PBS to pull together all of the country's best math projects in one umbrella service. Aside from public television, no broadcast or cable company has a national system of 346 local stations that have long-standing, productive partnerships with their local school systems.

Here are a few of the projects envisioned for the service: video modeling for professional teacher development, based on the new NCTM standards; an electronic online resource center that will allow teachers across the country to share their best work; a national recognition program for teachers who make effective use of new technologies; national videoconferences involving teachers, administrators, and school board members to build local support for the new standards; summer telecolloquia to give teachers extended periods for math study; and national broadcast television programs, including a math game show series for kids, a family math series, and the Mathematical Sciences Education Board's second "Report to the Nation," all to raise awareness and support among the 100 million adults who have an interest in their children's or grandchildren's math education.

To ensure the success of the Math Service, PBS has established partnerships and collaborations with leading professional organizations—those at the forefront of the nation's school reform movement. The National Council of Teachers of Mathematics (NCTM) is working closely with PBS by helping to organize, and by serving as *ex officio* members of, the PBS Math Service Advisory Committee. In addition, working relationships have been established with the Mathematical Sciences Education Board, the Council of Chief State School Officers, the National Education Association, and the National School Boards Association.

POTENTIAL CONTRIBUTIONS

The PBS Math Service will enable teacher, students, and parents:

1. To implement the national curriculum and teaching standards quickly and effectively;

2. To share resources with one another;

3. To view the best practices of standards-based instruction;

4. To link school and home use of educational technologies;

5. To increase parental involvement in children's learning;

6. To secure support for change from school administrators and school boards; and

7. To access teaching materials when and where needed.

Ultimately, students all across the United States—from the poorest to the richest, in cities and in suburbs, and in our most isolated and remote settings—will have the best chance ever to achieve a new, world-class standard of math understanding and performance. They will be students who can solve problems; students who know how to ask difficult, analytical questions; students who want to continue to learn and use math throughout their lives; students who are able to work confidently with high-technology concepts and equipment.

The Whittle Educational Network
(Channel One, The Classroom Channel,
The Educators' Channel)

Jim Ritts
President of Network Affairs
Whittle Educational Network

The Whittle Educational Network (WEN) is a serious commitment to providing quality programming and technology to America's secondary schools. WEN was developed in 1989 in response to the concerns of parents and teachers in local communities who were seeking innovative public/private partnerships to provide resources for undersupported schools. With an investment of more than $300 million, WEN represents the largest single infusion of video technology and programming to secondary schools in United States history.

WHAT WEN OFFERS

Quality Programming

A secondary school that contracts for WEN services receives:

1. *Channel One*, a daily 12-minute news and issues program designed specifically for a teenage audience. Produced at our studios in Los Angeles by a staff of more than 60 experienced journalists and news producers, *Channel One* covers the events that shape the nation and the world each 24 hours. The following mission statement governs the production of *Channel One*:

The Purpose

- Use news and current events information as a tool to educate and engage young adults in world happenings.

- Make the daily news accessible, relevant, and exciting to younger viewers.

- Promote awareness of the relationship between national and world events and every teen's individual life.

- Encourage young people to become productive and active adult citizens by proving to them that they are participants in history, not just witnesses to it.

The Commitment

- Report the news from a perspective with which young people are familiar and capable of understanding.

- Seek angles that make the importance and explanation of news stories clear to young viewers.

- Produce in-depth studies of how current events affect teens around the world.

- Present issues as opportunities in which young people can play an active role, rather than as overwhelming problems no one can solve.

The Standards

- Demand the highest possible editorial standards and ensure that stories be covered in a measured and responsible fashion.

- Tell the truth objectively, without sensationalism or condescension, and trust an informed public to make its own judgments.

- Present *Channel One* with a special sensitivity to our audience in our usage of pictures and our choice of angles on all stories.

2. *The Classroom Channel*, which provides several hundred hours of noncommercial instructional support and curriculum-driven programming each academic year to participating WEN schools. *The Classroom Channel* is managed by the Pacific Mountain Network, an association of 43 public television stations in the western United States. Programming on *The Classroom Channel* is satellite-transmitted to each school between 3:30 a.m. and 6:00 a.m. (EST) Monday through Friday and is automatically recorded on the WEN equipment. Programming is divided into four broad categories: history/current events, foreign language/literature, math/science, and life skills/teen issues.

3. *The Educators' Channel*, which provides programming for teachers and school administrators addressing a variety of developments in research, key teaching issues, and classroom management. Programming has included the landmark series, "... And Learning for All." Based on a wealth of educational research, this seven-part series covers a range of important conceptual innovations, from learner-centered models to authentic assessment. The series, which features inspirational stories about communities that identify priorities and develop solutions, begins with an overview of education in America and provides provocative arguments for changes in the system. Subsequent programs address the following topics: school readiness for implementing new programs, the importance of safe and supportive schools, the need for excellence in math and science, the advantages of fostering citizenship and a sense of shared responsibility in our graduates, strategies for helping more students complete high school and learn how to succeed in life, and methods of nurturing a lifelong love of learning. Partners in the "... And Learning for All" project include Pacific Mountain Network (administrator of *The Classroom Channel*), Mid-Continent Regional Educational Laboratory, Western Cooperative for Educational Telecommunications, PBS station KRMA-TV, Mind Extension University, Colorado 2000 Communities, and the National School Public Relations Association.

4. *International and National High School Assemblies*, a series of one-hour special programs produced by the WEN news team in reaction to major global events and presented live to the WEN schools for broadcast. Programs have included "Sharing Freedom," a program developed in the wake of the failed Russian coup attempt of August 1991. This programming allowed Russian and American teenagers to speak directly and openly via a satellite space-bridge regarding the recent historical events in Moscow and the ensuing search for freedom. "Sharing Freedom" was moderated by NBC news anchor Tom Brokaw from a WEN school in Dayton, Ohio. "South Central" was a one-hour live program broadcast from a WEN school on South Central Boulevard in Los Angeles one week following the violence that erupted in that city in reaction to the verdict in the Rodney King trial. WEN brought 250 students from across the Los Angeles area to meet with local, state, and national leaders. The live program, moderated by Arsenio Hall, allowed Los Angeles students at the WEN school broadcast site

and teens across the nation via satellite to express their fears, frustrations, and anger over the events that were unfolding in California. The most recent live special was held in October 1992 and was entitled the "OneVote." The "OneVote" was an effort to educate, spark enthusiasm, and increase the number of teenage voters in the 1992 presidential election. WEN and the National Association of Secondary School Principals (NASSP) held the nation's largest election exclusively for middle and high school students. Ballots were cast by 3.5 million teenagers on October 19 and 20 and the results were presented in a special live "OneVote" broadcast on October 21. In preparation for the "OneVote," WEN and the NASSP assembled an extensive programming package to help teenagers better understand the electoral process. This package included comprehensive analysis of the key political issues, interviews with candidates, and teachers' guides distributed to every participating school.

5. *Closed Captioning—Channel One* is the first program for students in schools that offers closed captioning. Deaf and hearing-impaired students can now benefit from the same news and information brought daily to over eight million students. Remedial readers and students who speak English as a second language can benefit, too. Research has shown that captioned television programs are an excellent instructional tool for helping students practice reading, vocabulary, and comprehension skills. Lesson plans are available to help teachers use closed captioning.

6. *Monthly Teacher Discussion Guides*. Each month WEN sends a 16- to 20-page guide to the more than 350,000 teachers participating in the WEN project. This guide previews all programming for the upcoming month and provides suggested classroom discussion and other correlated activities.

Technology

For each participating school, WEN installs, insures, and services an in-house television system that educators may use for any purpose. The system at each school includes:

1. A rooftop KU-band satellite dish;

2. Central receiving center, including two VCRs capable of receiving all signals from the satellite and any other signal source, including cable and antenna;

3. Ceiling-mounted color television monitor in every participating classroom; and

4. Cabling and wiring connecting all in-class televisions with the central receiving and broadcasting equipment.

How the Programming and Technology Work in Concert

All programming (with the exception of live event coverage) is transmitted to schools via satellite before 6:00 a.m., where it is automatically recorded by one of the WEN VCRs. The prerecording of *Channel One* each day allows a designated school person or school group to preview the program and determine whether to show *Channel One* for that day.

THE FUNDING

The entire package of programming and technology is provided to each participating WEN school at no cost. Funding for all aspects of this project is derived from 2 minutes of commercials that appear in the 12-minute daily *Channel One* news program.

THE COMMERCIAL GUIDELINES

The following standards and guidelines were developed in concert with parents and educators to govern the commercials that appear in *Channel One*. These guidelines are a part of the contract signed by every school in the Whittle Educational Network.

1. Policy Statement

It is the policy of *Channel One* to present advertising that is truthful and tasteful and not misleading or deceptive. *Channel One* recognizes that it has a special responsibility to its teenage audience because of that age and the educational environment in which the programming is viewed. Careful attention will be given to all guidelines to assure that practices and behavior that are inconsistent with the learning environment, as well as the community at large, will be avoided in commercial programming. Additionally, strict separation of advertising messages and editorial content will be maintained.

2. Products and/or Services That Will Not Be Considered for Channel One

Abortion clinics; alcoholic beverages (including beer, wine, and distilled spirits); contraceptive products; firearms, ammunition, and fireworks; gambling; "head shops" or other establishments whose activity concentrates on drug-related paraphernalia; lotteries; motion pictures rated "R" or "X" by the MPAA; prescription drugs; tampons or other feminine hygiene products; political advertisements; religious time; solicitation of funds; tobacco products (including cigarettes, cigars, pipe tobacco, and "smokeless" tobacco).

3. General Guidelines

Channel One reserves the right to accept or reject at any time advertising for any product or service submitted for airing over its facilities. The following general guidelines will be developed to aid sponsors in the development of appropriate advertising:

A. *Advertising/Programming Distinction*

Any creative technique that may confuse the viewer by blurring the distinction between programs and commercials is unacceptable.

B. *Audio/Visual Misrepresentation*

Advertisements will avoid audio and video techniques that in any way misrepresent, distort, exaggerate, or overglamorize their attributes or functions.

C. *Community Sensibilities*

Advertising that belittles any group based on its social, racial, ethnic, or religious traits or any person because of his or her age, sex, or handicaps is unacceptable.

D. *Comparative Advertising*

Comparative advertising may not distort or exaggerate differences between competitive products or services or otherwise create a false, deceptive, or misleading impression.

E. *Controversial Issues*

Advertising that takes a position on a controversial issue of public importance is unacceptable. A *controversial issue of public importance* is defined as one that involves matters having significant impact on society or its institutions, and as to which there is a current public debate with substantial segments of the community taking opposing positions.

F. *Criminal Activity*

Advertising that promotes or accepts violence, crime, or obscenity is unacceptable. Advertising may not contain the portrayal of specific detailed techniques involved in the commission of crimes, the use of weapons, the avoidance of detection, or any other forms of antisocial behavior.

G. *Dramatizations, Reenactments, and Simulations*

A commercial that utilizes a dramatization, reenactment, or simulation must accurately depict the product, service, or event involved.

H. *Endorsements*

Endorsements must reflect the honest opinions, beliefs, findings, or experience of the endorser. Endorsements may not contain any claims that could not be substantiated if made directly by the advertiser.

I. *Safety*

Advertisements and products advertised must be consistent with generally recognized safety standards. All advertising that disregards normal safety precautions is unacceptable.

J. *Subliminal Perception*

Any advertising utilizing the technique of "subliminal perception" or any similar technique is unacceptable.

4. Development of Audience-Specific Advertising

Although the ultimate responsibility of developing advertising rests with the individual sponsors, *Channel One* will encourage the development of specific messages that accomplish the following objectives:

A. Include a balanced representation of individuals from a variety of social, racial, ethnic, or gender groups;

B. Provide positive role models for all members of the viewing audience;

C. Include and portray individuals with physical and mental impairments;

D. Place an emphasis on the importance of education and remaining in school; and

E. Communicate a strong message against all forms of antisocial behavior, including drug use, violence, prejudice, and the like.

THE NATION'S RESPONSE TO THE WHITTLE EDUCATIONAL NETWORK

- Almost 12,000 middle and high schools (40 percent of U.S. secondary schools), with 347,000 classrooms across the nation, are part of WEN.

- More than eight million students view the news daily through *Channel One*. This is five times the combined total of teenagers that view the evening news each day on ABC, CBS, and NBC.

- *Channel One* is available in all of the following states:

Public, Private, and Parochial Schools

Alabama	Indiana	Montana	Rhode Island
Arizona	Iowa	Nebraska	South Carolina
Arkansas	Kansas	Nevada	South Dakota
California	Kentucky	New Hampshire	Tennessee
Colorado	Louisiana	New Jersey	Texas
Connecticut	Maine	New Mexico	Utah
Delaware	Maryland	North Carolina	Vermont
District of Columbia	Massachusetts	North Dakota	Virginia
Florida	Michigan	Ohio	Washington
Georgia	Minnesota	Oklahoma	West Virginia
Idaho	Mississippi	Oregon	Wisconsin
Illinois	Missouri	Pennsylvania	Wyoming

Private and Parochial Schools Only

New York

RESEARCH

Although literally hundreds of national, statewide, and local research projects involving WEN and *Channel One* are being conducted, the most widely referenced study is the three-year examination being conducted by the Institute for Social Research at the University of Michigan and Interwest Applied Research in Beaverton, Oregon. This longitudinal study was commissioned by WEN to provide an objective assessment of the educational impact of this project and to guide the evolution of programming and implementation of the project at the school level. The following are the main findings of the first-year report, which focuses on the student and teacher ratings of *Channel One* and on the current events knowledge of high school students who watched the programs between September 1990 and May 1991.

Teachers in the *Channel One* schools gave *Channel One* programming high marks, ranging from A- to B+. The marks were for news content and understandability to a teenage audience. Sixty percent of the teachers said they would recommend *Channel One* "strongly" or "very strongly" to other schools and teachers. Twenty-eight percent would recommend it, but "with some reservations." Forty-seven percent of the students felt that they learned something important "always" or "most of the time."

On a test of current events knowledge, *Channel One* viewers, *on average,* knew more about current events than their nonviewing counterparts, but the advantage was very small— one more item correct on a 30-item test or an advantage of 3.3 percent. "A" and "B" students showed an advantage of 6 percentage points. There were big differences from school to school. In four of the schools, the advantage from viewing was 6-9 percentage points.

The average *Channel One* viewer knew more than nonviewers about secondary news stories—what was happening in Russia, South Africa, and Poland. They also were more likely to know where (on a map) news events were occurring.

The second phase of this research study was released late in 1993 and reports case study findings that examined the implementation of *Channel One* in several schools participating in the phase one research. The goal of this second phase was to garner a better understanding of the variance of learning and acceptance that occurred among the sample schools.

RECENT DEVELOPMENTS

- The Armed Forces Radio and Television Service (AFRTS) announced the selection of *Channel One* as its educational news program for the more than one million U.S. military personnel and their families in over 130 countries.

- In December 1992, six WEN pilot schools in Russia began receiving *Channel One*. Nearly 3,000 Russian students began viewing the daily news program on equipment installed by WEN as part of this international educational partnership.

- The 1993 Board of Directors and Foundation Trustee of American Women in Radio and Television selected *Channel One* programming for commendable achievement in presentation of areas of interest to women.

- As part of the WEN Curriculum Development Project, designed to assist teachers in using *Channel One* as an educational tool in the classroom, WEN solicits proposals for lesson plans from participating schools. A selection committee reviews the submissions and awards stipends to the teachers whose lesson plans are selected. The stipend allows full development of their proposals to integrate *Channel One* into current curriculum. A portfolio of lesson plans is now available in virtually every subject area.

For information regarding the Whittle Educational Network, write to: Whittle Educational Network, The Education Resources Department, 333 Main Street, Knoxville, TN 37902.

Curricular Help on Integrating Computers in Education
Transforming Teachers

Deborah Y. Bauder
Director, Learning Center

Mary Planow
Assistant Professor of Computer Science

Ron Sarner
Professor of Computer Science
State University of New York Institute of Technology at Utica/Rome

David Carr
Dean of Social Sciences
Stockton State College

Early attempts at introducing computers into the classroom centered around introductory inservice courses that often left teachers frustrated and alienated. This study discusses a project designed to prepare teachers to integrate computers into the curriculum. Pre- and post-tests were designed to capture teachers' perceptions of computers and of their comfort and skill levels with respect to using computers for instruction. Changes in attitudes were measured by t-test analyses using paired samples.

INTRODUCTION

As computers and related technologies become increasingly woven into nearly every aspect of daily life, it is only natural to expect that they would become an integral part of the educational system as well. The promises of yesteryear indicated that computers would revolutionize education and produce the generations of technologically literate independent thinkers required for the transformation into the Information Age. Seymour Papert suggests these two theses in his introduction to *Mindstorms* (1980): "The computer presence will enable us to so modify the learning environment outside the classrooms that much if not all the knowledge schools presently try to teach with such pain and such expense and such limited success will be learned as the child learns to talk, painlessly, successfully, and without organized instruction" (p. 9). Although not advocating the abolition of schools, he was suggesting that schools must be able to adapt in form and function to a rapidly changing technological world.

Yet today, 13 years later, in many schools, integration of the computer into the classroom has been minimal, characterized by limited use of the technology as an add-on rather than as integral to teaching and learning (Zappone 1991). The overall effect appears to be merely a ripple on the surface of the system while, for the most part, education continues as it has for the past several decades.

In their paper "The State of the Art in Computer Education," Maddux, Johnson, and Harlowe (1992) compare the current status of educational computing to a "good news, bad news" joke:

The good news is that computers have found their way into classrooms across the country, and they are here to stay. They have become so ingrained in mainstream culture that a place in the subculture of schooling is assured....

The bad news is that the entire process of bringing students and computers together in schools is being carried out in ways that are often inefficient, poorly planned, and incredibly chaotic (p. 119).

One problem is that the growth of computer usage by the schools was neither preceded nor accompanied by a plan; the past 10 years or more have been an age of experimentation. To compound this problem, the technological horizons are moving so fast that today's techniques and even today's concerns are often outmoded by tomorrow. Many teachers, while being bombarded with promises of tomorrow's technology, are still struggling to make efficient and effective use of yesterday's hardware and software. Current practice is rooted in the limitations of these older resources and in lack of training.

In more recent years, an emphasis has been on the use of the computer as a tool to achieve curricular objectives. The development of Integrated Learning Systems (ILS), beginning with early systems such as Plato, has exploded with the introduction of multimedia technology. Certainly, newer hypermedia technology has potential, but even more traditional software can be integrated into classroom practice. The most often cited barriers to this integration are lack of resources and lack of training (OTA 1988; Knupfer 1989).

According to the report *Power On!* from the Congressional Office of Technology Assessment (OTA 1988), only one-third of the nation's teachers have had as much as 10 hours of computer training. Most of this training has been about computers rather than about how to teach with computers. The response from teachers has been that this type of training leaves them with an overwhelming realization of the necessity to learn more.

Though access to resources and training has always been considered necessary for the integration of computers into teaching and instruction, support is a third element that is often overlooked. In this respect, administrative support is the key to access and training (Jongejan 1990). Another type of support often lacking is follow-up support beyond initial training periods (Hall and Hord 1987).

Project CHOICE: Curricular Help on Integrating Computers in Education

Recognition of the importance of training, support, and resources to the integration of computers into the curriculum was the cornerstone of the Project CHOICE design (Bauder, Planow, and Sarner 1990). The two-year program was offered at the State University of New York Institute of Technology at Utica/Rome, beginning in June 1990. It was funded through a grant from the U.S. Department of Education's Office of Educational Research and Improvement through the Secretary's Fund for Innovation Program (PR/Award #R215A92073).

This comprehensive program aimed to help teachers acquire the skills necessary to integrate use of the computer into the curriculum and to ensure that resources and support would be available as necessary. To do so, the project went beyond the traditional inservice training workshop.

Central to the project was the development of four graduate-level courses for teachers and the provision of software and related hardware (interface boards) to their schools. For the first year of the project, courses were designed using software based on the Logo programming language (LEGO Logo and LogoWriter). The primary reason for this choice was that these products can be used for a wide range of grade levels, subject areas, and teaching methods. Also, the products chosen are available for the type of equipment most commonly found in today's schools and do not require extensive retraining to adjust from one platform to another.

For the second year of the project, a course using a presentation graphics package and video output capability was added.

Support for the teachers was twofold. The two-week intensive summer courses were augmented by follow-up meetings during the school year, and by on-site visits by the Project CHOICE team. These facets of the program gave participants the opportunity to share experiences and concerns with each other and with project staff.

School-based support for the project was also important. Participating teachers were selected through a process that required signatures of support from administrators and union leaders (where teachers were represented by a union). This ensured that teachers would be given release time to attend follow-up meetings and would be allocated resources and time to field-test lessons and materials developed through the project.

Teachers were expected to develop and test at least one lesson using the software and to offer inservice training in their home districts or through the local teacher center. No specific requirements for inservice training were given, as this is often a locally controlled contractual agreement.

In the first year of the project, June 1990 through June 1991, 36 teachers in 34 different schools and 24 districts participated. Teachers represented nearly all grade levels and subject areas and came from a 100-mile radius of Utica, although most were from the Utica/Rome area. Thirteen teachers were enrolled in the LEGO Logo course and 23 took the LogoWriter course.

June 1991 began the second year of the project. A total of 42 teachers representing over 30 districts participated. Seven of those teachers had also participated in the first year of the project.

METHODOLOGY

A pre- and post-test questionnaire was developed to measure teachers' attitudes toward the educational use of computers, their own perceived comfort and knowledge levels, and their perceptions of the level of support and planning in their districts. The questionnaire was administered to teachers at the beginning of their participation in June 1990 or June 1991, and again at the end of their year of participation (May 1991 or May 1992).

Participant attitudes were measured by reaction to 18 statements along three dimensions: (1) general attitudes with respect to computer use, (2) level of comfort with respect to computer use, and (3) perception of their own skill level. Responses were coded on a nine-point scale and statements were both positive and negative to detect response biases. Twenty-nine of 36 participants in the first year and 28 of 40 participants in the second year completed both the pre- and post-test questionnaires.

Because a central premise of Project CHOICE was that attitudes would be altered as a result of participation, analysis of each item necessitated excluding cases in which the participant indicated the most favorable outcome for an item on the pre-test. Thus, for example, a participant who indicated complete agreement with the statement "All teachers should be skilled users of microcomputers" would be removed from analysis of that item, as it was not possible to improve the score of a respondent already at the ceiling. The remaining pool of respondents were included in t-test analyses using paired samples.

RESULTS

Seven of the questions probed general attitudes with respect to computer use. Typical of this group were statements like "Microcomputers are important pedagogical tools," "Microcomputers can assist the teacher in accomplishing a wide variety of educational tasks," and "All teachers should have a microcomputer in their classroom." On all of these items, no significant change was observed in at least one of the two years, and the pattern was inconsistent. This lack of change was not unexpected, as the selection process began with self-nomination by the teachers within their own school district. The participants would not have been likely to become involved in this type of project unless they already felt that computers were worthwhile tools. Once the participants were nominated, they had to be endorsed by their administrations and by their bargaining agents. If either of these did not feel that a potential participant was appropriately motivated, it is not likely that the nominee would have been granted the necessary support by the school district to participate in the program.

Two of the questions dealt with participants' comfort with respect to computer use. On the first, "In general I feel comfortable using microcomputers to accomplish educational goals/objectives," 12 of the 29 respondents in year one and 10 of the 28 respondents in year two indicated complete agreement with the statement. The degree of change in the remaining participants was not significant in the first year, and was significant at the .01 level in the second year. Again, the selection process caused only those with a fair amount of comfort using the computer to participate. The other question asked the participants to compare their comfort levels with those of their peers. The change in this item was significant ($p < .01$) in both years. This change could be seen as a result of the multiple facets of Project CHOICE. The intensive two-week summer course was a major catalyst. It was designed to include more than 45 hours of hands-on training, an amount that far exceeds the usual inservice course offerings. In addition, the project team served as a support group for the participants once they went back to their school districts. The team answered questions over the phone and went onsite to solve problems when necessary. Although not many of the participants took advantage of the support, several expressed a sense of security that it existed. The follow-up sessions held throughout the school year also gave participants a chance to ask questions and get help if needed.

The third dimension of the questionnaire, consisting of seven items, was concerned with participants' perception of their own microcomputer skills. By far the most concrete of the three dimensions, skill level is also the most easily altered. It was in this dimension that Project CHOICE scored its most notable and consistent successes. Typical items in this area were "I am not knowledgeable enough about microcomputers to make effective use of them in the classroom," "When I face a new educational problem or task, I have sufficient knowledge to integrate the microcomputer in the accomplishment of the task," and "I know enough about microcomputers to teach others in my school/district." With the ceiling effect again controlled for, significant results ($p < .05$) were achieved on six of the seven items in both years. Changes in this dimension are most likely to be associated with the intensive summer course and follow-up support. Another possible component is that of access. Participation in the program required that teachers be given sufficient resources to incorporate materials developed into classroom use. For some, this meant regular access to computers in the classroom or lab for the first time.

The sole item on which significant change did not occur was "When I use a microcomputer in the classroom, it is usually because someone else has shown me how to do it." Teachers may attribute their own growth in skill level to the coursework and to experiences shared with peers during the follow-up sessions.

Project CHOICE was effective in raising the skill levels of participants. The assumption that they would bring to the program positive attitudes and a relative level of comfort in using computers was substantiated. Because these participants were sophisticated, having had considerable experience in computer usage, it is not surprising that attitudes and comfort level did not change appreciably. As participants were exposed to new, integrative computer activities, and as their skill levels were enhanced, our evidence suggests that they discerned distinct performance differences between colleagues using computers and those who did not. Furthermore, all three items calling for peer comparisons showed increases in participants' perceived competency relative to their peers.

The change literature suggests that the full impact of intervention programs will not be immediately evident. Work in progress will examine diffusion patterns in the participants' schools and will relate them to teachers' perceptions of conditions associated with technological change.

REFERENCES

Bauder, D. Y., Planow, M. M., and Sarner, R. (1990). CHOICE: A model for computer integration in the K-12 curriculum. *Research & Creative Expression*, 2(2), 4-9.

Hall, G. E., and Hord, S. M. (1987). *Change in the schools: Facilitating the process*. Albany, NY: State University of New York Press.

Jongejan, T. (1990). Teacher training for technology education in schools of education. *Journal of Computing in Teacher Education*, 7(1), 3-11.

Knupfer, N. N. (1989). The teacher as a critical component of computer education and school change. *Journal of Computing in Teacher Education*, 6(2), 16-29.

Maddux, C., Johnson, L., and Harlowe, S. (1992). The state of the art in computer education. In *Technology and teacher education annual 1992*, ed. D. Carey, R. Carey, D. Willis, and J. Willis (Charlottesville, VA: Association for the Advancement of Computing in Education), 119-22.

OTA (Office of Technology Assessment). (1988). *Power on! New tools for teaching and learning*. OTA-SET-379. Washington, DC: U.S. Government Printing Office.

Papert, S. (1980). *Mindstorms*. New York: Basic Books, Inc.

Zappone, F. (1991). Using technology in education—steps to the future. *Computers in the Schools*, 8(13), 83-87.

Deborah Bauder is Director of the Learning Center at the State University of New York Institute of Technology at Utica/Rome, P.O. Box 3050, Utica, NY 13504-3050 e-mail: debbie@sunyit.edu.

David Carr is Dean of Social Sciences at Stockton State College, Pomona, NJ.

Mary Planow is Assistant Professor of Computer Science at the State University of New York Institute of Technology at Utica/Rome, P.O. Box 3050, Utica, NY 13504-3050 e-mail: mary@sunyit.edu.

Ron Sarner is Professor of Computer Science at the State University of New York at Utica/Rome, P.O. Box 3050, Utica, NY 13504-3050 e-mail: ron@sunyit.edu.

Teaching Teachers with Telematics*

John C. Hedberg and Barry Harper
Faculty of Education
University of Wollongong

Suzanne McNamara
Faculty of Education
Monash University

This paper explores ideas through which educational programs can be provided at a distance. It examines the link between the student and teacher and the technology that facilitates communication over this link. Secondly, it examines the changing nature of the information design and methods of accessing and linking remote information, which provide learners at a distance with a variety of possible new methods to access and control their learning. It also suggests that there should be some organizational changes to facilitate the use of information technology to create new links between teacher and learner.

Although it is always difficult to predict a scenario of what teaching and learning strategies might be employed with developing technologies, it already appears that the information age challenges us to rethink the strategies we use for learning. Information technology provides a substrate on which many activities and information exchanges are based. Current technologies allow for a knowledge base to be accessed as required by the user or as directed by a tutor. This trend is evident in the use and application of information technology in business and industry and is increasingly evident in education. The trend that may be the most significant for education, however, is the facility to access information through telecommunication networks, both for the student and the instructor.

In constructing a model for the development of technology to support the professional development of teachers, it is important to examine some assumptions about technology's role in learning and teaching in the immediate future. The use of technologies in instruction tends to have an inbuilt assumption that the pedagogy employed is sound. A definition of *educational technology* is understood to encompass its widely recognized meaning of teaching/learning via *media*, including the traditional audiovisual media and now including educational computing and various forms of telecommunications, as well as interactive media such as videodisc and compact disc. However, the term *educational technology* also includes a *process* aspect, which has been defined as:

> A systematic way of designing, carrying out, and evaluating the total process of teaching and learning in terms of specific objectives, based on research in human learning and communication, and employing a combination of human and non-human resources to bring about more effective instruction. (Commission on Instructional Technology 1970)

*Paper presented at the Annual Conference of the Association for Educational Communications and Technology in Washington, DC, February 5-8, 1992.

An important aspect of delivery technologies in the 1990s and their impact on all education is the extent to which digital encoding is causing the different modes of storing, transmitting, and manipulating information to converge. This has significant implications on the equipment, facilities, and functions of institutions involved with supporting distance education students into the next decade.

The development and delivery of educational materials is rapidly evolving toward the situation where, from any representational starting point, the final delivery is purely one of choice of the instructor (or in some cases the learner). This is represented in Figure 1.

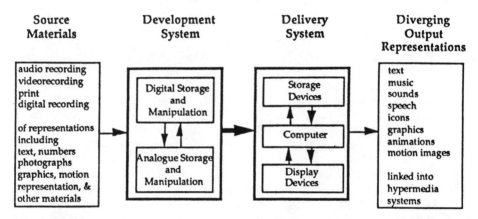

Fig. 1. Convergent technologies for developing and deliverying educational products (Hedberg and Harper 1992).

ORGANIZATIONS AND DELIVERY

Formal organizational systems often fail to adapt quickly enough to meet technological changes. The introduction of alternative technological systems of communication between teacher and students, such as electronic mail, computer bulletin boards, and the host of individual variations on this theme, poses such a challenge. This challenges every educational institution to provide educational services to their students on and off campus. In this context, the concept of distance is largely irrelevant to the categorization of the relationship. The growth of electronic links has generated "virtual" institutions, which exist only to provide specialized educational services. Further, this may mean the partnership should be largely with telecommunications carriers, with the educational institution providing the value-added educational services.

Technological innovations can at times work to create interesting links between members of the same institution, which do not follow the expected organizational charts beloved of senior administrators. Even though the technological change might be imposed by senior management, if it does actually provide an advantage for those working at the front, it will be employed in creating new and useful links between individuals.

There are a number of important aspects to these links in the distance education setting. First is the increasing use of delayed (versus real-time) links between teacher and students, achieving less unnecessary movement and increased convenience for both parties. This has always been paramount when the link was based on written or printed materials, but is further extended by the electronic metaphor, as it is now possible to bring the post office into the home, eliminating one element in the chain.

The second element of the link is its potential for increased individualized (versus large-group) contact between instructor and students. The third aspect is the absence of significance of geographical boundaries, save for that of allowing additional types of links such as site visits and face-to-face (nonmediated) conversations. A growing fourth aspect is the possibility of including alternative means of delivery in presenting the concepts or raising questions.

All these assertions should be viewed in terms of changing structures and definitions. For example, some basic infrastructure in most institutions now includes:

- **A hardware network**: A campus-wide, high-capacity communication network linking all teaching/learning, research, and administrative areas, enabling the sharing of information in various forms, including data, video, and audio.

  It is interesting to note that in times not too long ago, in places very close to home, the two areas of academic services (computing services and audiovisual) did not coexist comfortably. If they do not have links in the future, then it will probably be at the expense of the institution's establishment of a high and creditable profile in information technology communications.

- **A resource-sharing network**: A campus-wide network of links amoung people to share skills, expertise, and resources such as hardware, software, and courseware.

- **A symbiotic relationship** between information storage (library) and information services (such as computer service departments, network management, and courseware development).

A similar comment might be made here about the links between library and other forms of information storage and delivery. No individual subcomponent of the organization can ignore the links between development of knowledge, its storage, and its delivery. Like efficiency in producing a commercial product, the links between the start and the end of the process must be as seamless as possible to enable generation of ideas to flow through to final implementation. This process today can occur with greater feedback and interaction than has previously been possible.

These basic elements of infrastructure provide a skeleton on which instruction and learning can occur. The existence of this technological platform allows the changing nature of the relationship between institution and student. In fact, the distinction between an internal and a distant student is starting to become very blurred, and most future students will be involved to some extent in off-campus learning. Consider the following scenarios:

- Students who are practice teaching might continue a subject they are repeating by submitting assignments through electronic mail from the school in which they are teaching. By these means, they do not miss out on completing their full course materials because they are over 100 kilometers from the main campus.

- A physically disabled student might only be able to drive to a satellite campus located in a local school. A course in "Sociology of the Classroom" might only be offered on the main campus, but by slow-scan television transmitted over the ISDN phone network, the student might watch the lecture and even ask questions over a return audio link.

- With the installation of new library computer systems, remote access to the library catalogues, and materials reservation facilities, individual students can identify sources of materials for research and study from their desks, whether they are on the campus or at a remote location.

This changing technological relationship enables the reconsideration of the type of institution in which learning occurs. Development of innovative programs can occur in a "virtual campus," which will allow a greater range of educational offerings and easier access to courses for teachers at remote locations, with little or no degradation in the quality of the course. It also enables the provision of development programs at convenient times throughout the working day, reducing travel and improving the productivity of the teachers' time.

The development of the concept of virtual institutions through telecommunication is now being employed in a number of settings (Davies and Jennings 1991). The concept of a virtual university that will promote a global perception of the wisdom and experience of all the world's cultures has considerable attraction to consumers who are distant from the source of instruction.

TECHNOLOGY AND TEACHING

In an earlier paper (Hedberg and McNamara 1989), we described technology as a mediator amoung the three human components of the interaction: the subject matter/content expert, the instructional designer, and the learner. Technology on its own is inanimate and lifeless; the human manipulation of the interaction creates the power of the technology for learning. The link between the original expert and the learner is mediated through the attributes of the technology employed and the skills of the instructional designer. The particular content organization and the employed attributes of the technology will help or hinder the learner's comprehension of the ideas to be learned. Learners, in turn, apply their own individual understanding or conceptual sets to the presented materials to achieve mastery of the knowledge and information presented.

With the integration of video, videodisc, telecommunications, and other disc technologies capable of high-resolution still and motion vision, *multimedia* is becoming a buzzword, and with it comes greater potential, greater complexity—and problems for the learner, the instructor, and the instructional designer. Technology-based instructional systems pose interesting challenges for learners faced with the "adventure" of interacting with and learning from such systems. The storage, transmission, and presentation mechanisms can become controllable by the learner, allowing greater individual control. The combination of resources can then be structured by the instructor or the learner. The latter requires the skills of information organization, form of representation, and retrieval to be paramount.

Several studies have supported refocusing emphasis on learning skills. For example, Law and Sissons (1985) noted that "trivial behaviors" were being developed at the expense of personal understanding in many so-called innovative computer courseware packages. Similarly, Edwards and McNamara (1989) suggested that often emphasis was placed on operational skills, as opposed to the more intellectually challenging skills of analysis and synthesis.

Several levels of encounter between people and technology can be identified. Each level can contribute to achieving an ideal, namely, technology transparency in the learning situation. Figure 2 models the levels involved in the human-technology instructional interaction. It is our belief that designers and developers must endeavor to utilize mechanisms that can emulate some of the teacher-student interaction of the classroom.

Users of technology in distance education are no different. It is easy to describe the potential offered by communications packages, bulletin boards, design packages, and the like, but until the need for their use arises, such descriptions fall into the realm of "nice information to be remembered at a later date." Many present technology users have come to their encounter with the technology through a need. Associated with this need are time constraints and often limited access to the technology. The humble telephone line is perhaps a simple but appropriate illustration of the potential and the problems of telematics. Overcoming the diversity of geographical locations is one of the more traditional roles of telephone technologies. Today, the integration of computer technology with the telephone network has generated a seemingly endless array of possible communication links, to such an extent that geographical isolation is now a comparatively minor concern for the delivery of education at a distance. In human terms, practicalities and operational skills are the more consequential concerns. Presumably, everyone knows how to hold a phone conversation, but not everyone has the immediate party-line skills required by teleconferencing, nor, at a higher level, do they have the required skills (or, in many cases, access) to tap into the vast array of technologies available at the other end of the phone line.

Often these devices can be accessed without requiring high-level operational expertise. The availability of the applications software enables the learner and the teacher, with the help of the instructional designer, to work at a distance without the need for as many specialized skills. Consider, for example, the use of prepared art materials, templates for financial analysis, or desktop publishing templates—all the execution can be controlled by simple, previously agreed-upon design decisions. Increasingly, groupware, when linked with appropriate user-understandable protocols, can enable joint sharing of information and equal user contribution to the end product. Bulletin boards and telememo systems are simple ways through which we can share thoughts and problems.

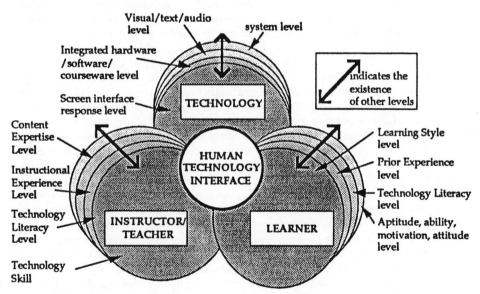

Figure 2: Levels of encounter at the instructional interface (Hedberg and McNamara 1989).

RECONCEPTUALIZING THE DESIGN

To refocus on the person for whom the system is meant to be catering, there are some common questions we have all asked: What are the learner's needs? Have data been collected from the learners and have the results been included in the final materials design? The learners bring to the interface their characteristics, experiences, and expertise, which will test the full potential of the technology, but how can the designer of open learning materials approach the human-technology match?

Such a concept forces us first to examine the reasons for using technology in the teaching/learning process. Recent work by Hedberg (1989) tried to reassess the functions of technology in terms of the types of tools required for different types of learning activities.

Consider four key activities for open learning: knowledge generation, knowledge presentation, knowledge communication, and information management. The designer needs first to focus on the underlying activity; then, secondly, to define a link between the concept presentation and how the students must work with the information to produce their own conceptual understanding of the ideas and issues. Foremost in this design concept is the idea of allowing the student to manipulate the concepts directly, not to require the designer to present information in a conceptual model where all has been decided in advance and the student can simply learn someone else's ideas.

In working with open learning modes of instruction, inevitably one finds an easier method after it is required. Although the manual might hold the solution, accessing the manual is often viewed as a divergence (and not always a worthwhile one) from the task at hand. Having to continually refer to a manual not only destroys valuable concentration, it can be confidence-destroying, if not soul-destroying. Similarly, the expectation of the user, who expected to find the particular article on the database, was disappointed to learn that his or her task also required a hunt through the library.

A broader focus of design considerations is required when using and providing technology-based delivery systems in open learning. The studies referred to in this paper highlighted some downfalls of the present provision of technological facilities for independent study by students. The technology alone will not improve the quality of the learning. It might allow for more aesthetic visual presentation, but to reach an effective human-technology match, an understanding is required that will ensure competent, efficient, and effective usage.

From the point of view of open learning, the technology of the computer must be supplemented by other appropriate mechanisms, such as the use of teleconferencing, video materials of some form, or direct contact with a human tutor. Courses employing technological delivery must ensure that participants not only have access to appropriate and compatible technologies, but also that they are aware of, understand, and are competent with the delivery technology to ensure smooth use. The focus should be on the information delivered via the technology, rather than on the technology itself, with packages viewed as a means to an end rather than as the most important element of the interaction. In terms of personality differences and the implications of differing learning styles, courses and packages utilizing technology-based materials must incorporate design measures that offer alternate paths and options for the successful learning encounter. Laurillard (1987) spoke of the development of multifaceted design models, and Hedberg (1988) mentioned the use of templates as simple ways to link the use of technology to regular tools that are in common (preferably daily) use by the student. For example, use of the simple device of a spreadsheet with a prepared mathematical model allows at least three levels of processing. First, students may type their own numbers into a prepared proforma. The package will calculate according to the prepared algorithms, and, by changes in different elements, will show a relationship between inputs and results. Changing the inputs allows the student to model different results based on the input assumptions. A second level might involve translation of the numbers into another form of representation, such as a chart. This second level may already have been prepared and the links simply updated as learners change the numbers in their first proforma, or the students might use the links between spreadsheet and charting routines to clarify or further investigate relationships (especially if they are visual learners). A third level would enable the student to change the underlying assumptions on which the analysis is based. The learner might decide to investigate the algorithms devised for the relationships between inputs and results. By changing the formulae, the learner can extend beyond the interaction designed by the subject matter expert and the instructional designer. At both the second and third levels, the learner is manipulating the technology to generate knowledge rather than simply to watch its presentation.

While recognizing that learners at a distance do not always have easy access to technology, we have the tools to manipulate information so that adult learners do not have to passively accept what is presented to them. Technology allows the user to decide on the representation and to change the assumptions and the algorithms. It is up to the other human side of the interface—the instructional designer—to meet the challenge of technology and design materials that are open-ended and support the distance learner.

ALTERNATIVE LINKS TO SUPPORT PROFESSIONAL DEVELOPMENT

Throughout the world, a variety of innovative projects are being undertaken to apply telecommunications to the concepts of distance education and open learning strategies and evaluate its effectiveness (some Australian examples are included in Hedberg and Harper [1992]). Some of the programs have been designed to maintain currency for professional teachers, some to offer teachers paths to postgraduate studies, and others to become integral parts of preservice offerings. As the trend leading to telecommunication facilities becoming available in many schools continues, so teachers' participation in e-mail-based inservice programs will rise rapidly.

The brief case studies outlined here exemplify the work being done to design efficient and effective course delivery to off-campus students.

Postgraduate Studies in Specialized Areas Using Telematics

The University of Wollongong is currently supporting a major initiative in the development of information technology expertise and interactive multimedia specialization, as part of the movement toward open learning approaches to professional development. The Faculty of Education has set up a state-of-the-art interactive multimedia laboratory for research and development in this area and is dedicated to the use of innovative technology in instruction. This facility is being used as a basis for the development of interactive multimedia materials and to support, through telecommunication systems, inservice and postgraduate studies for teachers.

The laboratory is well equipped with facilities to develop software and audiovisual resources to test and evaluate prototype laserdisc materials. The facility includes 10 workstations with large storage capacity, which are equipped with laserdisc and CD-ROM players as well as video and audio digitizing and video editing units. The laboratory is attached to a University-wide e-mail system that can be accessed through external electronic mail networks available to teachers in schools.

Development of the system at Wollongong is based on supporting teachers and postgraduate students through linking them directly to lecturers via a simple and inexpensive existing e-mail system. The University of Wollongong, through its Information Technology Services unit, has established a campus-wide network that takes full advantage of the interconnectivity now being developed for desktop personal computers. The desktop machines of staff members are interconnected through either Ethernet or Appletalk networks, which are linked through routers to the campus-wide fiber optic system. Access to the library system (PALS), administrative student data, and international e-mail through the Australian Academic and Research Network (AARNet) and the international Internet system are at the fingertips of academic staff.

The Faculty of Education has three Appletalk fileservers, all with excess storage capacity. This excess capacity has been put to use to support a pilot study in course support through student access to the networks via network modems. Postgraduate students are assigned a folder to download assignments and submissions or questions for their lecturers. Furthermore, a folder for distribution of information to students has been set up, so that relevant information or instructional materials in the form of text or in hypertext-type applications (such as HyperCard stacks) can be downloaded when students sign on. This system has proved to be reliable and inexpensive for the faculty to set up, considering that the only extra cost has been for network modems. Experience has shown that most of our students purchase a computer to use in their work, and the added cost of a modem seems to be an attractive alternative to campus visits, phone calls, and submitting assignments by mail. This program was developed as a prototype for providing specialized postgraduate courses at greater distances without the cost of highly designed materials, which are expensive for small numbers, and in which it is difficult to maintain currency in highly volatile content areas.

Christopher Columbus Links Between Schools and University

Apple Computer Australia and the University of Wollongong have embarked on a joint project called the *Christopher Columbus Program—Down Under*. Just as Columbus discovered new worlds, this program aims to discover new ways of learning.

The project aims to research effective applications of interactive multimedia in education and training, and to develop educational courseware for both learners and teachers/trainers for Australian and overseas markets. It is also investigating the use of international telecommunication systems in learning environments, through electronic mail links between Australian and the worldwide network of centers participating in the program. This network is part of the Apple Global Educational Network.

The University of Wollongong site is the first Australian representative in the Christopher Columbus program, which is based in the United States and incorporates more than 20 similar collaborating centers throughout the world. The projects that are developed from the program will be based in the interactive multimedia laboratory, which was established by the Education Policy Program on behalf of the Faculty of Education.

The project focuses on working with selected local schools to develop cost-effective uses of interactive multimedia in the K-12 curriculum and to investigate the use of electronic mail systems in support of teachers and students in these developments.

Apple Computer Australia is supporting the program by supplying links to international telecommunication systems, supplying experimental software and technology to the University and collaborating schools, and funding production costs for an initial interactive multimedia package on ecology, which is being designed for use in the years 11-12 Biology curricula throughout Australia.

The Pegasus Network

Gert Gast (1991) reported on an experiment that made use of the Pegasus networks for distance education. The experiment involved facilitating telemetric access to a campus in California for an isolated student in Australia. The student had access to a virtual campus, through which she was able to electronically attend lectures and seminars from her own computer, write assignments and essays, and communicate with her lecturers and tutors online. This was achieved through use of a modem and computer by a student with limited experience in computer use. Pegasus Networks Communications Pty. Ltd. is a wholly Australian-owned company established to make the latest developments in electronic information and communications readily available and affordable to as many people as possible in the Australian community. The network has a variety of gateway facilities that allow the user to access a large number of networks worldwide. Thousands of academics at major universities, as well as millions of commercial network users, are accessible. The system's international connections also offer shared conference material, electronic mail services, and a variety of other resources.

The WorldWideWeb Project

The WorldWideWeb (WWW) project seeks to merge the techniques of information retrieval and hypertext to make an easy but powerful global information system accessible to users of international e-mail systems. The project, based at C.E.R.N. in Geneva, started with the philosophy that academic information should be freely available to any prospective user and that information sharing should be readily available to internationally dispersed teams.

The WWW consists of documents, links to documents, and indexes of these links. Users may browse the preconstructed links or generate a web of their own construction, using keyword searches of remote information servers via the browsing software designed for the project. The web contains documents in many formats. Documents that are hypertext (real or virtual) contain links to other documents or places within documents. All documents available to the system, whether real, virtual, or indexes, look similar to the reader and are contained within the same addressing scheme.

This type of development opens up a broad range of possibilities for information access for educational programs at a distance. Specialized resources of this type might be all that is needed for advanced-level students to compile their own knowledge structures and learning strategies. Efficient document caching, the reduction of redundant and out-of-date copies, and elimination of many of the irrelevant hardcopy documents currently commonly obtained by distance education students through traditional library loan systems will be a distinct advantage of such a system. This type of network could be accessed by any distance student who can connect to AARNet in Australia and have network access.

The Victorian Telematics Experience

In late 1986, the Victorian Government commenced a project to use electronic means of curriculum dissemination to improve retention rates in small rural secondary schools. Seventy-nine state postprimary schools formed themselves into 16 clusters to devise ways of improving curriculum choice for their students.

An audiographic system consisting of voice, document, and real-time simulated blackboard links was chosen. Computer software designed to simultaneously link two or more Macintosh computers together to transmit screens of graphics was developed. When the software is used in conjunction with a paint program such as MacPaint and with a graphics tablet, a very powerful blackboard is simulated.

As well as communication links, most clusters identified a need for more curriculum materials in areas such as technology and technical studies, health sciences, community languages, and music. To provide this additional curriculum cost-effectively, they developed technology packages (TEKPAKS) consisting of mobile resources of working models, teacher guides, student materials, and sometimes tool kits, which circulate amoung schools in the cluster on a preplanned schedule. They provide students with valuable practical experience in a range of technology and save individual schools and the Ministry the cost of fully equipped workshops for small numbers of students.

This complex initiative has achieved many outcomes, some predictable and some unanticipated. Approximately 130 hours of instruction are provided each week by clusters using telematics to link small groups of students in neighboring schools. In addition, the audiographic network has been used to deliver professional development seminars to teachers in remote schools. A more subtle outcome has been the increase in contact between schools and sharing of expertise and other resources. This has helped schools explore ways of improving their capacity to provide a more comprehensive curriculum, particularly at senior levels. Further, there has been significant growth in teacher expertise and self-esteem as a result of participating in a project that not only provides them with new skills, but also gives them the feeling of being part of something new and exciting.

CONCLUSION

The new technologies offer significant opportunities for distance learners in the places where they work. The development of new relationships between institution and student enables a wider range of course offerings for both professional development and postgraduate degree studies. Apart from the convenience, the potential increase in effective time management can reduce the personal costs of professional development. The obvious gains are continued immediacy, responsiveness of the provider, and personalization.

Importantly, access and equality of opportunity are enhanced at possibly less cost than attended programs, and at less cost than the professionally designed distance education courses that have been considered necessary as part of the distance education program. This latter issue might be contested by those arguing for quality learning materials, but the economics of providing specialized courses or courses with highly volatile content through means of telecommunications support must be considered in an age of reduced resources.

Linking the student and instructor through telematics allows dynamic and current knowledge structures to be accessed in ways that traditional distance education systems do not possess. The change in locus of control from instructor to learner raises a series of hypermedia issues about cognition, motivation, and navigation that beg to be explored (Grabowski and Curtis 1991). It is also possible to extend (or encapsulate) the model of the WWW into local computer networks; the latest operating systems available on microcomputers enable the current versions of notes, diagrams, sound files, or digitized images to be "published" and users to "subscribe." The implications for creating dynamic knowledge structures and the organization of learning experiences are profound.

As these case studies have illustrated, Australian institutions are beginning to expand their approaches to open learning through telecommunications. The current experiments range from simple, cheap solutions to quite novel and more expensive solutions. With the development of national policies, there is likely to be a major change in the way institutions view their role and their teaching functions. Increased pressure is being placed on institutions that do not see themselves as holding a national mission and view their relationship with their clientele as being one of personal, face-to-face contact. The alternative view of the virtual institution should appeal both politically and individually as a method of addressing needs specific to current national and personal development priorities.

If alternative systems of delivery are to be developed in institutions purely to service their existing students, even if they are not formally distance education institutions, any educational institution today must consider maximizing the methods through which its staff and students communicate. Failure to do so will ensure the increasing regionalization and general lack of access to the best students. Further, if there are specializations, then they are immediately available to any interested party virtually anywhere. National boundaries are no longer important in this equation; quality of staff and the ideas that drive the students and research program are the currency with which students will purchase the product. In fact, it is only quality that will make us unique, and bring students to believe that spending their time and effort in contact with us will result in something of value.

REFERENCES

Commission on Instructional Technology. (1970). *To improve learning: An evaluation of instructional technology.* New York: R. R. Bowker.

Davies, D., and Jennings, C. (1991). *Distributed learning systems: Telecommunications, telematics and organizations.* Paper presented at Current and Future Developments and Applications of Technology Based Training: Networks and Telecoms. Coventry, United Kingdom.

Edwards, P., and McNamara, S. (1989). *Developing a distance education facility within a faculty of education.* Monash University Research Report.

Gast, G. (1991, March). A viable approach. *Adult Education News*, 9-12.

Grabowski, B. L., and Curtis, R. (1991). Information, instruction, and learning: A hypermedia perspective. *Performance Improvement Quarterly*, 4(3), 2-12.

Hedberg, J. G. (1988). Technology, continuing education and open learning or Technology 1-Bureaucracy 0. In *Designing for learning in industry and education*, ed. J. Steele and J. G. Hedberg. (Canberra: Australian Society for Educational Technology), 90-94.

Hedberg, J. G. (1989). The relationship between technology and mathematics education: Implications for teacher education. In Department of Employment, Education and Training, *Discipline Review of Teacher Education in Mathematics and Science*, vol. 3 (Canberra, ACT: Australian Government Publishing Service), 103-37.

Hedberg, J. G., and Harper, B. (1992). Supporting and developing teachers through telecommunications. In *Distance education and teacher training*, ed. R. Cornell (Paris: International Council for Educational Media).

Hedberg, J. G., and McNamara, S. E. (1989). The human-technology interface: Designing for open and distance learning. *Educational Media International*, 26(2), 73-81.

Laurillard, D. (1987). *Interactive media: Working methods and practical applications.* London: John Wiley.

Law, M., and Sissons, M. (1985). The challenge of distance education. In *Involving adults in the educational process: New directions for continuing education*, ed. R. H. Rosenblum (San Francisco: Jossey-Bass).

Matthews, W., and Brookshaw, J. (1988). Distance education in the Mallee Secondary College Cluster. In *Designing for learning in industry and education*, ed. J. Steele and J. G. Hedberg (Canberra: Australian Society for Educational Technology), 113-16.

McNamara, S. E. (1989a, February). *Support services for RA3 (Telematics in distance education projects)—Staff development and course design and delivery.* Unpublished report for the Victorian Ministry of Education.

McNamara, S. E. (1989b). Distance education by interactive telematics. In *Teaching tips from the inexperienced*, ed. N. Elliot (the Victorian telematics manual). Melbourne: Ministry of Education.

Dr. John Hedberg is Associate Professor in Information Technology in Education at the University of Wollongong. Address: Faculty of Education, University of Wollongong, PO Box 1144, Wollongong, NSW, 2500. Dr. Barry Harper is a Senior Lecturer in the Faculty of Education, University of Wollongong, and Dr. Suzanne McNamara is a lecturer at Monash University in Clayton, Victoria.

Telecommunications and Teachers
Preliminary Findings from a National Survey*

Margaret Honey and Andres Henriquez
Center for Technology in Education
Bank Street College of Education

INTRODUCTION

Providing educators with access to basic telecommunications technology—computers, modems, and telephone lines—is currently being discussed as an essential component of the educational reform agenda (Hunter 1992; Lavin and Phillepo 1990). Teachers can use networks to access a wealth of information ranging from reports on educational research to curriculum sources and lesson activities. The conferencing capabilities of bulletin boards and networks are a promising means for teachers to exchange ideas with colleagues (Merseth 1991; Weir 1992). Many networks now feature discussion centers and teacher forums on a wide range of topics, including school-based management, alternative assessment, and equity and education issues. Anecdotal reports have long suggested that collaborations that take place over telecommunications networks help to erase experiences of professional isolation common among teachers.

In addition, there is widespread agreement that telecommunications can enhance the range and scope of what students learn in the classroom (Brienne and Goldman 1988; Cohen and Reil 1986; Levin and Cohen 1985; Newman, Brienne, Goldman, Jackson, and Magzamen 1988; Reil 1985; Reil and Levin 1990; Ruopp 1993; Waugh and Levin 1989). With the aid of creative teachers, students are using telecommunications systems to gather and exchange science information, to carry out creative writing projects, and to exchange cultural and social information (Foster, Julyan, and Mokros 1988; Riel 1987; Rogers 1992). In the last five years, the use of telecommunications in the classroom has moved beyond the research and development phase and has become a widespread component of numerous technology integration efforts.

Although there exists a wealth of descriptive information on the kinds of projects that are being carried out, there has been no systematic analysis of the range and type of telecommunications activities being conducted by teachers for either professional development or student learning. As a result, the national Center for Technology in Education at Bank Street College conducted, during 1992, a nationwide survey of K-12 educators' use of telecommunications systems for two principal purposes: professional enhancement (i.e., communicating with colleagues, downloading curriculum materials, online research activities) and student learning (i.e., classroom exchange projects, online research activities). The survey was designed to gather a systematic profile of the range of activities currently being undertaken by teachers to adequately advise school officials, policymakers, industry, and teachers themselves on strategies for the creative use of this technology. Based on the responses of 550 educators from 48 states, this survey represents the first systematic and large-scale profile

*This research was supported by the Center for Technology in Education under Grant No. R117F80011 from the Office of Educational Research and Improvement (OERI), U.S. Department of Education to Bank Street College of Education.

of the benefits of and obstacles to using telecommunications effectively as a professional resource and learning tool. The following report presents a summary of the major findings from the survey.

DEVELOPING THE QUESTIONNAIRE

Our goal in developing the survey instrument was to create a questionnaire that would adequately reflect and capture the array of experiences that are relevant to educators who are actively involved in telecommunications. Using our network of professional contacts, we put together a total of five focus groups in the New York metropolitan region. Thirty-one teachers, administrators, and computer and media specialists who were using a range of telecommunications networks for professional and student learning purposes participated in these groups.

The focus groups addressed a broad range of topics that we wanted the survey to cover. We asked educators how and why they first became involved with telecommunications, the kinds of training they received, and what their own individual learning curves looked like. We asked them to describe what they used network services for, including the kinds of professional collaborations they were involved in, as well as their student-based projects. We asked them about the pros and cons of networking, and whether telecommunications had had an impact on their teaching and their students' learning. Finally, we discussed the factors that make telecommunications activities successful, as well as the barriers that prevent the effective use of this technology.

Out of these discussions we developed a 27-page questionnaire that gathered information about the following:

I.   *Background as an educator:* Respondents' educational background and their experience with computer technology.

II.   *Background and experience in telecommunications:* Respondents' general experience using telecommunications for both student learning activities and professional development activities.

III. *Practical and technical aspects of telecommunications:* Respondents' experience with the practical (e.g., where do they telecommunicate from) and technical (e.g., kind of computer hardware, baud rates) dimensions of telecommunicating for both student learning and professional activities.

IV.   *Telecommunications and student learning:* Kinds of telecommunications activities respondents engage in with students and how they perceive the effectiveness of these activities, including factors that make telecommunications activities successful and factors that have encouraged the respondents to pursue such activities with their students.

V.   *Telecommunications and professional activities:* Kinds of telecommunications activities that respondents engage in for professional purposes and how they perceive the effectiveness of these activities, along with the factors that have encouraged the use of telecommunications for professional development.

VI.   *Telecommunications at respondents' schools:* What telecommunications looks like at each respondent's school, including the role they play in relation to their colleagues, how telecommunications activities first got under way, and how their school supports faculty's use of telecommunications.

VII. *Barriers:* Extent to which respondents have experienced both past and present barriers in the process of attempting to get telecommunications projects under way in their schools.

VIII. *Background about computers at respondents' schools:* What computer technology in general looks like at the respondents' schools.

IX.   *School demographics:* Demographic information about the respondents' schools.

DEVELOPING THE SAMPLE

Because we were interested in learning about educators who were actively involved in using telecommunications, we developed the survey sample by posting online announcements on more than 50 educational, commercial, and state-run telecommunications networks. The announcement read as follows:

> The national Center for Technology in Education at Bank Street College will be conducting, in 1992, a nation-wide survey of teachers who use telecommunications systems for professional development and student learning. We are interested in surveying K-12 teachers who use bulletin boards, online commercial services, or online education services for a range of activities.

We also solicited respondents through mailing lists (FrEdMail, ISTE, K-12 Net, Learning Initiatives, NYSERNET), conferences, state education departments, and professional contacts. As a result, all of the educators who responded to the survey volunteered to participate. Fifty percent of the educators who volunteered to be part of this study returned the questionnaire (550 out of 1,100).

SCHOOL PROFILE

To understand how our voluntary sample is similar to and different from our nation's schools and the teachers who teach in them, we compared the demographics of our sample to national averages collected by the National Center for Education Statistics. We found that across size, type of school, and ethnic and economic representation, the respondents' schools are comparable to national averages (NCES 1992). Although there is a trend toward more suburban schools in our sample than is the case nationally, our economic data suggest that our sample does not overrepresent more affluent communities. The sample is concentrated in the Northeast and West and underrepresentative of the South and Midwest.

The schools in our sample are well endowed with computer and distance learning technologies. The average number of computers in these schools, 66.5, is more than double the average of 26 reported in a random survey of U.S. schools (Becker 1989). These schools also have a range of distance learning technologies available to them, including cable television systems (75 percent); microwave hookups (38 percent); satellite (35 percent); and broadcast technologies (30 percent).

RESPONDENT PROFILE

Our sample is on average older than the nation's teachers as a whole (44.9 versus 40.2 years), and almost entirely Caucasian (95 percent—the national average is 88.1 percent). There are also many more men in our sample (43 percent of the total) than are represented in national averages (the national teaching population is 71 percent female, 29 percent male).

These educators are experienced and well-educated teachers. Eighty-three percent have taught for ten or more years (the national average is 57 percent). Most (79 percent) of our respondents have done graduate work at or beyond the master's level; this is 32 percent higher than the national average.

Our respondents work with students spanning the K-12 age groups. Approximately one-fifth (20 percent) are elementary school teachers, suggesting that educators are finding that telecommunications can support a range of activities that are meaningful for teachers who work with younger children as well as older students. Twenty-three percent of the respondents identified their primary teaching assignment as general computer-based instruction (as distinct from computer science); and 14 percent percent listed their primary teaching assignment as library/media specialists.

> A new and growing specialty in which technology and telecommunications activities are taking place is among library media specialists. We first noticed this trend when we conducted focus groups to help us design the survey instrument. According to the Bureau of School Library Media Programs, what distinguishes a library media specialist from a school librarian is that they are certified K-12 teachers. "A school library media specialist assures full integration of the library media program into the curriculum of the school through a partnership established among the library media specialist, district level personnel, administrators, teachers, and parents..." (SMLSGram 1992).

The sciences (13 percent), including biology, chemistry, physics, earth science, and geology, represented the largest content-specific discipline for these telecommunicating educators. This was followed by math and computer science (8 percent); other special areas (art, music, reading, health, physical education, industrial arts, business education—6 percent); English/language arts (4 percent); social studies/social sciences (3 percent); gifted education (3 percent); special education (2 percent); vocational education (2 percent); foreign language (2 percent); bilingual/ESL (.4 percent); and basic skills (.4 percent). When these figures are compared to national averages compiled by the National Center for Education Statistics, it becomes clear that our sample of telecommunicating educators is heavily concentrated in jobs that are directly related to using technology in instruction.

The majority (83 percent) of our respondents are experienced computer users, reporting that they have been using computers for five or more years. Almost all have access to computers at home (91 percent), and they are involved in a wide range of computer-based practices, from word processing to robotics. They also report that they are self-taught technology users (96 percent), and attend conferences and workshops on their own time (72 percent).

Eighty percent of the respondents to an earlier study also reported that they had been using computers in their teaching for five or more years. In 1989, the Center for Technology in Education carried out a national survey of teachers nominated as accomplished users of educational technology. According to teachers' descriptions of their practices and the amount of time they had been using technologies in their teaching, we were able to determine that it takes, on average, five to seven years for a teacher to become a comfortable, confident user of educational technology. By the fifth year, use of drill and practice and tutorial software dropped, and teachers started expanding the number and kind of technologies they used in their classrooms. Similarly, our sample reports an average of five years of computer use, and a much lower level of use of drill and practice and tutorial software than the teachers in the "Accomplished Teachers" survey. The five years of technology use (and the kinds of applications used) that our respondents report suggest that one common path to telecommunications may be completing an "early" phase of technology use, and moving on to explore new technologies at the end of that phase.

Motivation, Experience, and Training

> *Being able to connect with other "techie" teachers really is exciting. The teachers in my building are not interested in technology, for the most part. So, using the modem connects me to a larger, more stimulating group of educators!**

---

*All quotations are taken from respondents' answers to open-ended survey questions.

Most of these educators describe themselves as "intermediate" (53 percent) or "very knowledgeable" (30 percent) about telecommunicating. The majority (88 percent) are self-taught and have been involved in telecommunicating for professional reasons for more than four years, and using telecommunications for student activities for more than three years.

Among this group of educators, telecommunications use has been driven largely by individual motivation rather than by school or district initiatives. Seventy-eight percent of the sample reported that they were "personally intrigued by the technology" and that this is why they initially got involved with telecommunications. The survey results strongly suggest that support for telecommunications activities at the school and district level is virtually nonexistent. In the absence of organized school-based support, a high degree of self-motivation appears to be a necessary component of undertaking telecommunication activities.

Although support is available in our respondents' schools for training in general *computer-based* activities, there is a notable absence of such support (on either a district or school level) for telecommunications. Forty-five percent of our respondents said that they learned how to use basic computer applications by taking courses offered at the district level, and 40 percent report taking courses offered in schools. In contrast, only 13 percent of the respondents report taking district-sponsored courses to learn basic telecommunications skills, and only 8 percent have taken telecommunications courses offered at their schools. Instead, respondents report learning about telecommunications activities mainly on their own (88 percent) and by attending workshops and conferences (45 percent).

TELECOMMUNICATING FOR PROFESSIONAL DEVELOPMENT

I have been able to meet and work and learn with such a variety (geographically and background) of education professionals that it is rather like being in continuous attendance at a large international conference.—A high school science teacher.

I have grown professionally by having others to collaborate with. This has helped me to be a better teacher. Having that global view keeps my classroom exciting.—A K-12 computer coordinator.

The educators in our sample are actively involved in using telecommunications for a number of professional activities, including sending e-mail to colleagues (76 percent), exchanging information on forums and bulletin boards (62 percent), accessing databases that contain information relevant to students (51 percent), and accessing information about educational research (49 percent). Approximately two-thirds are accessing information services and carrying out collegial exchanges, on average, once a week or more. The majority (69 percent) of these educators conduct professional telecommunications activities on their own time, from their homes, using both free and commercial networks, and subscribe to an average of four different telecommunications services.

What About the Internet?

- Slightly less than half (48 percent) of the respondents have access to the Internet.

- The Internet is used by twice as many of the respondents for professional activities as for student learning activities.

- Exchanging e-mail (91 percent), accessing news and bulletin boards (63 percent), and gaining remote access to other computers (48 percent) are the activities most frequently engaged in for professional purposes.

- Access to the Internet is supplied most frequently through a university computer (46 percent) or through an educational telecommunication service (37 percent).

TELECOMMUNICATING WITH STUDENTS

My students have learned to think more about the world as classroom—we are able to visualize the children of other nations as students, just like ourselves. I've not been able to get this idea across effectively before.—An elementary school computer coordinator.

It allows me to do real science with others who choose to do real work, and allows students the chance to have a real role in global affairs while doing scientific work that matters.—A high school science teacher.

Students are more actively involved, question more, contribute more, work cooperatively, initiate learning.—A middle school media specialist.

Pen-pal exchanges (41 percent), scientific data collection (34 percent), and social awareness and opinion exchanges (33 percent) represent the range of activities most frequently done as classroom exchange projects. When students are conducting research projects, encyclopedias (57 percent), news retrieval services (54 percent), weather information (50 percent), and educational databases (48 percent) are the resources most frequently used.

Much of the telecommunications activity done with students takes place in the educator's classroom (42 percent), but these respondents also telecommunicate from computer labs (33 percent), library media centers (32 percent), and their own homes (30 percent).

The most commonly used network services include commercial educational networks (97 percent)—for example, Learning Link, AT&T Learning Circles, National Geographic Kids Network—and free educational networks (81 percent)—for example, FrEdMail, FreeNet, K-12 Net.

Service offerings, expense, and ease of use are the three factors most important in determining which network services are selected.

The same factors that influence the success of any shared learning activity are important to the success of a telecommunications project: planning, cooperation, and well-defined and relevant project goals.

Educators rate science and social awareness projects as the most effective kinds of classroom exchange activities. News retrieval services, scientific databases, encyclopedias, ERIC, and social studies databases are perceived to be the most effective information resources to use with students.

Our students are from small rural communities and very few have had the experience of traveling far from home. Last fall we were involved with the AT&T Learning network where we communicated with nine other schools in North America. This really sparked the interest in geography, writing (penpals), and work in small groups to complete assignments.—A middle school computer science teacher.

University of Michigan Arab-Israeli Peace Conference Simulation. Have done it twice and will expand to two classes next year. Involves every student telecommunicating every day. Works because we have 25 individual computers and modems. Works because Michigan is organized and facilitates, provides feedback, solves problems.—A high school social studies teacher.

We are involved in the International Arctic Project which is an environmental initiative focusing on the Arctic. We are following a 5-week expedition from Hudson Bay to Nueltin Lakes by four explorers on dog sled. It is the most exciting project we have ever been involved with. We are tracking the real movements of polar bears, exchanging questions and answers with the explorers, and learning about other schools.—A middle school media specialist.

Last year we set up a weather exchange on K-12 Net. We received weather data from all over the world. Our sixth grade class became interested in learning more about an Ojibway tribe that sent weather data from N. Canada. We sent them some questions, they responded and sent us some questions also. After several exchanges, we decided to exchange videotapes. Our student council also sent them some hockey equipment. It seemed that both groups learned a lot!

INCENTIVES FOR TELECOMMUNICATING

The educators in this study report a range of incentives for using telecommunications as a professional resource. Using a six-point scale, in which 1 represented strong disagreement and 6 represented strong agreement, respondents rated a list of statements describing the pros and cons of telecommunications. The most highly rated incentives for using telecommunications as a professional resource included opportunities to communicate with other educators and share ideas (5.4); access to information that would otherwise be difficult to obtain (5.1); and combating the isolation that so many educators experience as part of their jobs (4.9).

Using the same six-point scale, educators also rated a series of statements describing the pros and cons of using telecommunications for purposes of student learning. Expanding students' awareness about the world in general (5.5); accessing information that would be difficult to get otherwise (5.3); and increasing students' inquiry-based and analytical skills (5.0) were the three most highly rated incentives.

Respondents report that one of the most important benefits of using this technology for instructional purposes is its impact on their students' higher-order thinking skills. The inquiry-based analytical skills, such as critical thinking, data analysis, problem solving, and independent thinking, develop when students use a technology that supports research, communication, and analysis. These educators report that students' involvement with telecommunications does not directly help to improve their performances on state- or city-mandated tests. This finding suggests that there is an enormous gap between what teachers *know* the creative use of telecommunications can do for their students, and what traditional measures of assessment *actually* account for.

BARRIERS TO USE

There should be a computer and phone on every teacher's desk.—A sixth grade teacher.

My limited use has given me a vision of its potential, but because of hardware and budget limitations we have not yet realized that potential at the elementary level.—An elementary school computer coordinator.

The barriers to effective use of telecommunications resources that were cited by our sample will sound familiar to most educators who have worked to introduce new technologies into their schools. Primary barriers described in the CTE Accomplished Teachers study in 1990—insufficient hardware, inflexible access to equipment, lack of administrative support—are still present for teachers working with telecommunications. However, new barriers appear with the advent of telecommunications technology, the most notable being insufficient telephone lines in the school building.

Other frequently mentioned barriers include lack of time in the school schedule, inadequate communication about telecommunications-related matters throughout school systems, lack of financial support, and inadequate district-level development of goals and plans for use of telecommunications.

Technical barriers related to telecommunications software, including availability of software, ease of use, and compatibility of software with hardware, were three of the least encountered barriers. In addition, the overall quality of telecommunications services was not experienced by this group of educators as a significant barrier. Neither the design of network interfaces nor "informational overload" (too many choices or complexity of choices) was rated as a significant obstacle.

CONCLUDING REMARKS

The findings of this survey suggest that, for this group of educators, telecommunications serves as a valuable resource for both professional and student learning activities. The findings also suggest that these educators represent a very specialized group. They are experienced and highly educated teachers. They are extremely knowledgeable about computer technology and have been using a range of computer-based applications in their classrooms for a number of years. Also, they are working in schools that are well endowed with computer resources.

Within this group, it is the computer and library media specialists who are taking the lead in telecommunications activities, serving as resource persons and facilitators for colleagues in their schools. Our data also suggest that there is *not* widespread administrative support for telecommunications activities on either the district or school level. Although the schools and districts represented in this study have invested in training teachers in general computer-based applications, training in telecommunications is almost nonexistent. The majority of our respondents are self-taught, and they tend to gather information about telecommunications activities by attending conferences or workshops on their own time.

Though their personal motivation for using telecommunications is extremely high, the findings also suggest that there are pragmatic incentives that encourage the use of telecommunications for both professional and student learning tasks. Combating isolation, exchanging ideas, and obtaining information are all important factors that motivate the use of telecommunications for professional purposes. Expanding students' awareness, accessing information resources, and increasing students' higher-order thinking skills are the factors that make telecommunications a particularly compelling resource to use with students.

The overall findings of this study speak to the largely beneficial and rewarding aspects of using telecommunications technology, but this research also raises an important question. How can this technology be made available to educators who are less technologically sophisticated and perhaps less personally motivated to become technological enthusiasts than the individuals represented in this study? The results suggest that, if the use of telecommunications technology is to become as widely based a practice as are general computer-based applications, then certain supports must be put in place.

First, schools and districts must get involved in training teachers in the use of telecommuni-cations. At a minimum, the same level of investment that schools and districts have made in computer-based training needs to be present for training teachers in the use of telecommunications.

Second, respondents' ratings of barriers make it clear that more time must be made available in the school schedule if teachers are to effectively integrate telecommunications into their ongoing classroom activities. Research on technology integration efforts (Sheingold and Hadley 1990) shows that typical 40-minute class periods are not adequate for projects that successfully *integrate* computer or multimedia technology into the curriculum.

Third, for teachers to feel confident that student-based telecommunications projects are academically justified, assessment measures must be devised that can adequately capture and account for the kinds of critical thinking and inquiry-based analytical skills that such activities appear to foster.

Fourth, more financial support must become available in schools for telecommunications projects (e.g., network fees, telephone lines, support personnel, curriculum development). Because schools are overextended financially, this support will have to come from other sources, including private corporations and foundations, as well as state and federal funding sources.

Finally, telephone lines must become much more widely available in schools. Teachers are the only group of professionals who do not have regular access to telephones, often because the cost of installing phone lines in school buildings is prohibitive. Ideally, regional phone companies need to develop pricing structures that encourage schools to invest in this technology for their teachers. Alternatively, schools can also consider installing local area networks—a solution that reduces the need for multiple phone lines in school buildings (Newman, Bernstein, and Reese 1992).

REFERENCES

Becker, H. J. (1989). [U.S. Administration of the 1989 IEA Computers and Education Survey, Johns Hopkins University Center for Social Organization of Schools]. Unpublished raw data.

Brienne, D., and Goldman, S. (1988). *Collaborative network activities for elementary earth science.* Working Paper. New York: Center for Children and Technology, Bank Street College of Education.

Cohen, M., and Reil, M. (1986). *Computer networks: Creating real audiences for students' writing. Technical Report No. 15.* San Diego, CA: Interactive Technology Laboratory, University of California.

Foster, J., Julyan, C. L., and Mokros, J. (1988). The National Geographic Kids Network from Technical Education Research Centers, Inc. (TERC). *Science and Children,* 25(8), 38.

Hunter, B. (1992). Linking for learning: Computer-and-communications network support for nationwide innovation in education. *Journal of Science Education and Technology,* 1(1), 23-34.

Lavin, R. J., and Phillepo, H. (1990). Improve school-based management through intelligent networking. *T.H.E. Journal,* 18(4), 69-71.

Levin, J., and Cohen, M. (1985). The world as an international science laboratory: Electronic networks for science instruction and problem solving. *Journal of Computers in Mathematics and Science Teaching,* 4(1), 33-35.

Merseth, K. K. (1991). Supporting beginning teachers with computer networks. *Journal of Teacher Education*, 42(2), 140-47.

National Center for Education Statistics (1992). *Schools and staffing in the United States: A statistical profile, 1987-88.* Washington, DC: U.S. Department of Education, Office of Educational Research and Improvement.

Newman, D., Bernstein, S. L., and Reese, P. A. (1992). *Local infrastructures for school networking: Current models and prospects. Technical Report #22.* New York: Bank Street College of Education.

Newman, D., Brienne, D., Goldman, S., Jackson, I., and Magzamen, S. (1988, April). *Computer mediation of collaborative science investigations.* Revision of a paper presented at the Symposium on Socializing Children into Science, American Educational Research Association.

Riel, M. (1985). The computer chronicles newswire: A functional learning environment for acquiring literacy skills. *Journal of Educational Computing Research*, 1(3), 317-37.

Riel, M. (1987). The InterCultural Learning Network. *Computing Teacher*, 14(7), 27-30.

Riel, M., and Levin, J. A. (1990). Building electronic communities: Success and failure in computer networking. *Instructional Science*, 19, 145-69.

Rogers, A. (1992). *Linking teachers and students around the world.* FrEdMail Foundation.

Ruopp, R. (1993). *LabNet: Toward a community of practice.* Hillsdale, NJ: Lawrence Erlbaum Associates.

Sheingold, K., and Hadley, M. (1990). *Accomplished teachers: Integrating computers into classroom practice. Special Report.* New York: Center for Technology in Education.

SMLSGram. (1992, Spring). New York Library Association. School Library Media Section.

Waugh, M., and Levin, J. A. (1989). Telescience activity: Educational uses of electronic networks. *Journal of Computers in Mathematics and Science Teaching*, 8, 29-33.

Weir, S. (1992). *Electronic communities of learners: Fact or fiction. Working paper 3-92.* Cambridge, MA: TERC.

Internet Basics*

Roy Tennant

This digest briefly describes the Internet computer network, the physical connections and logical agreements that make it possible, and the applications and information resources the network provides.

THE INTERNET

The Internet is a worldwide network of computer networks. It is composed of thousands of separately administered networks of many sizes and types. Each of these networks is comprised of as many as tens of thousands of computers; the total number of individual users of the Internet is in the millions. This high level of connectivity fosters an unparalleled degree of communication, collaboration, resource sharing, and information access. In the United States, the National Science Foundation Network (NSFNet) comprises the Internet "backbone" (a very high speed network that connects key regions across the country). The NSFNet will likely evolve into the National Research and Education Network (NREN) as defined in the *High-Performance Computing Act of 1991* (P.L. 102-194, signed into law by President Bush on December 9, 1991).

PHYSICAL CONNECTIONS AND LOGICAL AGREEMENTS

For the Internet to exist, there must be connections between computers and agreements on how they are to communicate. Connections can consist of any of a variety of communication media or methods: metal wires, microwave links, packet radio or fiber optic cables. These connections are usually established within areas or regions by the particular networking organization with authority or economic interest in that area. For example, a university academic department may lay Ethernet cable to connect its personal computers and workstations into a local area network (LAN), which is then connected to the cables the campus laid to connect its buildings together, which is then linked to cables laid by a regional network, which itself ties into the NSFNet backbone, the infrastructure for which was funded by the U.S. government. Therefore the path between any two points on the Internet often traverses physical connections that are administered by a variety of independent authorities.

*This digest was prepared for the ERIC Clearinghouse on Information Resources by Roy Tennant, Public Service Automated Systems Coordinator, The Library, University of California, Berkeley. September 1992.

ERIC Digests are in the public domain and may be freely reproduced and disseminated.

This publication was prepared with funding from the Office of Educational Research and Improvement, U.S. Department of Education, under contract no. RI88062008. The opinions expressed in this report do not necessarily reflect the positions or policies of OERI or ED.

For disparate computers (from personal computers to mainframes) to communicate with other computers over a network, there must be agreements on how that should occur. These agreements are called *communication protocols.* At present, the Transmission Control Protocol/Internet Protocol (TCP/IP) suite of protocols defines how Internet computers are to communicate. In the future, the Open Systems Interconnection (OSI) suite of protocols promulgated by the International Standards Organization (ISO) may be supported on the Internet as well. These protocols define how certain applications are to be accomplished: electronic messaging, online connections, and the transfer of files.

ELECTRONIC MAIL

Electronic mail, or e-mail, is a fast, easy, and inexpensive way to communicate with other Internet users around the world. In addition, it is possible for Internet users to exchange e-mail with users of other independent networks such as CompuServe, Applelink, the WELL, and others. Internet users often find that the expanded capability to communicate with colleagues around the world leads to important new sources of information, collaboration, and professional development.

Besides basic correspondence between two network users, e-mail presents additional opportunities for communication. Through various methods for distributing e-mail messages to lists of "subscribers," e-mail supports electronic discussions on a wide range of topics. These discussions bring together like-minded individuals who use such forums for discussing common problems, sharing solutions, and arguing issues.

Another type of electronic communication that is growing in popularity is the electronic journal, or "e-journal." Although some e-journals require certain types of software and hardware to display each issue, most e-journals are distributed to a list of subscribers as an e-mail text message, either complete as one issue, or retrievable at the article level by mailing a command to a software program that automatically sends the appropriate file. The very definition of a "journal" is undergoing change in the electronic environment, as e-journal publishers experiment with different publication models (e.g., sending articles out individually as soon as they are ready rather than waiting until a group of articles are gathered for an "issue").

REMOTE LOGIN

Remote login is the ability of a computer user in one location to establish an online connection with another computer elsewhere. Once a connection is established with a remote computer, the users can use that remote system as if their computer were a hard-wired terminal of that system. Within the TCP/IP protocol suite, this facility is called *Telnet.* Utilizing Telnet, an Internet user can establish connections with a multitude of bibliographic databases (primarily library catalogs), campus information systems of various universities, full-text databases, data files (e.g., statistics, oceanographic data, meteorologic data, geographic data, etc.), and other online services. Many of these systems are available for any Internet user to access and use without an account.

What makes this application truly remarkable is that ease and speed of access are not dependent upon proximity. An Internet user can connect to a system on the other side of the globe as easily as (and generally not much slower than) he or she can connect to a system in the next building. In addition, since many Internet users are not at present charged for their network use by their institutions, or at least are not charged by the level of their use, cost is often not a significant inhibitor of usage. Therefore the barriers of distance, time, and cost, which are often significant when using other forms of electronic communication, can be reduced in the Internet environment. A compensating disadvantage is that initial costs for Internet connection can be high, and access can be technically demanding.

FILE TRANSFER

Another application of the Internet is the ability to transfer files from one Internet-connected computer to another. This function is provided by the *File Transfer Protocol* (FTP) of the TCP/IP protocol suite. In a method similar to using Telnet, network users initiate an online connection with another Internet computer via FTP. But unlike Telnet, this online connection can perform only functions related to locating and transferring files. This includes the ability to change directories, list files, retrieve files, etc.

Types of files that can be transferred using FTP include virtually every kind of file that can be stored on a computer: text files, software programs, graphic images, sounds, files formatted for particular software programs (e.g., files with word processing formatting instructions), and others. Many computer administrators have set aside portions of their machines to offer files for anyone on the Internet to retrieve. These archive sites support "anonymous" logins that do not require an account to access, and therefore are called *anonymous FTP sites.* To locate files, Internet users can use the Archie service, which indexes files from over 900 separate anonymous FTP sites (Tennant 1993).

EXTENDED SERVICES

The three basic Internet applications of electronic mail, remote login, and file transfer are also building blocks of more sophisticated applications that usually offer increased functionality and ease of network use. Tools such as Gopher, WAIS, and World Wide Web go beyond the three basic Internet functions to make information on the network easier to locate and use. Gopher is a project of the University of Minnesota that uses a series of menus to organize and automate access to information and other online systems wherever they reside on the Internet. The Wide Area Information Servers (WAIS) project of Thinking Machines, Apple Computer, Dow Jones & Co., and KPMG Peat Marwick seeks to provide a common interface to a multitude of Internet databases. World Wide Web is a hypertext interface to Internet information resources that was developed at CERN in Switzerland (Tennant 1993). This trend toward more powerful, user-friendly networked information resource access systems is likely to continue as the Internet grows and matures.

FUTURE POSSIBILITIES

The backbone infrastructure for the United States portion of the Internet (the NSFNet, or the Interim NREN) is largely supported through federal government funding. For this reason, use of the network has been limited to nonprofit research and educational uses, and commercial companies have established networking arrangements that avoid using the NSFNet. Most recently, however, dialogues have begun about commercialization and privatization of the NSFNet infrastructure. The full effects of such a move on current Internet users, especially research and educational institutions, has yet to be seen. One certainty is that the breadth of information and the services offered on the Internet will continue to burgeon, at an ever more rapid rate.

FURTHER READING

Bishop, Ann P. (1991, December). *The National Research and Education Network (NREN): Update 1991.* ERIC Digest. Syracuse, NY: ERIC Clearinghouse on Information Resources. (EDO-IR-91-9). [Also in ERIC as ED 340 390.]

Farley, Laine, ed. (1991). *Library resources on the Internet: Strategies for selection and use.* Chicago, IL: Reference and Adult Services Section, American Library Association.

Kehoe, Brendan P. (1993). *Zen and the art of the Internet: A beginner's guide to the Internet.* 2d ed. Englewood Cliffs, NJ: Prentice Hall.

Lynch, Clifford, and Preston, Cecilia. (1990). Internet access to information resources. In Martha E. Williams, ed., *Annual review of information science and technology,* vol. 26 (Medford, NJ: Learned Information), 263-312.

Malkin, Gary Scott, and Marine, April N. (1992). *FYI on questions and answers: Answers to commonly asked "new Internet user" questions.* Network Working Group, Request for Comments 1325. [Available through anonymous FTP from host ftp.nisc.sri.com, directory rfc, filename rfc1325.txt.]

Polly, Jean Armour. (1992). Surfing the Internet: An introduction. *Wilson Library Bulletin,* 66(10), 38-42+.

Scientific American. (1991). Special issue: Communications, computers, and networks. 265(3).

Stanton, Deidre E. (1992). *Using networked information resources: A bibliography.* Perth, WA: Author. [Available through anonymous FTP from host infolib.murdoch.edu.au, directory pub/bib, filename stanton.bib or stanton.bib.wp.]

Tennant, Roy; Ober, John; and Lipow, Anne G. (1993). *Crossing the Internet threshold: An instructional handbook.* Berkeley, CA: Library Solutions Press.

U.S. Congress. (1991). *High-Performance Computing Act of 1991. Public Law 102-194, December 9, 1991.* Washington, DC: U.S. Government Printing Office. [Available through anonymous FTP from host nnsc.nsf.net, directory nsfnet, filename nrenbill.txt.]

Networking
K-12*

Michael B. Eisenberg

INTRODUCTION

At-risk high school students in the states of Washington, Texas, Massachusetts, and California "meet" online to discuss teenage pregnancy, drug prevention, Middle East foreign policy, and other topics of current interest (Jensen 1991/92).

Students of all ages collaboratively produce a newspaper, *GlobalVillage News*, using input from dozens of worldwide student "news bureaus" linked through more than 15,000 free computer bulletin boards in over 50 countries. The paper is distributed to thousands of users throughout the world (Rose 1992).

Students from the United States and other countries go on a simulated space shuttle journey, assuming various roles including secondary mission control, selecting alternative landing sites, and docking other shuttles (Clement 1992).

What makes these common educational experiences exciting and unique? They all involve students and teachers from around the world interacting through computer networks.

THE BENEFITS OF NETWORKING

Long-distance, or wide-area, computer networking can change teaching and learning dramatically. Teachers and students with access to a computer, a modem, and phone lines are freed from the physical limits of a school building and the time limits of an 8 a.m. to 3 p.m. school day. They can communicate with peers and gain access to electronic resources as they wish, making individualized instruction and personal inquiry the norm, not the exception. Interaction through networks helps break down communication barriers and inhibitions that often stifle the open exchange of ideas in traditional classrooms. There is also a strong motivational aspect to network use: kids bring an energy and enthusiasm to it that's often missing in traditional classrooms, and teachers are thrilled to be able to share ideas, problems, and solutions with colleagues across the country as easily as if they were next door.

The excitement and enthusiasm for networking is not wistful speculation based on theoretical possibilities—it's happening right now. Thousands of students and teachers are tapping into networks, sharing experiences, and engaging in a wide range of learning activities. As the pace of networking accelerates, so too will the creative uses and the overall impact of the movement.

*Written by Michael B. Eisenberg, Director, ERIC Clearinghouse on Information Resources, Syracuse University, Syracuse, New York. December 1992. This digest was adapted from: Eisenberg, Michael B., & Ely, Donald P. Plugging Into the 'Net. *The ERIC Review*, 2(3), 1-29, forthcoming. For a free copy, contact ACCESS ERIC, 1-800-LET-ERIC; ACCERIC@GWUVM.GWU.EDU.

ERIC Digests are in the public domain and may be freely reproduced and disseminated.

This publication was prepared with funding from the Office of Educational Research and Improvement, U.S. Department of Education, under contract no. RI88062008. The opinions expressed in this report do not necessarily reflect the positions or policies of OERI or ED.

HOW ARE NETWORKS USED?

Whether connected to a state, regional, or private network, or to the Internet (the worldwide "network of networks"), network users can undertake three primary activities: electronic mail, computer conferencing, and accessing information from remote sources. Each of these offers opportunities to expand the learning environment, foster better communication, and excite learners and educators.

Electronic Mail (or E-Mail)

Using e-mail, learners can exchange information with teachers or other learners, and teachers can communicate with students or colleagues, locally and worldwide. E-mail messages offer immediate access to others on the same network.

- Teachers, administrators, librarians, and other educators can consult with colleagues in the district and across the country on curriculum, policies, technology, and other concerns.

- Students can "talk" to others across time zones and continents and get responses much more quickly than by mail.

- Texts, or files, can be transferred through e-mail, facilitating the exchange of papers, reports, and resource materials for teachers, administrators, and students.

Group Communication

Network communication also makes it easy for groups of people to work cooperatively and share information without having to be in close physical proximity. It is possible to create "global classrooms" where students work with others as if they were in the same location. Educators and students can join organized discussion groups on specific topics. The networks are filled with hundreds of such groups (sometimes called "listservs"), many having international membership. LM_NET, for example, is an Internet discussion group for the library media field; EDTECH-L is dedicated to educational technology.

Remote Information Access

Through computer networking, information from around the world becomes available in the local school and even in the individual classroom or library media center. A few examples of the wealth of information available to students include:

- Research data, discussions, libraries, and additional services related to drug and alcohol abuse from California's Drug and Alcohol Abuse Prevention Net.

- Text and commentaries of Supreme Court decisions, information on space flights and space science, and data from the U.S. Commerce Department through the Cleveland Free-Net.

- The full text of the Federalist Papers, the U.S. Constitution, the Koran, and a host of other books through Project Gutenberg, a nonprofit organization seeking to prepare electronic editions of more than 10,000 books by the year 2001.

GETTING STARTED

To get into wide-area networking, you need to know: (1) how to operate your own computer, modem, and telecommunications software; (2) how to connect to and communicate with a computer already linked to the network; and (3) how to use the network to communicate with others. User manuals, classes, and general reference books (for example, Roberts 1990; Glossbrenner 1989) can help you master these basics.

Finding a connection to a computer on a network is not always an easy task. Options include:

- Local bulletin board systems (bbs). Telephone dial-up to a local bulletin board is a readily available and generally free connection to a computer network. Computer stores, the public library, education agencies, or computing centers at local colleges should be able to provide information about bulletin boards in your area.

- College and university computer systems. Most colleges and universities provide free or low-cost accounts on their computer systems to all students. These systems usually connect to BITNET or some other network that in turn provides access to the Internet. Educators who are enrolled in college or university courses should inquire about network access.

- Statewide and regional systems. A growing number of states, including Texas, Virginia, Florida, and North Dakota, provide low-cost or free connections to schools and/or teachers, administrators, and students within the state. These networks generally provide some statewide services (e.g., bulletin boards, conferencing, curriculum resources sharing, administrative data transfer) as well as a gateway to the Internet and other networks. In addition, some of the National Science Foundation mid-level and regional networks are providing fee-based access to the Internet. Contact state education agencies for information.

- School computing facilities. Local schools and districts are just beginning to develop wide-area network capabilities. Check with your building or district computer support personnel to see what is available to you.

- Commercial vendors. Commercial vendors provide a wide range of fee-based information resources and services, including electronic mail and messaging. Many of the commercial systems offer, or intend to offer, connections to the Internet (see Notess, 1992 for list).

SELECTED K-12 NETWORK RESOURCES

Academy One. Affiliated with the National Public Telecomputing Network (NPTN) and the Cleveland Free-Net, this program aims to create a "national online information cooperative for K-12 telecomputing activities." Schools throughout the world access the resources of Academy One's community computer systems and participate in a variety of online projects and events. Contact: Linda Delzeit, NPTN Director of Education, Box 1987, Cleveland, OH 44106; (216) 368-2733. Internet: AA002@NPTN.ORG.

AppleLink. This official online information resource of the Apple Computer community offers a K-12 Education Area with discussion forums, software reviews, conference listings, lesson plans, and research results. Contact: Lisa Bauer, Mail Stop 41-D, Apple Computer, Inc., 20525 Mariani Ave., Cupertino, CA 95014; (408) 996-1010.

Commercial Vendors. Following are some of the many commercial networks offering some resources and services specifically for education: **America Online**, 8619 Westwood Center Drive, Vienna, VA 22182, 800-827-6364. **America Tomorrow**, P.O. Box 2310, W. Bethesda,

MD 20827-2310, 800-456-8881. **GTE Education Services**, West Airfield Drive, P.O. Box 619810, D/FW Airport, TX 75261-9810, 800-927-3000.

FrEdMail. The "Free Educational Mail Network," the oldest and largest educational network in the U.S., uses the Internet to link more than 150 electronic bulletin boards operated by individuals and institutions (see Rogers 1992). FrEdMail offers collaborative activities designed to help students become better writers and learners. It also promotes the sharing of resources and experiences among teachers. For information on finding a local node or setting up your own electronic mail center, contact: Al Rogers, FrEdMail Foundation, P.O. Box 243, Bonita, CA 91908; (619) 475-4852. Internet: AROGERS@BONITA.CERF.FRED.ORG.

K12Net. This bulletin board-based system works through "echo" forums around major curriculum areas for teachers and students interested in particular topics. These forums facilitate cooperative projects such as *Global Village News* (see opening). Access to K12Net is through **FidoNet**, a free general-interest computer network that joins more than 15,000 computer bulletin boards in more than 50 countries. Participation is free to anyone with local bulletin board access. To find active bulletin boards in your region, call a local computer store or your public library (Rose 1992).

KIDSNET. Accessible through the Internet, KIDSNET is a global discussion group for teachers and others interested in networking for children and education. (See Join KIDSNET!, 1991.) Participants discuss general questions regarding computer networking and user interfaces, and specific projects that link teachers and students using the Internet. KIDS is an associated list just for children. To subscribe to KIDSNET, send an Internet request to: JOINKIDS@PITTVMS.BITNET. Children with access to the Internet can post messages to KIDS by sending mail to: KIDS@PITTVMS.BITNET.

REFERENCES AND READINGS

Clement, John. (1992, January/February). Network-based collaborations: How universities can support K-12 reform efforts. *EDUCOM Review*, 27(1), 8-12.

Glossbrenner, Alfred. (1989). *The complete handbook of personal computer communications: Everything you need to go online with the world*. 3d ed. New York: St. Martin's Press.

Jensen, Eric. (December 1991/January 1992). At-risk students online. *The Computing Teacher*, 19(4), 10-11.

Join KIDSNET! (1991, December). *NYSERNET User*, 2(2), 6.

Kochmer, Jonathan. (1991). *NorthWestNet User Services Internet Resource Guide (NUSIRG)*. 3d ed. Bellevue, WA: NorthWestNet.

Notess, Greg R. (1992, September). Gaining access to the Internet. *Online*, 16(5), 27-34.

Polly, Jean Armour. (1992, June). Surfing the Internet: An introduction. *Wilson Library Bulletin*, 66(10), 38-42, 155.

Polly, Jean Armour. (1992, December). *Surfing the Internet, Volume 2*. Available through anonymous ftp at host nysernet.org, directory/pub/resources/guides, filename surfing.the.internet.2.0.txt.

Roberts, N., Blakeslee, G., Brown, M., & Lenk, C. (1990). *Integrating telecommunications into education*. Englewood Cliffs, NJ: Prentice-Hall.

Rose, Mike. (1992, May/June). Are you plugged into the global classroom? *American Teacher*, 76(6), 8-9.

Strategies for Teaching at a Distance*

Barry Willis

Effective teaching at a distance is more the result of preparation than innovation. The distance educator can employ a number of strategies focusing on planning, student understanding, interaction, and teaching to ensure a successful distance delivered course.

WHAT'S DIFFERENT ABOUT DISTANCE TEACHING?

Classroom teachers rely on a number of visual and unobtrusive cues from their students to enhance their delivery of instructional content. A quick glance, for example, reveals who is attentively taking notes, pondering a difficult concept, or preparing to make a comment. The student who is frustrated, confused, tired, or bored is equally evident. The attentive teacher consciously and subconsciously receives and analyzes these visual cues and adjusts the course delivery to meet the needs of the class during any particular lesson.

In contrast, the distant teacher has few, if any, visual cues. Those cues that do exist are filtered through technological devices such as video monitors. It is difficult to carry on a stimulating teacher-class discussion when spontaneity is altered by technical requirements and distance.

Without the use of a real-time visual medium such as television, the teacher receives no visual information from the distant sites. The teacher might never really know, for example, if students are asleep, talking among themselves, or even in the room. Separation by distance also affects the general rapport of the class. Living in different communities, geographic regions, or even states deprives the teacher and students of a common community link.

WHY TEACH AT A DISTANCE?

The challenges posed by distance teaching are countered by opportunities to reach a wider student audience; to meet the needs of students who are unable to attend on-campus classes; to involve outside speakers who would otherwise be unavailable; and to link students from different social, cultural, economic, and experiential backgrounds. Many teachers feel the opportunities offered by distance education outweigh the obstacles. In fact, instructors often comment that the focused preparation required by distance teaching improves their overall teaching ability and empathy for their students.

*This digest is based in part on *Distance Education: A Practical Guide*, by Barry Willis, 1993.

This digest was prepared for the ERIC Clearinghouse on Information Resources by Barry Willis, Statewide Director of Distance Education, University of Alaska System. November 1992.

ERIC Digests are in the public domain and may be freely reproduced and disseminated.

This publication was prepared with funding from the Office of Educational Research and Improvement, U.S. Department of Education, under contract no. RI88062008. The opinions expressed in this report do not necessarily reflect the positions or policies of OERI or ED.

IMPROVING PLANNING AND ORGANIZATION

In developing or adapting distance instruction, the core content remains basically unchanged, although its presentation requires new strategies and additional preparation time. Suggestions for planning and organizing a distance delivered course include:

- Begin the course planning process by studying distance education research findings. There are several excellent research summaries available (see Blanchard 1989; Moore and Thompson 1990).

- Before developing something new, check and review existing materials for content and presentation ideas.

- Analyze the strengths and weaknesses of possible delivery approaches, in terms of learner needs and course requirements, before selecting a mix of instructional technology. Avoid "technological solutions in search of instructional problems."

- Hands-on training with the technology of delivery is critical for both teacher and students. Consider a pre-class session in which the class meets informally using the delivery technology and learns about the roles and responsibilities of technical support staff.

- At the start of class initiate a frank discussion to set rules, guidelines, and standards. Once procedures have been established, consistently uphold them.

- Make sure each site is properly equipped with functional and accessible equipment. Provide a toll-free "hotline" for reporting and rectifying problems.

- If course materials are sent by mail, make sure they are received well before class begins. To help students keep materials organized, consider binding the syllabus, handouts, and other readings prior to distribution.

- Start off slowly with a manageable number of sites and students. The logistical difficulties of distant teaching increase with each additional site.

- Understand the strengths and weaknesses of the instructional delivery systems available to you (e.g., audio, video, data, and print) as well as the technical means by which they are delivered (e.g., satellite, microwave, fiber optic cable, etc.).

MEETING STUDENT NEEDS

To function effectively, students must quickly become comfortable with the nature of teaching and learning at a distance. Efforts should be made to adapt the delivery system to best motivate and meet the needs of the students, in terms of both content and preferred learning styles (see Coldeway, Spencer, and Stringer 1980). Consider the following strategies for meeting students' needs:

- Make students aware of and comfortable with new patterns of communication to be used in the course (see Holmberg 1985).

- Learn about students' backgrounds and experiences. Discussing the instructor's background and interests is equally important.

- Be sensitive to different communication styles and varied cultural backgrounds. Remember, for example, that students may have different language skills, and that humor is culturally specific and won't be perceived the same way by all (see Sponder 1990).

- Remember that students must take an active role in the distance-delivered course by independently taking responsibility for their learning.

- Assist students in becoming familiar and comfortable with the delivery technology and prepare them to resolve the technical problems that will arise. Focus on joint problem solving, not placing blame for the occasional technical difficulty.

- Be aware of students' needs in meeting standard university deadlines, despite the lag time often involved in rural mail delivery.

IMPROVING INTERACTION AND FEEDBACK

Using effective interaction and feedback strategies will enable the instructor to identify and meet individual student needs while providing a forum for suggesting course improvements. To improve interaction and feedback, consider the following:

- Integrate a variety of delivery systems for interaction and feedback, including one-on-one and conference calls, fax, electronic mail, video, and computer conferencing. When feasible, consider personal visits as well.

- Contact each site (or student) every week if possible, especially early in the course. Take note of students who don't participate during the first session, and contact them individually after class.

- Make detailed comments on written assignments, referring to additional sources for supplementary information. Return assignments without delay, using fax or electronic mail, if practical.

- Arrange telephone office hours using a toll-free number. Set evening hours if most of your students work during the day.

- Early in the course, require students to contact you and interact among themselves via electronic mail, so that they become comfortable with the process. Maintaining and sharing electronic journal entries can be very effective toward this end.

- Use pre-class study questions and advance organizers to encourage critical thinking and informed participation on the part of all learners. Realize that it will take time to improve poor communication patterns.

- Have students keep a journal of their thoughts and ideas regarding the course content, as well as their individual progress and other concerns. Have students submit journal entries frequently.

- Use pre-stamped and addressed postcards and out-of-class phone conferences for feedback regarding course content, relevancy, pace, delivery problems, and instructional concerns.

- Call on individual students to ensure that all participants have ample opportunity to interact. At the same time, politely but firmly discourage individual students or sites from monopolizing class time.

- Use an on-site facilitator to stimulate interaction when distant students are hesitant to ask questions or participate. In addition, the facilitator can act as the instructor's onsite "eyes and ears."

USE EFFECTIVE DISTANCE TEACHING SKILLS

For the most part, effective distance teaching requires enhancing existing skills, rather than developing new abilities. Pay special attention to the following:

- Develop strategies for student reinforcement, review, repetition, and remediation. Toward this end, one-on-one phone discussions and electronic mail communication can be especially effective.

- Realistically assess the amount of content that can be effectively delivered in the course. Because of the logistics involved, presenting content at a distance is usually more time-consuming than presenting the same content in a traditional classroom setting.

- Diversify and pace course activities and avoid long lectures. Intersperse content presentations with discussions and student-centered exercises.

- Be aware that student participants will have different learning styles. Some will learn more easily in group settings, while others will excel when working independently. While the same is true in traditional classroom settings, preferred student learning styles may be more difficult to determine at a distance.

- Humanize the course by focusing on the students, not the delivery system.

- Consider providing a strong print component to supplement nonprint materials (see Graham and Wedman 1989).

- Use locally relevant case studies and examples as often as possible to assist students in understanding and applying course content.

- Be concise. Use short, cohesive statements and ask direct questions, realizing that technical linkages might increase the time it takes for students to respond.

- Personalize instructor involvement, realizing that distance teaching does not replace the value of face-to-face contact and small group interaction. If budget and time permit, teach at least one session from each site. Typically, the earlier in the course this is done, the better.

- And finally ... Relax. Participants will quickly grow comfortable with the process of distance education and the natural rhythm of effective teaching and learning will return.

REFERENCES

Blanchard, W. (1989). *Telecourse effectiveness: A research-review update.* Olympia, WA: Washington State Board for Community College Education. (ED 320 554.)

Coldeway, D. E., Spencer, R., and Stringer, M. (1980). *Factors effecting learner motivation in distance education: The interaction between learner attributes and learner course performance. REDEAL Research Report #9.* Project REDEAL Research and Evaluation of Distance Education for the Adult Learner. Edmonton, Alberta, Canada: Athabasca University. (ED 249 346.)

Graham, S. W., and Wedman, J. F. (1989). Enhancing the appeal of teletraining. *Journal of Instructional Psychology*, 16(4), 183-91.

Holmberg, B. (1985). Communication in distance study. In *Status and trends of distance education.* Lund, Sweden: Lector Publishing.

Moore, M. G., and Thompson, M. M., with Quigley, A. B., Clark, G. C., and Goff, G. G. (1990). *The effects of distance learning: A summary of the literature. Research Monograph No. 2.* University Park, PA: The Pennsylvania State University, American Center for the Study of Distance Education. (ED 330 321.)

Sponder, B. (1990). *Distance education in rural Alaska: An overview of teaching and learning practices in audioconference courses. University of Alaska Monograph Series in Distance Education No. 1.* Fairbanks, AK: University of Alaska, Center for Cross-Cultural Studies. (ED 325 276.)

Willis, B. (1993). *Distance education: A practical guide.* Englewood Cliffs, NJ: Educational Technology Publications.

Instructional Development for Distance Education*

Barry Willis

INTRODUCTION

Instructional development provides a procedure and framework for systematically planning, developing, and adapting instruction based on identifiable learner needs and content requirements. This process is essential in distance education, where the instructor and students may share limited common background and typically have little face-to-face contact.

Although instructional development models and processes abound (see Dick and Carey 1990; Gustafson and Powell 1991), the majority follow the same basic stages of design, development, evaluation, and revision. While it is possible, even appropriate on occasion, to shorten the instructional development process, it should be done only after considering the needs of the learner, the requirements of the content, and the constraints facing both teacher and students.

THE DESIGN STAGE

The design stage focuses on gathering information to help understand the instructional gap between what is and what should be. Steps include defining the problem or need, understanding the audience, and identifying instructional goals and objectives.

In defining the problem or need, determine why the instruction is required, what external data verify the need, what factors led to the instructional need, and what past experiences indicate that the instruction being planned can effectively meet this need.

To better understand the distant learners and their needs, consider their ages, cultural backgrounds, interests, and educational levels. In addition, assess their familiarity with the various instructional methods and delivery systems being considered, determine how they will apply the knowledge gained in the course, and note whether the class will consist of a broad mix of students or discrete subgroups with different characteristics (e.g., urban/rural, undergraduate/graduate). When possible, the instructor should visit distant sites and interview prospective students, both individually and in small groups. This personalized attention will also show students that the instructor is more than an anonymous presence, linked by electronic technology. If on-site interaction is impossible, students should be contacted by telephone. Colleagues who have worked with the target population can also offer advice to the distance educator.

*This digest is based in part on *Distance Education: A Practical Guide*, by Barry Willis, 1993.

This digest was prepared for the ERIC Clearinghouse on Information Resources by Barry Willis, Statewide Director of Distance Education, University of Alaska System. November 1992.

ERIC Digests are in the public domain and may be freely reproduced and disseminated.

This publication was prepared with funding from the Office of Educational Research and Improvement, U.S. Department of Education, under contract no. RI88062008. The opinions expressed in this report do not necessarily reflect the positions or policies of OERI or ED.

Based on the nature of the problem as well as student needs and characteristics, establish instructional goals and objectives. Goals are broad statements of instructional intent, while objectives are specific steps leading to goal attainment.

THE DEVELOPMENT STAGE

The first step in development is to create a content outline based on the instructional problem, the audience analysis, instructional goals and objectives, and an understanding of the desired course content. Next, the instructor should review existing materials. Instructional materials should not be used solely because they are readily available or have been effective in traditional classroom settings (see Beare 1989). This is especially true if prepackaged materials, such as telecourses, are being considered (see Earl 1989). Whereas many prepackaged instructional tools are developed and marketed to reach students with similar backgrounds and experiences, they may have little relevance for distant learners who come to the course with widely varied and nontraditional experiential backgrounds. If prepackaged instructional materials are to be used, consider developing "wrap-around" introductions, conclusions, and summaries that specifically relate the learning materials to the instructional context of the distant student.

Perhaps the greatest challenge facing the distance educator is creating student-relevant examples. Content, for the most part, is taught by using examples to relate the content to a context understood by the students. The best examples are "transparent," allowing the learners to focus on the content being presented. If examples are irrelevant, learning is impeded. This is a special challenge in rural and multicultural settings where the teachers' realm of experience and content examples may be foreign to distant learners. To address this problem, discuss potential content examples with a sampling of the target audience.

In critiquing course content and presentation strategies, find reviewers who have content expertise and experience teaching the target learner population. Use informal peer networks to identify these individuals and consult with local school teachers and community school personnel, who often cater to the needs of distant learners.

The development of instructional materials and selection of delivery methods will often require integrating voice, video, and data technology with print resources. The challenge here is to select instructional technology based on identifiable learner needs, content requirements, and technical constraints. For example, it does little good to rely on delivery technology that is unavailable or relatively inaccessible to some class members. If unusual delivery systems are required, make sure they are available to all distant learners to avoid having to create parallel learning experiences based on the different delivery systems available to class members.

THE EVALUATION STAGE

The primary purpose of evaluation is to provide information to decision makers. According to Brookfield (1990), the utility of educational evaluation is enhanced by immediacy, clarity, regularity, accessibility, and future orientation. With this in mind, there are two approaches to evaluation, formative and summative.

Formative evaluation is ongoing throughout the instructional development process and helps ensure that the course or instructional product will achieve its stated goals (Flagg 1990). One evaluation method for the distance educator to consider is giving students pre-addressed and stamped postcards to complete and mail after each class session. These "mini-evaluations" might focus on course strengths and weaknesses, technical or delivery concerns, and content areas in need of further coverage.

Summative evaluation is conducted upon course completion and is used to determine the overall effectiveness of the class or instructional product. Summative evaluation usually focuses on student performance, course relevancy, learner attitudes toward the delivery methods used, and the instructor's teaching style and effectiveness. Following course completion, consider a summative evaluation session in which students informally brainstorm ways to improve the course. Consider having a local facilitator run the evaluation session to encourage a more open exchange of evaluative information.

Within the context of formative and summative evaluation, data are collected through quantitative and qualitative methods. Quantitative techniques rely on a breadth of response and are patterned after experimental research focused on the collection and manipulation of statistically relevant quantities of data. In contrast, qualitative evaluation focuses on depth of response and usually involves gathering more subjective data and anecdotal information from a relatively small, and possibly statistically insignificant, group of respondents. Guba (1978) identifies a number of qualitative methods for collecting evaluative data, including open-ended questioning, participant observation, nonparticipant observation, content analysis, interviews, and unobtrusive measures.

Qualitative approaches may be of special value to the distance educator because the diversity of students may defy statistically relevant stratification and analysis. The best approach often combines quantitative measurement of student performance with open-ended interviewing and nonparticipant observation to collect and assess information about attitudes toward the course's effectiveness and the delivery technology.

THE REVISION STAGE

There is room for improvement in even the most carefully developed distance-delivered course, and the need for revision should be anticipated. In fact, there will likely be more confidence in a course that has been significantly revised than in one that was considered flawless the first time through.

Revision plans typically are a direct result of the evaluation process in tandem with feedback from colleagues and content specialists. The best source of revision ideas may be the instructor's own reflection on course strengths and weaknesses. For this reason, revision should be planned as soon as possible after the course ends.

Often, course revisions will be minor, such as breaking a large and unwieldy instructional unit into more manageable components, increasing assignment feedback, or improving student-to-student interaction. On other occasions, greater revisions will be needed. Revisions should be made according to priority, and significant course changes should be field-tested prior to future course scheduling.

To test revision ideas, contact and reconvene small groups of distant learners, content specialists, and colleagues, and ask them to review and critique the revision ideas being considered. Results of this process should be tempered by the knowledge that the characteristics of each distance-delivered class will vary and that revisions required for one learner group may be inappropriate for a different student population.

IN CONCLUSION

Adhering to sound principles of instructional development won't overcome all of the obstacles one encounters en route to developing effective distance education programs. It will, however, provide a process and procedural framework for addressing the instructional challenges that will surely arise.

REFERENCES

Beare, P. L. (1989). The comparative effectiveness of videotape, audiotape, and telelecture in delivering continuing teacher education. *American Journal of Distance Education*, 3(2), 57-66.

Brookfield, S. D. (1990). *The skillful teacher: On technique, trust, and responsiveness in the classroom.* San Francisco, CA: Jossey-Bass.

Dick, W., and Carey, L. (1990). *The systematic design of instruction.* 3d ed. Glenview, IL: Scott, Foresman, and Co.

Earl, A. W. (1989). *Design of a telecourse: From registration to final exam.* Paper presented at the Annual Conference on Emerging Technologies in Education and Training, Augusta, Maine, September 29, 1989. (ED 317 182.)

Flagg, B. N. (1990). *Formative evaluation for educational technologies.* Hillsdale, NJ: Lawrence Erlbaum Associates.

Guba, E. G. (1978). *Toward a methodology of naturalistic inquiry in educational evaluation. CSE Monograph Series in Education, 8.* Los Angeles, CA: University of California, Center for the Study of Evaluation. (ED 164 599.)

Gustafson, K. L., and Powell, G. C. (1991). *Survey of instructional development models with an annotated ERIC bibliography.* 2d ed. Syracuse, NY: ERIC Clearinghouse on Information Resources. (ED 335 027.)

Willis, B. (1993). *Distance education: A practical guide.* Englewood Cliffs, NJ: Educational Technology Publications.

Part Four
Leadership Profile

Introduction

For the past six years, one of the features of the *Yearbook* has been this part highlighting the people who have made significant contributions to the field of educational media and technology. Each person profiled has made special contributions through research, writing, and service to the profession. The names each year are selected by the editors. There is no nomination process, no voting, no awards—only the recognition of unique individuals who have reached the pinnacle of the profession through their achievements and personal influence on colleagues and students.

Each "portrait" is painted by a person who knows the leader well. In most cases, the authors are or have been colleagues. Their articles are labors of love, respect, and admiration. They offer genuine insights into the leader that go beyond the usual biographical sketch.

The person profiled this year—Dr. Harry A. Johnson—has been active in the field in the international arena, throughout the United States, and in his home state of Virginia. He has served as the president of the Virginia Association for Educational Communications and Technology, which recently awarded him its Life Time Achievement Award, and as a member of the board of the Association for Educational Communications and Technology. This article describes fully the person and his contributions.

Each edition of the *Yearbook* will continue to carry leadership profiles. At the risk of creating a contest, the editors would like to invite nominations for individuals who deserve to be honored in this fashion.

Harry Alleyn Johnson

Vykuntapathi Thota
*Director, University Center for Instructional Media and Technology and
Professor, Virginia State University, Petersburg*

Dr. Harry Alleyn Johnson, Professor Emeritus at Virginia State University, was born in Norfolk, Virginia, the youngest child of Ozeas and Blanch Johnson. He received his early education in the public schools of Norfolk. Upon graduation from Booker T. Washington High School, he entered Virginia State College, where he received a B.S. degree. This was followed by a stint with the United States Army in the Pacific Theater, where he was awarded two oak leaf clusters. Commissioned a first lieutenant in the field, he remained active with the reserves until his retirement as a captain in the Retired Reserves.

After the war, Johnson taught in the public school system of Charlottesville, Virginia, until his appointment to the Virginia State College faculty in 1949. As a Virginia State faculty member, he completed the Doctor of Education degree at Teachers College, Columbia University, where he had received his master's degree four years earlier.

Early in his career, Johnson won a Fulbright Scholars' Post Doctoral Fellowship to Paris, France, where he worked at the École Normale Supérieure and studied at the Sorbonne (University of Paris). Later, he served as communications media advisor to the Sierra Leone Government, West Africa, through a contract with Indiana University and the United States Agency for International Development. During this time, he founded and organized the first audiovisual center in Sierra Leone for training teachers.

In April 1962, Dr. Johnson served as a consultant in Milan, Italy, for the First International Conference on the use of audiovisual aids for education and professional training in Africa. On several invitations from the government of Norway, Dr. Johnson lectured and held workshops at the University of Trondheim, the University of Berogen, and the University of Oslo. He held faculty workshops on communication media and teaching methodology that included use of educational radio and television in higher education. He directed the first National Educational Media Institute held in Oslo, Norway, for participants representing 21 Norwegian institutions of higher education. He also served as a consultant at the University of Sussex in England.

A change in geographic direction then took Dr. Johnson to the University of Puerto Rico, School of Education, where he served as consultant on curriculum and mediated instruction. These seminars included English as a second language and an institute for teachers of disadvantaged youth. A later project took him to Asilomar, California, to participate in a 10-day international invitational seminar on "Curriculum and Instruction," which was attended by more than 100 American and 300 foreign educators. This was the beginning of the World Council on Curriculum and Instruction, sponsored by the National Education Association and the Association for Supervision and Curriculum Development.

Dr. Johnson's special services to the educational media field have benefited Virginia State in many ways. He wrote proposals and won federal contracts for educational media institutes for advanced study at Virginia State University for seven consecutive years, which brought the university more than a quarter of a million dollars through the National Defense Education Act (NDEA) programs. Dr. Johnson feels, however, that one of his greatest challenges was the five-year stint as chair of the Education Building Committee at Virginia State University, which planned, helped design, and saw to fruition what is now Harris Hall Education Building.

Dr. Johnson has authored and compiled three books, two published by R. R. Bowker Company of New York and London, and the third, *Negotiating the Mainstream: The Afro-American Experience*, by the American Library Association. Dr. Johnson was invited by a number of universities to serve as visiting professor, including the University of Maine, Michigan State University, California State University at Hayward, and the University of Washington at Seattle. He also had the distinction of serving on the National Advisory Board of the ERIC Clearinghouse on Educational Media at Stanford University for six years. Dr. Johnson was named an Honorary Life Member to CINE, which screens American-made films for foreign film festivals. He was the first black to be president of the Virginia Association for Educational Communications and Technology (now VEMA), and was recently awarded its Life Time Achievement Award. He was also the first minority member elected to the AECT Board (then DAVI).

Recent assignments have included research papers presented in Manila, the Philippines, at the World Council on Curriculum and Instruction; the Fifth International Seminar for Teacher Education, held at the University of Aveiro in Portugal; and the World Educators Conference, held at the University of Hawaii at Honolulu.

Dr. Johnson's career at Virginia State University was marked by prodigious productivity in a number of research areas. The great bulk of his research is in the areas of multicultural education and Afro-American studies. It would be hard to single out a particular publication as his most important contribution in these areas, but to me, the most impressive are those dealing with the multimedia materials for Afro-American and ethnic American minorities. This somewhat brief examination of Dr. Johnson's major research efforts does not do justice to his many contributions.

Over the years, Dr. Johnson has contributed greatly to educational media and technology through his graduate teaching. At the graduate level, he has taught courses on radio and television, the selection and utilization of instructional materials, and individualizing instruction, as well as seminars and independent study. He has probably had more influence on his students than anyone else in the department, not only because his teaching has had great relevance to their work, but also because he has been a patient, understanding, and tolerant person, who is more concerned with the professional development of his students than with his own aggrandizement.

In his more than 40 years at Virginia State, Dr. Johnson has served as a major professor to more than 130 students who were awarded M.Ed. degrees. In all of the years I have known Dr. Johnson, I have never seen him give way to anger or be unkind to any student or colleague.

He has always treated his students as colleagues. He has always been considerate of his students and helped them to achieve high standards of academic performance. In his modest way, he has contributed greatly to educational media and, more than any other person, is responsible for the preeminent reputation of Virginia State's educational program throughout the world.

Working with Dr. Harry A. Johnson at Virginia State University for more than 15 years has given this writer a whole new perspective and level of appreciation for a truly great and generous man. That period proved to be one of the most rewarding and memorable experiences of my professional career.

Dr. Johnson is a member of Gillifield Baptist Church and Kappa Alpha Psi and Sigma Pi Phi fraternities. He has received numerous honors, including membership in the Phi Delta Kappa and Kappa Delta Pi honor societies and a number of educational organizations. Recently, Dr. Johnson was sworn in as the new Chesterfield County School Board member. Dr. Johnson, who represents the Matoaca District of the Commonwealth of Virginia, is the first black board member in the county's history. Dr. Johnson is married to Dr. Mae Coleman Johnson, herself a seasoned and polished writer and teacher. Their two children, Lynne Johnson and Jeffrey A. Johnson, reside and teach in Petersburg, Virginia.

Part Five
The Year in Review

Introduction

There are many professional associations in the field of educational media and technology. The seven that are included in this edition are considered to be the major organizations in North America. Their inclusion is based on longevity, number of members, professional journals published, and visibility. Additional professional associations are listed in part 6, Organizations and Associations in North America.

People in a field organize themselves to improve communications among a group of people with common interests and objectives. They advance the profession by establishing performance standards and usually a code of ethics. All of the associations featured in this part have received recognition for their contributions to the advancement of educational media and technology. In some cases, the scope of interest of one organization overlaps that of another. Some professionals realize that their interests are not contained only within one association, and, therefore, join others that also are compatible with their interests, values, and goals.

The editors plan to continue this section in the *Yearbook* as an important component of an annual status report to the profession.

ADCIS
Association for the Development of Computer-Based
Instructional Systems

ADCIS is an international association with a worldwide membership of professionals who are actively involved in the development and use of computer-based instructional technologies. Members work in a wide variety of settings, including business and industry; elementary and secondary schools; junior colleges, colleges, and universities; and vocational and specialized schools; as well as the military and the government.

ADCIS brings together people of many different perspectives and careers, who share the common goal of excellence in instruction through the effective use of computer technology. Their interests range from the most basic concepts of computer literacy to the most advanced concepts in interactive video and artificial intelligence. Information shared is based on the highest-quality research available.

The Association provides an international forum for:

- Intellectual leadership in the field;

- Professional growth opportunities; and

- Integration of theory and practice.

THE ADCIS MISSION AND MEMBERSHIP

The mission of ADCIS is to promote human learning and performance through the use of computer-based technologies. All ADCIS members receive a free subscription to the *Journal of Computer-Based Instruction (JCBI)*, a quarterly periodical that is highly respected as one of the most scholarly publications in the field of computer-based instruction.

ADCIS members also receive reduced registration fees to the annual ADCIS International Conference. This conference attracts more than 750 conferees from around the world. During the five-day meeting, more than 300 presentations are made in the 15 interest areas covered by the Special Interest Groups (SIGs). These presentations are selected from juried papers and bound in a 400-plus page *Proceedings*, which is received by all conferees. The 36th International Conference will be held February 16-20, 1994, in Nashville, Tennessee, in conjunction with the Annual Conference of the Association for Educational Communications and Technology.

The ADCIS membership divides itself into four divisions and 15 Special Interest Groups (SIGs). Members receive one free membership in a SIG of their choice; additional SIGs may be joined for $5 each. The 15 SIGs are listed by division:

Computers in Training Division

- SIGCBT   Computer-Based Training
- MISIG   Management Issues

Multimedia, Authoring, and Delivery Systems Division

- HYPERSIG — Hypermedia
- SIGIVA — Interactive Video/Audio
- SIGPILOT — PILOT User's Group
- PUG — Plato User's Group
- SIGTELE — Telecommunications

Technologies Division

- ETSIG — Emerging Technologies
- SIGTAR — Theory and Research

Computers in Education Division

- ELSECJC — Elementary/Secondary/Junior College
- HESIG — Health Education
- HOMEC — Home Economics
- SIGAC — Academic Computing
- MUSIC — Association for Technology in Music
- SIGHAN — Educators of the Handicapped

NEWSLETTERS

ADCIS members receive the *ADCIS News*, an association newsletter that keeps members up-to-date on important developments in the field of computer-based technologies. Each SIG also publishes a newsletter for its members.

NETWORKING AND JOB OPPORTUNITIES

Contacts with professionals who have similar interests or who are working on similar projects or problems are coordinated through the ADCIS headquarters office and through the SIG structure. Members stay in touch with each other through electronic mail. A membership directory is provided to facilitate communication among members.

The ADCIS headquarters office serves as a clearinghouse, posting job openings within the profession that are listed with the ADCIS Job Opening Service.

CURRENT OFFICERS

Tim Spannaus, President; Ed Schwartz, Vice President; Lloyd Rieber, Immediate Past President; Tim Spannaus, Immediate Past Vice President; Celia Kraatz, Program Chair; and Carol Norris, Account Manager.

ACCESSING ADCIS SERVICES

Individuals interested in joining ADCIS, subscribing to the *Journal of Computer-Based Instruction*, or receiving registration information for the International Conference should contact ADCIS International Headquarters, 1601 West Fifth Avenue, Suite 111, Columbus, OH 43212. (614) 487-1528. Fax (614) 488-8354. Carol Norris, contact person.

AECT
Association for Educational Communications and Technology

Established in 1923, the Association for Educational Communications and Technology is an international professional association dedicated to the improvement of instruction through the utilization of media and technology. The mission of the association is to provide leadership in educational communications and technology by linking professionals holding a common interest in the use of education technology and its application to the learning process. In the past few years, convention topics have focused on hypermedia, teleconferencing, and converging technologies, and AECT cosponsored the teleconference, "Teaching and Technology: A Critical Link," which addressed issues on the restructuring of public schools and the role of technology. AECT also honors outstanding individuals or groups making significant contributions to the field of educational communications and technology or to the association. (See the separate listing for full information on these awards.)

MEMBERSHIP

AECT members include instructional technologists; media or library specialists; university professors and researchers; industrial/business training specialists; religious educators; government media personnel; school, school district, and state department of education media program administrators and specialists; educational/training media producers; and numerous others whose professional work requires improvement of media and technology in education and training. AECT members also work in the armed forces, in public libraries, in museums, and in other information agencies of many different kinds, including those related to the emerging fields of computer technology.

MEMBERSHIP SERVICES

AECT serves as a central clearinghouse and communications center for its members. The association maintains TechCentral, a national electronic mail network and bulletin board service. Through its various committees and task forces, it compiles data and prepares recommendations to form the basis of guidelines, standards, research, and information summaries on numerous topics and problems of interest to the membership. AECT professional staff members report on government activities of concern to the membership and provide current data on laws and pending legislation relating to the educational media/technology field. AECT also maintains the ECT Foundation, through which it offers a limited number of financial grants to further the association's work. Archives are maintained at the University of Maryland.

CONFERENCES

The Annual Conference will be held at the Opryland Hotel and Exhibit Hall in Nashville, Tennessee, on February 16-20, 1994. It will be accompanied by the first International Computing and Instructional Technology Exposition, which will be open February 17-19, 1994.

PUBLICATIONS

AECT maintains an active publication program which includes *TechTrends for Leaders in Education and Training* (6/yr., free with membership); *Educational Technology Research & Development* (4/yr.); various division publications; and a number of books and videotapes, including the following recent titles: *Adoptable Copyright Policy: Copyright Policy and Manuals Designed for Adoption by Schools, Colleges and Universities* (1992); *Library Copyright Guide* (1992); *Appraising Audiovisual Media: A Guide for Attorneys, Trust Officers, Insurance Professionals, and Archivists in Appraising Films, Video, Photographs, Recordings, and Other Audiovisual Assets* (1993); *Compressed Video: Operations and Applications* (1993); *The 1992-93 Educational Software Preview Guide* (1992); *Educational Technology: A Review of the Research* (1992); *Evaluating Computer Integration in the Elementary School: A Step by Step Guide* (1990); *Focus on Reform: State Initiatives in Educational Technology* (1992); *Graduate Curricula in Educational Communications and Technology: A Descriptive Directory* (4th ed., 1992); *Videographing the Pictorial Sequence: AECT Presidents' Library Vol. II* (1991); and *Teaching and Learning through Technology, the Star Schools Videotape* (one VHS tape, 1989).

AFFILIATED ORGANIZATIONS

Because of similarity of interests, a number of organizations have chosen to affiliate with AECT. These include the Association for MultiImage (AMI); Association for Special Education Technology (ASET); Community College Association for Instruction and Technology (CCAIT); Consortium of University Film Centers (CUFC); Federal Educational Technology Association (FETA); Health Science Communications Association (HeSCA); International Association for Learning Laboratories (IALL); International Visual Literacy Association (IVLA); Minorities in Media (MIMS); National Association of Regional Media Centers (NARMC); National Instructional Television Fixed Service Association (NIA/ITFS); New England Educational Media Association; Northwest College and University Council for the Management of Educational Technology; Southeastern Regional Media Leadership Council (SRMLC); and State University of New York Educational Communications Center.

Two additional organizations are also related to the Association for Educational Communications and Technology: the AECT Archives and the AECT ECT Foundation.

AECT DIVISIONS

AECT has nine divisions: Division of Educational Media Management (DEMM); Division of Interactive Systems and Computers (DISC); Division of Instructional Development (DID); Division of School Media Specialists (DSMS); Division of Telecommunications (DOT); Industrial Training and Education Division (ITED); International Division (INTL); Media Design and Production Division (MDPD); and Research and Theory Division (RTD).

CURRENT OFFICERS/MEMBERS OF THE
AECT BOARD OF DIRECTORS

Stanley D. Zenor, Executive Director; Addie Kinsinger, President; Larry Kitchens, Past President; Kent Gustafson, President Elect; David Graf, Secretary-Treasurer; and Kay Bland, Roberts S. Braden, William J. Burns, Joaquin Holloway, Lynn Milet, Ron Payne, Jim Stonge, and Rusty Russell, Board Members.

Further information is available from AECT, 1025 Vermont Avenue NW, Suite 820, Washington, DC 20005. (202) 347-7834. Fax (202) 347-7839.

AMTEC
Association for Media and Technology
in Education in Canada
L'Association des Media et de la Technologie
en Education au Canada

PURPOSE

Canada's national association for educational media and technology professionals, AMTEC is a forum concerned with the impact of media and technology on teaching, learning, and society. As an organization, AMTEC provides national leadership through annual conferences, publications, workshops, media festival awards, ongoing reaction to media and technology issues at the international, national, provincial, and local levels, and linkages with other organizations with similar interests.

MEMBERSHIP

AMTEC's membership is geographically dispersed and professionally diversified. Membership stretches from St. John's, Newfoundland, to Victoria, British Columbia, and from Inuvik, Northwest Territories, to Niagara Falls, Ontario. Members include teachers, consultants, broadcasters, media managers, photographers, librarians/information specialists, educational technology specialists, instructional designers/trainers, technology specialists, artists, and producers/distributors. They represent all sectors of the educational media and technology fields: elementary and secondary schools, colleges, institutes of technology, universities, provincial governments, school boards, military services, health services libraries, and private corporations.

ACTIVITIES

Workshops. AMTEC offers workshops in cooperation with other agencies and associations based on AMTEC members' needs, in addition to the in-depth workshops at the AMTEC annual conference.

Annual Conference. The AMTEC annual conference provides opportunities to meet delegates from across the nation and to attend sessions on the latest issues and developments in such areas as copyright law, instructional design, distance education, library standards, media production, broadcasting and educational technology, media utilization, and visual literacy. AMTEC 93 was held June 13-16, 1993, in Windsor, Ontario, and AMTEC 94 is scheduled to be held in May, 1994, in Lethbridge, Alberta.

Awards. AMTEC annually recognizes outstanding individual achievement and leadership in the field through the EMPDAC (Educational Media Producers and Distributors Association of Canada) Achievement Award and the AMTEC Leadership Award. In addition, AMTEC acts as the correspondent for the Commonwealth Relations Trust Bursary for educational broadcasters. This annual bursary provides a three-month study tour of educational broadcasting in the United Kingdom.

Reaction to Issues. AMTEC provides opportunities for members to contribute to educational media and technology issues and their solutions. The association frequently communicates with other associations and levels of government to resolve issues of concern to the membership.

Publications. Publications include:

- *The Canadian Journal of Educational Communications (CJEC)* is a quarterly covering the latest in research, application, and periodical literature. It also publishes reviews on significant books and films and critiques on computer programs.

- *Media News* is a quarterly newletter that covers the news in the field, including helpful tips, future conferences, comments on current projects, and information about AMTEC members and the AMTEC Board.

- *Membership Directory* expands the professional network of members.

In addition, occasional publications are produced to assist members in keeping abreast in the field. These include directories, guidelines, and monographs.

CURRENT OFFICERS

The AMTEC Board of Directors includes the association's President, Barbara Martin; Past President, David A. Mappin; President-Elect, Ross Mutton; Secretary/Treasurer, Lillian Carefoot; and three Directors, Esio Marzotto, Dan Malone, and Bob Christie.

Additional information may be obtained from AMTEC, 3-1750 The Queensway, Suite 1818, Etobicoke, Ontario, Canada M9C 5H5.

ISTE
International Society for Technology in Education

PURPOSE

The International Society for Technology in Education is a nonprofit professional society of educators. Its goals include the improvement of education through the appropriate use of computer-related technology and the fostering of active partnerships between businesses and educators involved in this field. The majority of ISTE's efforts are aimed at precollege education and teacher preparation.

MEMBERSHIP

ISTE members are teachers, administrators, computer coordinators, curriculum coordinators, teacher educators, information resource managers, and educational technological specialists. Approximately 85 percent of the 7,000-person membership is in the United States, 10 percent is in Canada, and the remainder is scattered throughout nearly 100 other countries.

ACTIVITIES

ISTE works to achieve its mission through its publication program, which includes 12 periodicals as well as a wide range of books and courseware, cosponsorship or sponsorship of a variety of conferences and workshops, and its extensive network of regional affiliates, a Private Sector Council, a distance education program, and membership in NCATE (National Council for the Accreditation of Teacher Education).

PUBLICATIONS

Periodical publications include membership periodicals: *The Computing Teacher* (8/yr.); the *Journal of Research on Computing in Education* (quarterly); and *ISTE Update: People, Events, and News in Education Technology* (newsletter, 8/yr.). Quarterly periodicals for special-interest groups include: *Logo Exchange*, for the Logo SIG; the *Journal of Computing in Teacher Education*, for the Teacher Educators SIG; *HyperNEXUS*, for the Hyper/Multi-Media SIG; the *Journal of Computer Science Education*, for the Computer Science SIG; *T.I.E. News*, for the Telecommunications SIG; and *SIGTC Connections*, for the Technology Coordinator SIG. Other periodicals include the *Educational Information Resource Manager (IRM) Quarterly*; *Microsoft Works in Education*, a quarterly for users of Microsoft Works; and *CAELL Journal* (Computer Assisted English Language Learning Journal), quarterly for teachers of English, foreign languages, and adult literacy.

ISTE also publishes a variety of books and courseware.

CONFERENCES

ISTE is the fiscal sponsor of the National Educational Computing Conference (NECC), which was held June 27-30, 1993, in Orlando, Florida. ISTE will also be running the Second International Symposium on Telecommunications in Education, which will be held November 10-13, 1993, in Dallas, Texas.

CURRENT OFFICERS

The current ISTE Board includes Sally Sloan, President; Lajeane Thomas, President-Elect; Bonnie Marks, Past President; Barry Pitsch; Peggy Kelly; Don Knezek; Kim Allen; Ruthie Blankenbaker; David Brittain; Francisco Caracheo; Sheila Cory; Terry Gross; Gail Morse; Connie Stout; and Dennis Bybee.

For further information, contact Maia Howes, ISTE Executive Secretary, at 1787 Agate Street, Eugene, OR 97403-1923. (503) 346-2414. Fax (503) 346-5890.

IVLA
International Visual Literacy Association

PURPOSE

IVLA, Inc., a nonprofit international association, was established in 1968 to provide a multidisciplinary forum for the exploration, presentation, and discussion of all aspects of visual communication and their applications through visual images, visual literacy, and literacies in general. The association serves as the organizational bond for professionals from many diverse disciplines who are creating and sustaining the study of the nature of visual experiences and literacies and their cognitive and affective bases, and who are developing new means for the evaluation of learning through visual methods. It also encourages the funding of creative visual literacy projects, programs, and research, and promotes and evaluates projects intended to increase the use of visuals in education and communications.

MEMBERSHIP

IVLA members represent a diverse group of disciplines, including fine and graphic artists, photographers, researchers, scientists, filmmakers, television producers, graphic and computer-graphic designers, phototherapists, business communication professionals, school administrators, classroom teachers, visual studies theorists and practitioners, educational technologists, photojournalists, print and electronic journalists, and visual anthropologists.

MEMBER SERVICES

Members of IVLA benefit from opportunities to interact with other professionals whose ideas may be challenging or reinforcing. Such opportunities are provided by the annual conference, information exchanges, research programs, workshops, seminars, presentation opportunities as an affiliate of the Association for Educational Communications and Technology (AECT), and access to the Visual Literacy Collection located in the Center for Visual Literacy at Arizona State University.

PUBLICATIONS

IVLA publishes two periodicals: the *Journal of Visual Literacy* (2 per year) and the *Review*, a visual literacy newsletter. It also publishes an annual book of selected conference readings.

CONFERENCES

The 25th anniversary conference will be held in Rochester, New York, October 13-17, 1993. The conference theme was "Visual Literacy in the Digital Age." The 1993 Symposium was held at the European Cultural Center of Delphi, Greece, June 26-29, 1993. The theme was "Verbo-Visual Literacy: Understanding and Applying New Educational Communication Media Technologies."

CURRENT OFFICERS

Nikos Metallinos, President; Ron Sutton, President-Elect; Darrell Beauchamp, Immediate Past President; Robert Griffin, Rune Pettersson, and Margaret Smith, Vice Presidents; Alice D. Walker, Executive Treasurer; and Rob Branch, Recording Secretary.

Further information may be obtained from Alice D. Walker, Treasurer, Virginia Tech, Educational Technologies-LRC, Old Security Building, Blacksburg, VA 24061-0232. (703) 231-8992.

NSPI
National Society for Performance and Instruction

NSPI is an international association dedicated to increasing productivity in the workplace through the application of performance and instructional technologies. Founded in 1962, the society promotes the improvement of human performance among governmental, legislative, business, corporate, and educational leaders, and through the national media.

MEMBERSHIP

The 5,000 members of NSPI are located throughout the United States, Canada, and 30 other countries. Members include performance technologists, training directors, human resource managers, instructional technologists, change agents, human factors practitioners, and organizational development consultants. They work in a variety of settings, including business, industry, universities, governmental agencies, health services, banks, and the armed forces.

SERVICES TO NSPI MEMBERS

NSPI offers its members opportunities to grow professionally and personally, to meet and know leaders in the field and learn about new things before they are published for the world at large, to make themselves known in the field, and to pick up new ideas on how to deal with their own political and technical challenges on the job. Membership benefits include subscriptions to *Performance & Instruction* and *News & Notes*; the *Annual Membership Directory*; participation in the annual conference and exposition; access to a variety of resources and individuals to help improve professional skills and marketability; a variety of insurance programs at group rates; leadership opportunities through participation in special projects, 12 major committees, and task forces, or serving as national or chapter officers; an executive referral service; and discounts on publications, advertising, conference registration and recordings, and other society services.

ACTIVITIES

The NSPI Endowment sponsors the Young Academic Program, an awards program for recent recipients of a doctoral degree currently working in academic positions. Designed to promote excellence in the field, the award is given for research on topics related to performance and instructional technology, including literature reviews and/or meta-analyses with implications for performance-enhancing interventions. The recipient of the award of $500 is required to prepare and make a presentation at the annual conference and submit a potentially publishable manuscript.

CONFERENCES

Annual Conference and Expo, Chicago, Illinois, April 12-16, 1993; San Francisco, California, April 4-8, 1994.

PUBLICATIONS

NSPI publications include *Performance & Instruction Journal*, (10/yr.); *Performance Improvement Quarterly*; *News & Notes* (10/yr.); and the *Annual Membership Directory*.

CURRENT OFFICERS

Kathleen Whiteside, President; William Coscarelli, President-Elect; Carol Valen, Vice President—Chapter Development; Noel Villa Corta, Vice President—Conferences; Darryl Sink, Vice President—Finance; C. J. Wallington, Vice President—Publications; Richard Pearlstein, Vice President—Research and Development; Paul Tremper, Executive Director.

Further information is available from NSPI, 1300 L Street NW, Suite 1250, Washington, DC 20005. (202) 408-7969. Fax (202) 408-7972.

SALT
Society for Applied Learning Technology

PURPOSE

The Society for Applied Learning Technology (SALT) is a nonprofit professional membership organization that was founded in 1972. Membership in the society is oriented to professionals whose work requires knowledge and communication in the field of instructional technology. The society provides members a means to enhance their knowledge and job performance by participation in society-sponsored meetings, through subscriptions to society-sponsored publications, by association with other professionals at conferences sponsored by the society, and through membership in special-interest groups and special society-sponsored initiatives and projects.

The society sponsors conferences that are educational in nature and cover a wide range of application areas, such as interactive videodisc in education and training, development of interactive instructional materials, CD-ROM applications in education and training, interactive instruction delivery, and learning technology in the health care sciences. These conferences provide attendees with an opportunity to become familiar with the latest technical information on application possibilities, on technologies, and on methodologies for implementation. In addition, they provide an opportunity for interaction with other professional and managerial individuals in the field.

In addition, the society offers members discounts on society-sponsored journals, conference registration fees, and publications.

PUBLICATIONS

- *Journal of Interactive Instruction Development.* This established quarterly journal meets the needs of instructional systems developers and designers by providing important perspectives on emerging technologies and design technologies.

- *Journal of Medical Education Technologies.* Now in its third year of publication, this exciting new journal helps keep readers abreast of developments utilizing technology-based learning systems to train health care professionals and educate students involved in the various health care disciplines.

- *Journal of Educational Technology Systems.* This quarterly publication deals with systems in which technology and education interface, and is designed to inform educators who are interested in making optimum use of technology.

- *Instruction Delivery Systems.* Society members are eligible to have a free subscription to this bimonthly magazine, which covers interactive multimedia applications and happenings. With up-to-date application descriptions and valuable reference editions, it is devoted to enhancing productivity through appropriate applications of technology in education, training, and job performance.

CONFERENCES

Conferences in 1993 were held February 26-28 in Orlando, Florida, and August 26-28 in Washington, D.C. Conferences for 1994 are scheduled for February 23-25 in Orlando, Florida, and August 24-26 in Washington, D.C.

CURRENT OFFICERS

Dr. Nathaniel Macon, Chairman; Raymond G. Fox, President; Dr. Stanley Winkler, Vice President; and Dr. Carl R. Vest, Secretary/Treasurer.

Further information is available from the Society for Applied Learning Technology, 50 Culpeper Street, Warrenton, VA 22186. (703) 347-0055. Fax (703) 349-3169.

Part Six
Organizations and Associations in North America

Introduction

This part of *EMTY 1993* includes annotated entries for several hundred associations and organizations headquartered in North America whose interests are in some manner significant to the fields of instructional technology/educational media, library and information science, communication, computer technology, training/management in business/industry, publishing, and others. They are organized into two general geographic areas: the United States and Canada. The section on the United States includes a classified list with headings designed to be useful in finding subject leads to the alphabetical list. Readers who know only the acronym for an association or organization of interest may refer to the index to obtain its full name.

It was not deemed necessary to include a classified list for Canada because the overall number of organizations listed is considerably smaller than for the United States.

All organizations listed in part 6 were sent a copy of the entry describing the organization that appeared in *EMTY 1992*. Respondents were invited to update and edit these entries, with the proviso that, if no response was received, information included in *EMTY 1992* would be repeated so that the organization or association would be represented in this directory. Entries for organizations that did not respond are indicated by an asterisk (*) before the name of the organization. Any organization that has had a name change since the 1992 edition is listed under the new name; a note referring the user to the new name appears under the former name. If information was received that an organization had ceased operations, a note to this effect appears under the organization name in the alphabetical listing.

The reader is reminded that changes in communications and media are frequent and extensive and that the information in this directory is as accurate as possible at the time of publication.

United States

CLASSIFIED LIST

Adult, Continuing, Distance Education

Audio (Records, Audiocassettes and Tapes, Telephone, Radio); Listening

Audiovisual (General)

Censorship

Children-, Youth-Related Organizations

Communication

Community Resources

Computers, Computer Software, Computer Hardware

Copyright

Databases; Networks

Education (General)

Education (Higher)

Equipment (Manufacturing, Maintenance, Testing, Operating)

ERIC-Related

Films—Educational/Instructional/Documentary

Films—Theatrical (Film Study, Criticism, Production)

Films—Training

Futures

Games, Toys, Drama, Play, Simulation, Puppetry

Graphics

Health-Related Organizations

Information Science

Instructional Technology/Design/Development

International Education

Libraries—Academic, Research

Libraries—Public

Libraries—Special

Libraries and Media Centers—General, School

Microforms; Micrographics

Museums; Archives

Photography

Print—Books

Production (Media)

Publishing

Religious Education

Research

Selection, Collections, Processing (Materials)

Special Education

Training

Video (Cassette, Broadcast, Cable, Satellite, Videodisc, Videotex)

Adult, Continuing, Distance Education
(ALA) Reference and Adult Services Division
(RASD)
Association for Continuing Higher Education (ACHE)
Association for Educational Communications and Technology (AECT)
ERIC Clearinghouse on Adult, Career, and Vocational Education (CE)
National University Continuing Education Association (NUCEA)
Network for Continuing Medical Education (NCME)
Superintendent of Documents

Audio (Records, Audiocassettes and Tapes, Telephone, Radio); Listening
American Women in Radio and Television (AWRT)
Clearinghouse on Development Communication
Corporation for Public Broadcasting (CPB)
Federal Communications Commission (FCC)
National Association for Better Broadcasting (NABB)
National Association of Broadcasters (NAB)
National Association of Business and Educational Radio (NABER)
National Public Radio (NPR)
Oral History Association
Radio Free Europe/Radio Liberty (RFE-RL)
Recording for the Blind
Recording Industry Association of America, Inc. (RIAA)

Audiovisual (General)
Association for Educational Communications and Technology (AECT)
(AECT) Division of Educational Media Management (DEMM)
(AECT) Division of School Media Specialists (DSMS)
Association of AudioVisual Technicians (AAVT)
HOPE Reports

Censorship
Freedom of Information Center (FOI)

Children-, Youth-Related Organizations
(ALA) Association for Library Service to Children (ALSC)

(ALA) Young Adult Library Services Association (YALSA)
Association for Childhood Education International (ACEI)
Children's Television International, Inc.
Close Up Foundation
Council for Exceptional Children (CEC)
(CEC) Technology and Media Division (TAM)
ERIC Clearinghouse on Elementary and Early Childhood Education (PS)
ERIC Clearinghouse on Disabilities and Gifted Education (EC)
National Association for the Education of Young Children (NAEYC)
National PTA

Communication
ERIC Clearinghouse on Information & Technology (IR)
ERIC Clearinghouse on Languages and Linguistics (FL)
ERIC Clearinghouse on Reading, English, and Communication (CS)
Freedom of Information Center (FOI)
International Association of Business Communicators (IABC)
International Communication Association
International Communications Industries Association (ICIA)
National Council of the Churches of Christ—Communication Unit
Speech Communication Association (SCA)
Women in Film (WIF)

Community Resources
Teachers and Writers Collaborative (T&W)

Computers, Computer Software, Computer Hardware
(AECT) Division of Interactive Systems and Computers (DISC)
Association for the Development of Computer-Based Instructional Systems (ADCIS)
Computer-Based Education Research Laboratory (CERL): PLATO and NovaNet
International Association for Computer Information Systems (formerly Association for Computer Educators [ACE])
International Society for Technology in Education (ISTE)
MECC (Minnesota Educational Computing Corporation)

OCLC (Online Computer Library Center)
SOFTSWAP
SpecialNet

Copyright
Copyright Clearance Center (CCC)
International Copyright Information Center (INCINC)

Databases; Networks
ERIC (Educational Resources Information Center) (See separate entries for the various clearinghouses.)
ERIC Document Reproduction Service (EDRS)
ERIC Processing and Reference Facility
SpecialNet

Education (General)
American Association of School Administrators (AASA)
American Montessori Society (AMS)
American Society of Educators (ASE)
Association for Childhood Education International (ACEI)
(AECT) Minorities in Media (MIM)
Association for Experiential Education (AEE)
Association of Teacher Educators (ATE)
Center for Instructional Research and Curriculum Evaluation
Council for Basic Education
Education Development Center, Inc.
ERIC Clearinghouse on Counseling and Student Services (CG)
ERIC Clearinghouse on Educational Management (EA)
ERIC Clearinghouse on Elementary and Early Childhood Education (PS)
ERIC Clearinghouse on Disabilities and Gifted Education (EC)
ERIC Clearinghouse on Rural Education and Small Schools (RC)
ERIC Clearinghouse for Science, Mathematics, and Environmental Education (SE)
ERIC Clearinghouse for Social Studies/Social Science Education (ERIC/ChESS)
ERIC Clearinghouse on Teaching and Teacher Education (SP)
ERIC Clearinghouse on Urban Education (UD)
National Association of Secondary School Principals (NASSP)

National Association of State Boards of Education (NASBE)
National Association of State Educational Media Professionals (NASTEMP)
National Association of State Textbook Administrators (NASTA)
National Center for Appropriate Technology (NCAT)
National Clearinghouse for Bilingual Education
National Council for Accreditation of Teacher Education (NCATE)
National Education Association (NEA)
National Endowment for the Arts (NEA)
National Endowment for the Humanities (NEH)
National Science Foundation (NSF)
National Science Teachers Association (NSTA)
Project in Distance Education
Project in Educational Technology
Social Science Education Consortium (SSEC)

Education (Higher)
American Association of Community and Junior Colleges (AACJC)
American Association of State Colleges and Universities
Association for Continuing Higher Education (ACHE)
(AECT) Community College Association for Instruction and Technology (CCAIT)
(AECT) Northwest College and University Council for the Management of Educational Technology
Association for Library and Information Science Education (ALISE)
ERIC Clearinghouse for Community Colleges (JC)
ERIC Clearinghouse on Higher Education (HE)
University Film and Video Association (UFVA)

Equipment (Manufacturing, Maintenance, Testing, Operating)
(ALA) Library and Information Technology Association (LITA)
American National Standards Institute (ANSI)
Association of AudioVisual Technicians (AAVT)
EPIE Institute
ERIC Clearinghouse on Assessment and Evaluation (TM)

International Communications Industries
    Association (ICIA)
ITA (formerly International Tape/Disc
    Association [ITA])
National School Supply and Equipment
    Association (NSSEA)
Society of Motion Picture and Television
    Engineers (SMPTE)

ERIC-Related
ACCESS ERIC
Adjunct ERIC Clearinghouse for United
    States-Japan Studies (ADJ/JS)
Adjunct ERIC Clearinghouse for ESL
    Literacy Education (ADJ/LE)
Adjunct ERIC Clearinghouse on Chapter 1
    (Compensatory Education)
    (ADJ/Chapter 1)
Adjunct ERIC Clearinghouse on Consumer
    Education (ADJ/CN)
ERIC (Educational Resources Information
    Center)
ERIC Clearinghouse on Adult, Career, and
    Vocational Education (CE)
ERIC Clearinghouse on Counseling and
    Student Services (CG)
ERIC Clearinghouse on Educational Manage-
    ment (EA)
ERIC Clearinghouse on Elementary and
    Early Childhood Education (PS)
ERIC Clearinghouse on Disabilities and
    Gifted Education (EC)
ERIC Clearinghouse on Higher Education
    (HE)
ERIC Clearinghouse on Information &
    Technology (IR)
ERIC Clearinghouse for Community Colleges
    (JC)
ERIC Clearinghouse on Languages and
    Linguistics (FL)
ERIC Clearinghouse on Reading, English,
    and Communication Skills (CS)
ERIC Clearinghouse on Rural Education
    and Small Schools (RC)
ERIC Clearinghouse for Science, Mathematics,
    and Environmental Education
    (SE)
ERIC Clearinghouse for Social Studies/Social
    Science Education (SO)
ERIC Clearinghouse on Teaching and
    Teacher Education (SP)
ERIC Clearinghouse on Assessment and
    Evaluation (TM)

ERIC Clearinghouse on Urban Education (UD)
ERIC Document Reproduction Service
    (EDRS)
ERIC Processing and Reference Facility

**Films—Educational/Instructional/Docu-
    mentary**
Anthropology Film Center (AFC)
Association of Independent Video and Film-
    makers/Foundation for Independent
    Video and Film (AIVF/FIVF)
Children's Television International, Inc.
CINE Information
Council on International Non-theatrical
    Events
Film Advisory Board (FAB)
Film Arts Foundation (FAF)
Film/Video Arts, Inc.
National Aeronautics and Space Administra-
    tion (NASA)
National Alliance for Media Arts and Cul-
    ture (NAMAC)
National Audiovisual Center (NAC)
National Film Board of Canada (NFBC)
National Information Center for Educational
    Media (NICEM)
Pacific Film Archive (PFA)
PCR: Films and Video in the Behavioral
    Sciences

**Films—Theatrical (Film Study, Criticism,
    Production)**
Academy of Motion Picture Arts and Sciences
    (AMPAS)
American Society of Cinematographers
Film Advisory Board (FAB)
Film Arts Foundation (FAF)
Hollywood Film Archive
National Film Information Service (NFIS)
The New York Festivals (International Film
    and TV Festival of New York)

Films—Training
American Film and Video Association
    (AFVA)
(AECT) Industrial Training and Education
    Division (ITED)
Association of Independent Video and Film-
    makers/Foundation for Independent
    Video and Film (AIVF/FIVF)
Council on International Non-theatrical
    Events
Great Plains National ITV Library (GPN)

National Audiovisual Center (NAC)
National Film Board of Canada (NFBC)
Training Media Association

Futures
Institute for the Future (IFTF)
Office of Technology Assessment (OTA)
World Future Society (WFS)

Games, Toys, Drama, Play, Simulation, Puppetry
North American Simulation and Gaming Association (NASAGA)
Puppeteers of America
Society for Computer Simulation (SCS)

Graphics
International Graphic Arts Education Association (IGAEA)

Health-Related Organizations
Health Science Communications Association (HeSCA)
Lister Hill National Center for Biomedical Communications of the National Library of Medicine
Medical Library Association (MLA)
National Association for Visually Handicapped (NAVH)
National Library of Medicine
Network for Continuing Medical Education (NCME)

Information Science
International Information Management Congress (IMC)

Instructional Technology/Design/Development
Agency for Instructional Technology (AIT)
Association for Educational Communications and Technology (AECT)
(AECT) Community College Association for Instruction and Technology (CCAIT)
(AECT) Division of Educational Media Management (DEMM)
(AECT) Division of Instructional Development (DID)
Association for the Development of Computer-Based Instructional Systems (ADCIS)
National Society for Performance and Instruction (NSPI)
Office of Technology Assessment (OTA)

Professors of Instructional Design and Technology (PIDT)
Society for Applied Learning Technology (SALT)

International Education
(AECT) International Division (INTL)
(AECT) International Visual Literacy Association, Inc. (IVLA)
Institute of Culture and Communication (East-West Center)
Institute of International Education
Office for International Networks in Education and Development (INET)
United Nations Department of Public Information, Dissemination Division

Libraries—Academic, Research
American Library Association (ALA)
(ALA) Association of College and Research Libraries (ACRL)
ERIC Clearinghouse on Information & Technology (IR)

Libraries—Public
American Library Association (ALA)
(ALA) Association for Library Service to Children (ALSC)
(ALA) Audiovisual Committee (of the Public Library Association)
(ALA) Library Administration and Management Association (LAMA)
(ALA) Library and Information Technology Association (LITA)
(ALA) Public Library Association (PLA)
(ALA) Reference and Adult Services Division (RASD)
(ALA) Technology in Public Libraries Committee (of the Public Libraries Association)
(ALA) Young Adult Library Services Association (YALSA)
ERIC Clearinghouse on Information & Technology (IR)

Libraries—Special
American Library Association (ALA)
(ALA) Association for Library Service to Children (ALSC)
(ALA) Association of Specialized and Cooperative Library Agencies (ASCLA)
ERIC Clearinghouse on Information & Technology (IR)

Special Libraries Association (SLA)
Theater Library Association

Libraries and Media Centers—General, School

American Library Association (ALA)
(ALA) American Association of School
Librarians (AASL)
(ALA) American Library Trustee Association (ALTA)
(ALA) Association for Library Collections
and Technical Services (ALCTS)
(ALA) Association for Library Service to
Children (ALSC)
(ALA Round Table) Continuing Library
Education Network and Exchange
(CLENE)
Association for Educational Communications and Technology (AECT)
(AECT) Division of School Media Specialists
(DSMS)
(AECT) National Association of Regional
Media Centers (NARMC)
Catholic Library Association (CLA)
Consortium of College and University Media
Centers
Council of National Library and Information
Associations
ERIC Clearinghouse on Information &
Technology (IR)
International Association of School Librarianship (IASL)
Library of Congress
National Alliance for Media Arts and Culture (NAMAC)
National Association of State Educational
Media Professionals (NASTEMP)
National Commission on Libraries and Information Science (NCLIS)
National Council of Teachers of English
(NCTE), Commission on Media
On-Line Audiovisual Catalogers (OLAC)

Microforms; Micrographics
See ERIC-related entries.

Museums; Archives
(AECT) Archives
American Federation of Arts (AFA)
Association of Systematics Collections
Computer Museum
Hollywood Film Archive

International Museum of Photography at
George Eastman House
Lawrence Hall of Science
Museum Computer Network, Inc. (MCN)
Museum of Holography
Museum of Modern Art
Museum of Television and Radio
National Gallery of Art (NGA)
Smithsonian Institution

Photography
International Center of Photography (ICP)
International Museum of Photography at
George Eastman House
Museum of Holography
National Press Photographers Association,
Inc. (NPPA)
Photographic Society of America (PSA)
Society for Imaging Science and Technology
(IS&T)
Society for Photographic Education (SPE)
Society of Photo Technologists (SPT)

Print—Books
American Library Association (ALA)
Association for Educational Communications and Technology (AECT)
Smithsonian Institution
United Nations Department of Public Information

Production (Media)
American Society of Cinematographers (ASC)
Association for Educational Communications and Technology (AECT)
(AECT) Media Design and Production Division
(MDPD)
Association of Independent Video and Filmmakers/Foundation for Independent
Video and Film (AIVF/FIVF)
Film Arts Foundation (FAF)
Women in Film (WIF)

Publishing
Association of American Publishers (AAP)
Government Printing Office (US GPO)
Magazine Publishers of America (MPA)
National Association of State Textbook
Administrators (NASTA)

Religious Education
Catholic Library Association (CLA)
National Religious Broadcasters (NRB)

Research

American Educational Research Association (AERA)

(AECT) ECT Foundation

(AECT) Research and Theory Division (RTD)

Center for Advanced Visual Studies (CAVS)

Center for Instructional Research and Curriculum Evaluation

Clearinghouse on Development Communication

Council for Educational Development and Research (CEDaR)

Education Development Center, Inc.

ERIC Clearinghouses. See ERIC-related entries.

Far West Laboratory for Educational Research and Development (FWL)

HOPE Reports

Institute for Development of Educational Activities, Inc. (IDEA)

Institute for Research on Teaching

National Technical Information Service (NTIS)

National Technology Center (NTC)

The NETWORK

Northwest Regional Educational Laboratory (NWREL)

Selection, Collections, Processing (Materials)

National Information Center for Educational Media (NICEM)

Special Education

Council for Exceptional Children (CEC)

ERIC Clearinghouse on Disabilities and Gifted Education (EC)

National Association for Visually Handicapped (NAVH)

National Technology Center (NTC)

Training

American Management Association (AMA)

American Society for Training and Development (ASTD)

Association for Educational Communications and Technology (AECT)

(AECT) Federal Educational Technology Association (FETA)

(AECT) Industrial Training and Education Division (ITED)

ERIC Clearinghouse on Adult, Career, and Vocational Education (CE)

National Society for Performance and Instruction (NSPI)

Training Modules for Trainers (TMT)

Video (Cassette, Broadcast, Cable, Satellite, Videodisc, Videotex)

Agency for Instructional Technology (AIT)

American Women in Radio and Television (AWRT)

Association for Educational Communications and Technology (AECT)

(AECT) Division of Telecommunications (DOT)

(AECT) National ITFS Association (NIA/ITFS)

Association of Independent Video and Filmmakers/Foundation for Independent Video and Film (AIVF/FIVF)

Central Educational Network (CEN)

Children's Television International, Inc.

Close Up Foundation

Corporation for Public Broadcasting (CPB)

Federal Communications Commission (FCC)

Great Plains National ITV Library (GPN)

International Telecommunications Satellite Organization (INTELSAT)

International Teleconferencing Association (ITCA)

International Television Association (ITVA)

ITA (formerly International Tape/Disc Association [ITA])

National Association for Better Broadcasting (NABB)

National Association of Broadcasters (NAB)

National Cable Television Institute (NCTI)

National Federation of Community Broadcasters (NFCB)

National Telemedia Council, Inc. (NTC)

Nebraska Videodisc Design/Production Group (VD-PG)

PBS Adult Learning Service (ALS)

PBS ENCORE

PBS VIDEO

Public Broadcasting Service (PBS)

Public Service Satellite Consortium (PSSC)

Society of Cable Television Engineers (SCTE)

Society of Motion Picture and Television Engineers (SMPTE)

Telecommunications Research and Action Center (TRAC)

Women in Film (WIF)

ALPHABETICAL LIST

*Academy of Motion Picture Arts and Sciences (AMPAS). 8949 Wilshire Blvd., Beverly Hills, CA 90211. (310) 247-3000. An honorary organization composed of outstanding individuals in all phases of motion pictures. Seeks to advance the arts and sciences of motion picture technology and artistry. Presents annual film awards; offers artist-in-residence programs; operates reference library and National Film Information Service. *Publications: Annual Index to Motion Picture Credits; Academy Players Directory.*

Agency for Instructional Technology (AIT). Box A, Bloomington, IN 47402-0120. (812) 339-2203. Fax (812) 333-4218. Michael F. Sullivan, Exec. Dir., Mardell Raney, Editor-in-Chief. AIT is a nonprofit U.S.-Canadian organization established in 1962 to strengthen education through technology. The Agency provides leadership and service through the development, acquisition, and distribution of technology-based instructional materials. AIT pioneered the consortium process to develop instructional series that meet learners' needs. It has cooperatively produced more than 32 series since 1970. Today, major funding comes from state and provincial departments of education, federal and private institutions, and corporate sponsors. *Publications: TECHNOS: Quarterly for Education and Technology* is the journal of the Agency for Instructional Technology. It is a forum for the discussion of ideas about the use of technology in education, with a focus on reform. A think piece for decision makers, *TECHNOS Quarterly*, focuses on the policy and pedagogical implications of the electronic revolution. ISSN 1060-5649. $20/yr. (four issues). AIT also publishes two product catalogs, one for audiovisual and one for broadcast customers. Materials include video programming, interactive videodiscs, computer software, and supporting print. Its series are broadcast on six continents, reaching nearly 34 million students in North American classrooms each year. Catalogs are available free on request.

*American Association of Community and Junior Colleges (AACJC). One Dupont Cir. NW, Suite 410, Washington, DC 20036-1176. (202) 728-0200. Dale Parnell, Pres. AACJC serves the nation's 1,211 community, technical, and junior colleges through advocacy, professional development, publications, and national networking. The annual convention draws more than 4,000 mid- and top-level administrators of two-year colleges. Staff and presidents offer expertise in all areas of education. Sixteen councils and six commissions address all areas of education. *Membership:* 1,110 institution, 150 international, 4 foundation, 75 corporate, 103 educational association. *Dues:* Vary for institutions, corporations, foundations, and individuals. *Publications: Community, Technical and Junior College Journal* (bi-mo.); *AACJC Letter* (mo.); *College Times*; Community College Press (books, monographs, etc.); publications program (directories, books, monographs, policy statements, etc.).

American Association of School Administrators (AASA). 1801 N. Moore St., Arlington, VA 22209. (703) 528-0700. Fax (703) 528-2146. Richard D. Miller, Exec. Dir. Represents professional administrators and managers in education in the United States and overseas; provides an extensive program of professional development through the National Academy for School Executives (NASE). Also produces publications and audiovisual programs to increase knowledge and skills of administrators. *Membership:* 18,500. *Dues:* $209. *Publications: The School Administrator; Leadership News*; numerous books and video programs.

American Association of State Colleges and Universities. One Dupont Cir. NW, Suite 700, Washington, DC 20036-1192. (202) 293-7070. James B. Appleberry, Pres. Membership is open to any regionally accredited institution of higher education, and those in the process of securing accreditation, that offers programs leading to the degree of bachelor, master, or doctor, and that are wholly or partially state-supported and state-controlled. Organized and operated exclusively for educational, scientific, and literary purposes, its particular purposes are to improve higher education within its member institutions through cooperative planning, studies, and research on common educational problems and the development of a more unified program of action among its members; and to provide other needed and worthwhile educational services to the colleges and universities it may represent. *Membership:* 375 institutions (university), 28 system, and 7 associate members. *Dues:* Based on current student enrollment at institution. *Publications: MEMO: To the President; The Center Associate; Office of Federal Program Reports; Office of Federal Program Deadlines.* (Catalogs of books and other publications available upon request.)

*American Educational Research Association (AERA). 1230 17th St. NW, Washington, DC 20036. (202) 223-9485. Fax (202) 775-1824. William J. Russell, Exec. Dir. A national professional organization of educators and behavioral scientists active and/or interested in educational research and its application to educational problems. Sponsors annual meetings featuring presentations of original research findings. *Membership:* 18,000. *Dues:* $45. *Publications: Educational Researcher; American Educational Research Journal; Journal of Educational Statistics; Educational Evaluation and Policy Analysis; Review of Research in Education; Review of Educational Research.*

The American Federation of Arts (AFA). Headquarters, 41 E. 65th St., New York, NY 10021. (212) 988-7700. Fax (212) 861-2487. Serena Rattazzi, Dir. National nonprofit museum program and service that organizes and circulates exhibitions of fine arts and media arts to museums, university art galleries, and art centers throughout the United States and abroad. Also provides specialized services to member museums, including reduced-rate programs of fine art insurance, air and surface transport of art, and professional management training. *Institutional Membership:* 520. *Dues:* $220 to $500, institutions; $100 (Friend) to $1,000 (Sustaining) individuals. *Publications:* Newsletter: *ART*, 3/yr.; *MEMO ·TO MEMBERS* (for institutional members only) (6/yr.). AFA exhibitions are accompanied by illustrated catalogs and/or illustrated brochures. AFA media arts exhibits are also accompanied by program notes.

American Film and Video Association (AFVA). 8050 N. Milwaukee Ave., P.O. Box 48659, Niles, IL 60714. (708) 698-6440. Fax (708) 823-1561. Kathryn Osen, Acting Exec. Dir.; Larry Skaja, Managing Dir. Formerly the Educational Film Library Association, the AFVA promotes and encourages the use, production, and distribution of quality nontheatrical film, video, and new technology in libraries, schools, and other institutions. *Membership:* 1,200. *Dues:* $55 individual, $210 institution, $315 corporation. *Publications: SightLines* (journal, 6/yr.); *AFVA Bulletin* (newsletter, 6/yr.); *AFVA Evaluations* (annual).

American Library Association (ALA). 50 E. Huron St., Chicago, IL 60611. (312) 944-6780. Fax (312) 440-9374. Peggy Sullivan, Exec. Dir. The ALA is the oldest and largest national library association. Its 55,000 members represent all types of libraries—state, public, school, and academic, as well as special libraries serving persons in government, commerce, the armed services, hospitals, prisons, and other institutions. Chief advocate of achievement and maintenance of high-quality library information services through protection of the right to read, educating librarians, improving services, and making information widely accessible. *Membership:* 55,000. *Dues:* Basic dues $38 first year, $75 renewing members. *Publications: American Libraries; Booklist; Choice; Book Links.*

(ALA) American Association of School Librarians (AASL). 50 E. Huron St., Chicago, IL 60611. (312) 280-4386. Fax (312) 664-7459. Ann Carlson Weeks, Exec. Dir. Interested in the general improvement and extension of school library media services for children and youth. Activities and projects of the association are divided among 55 committees and 3 sections. *Membership*: 7,400. *Dues:* Membership in ALA (1st yr., $38; 2d yr., $49; 3d yr., $60; 4th and subsequent yrs., $75) plus $35. Student membership rates available. *Publications: School Library Media Quarterly* (journal, q.); *Presidential Hotline* (newsletter, 2/yr.).

***(ALA) American Library Trustee Association (ALTA)**. 50 E. Huron St., Chicago, IL 60611. (312) 280-2160. Fax (312) 280-3257. Sharon L. Jordan, Exec. Dir. Interested in the development of effective library service for people in all types of communities and libraries. Members, as policymakers, are concerned with organizational patterns of service, the development of competent personnel, the provision of adequate financing, the passage of suitable legislation and the encouragement of citizen support for libraries. *Membership:* 1,710. *Dues:* $40 plus membership in ALA. *Publications: ALTA Newsletter; Trustee Digest.*

(ALA) Association for Library Collections and Technical Services (ALCTS). 50 E. Huron St., Chicago, IL 60611. (312) 944-6780. Karen Muller, Exec. Dir; Liz Bishoff, Pres., July 1992-June 1993. Dedicated to acquisition, identification, cataloging, classification, and preservation of library materials, the development and coordination of the country's library resources, and aspects of selection and evaluation involved in acquiring and developing library materials and resources. Sections include Acquisition of Library Materials, Cataloging and Classification, Collection Management and Development, Preservation of Library Materials, Reproduction of Library Materials, and Serials. *Membership:* 5,946. *Dues:* $35 plus membership in ALA. *Publications: Library Resources & Technical Services* (q.); *ALCTS Newsletter* (6/yr.).

(ALA) Association for Library Service to Children (ALSC).50 E. Huron St., Chicago, IL 60611. (312) 280-2163. Fax (312) 280-3257. Susan Roman, Exec. Dir. Interested in the improvement and extension of library services for children in all types of libraries, evaluation and selection of book and nonbook library materials, and improvement of techniques of library services for children from preschool through the eighth grade or junior high school age. Annual conference and midwinter meeting with the ALA. Committee membership open to ALSC members. *Membership:* 3,600. *Dues:* $35 plus membership in ALA. *Publications: Journal of Youth Services in Libraries*; *ALSC Newsletter.*

(ALA) Association of College and Research Libraries (ACRL). 50 E. Huron St., Chicago, IL 60611-2795. (312) 280-3248. Fax (312) 280-2520. Althea H. Jenkins, Exec. Dir. Represents librarians and promotes libraries of postsecondary, research, and specialized institutions. Has available library standards for colleges, universities, and two-year institutions. Publishes statistics on academic libraries. Committees include Academic Status, Audiovisual, Professional Education, Legislation, Publications, and Standards and Accreditation. Free list of materials available. *Membership:* 11,000. *Dues:* $35 (in addition to ALA membership). *Publications: College & Research Libraries*; *College & Research Libraries News*; *Rare Books and Manuscripts Librarianship*; 11 section newsletters; *Choice.*

(ALA) Association of Specialized and Cooperative Library Agencies (ASCLA). 50 E. Huron St., Chicago, IL 60611. (800) 545-2433, ext. 4399. Fax (312) 280-3257. Andrew Hansen, Exec. Dir. Represents state library agencies, multitype library cooperatives, and libraries serving special clienteles to promote the development of coordinated library services with equal access to information and material for all persons. The activities and programs of the association are carried out by 21 committees, 3 sections, and various discussion groups. Write for free checklist of materials. *Membership:* 1,300. *Dues:* (in addition to ALA membership) $30 for personal members, $50 for organizations, $500 for state library agencies. *Publications: Interface.*

(ALA) Library Administration and Management Association (LAMA). 50 E. Huron St., Chicago, IL 60611. (312) 280-5038. Karen Muller, Exec. Dir.; James G. Neal, Pres., July 1992-June 1993. Provides an organizational framework for encouraging the study of administrative theory, for improving the practice of administration in libraries, and for identifying and fostering administrative skills. Toward these ends, the association is responsible for all elements of general administration that are common to more than one type of library. These may include: Buildings and Equipment Section (BES); Fundraising & Financial Development Section (FRFDS); Library Organization & Management Section (LOMS); Personnel Administration Section (PAS); Public Relation Section (PRS); Systems & Services Section (SASS); Statistic Section (SS). *Membership:* 5,097. *Dues:* $35 (in addition to ALA membership). *Publication: Library Administration & Management* (q.).

*(ALA) Library and Information Technology Association (LITA). 50 E. Huron St., Chicago, IL 60611. (312) 280-4270; (voice) (800) 545-2433, ext. 4270. Fax (312) 280-3257. Linda J. Knutson, Exec. Dir. Concerned with library automation, the information sciences, and the design, development, and implementation of automated systems in those fields, including systems development, electronic data processing, mechanized information retrieval, operations research, standards development, telecommunications, video communications, networks and collaborative efforts, management techniques, information technology, optical technology, artificial intelligence and expert systems, and other related aspects of audiovisual activities and hardware applications. *Membership:* 5,000. *Dues:* $35 plus membership in ALA, $15 for library school students. *Publications: Information Technology and Libraries; LITA Newsletter.*

(ALA) Public Library Association (PLA). 50 E. Huron St., Chicago, IL 60611. (312) 280-5PLA. Fax (312) 280-5029. Bridget Bradley, Acting Exec. Dir.; Elliot Shelkrot, Pres. Concerned with the development, effectiveness, and financial support of public libraries. Speaks for the profession and seeks to enrich the professional competence and opportunities of public libraries. Sections include Adult Lifelong Learning, Community Information, Metropolitan Libraries, Public Library Systems, Small and Medium-sized Libraries, Public Policy for Public Libraries, and Marketing of Public Library Services. *Membership:* 7,270. *Dues:* $35, open to all ALA members. *Publications: Public Libraries* (q.).

(ALA) Audiovisual Committee (of the Public Library Association). 50 E. Huron St., Chicago, IL 60611. (312) 280-5752. Promotes use of audiovisual materials in public libraries.

(ALA) Technology in Public Libraries Committee (of the Public Library Association). 50 E. Huron St., Chicago, IL 60611. (312) 944-6780. Collects and disseminates information on technology applications in public libraries.

(ALA) Reference and Adult Services Division (RASD). 50 E. Huron St., Chicago, IL 60611. (312) 280-5752; (800) 545-2433, ext. 4398. Fax (312) 280-3257. Andrew M. Hansen, Exec. Dir. Responsible for stimulating and supporting in every type of library the delivery of reference information services to all groups and of general library services and materials to adults. *Membership:* 5,500. *Dues:* $35 plus membership in ALA. *Publications: RQ* (q.); *RASD Update*; others.

(ALA) Young Adult Library Services Association (YALSA) (formerly Young Adult Services Division). 50 E. Huron St., Chicago, IL 60611. (312) 280-4390. Fax (312) 664-7459. Linda Waddle, Deputy Exec. Dir.; Elizabeth O'Donnell, Pres. Seeks to advocate, promote, and strengthen service to young adults as part of the continuum of total library services, and assumes responsibility within the ALA to evaluate and select books and nonbook media, and to interpret and make recommendations regarding their use with young adults. Committees include Best Books for Young Adults, Recommended Books for the Reluctant Young Adult Reader, Media Selection and Usage, Publishers' Liaison, and Selected Films for Young Adults. *Membership:* 2,223. *Dues:* $35 (in addition to ALA membership), $15 for students. *Publications: Journal of Youth Services in Libraries* (q.).

(ALA Round Table) Continuing Library Education Network and Exchange (CLENE). 50 E. Huron St., Chicago, IL 60611. (312) 280-4278. Laura Kimberly, Pres. Seeks to provide access to quality continuing education opportunities for librarians and information scientists and to create an awareness of the need for such education in helping individuals in the field to respond to societal and technological changes. *Membership:* 350. *Dues:* Open to all ALA members; individual members $15, $50 for organizations. *Publications: CLENExchange* (q.), available to nonmembers by subscription at $20/yr. U.S. zip, $25 non-U.S. zip.

*American Management Association (AMA). 135 W. 50th St., New York, NY 10020. (212) 586-8100. David Fagiano, Chairman and CEO. The AMA is an international educational organization—membership-based and not-for-profit—dedicated to broadening the management knowledge and skills of people and, by so doing, strengthening their organizations. The AMA operates management centers and offices in the United States and, through AMA/International, in Brussels, Belgium; São Paulo, Brazil; Toronto, Canada; and Mexico City, Mexico. The AMA offers public meetings through the Center for Management Development, Padgett-Thompson, Presidents Association, AMA/International, AMA On-Site, and Operation Enterprise (young adult program), and provides interchange of management information, ideas, and experience on a wide variety of management topics through national conferences, seminars, and membership briefings. Services offered include the Extension Institute (self-study programs in both print and audio formats); the Information Resource Center (for members only), a management information and library service; and four AMA bookstores. The AMA publishes approximately 60 books per year, as well as numerous research surveys, research reports, and management briefing reports; AMA Video (based in Boston) produces a variety of videotapes. *Membership:* approx. 70,000. *Publications* (periodicals): *Management Review* (membership); *The President*; *Personnel*; *Organizational Dynamics*; *Service Savvy*; *Small Business Reports*; *Supervisory Management*; *Supervisory Sense*; *Trainer's Workshop*.

*American Montessori Society (AMS).150 5th Ave., New York, NY 10011. (212) 924-3209. Fax (212) 727-2254. Bretta Weiss, Natl. Dir. Dedicated to promoting better education for all children through teaching strategies consistent with the Montessori system. Membership is composed of schools in the private and public sectors employing this method, as well as individuals. It serves as a resource center and clearinghouse for information and data on Montessori, affiliates teacher training programs in different parts of the country, and conducts a consultation service and accreditation program for school members. Sponsors two regional and one national educational conference per year and four professional development symposia under the auspices of the AMS Teachers' Section. *Dues:* Teachers, schoolheads, $33.50/yr.; parents, $26.50/yr.; institutions, from $215/yr. and up. *Publications: AMS Montessori LIFE* (q.); *Schoolheads* (newsletter); occasional papers.

*American National Standards Institute (ANSI). 11 W. 42d Street, New York, NY 10036. (212) 642-4900. Fax (212) 302-1286. Manuel Peralta, Pres.; James N. Pearse, Chairman of the Board. ANSI is the coordinator of the U.S. voluntary standards system, approves American National Standards, and represents the United States in the International Organization for Standardization (ISO) and the International Electrotechnical Commission (IEC). The Institute does not write standards or codes, but coordinates those developed through an open consensus process by the more than 240 organizations, 1,000 businesses, and 20 government agencies that compose its membership. *Publications: Catalog of Standards* (annual) lists more than 8,000 standards for all topic areas; *ANSI Reporter* (mo.), newsletter of the national and international standards community; *Standards Action* (bi-weekly), listing of status of revisions on standards in the United States, international community, Europe, and other foreign national bodies.

*American Society for Training and Development (ASTD). 1640 King St., Box 1443, Alexandria, VA 22313. (703) 683-8100. Fax (703) 683-8103. Curtis E. Plott, Exec. V.P. Leading professional organization for individuals engaged in employee training and education in business, industry, government, and related fields. Members include managers, program developers, instructors, consultants, counselors, suppliers, and academics. The purpose of its extensive professional publishing program is to build an essential body of knowledge for advancing the competence of training and development practitioners in the field. Many special-interest subgroups relating to industries or job functions are included in the organization. *Membership:* 55,000 national plus chapter. *Dues:* $150/yr. individual (group discounts available). *Publications: Training and Development Magazine; Info-Line; ASTD Video Directories; Competency Analysis for Trainers: A Personal Planning Guide; ASTD Directory of Academic Programs in T&D/HRD; Evaluating Training Programs; Training and Development Handbook; National Report; Technical & Skills Training Magazine.* Newsletters: *Focus* (chapter newsletter); *Management Development Report; The Business of Training; Technical Trainer/Skills Trainer.* ASTD also has recognized professional areas, networks, and industry groups, most of which produce newsletters.

American Society of Cinematographers (ASC). 1782 N. Orange Dr., Hollywood, CA 90078. (213) 876-4333. Fax (213) 876-4973. William A. Fraker, Pres. ASC is an educational, cultural, and professional organization. Membership is by invitation to those who are actively engaged as directors of photography and have demonstrated outstanding ability. ASC membership has become one of the highest honors that can be bestowed upon a professional cinematographer, a mark of prestige and excellence. *Membership:* 271. *Publication: American Cinematographers Magazine.*

*American Society of Educators (ASE). 1429 Walnut St., Philadelphia, PA 19102. (215) 563-3501. Fax (215) 563-1588. Andrea Epstein, Mng. Ed. A multifaceted professional organization that serves the nation's teachers by providing information and evaluation of media resources and technologies for effective classroom use. *Membership:* 41,000. *Dues:* $29/yr., $47/yr. foreign. *Publications: Media and Methods; School Executive.*

American Women in Radio and Television (AWRT). 1101 Connecticut Ave. NW, Suite 700, Washington, DC 20036. (202) 429-5102. Donna Cantor, Exec. Dir. Organization of professionals in the electronic media, including owners, managers, administrators, and those in creative positions in broadcasting, satellite, cable, advertising, and public relations. The objectives are to work worldwide to improve the quality of radio and television; to promote the entry, development, and advancement of women in the electronic media and allied fields; to serve as a medium of communication and idea exchange; and to become involved in community concerns. Organized in 1951. Student memberships available. *Membership:* 47 chapters. *Dues:* $125/yr. *Publications: News and Views; Resource Directory; Careers in the Electronic Media.*

*Anthropology Film Center (AFC). Box 493-87504, 1626 Canyon Rd., Santa Fe, NM 87501. (505) 983-4127. Carroll Williams, Dir. Offers the Documentary Film Program, a 34-week full-time course in 16mm film production and theory and summer workshops. Also provides consultation, research, 16mm film equipment sales and rental, facilities rental, occasional seminars and workshops, and a specialized library. *Publications: An Ixil Calendrical Divination* (16mm color film); *First Impressions of Ixil Culture* (16mm color film).

*Association for Childhood Education International (ACEI). 11501 Georgia Ave., No. 315, Wheaton, MD 20902. (301) 942-2443. Lucy Prete Martin, Ed. and Dir. of Publications. Concerned with children from infancy through early adolescence. ACEI publications reflect careful research, broad-based views, and consideration of a wide range of issues affecting children. Many are media-related in nature. The journal (*Childhood Education*) is essential for teachers, teachers-in-training, teacher educators, day care workers, administrators, and parents. Articles focus on child development and emphasize practical application. Regular departments include book reviews (child and adult); reviews of films, pamphlets, and software; research; and classroom idea-sparkers. Articles address timely concerns: of the five issues published yearly, one is a theme issue devoted to critical concerns. *Membership:* 15,000. *Dues:* $45/yr. *Publications: Childhood Education* (official journal); *ACEI Exchange* (newsletter); *Journal of Research in Childhood Education.*

Association for Computer Educators (ACE). See listing for International Association for Computer Information Systems.

Association for Continuing Higher Education (ACHE). 620 Union Dr., Rm. 143 North, Indiana University, Purdue University at Indianapolis, Indianapolis, IN 46202-5171. (317) 274-2637. Fax (317) 274-4016. Dr. Scott E. Evenbeck, Exec. V.P.; Patricia A. Mills, Admin. Asst. The Association for Continuing Higher Education is an institution-based organization of colleges, universities, and individuals dedicated to the promotion of lifelong learning and excellence in continuing higher education. ACHE encourages professional networks, research, and exchange of information for its members and advocates continuing higher education as a means of enhancing and improving society. *Membership:* 1,622 individuals in 674 institutions. *Dues:* $50/yr. professionals, $225/yr. institutional. *Publications: Journal of Continuing Higher Education* (3/yr.); *5 Minutes* (newsletter, 10/yr.); *Proceedings* (annual).

Association for Educational Communications and Technology (AECT).1025 Vermont Ave. NW, Suite 820, Washington, DC 20005. (202) 347-7834. Fax (202) 347-7839. Stanley Zenor, Exec. Dir; Addie Kinsinger, Pres. AECT is an international professional association concerned with the improvement of learning and instruction through media and technology. It serves as a central clearinghouse and communications center for its members, who include instructional technologists; media or library specialists; religious educators; government media personnel; school, school district, and state department of education media program administrators and specialists; and educational/training media producers. AECT members also work in the armed forces, in public libraries, in museums, and in other information agencies of many different kinds, including those related to the emerging fields of computer technology. The AECT National Convention and InCITE Exposition will be held February 16-20, 1994, in Nashville, Tennessee, at the Opryland Hotel. *Membership:* 5,000, plus 9,000 additional subscribers, 9 divisions, 15 national affiliates, 46 state and territorial affiliates, and more than 30 national committees and task forces. *Dues:* $65/yr. regular, $26/yr. student and retired. *Publications: TechTrends* (6/yr., free with membership; $30/yr. nonmembers); *Report to Members* (6/yr., newsletter); *Educational Technology Research and Development* (q., $30/yr. member; $20/yr. student and retired; $45/yr. nonmembers); various division publications; several books; videotapes.

Because of similarity of interests, the following organizations have chosen to affiliate with the Association for Educational Communications and Technology. (As many as possible have been polled for inclusion in *EMTY*.)

- Association for Multi-Image (AMI)
- Community College Association for Instruction and Technology (CCAIT)
- Consortium of University Media Centers
- Federal Educational Technology Association (FETA)
- Health Science Communications Association (HeSCA)
- International Association for Learning Laboratories (IALL)
- International Visual Literacy Association (IVLA)
- Minorities in Media (MIM)
- National Association of Regional Media Centers (NARMC)
- National Instructional Television Fixed Service Association (NIA/ITFS)
- New England Educational Media Association
- Northwest College and University Council for the Management of Educational Technology (NW/MET)
- Southeastern Regional Media Leadership Council (SRMLC)
- State University of New York Educational Communications Center (SUNY)

Two additional organizations are also related to the Association for Educational Communications and Technology:

- AECT Archives
- AECT ECT Foundation

Association for Educational Communications and Technology (AECT) Divisions:

(AECT) Division of Educational Media Management (DEMM). 1025 Vermont Ave. NW, Suite 820, Washington, DC 20005. (202) 347-7834. Ron Payne, Pres. Seeks to develop an information exchange network and to share information about common problems, solutions, and program descriptions of educational media management. Develops programs that increase the effectiveness of media managers; initiates and implements a public relations program to educate the public and administrative bodies as to the use, value, and need for educational media management; and fosters programs that will help carry out media management responsibilities effectively. *Membership:* 780. *Dues:* One division membership included in the basic AECT membership; additional division memberships $10/yr. *Publications: Media Management Journal.*

(AECT) Division of Instructional Development (DID). 1025 Vermont Ave. NW, Suite 820, Washington, DC 20005. (202) 347-7834. Ann Shore, Pres. DID is composed of individuals from business, government, and academic settings concerned with the systematic design of instruction and the development of solutions to performance problems. Members' interests include the study, evaluation, and refinement of design processes; the creation of new models of instructional development; the invention and improvement of techniques for managing the development of instruction; the development and application of professional ID competencies; the promotion of academic programs for preparation of ID professionals; and the dissemination of research and development work in ID. *Membership:* 726. *Dues:* One division membership included in the basic AECT membership; additional division memberships $10/yr. *Publications: DID Newsletter*; occasional papers.

(AECT) Division of Interactive Systems and Computers (DISC). 1025 Vermont Ave. NW, Suite 820, Washington, DC 20005. (202) 347-7834. Kurt Miles, Pres. Concerned with the generation, access, organization, storage, and delivery of all forms of information used in the processes of education and training. DISC promotes the networking of its members to facilitate sharing of expertise and interests. *Membership:* 883. *Dues:* One division membership included in the basic AECT membership; additional division memberships $10/yr. *Publication:* Newsletter.

(AECT) Division of School Media Specialists (DSMS). 1025 Vermont Ave. NW, Suite 820, Washington, DC 20005. (202) 347-7834. Mary Mock Miller, Pres. DSMS promotes communication among school media personnel who share a common concern in the development, implementation, and evaluation of school media programs; and strives to increase learning and improve instruction in the school setting through the utilization of educational media and technology. *Membership:* 902. *Dues:* One division membership included in the basic AECT membership; additional division memberships $10/yr. *Publication:* Newsletter.

(AECT) Division of Telecommunications (DOT). 1025 Vermont Ave. NW, Suite 820, Washington, DC 20005. (202) 347-7834. Mark Rainey, Pres. Seeks to improve education through use of television and radio, video and audio recordings, and autotutorial devices and media. Aims to improve the design, production, evaluation, and use of telecommunications materials and equipment; to upgrade competencies of personnel engaged in the field; to investigate and report promising innovative practices and technological developments; to promote studies, experiments, and demonstrations; and to support research in telecommunications. Future plans call for working to establish a national entity representing instructional television. *Membership:* 607. *Dues:* One division membership included in the basic AECT membership; additional division memberships $10/yr. *Publication:* Newsletter.

(AECT) Industrial Training and Education Division (ITED). 1025 Vermont Ave. NW, Suite 820, Washington, DC 20005. (202) 347-7834. Joanne Willard, Pres. Seeks to promote the sensitive and sensible use of media and techniques to improve the quality of education and training; to provide a professional program that demonstrates the state of the art of educational technology as a part of the AECT convention; to improve communications to ensure the maximum use of educational techniques and media that can give demonstrable, objective evidence of effectiveness. *Membership:* 273. *Dues:* One division membership included in the basic AECT membership; additional division memberships $10/yr. *Publication:* Newsletter.

(AECT) International Division (INTL). 1025 Vermont Ave. NW, Suite 820, Washington, DC 20005. (202) 347-7834. Robert Stephens, Pres. Seeks to improve international communications concerning existing methods of design; to pretest, use, produce, evaluate, and establish an approach through which these methods may be improved and adapted for maximum use and effectiveness; to develop a roster of qualified international leaders with experience and competence in the varied geographic and technical areas; and to encourage research in the application of communication processes to support present and future international social and economic development. *Membership:* 295. *Dues:* One division membership included in the basic AECT membership; additional division memberships $10/yr. *Publication:* Newsletter.

(AECT) Media Design and Production Division (MDPD). 1025 Vermont Ave. NW, Suite 820, Washington, DC 20005. (202) 347-7834. Donna Zingelman, Pres. Seeks to provide formal, organized procedures for promoting and facilitating interaction between commercial and noncommercial, nontheatrical filmmakers, and to provide a communications link for filmmakers with persons of similar interests. Also seeks to provide a connecting link between creative and technical professionals of the audiovisual industry. Advances the informational film producer's profession by providing scholarships and apprenticeships to experimenters and students and by providing a forum for discussion of local, national, and universal issues. Recognizes and presents awards for outstanding films produced and for contributions to the state of the art. *Membership:* 318. *Dues:* One division membership included in the basic AECT membership; additional division memberships $10/yr. *Publication:* Newsletter.

(AECT) Research and Theory Division (RTD). 1025 Vermont Ave. NW, Suite 820, Washington, DC 20005. (202) 3477834. James D. Klein, Pres. Seeks to improve the design, execution, utilization, and evaluation of audiovisual communications research; to improve the qualifications and effectiveness of personnel engaged in communications research; to advise the educational practitioner as to use of the research results; to improve research design, techniques, evaluation, and dissemination; and to promote both applied and theoretical research on the systematic use of all forms of media in the improvement of instruction. *Membership:* 452. *Dues:* One division membership included in the basic AECT membership; additional division memberships $10/yr. *Publication:* Newsletter.

Association for Educational Communications and Technology (AECT) Affiliate Organizations:

(AECT) Community College Association for Instruction and Technology (CCAIT). New Mexico Military Institute, 101 W. College Blvd., Roswell, NM 88201. (505) 624-8381. Bruce McLaren, Pres. A national association of community and junior college educators interested in the discovery and dissemination of information about problems and processes of teaching, media, and technology in community and junior colleges. Facilitates member exchange of data, reports, proceedings, personnel, and other resources; sponsors AECT convention sessions and social activities. *Membership:* 200. *Dues:* $10. *Publications:* Regular newsletter; irregular topical papers.

(AECT) Federal Educational Technology Association (FETA). Science Applications International Co., Inc., 723 W. King St., Martinsburg, WV 25401. Trish Cavaleri, Pres. FETA is dedicated to the improvement of education and training through research, communication, and practice. It encourages and welcomes members from all government agencies, federal, state, and local; from business and industry; and from all educational institutions and organizations. FETA encourages interaction among members to improve the quality of education and training in any arena, but with specific emphasis on government-related applications.

(AECT) Health Science Communications Association (HeSCA). See separate listing.

(AECT) International Visual Literacy Association, Inc. (IVLA). Concordia University, 7141 Sherbrook St. West, Montreal, Quebec H4B 1R6, Canada. Nikos Metallinos, Pres. Provides a multidisciplinary forum for the exploration of modes of visual communication and their application through the concept of visual literacy; promotes development of visual literacy and serves as a bond between the diverse organizations and groups working in that field. *Dues:* $40 regular; $20 student. *Publications: Journal of Visual Literacy; Readings from Annual Conferences.*

(AECT) Minorities in Media (MIM). Center for Instructional Media and Technology, Virginia State University, Box 5002-N, Petersburg, VA 23803. Dr. Vykuntapathi Thota, Pres. Seeks to encourage the effective use of educational media in the teaching/learning process; provide leadership opportunities in advancing the use of technology as an integral part of the learning process; provide a vehicle through which minorities might influence the use of media in institutions; develop an information exchange network to share information common to minorities in media; study, evaluate, and refine the educational technology process as it relates to the education of minorities; and encourage and improve the production of materials for the education of minorities. *Membership:* 100. *Dues:* $10. *Publication:* Annual newsletter.

(AECT) National Association of Regional Media Centers (NARMC). Special Projects Center, 1150 Education Ave., Punta Gorda, FL 33950. Janet Williams, Pres. Seeks to foster the exchange of ideas and information among educational communications specialists responsible for the administration of regional media centers, through workshops, seminars, and national meetings. Studies the feasibility of developing joint programs that could increase the effectiveness and efficiency of regional media services. Disseminates information on successful practices and research studies conducted by regional media centers. *Membership:* 268 regional centers, 70 corporations. *Dues:* $45. *Publications: etin* (q. newsletter); *Annual Report.*

(AECT) National ITFS Association (NIA/ITFS). Academic Media Services, University of Colorado, Campus Box 379, Boulder, CO 80309-0379. (303) 492-7345. Fax (303) 492-7017. Dr. Daniel Niemeyer, Pres. Established in 1978, NIA/ITFS is a nonprofit, professional organization of Instructional Television Fixed Service (ITFS) licensees, applicants, and others interested in ITFS broadcasting. The goals of the Association are to gather and exchange information about ITFS, to gather data on utilization of ITFS, and to act as a conduit for those seeking ITFS information or assistance. The NIA/ITFS provides members with information on excess capacity leasing and license and application data, and represents ITFS interests for the FCC, technical consultants, and equipment manufacturers. *Publications:* Newsletter (q.); FCC regulation update.

(AECT) Northwest College and University Council for the Management of Educational Technology. University of Lethbridge, 4401 University Dr., Lethbridge, AB T1K 3M4, Canada. George Berg, Pres. The first regional group representing institutions of higher education in Alberta, Alaska, British Columbia, Idaho, Montana, Oregon, and Washington to receive affilate status in AECT. Membership is restricted to media managers with campus-wide responsibilities for educational technical services in the membership region. Corresponding membership is available to those who work outside the membership region. An annual conference and business meeting are held the last weekend of October each year, rotating throughout the region. Current issues under consideration include managing emerging telecommunication technologies, copyright, accreditation, and certification. Organizational goals include identifying the unique status problems of media managers in higher education and improving the quality of the major publication. *Membership:* approx. 85. *Dues:* $35. *Publication: NW/MET Bulletin.*

Other AECT-Related Organizations:

(AECT) Archives. University of Maryland at College Park, The University Libraries, c/o Lauren Brown, Curator, Historical Mss. & Archivist, College Park, MD 20742. (301) 405-9059. A collection of media, manuscripts, and related materials representing important developments in visual and audiovisual education and in instructional/educational technology. The collection is housed as part of the National Public Broadcasting Archives. Maintained by the University of Maryland at College Park in cooperation with AECT. Open to researchers and scholars.

(AECT) ECT Foundation. 1025 Vermont Ave. NW, Suite 820, Washington, DC 20005. Hans-Erik Wennberg, Pres. The ECT Foundation is a nonprofit organization whose purposes are charitable and educational in nature. Its operation is based on the conviction that improvement of instruction can be accomplished, in part, by the continued investigation and application of new systems for learning and by periodic assessment of current techniques for the communication of information. In addition to awarding scholarships, internships, and fellowships, the Foundation develops and conducts leadership training programs for emerging professional leaders.

*Association for Experiential Education (AEE). CU Box 249, Boulder, CO 80309. (303) 492-1547. Fax (303) 492-7090. Daniel Garvey, Exec. Dir. The AEE believes that the learner and the teacher should use the most powerful and effective means to interact with each other and their environments, and to deal with the tasks at hand. Experience-based education emphasizes direct experience to increase the quality of learning. The AEE helps to advance, expand, conceptualize, and formalize this learning process. *Membership:* 1,600. *Dues:* $35-$50 individuals, $125 institutions. *Publications: Jobs Clearinghouse*; *The Journal of Experiential Education*; books and directories.

*Association for Library and Information Science Education(ALISE). Sally Nicholson, Exec. Dir., 4101 Lake Boone Trail, Suite 201, Raleigh, NC 27607-4916. Seeks to advance education for library and information science and produces annual *Library and Information Science Education Statistical Report*. Open to professional schools offering graduate programs in library and information science; personal memberships open to educators employed in such institutions; other memberships available to interested individuals. *Membership:* 650 individuals, 85 institutions. *Dues:* institutional, $250 full; $150 associate; $75 international; personal, $40 full-time; $20 part-time, student, retired. *Publications: Journal of Education for Library and Information Science*; directory; *Library and Information Science Education Statistical Report*.

Association for the Development of Computer-Based Instructional Systems (ADCIS). International Headquarters, 1601 W. Fifth Ave., Suite 111, Columbus, OH 43212. (614) 487-1528. Fax (614) 488-8354. Carol Norris, contact person. Tim Spannaus, Pres. International association with a worldwide membership of professionals who are actively involved in the development and use of computer-based instructional technologies. Members work in business and industry; elementary and secondary schools; junior colleges, colleges, and universities; vocational and specialized schools; and the military and the government. An annual international conference, membership in special-interest groups, and networking for members provide an international forum for intellectual leadership in the field, professional growth opportunities, and the integration of theory and practice. *Membership:* 1,650. *Dues:* individuals, $60; students, $25. *Publications: ADCIS News* (members only); *The Journal of Computer-Based Instruction (JCBI)* (q.); *The Conference Proceedings* (annual).

Association of American Publishers (AAP). 220 E. 23d St., New York, NY 10010. (212) 689-8920. Ambassador Nicholas A. Veliotes, Pres. A group of approximately 220 companies whose members produce the majority of printed materials sold to U.S. schools, colleges, libraries, and bookstores, as well as to homes. Range of member interests is reflected in textbooks; religious, scientific, and media books; instructional systems; software; audio and videotapes; records; cassettes; slides; transparencies; and tests. Provides its members with information concerning trade conditions, markets, copyrights, manufacturing processes, taxes, duties, postage, freight, censorship movements, government programs, and other matters of importance. *Membership:* 220 companies. *Dues:* Vary. *Publication: AAP Monthly Report.*

Association of Audio-Visual Technicians (AAVT). P.O. Box 101264, Denver, CO 80250-1264. (303) 698-1820. Fax (303) 777-3261. Elsa C. Kaiser, Exec. Dir. Proposes to increase communication and to assist audiovisual services and production technicians in their work; holds seminars in conjunction with most of the major audiovisual shows. Also has a lending library of old service manuals for rent by AAVT members. *Membership:* 1,200. *Dues:* $35 individuals, $65 institutions. *Publication: Fast Forword.*

Association of Independent Video and Filmmakers/Foundation for Independent Video and Film (AIVF/FIVF). 625 Broadway, 9th Floor, New York, NY 10012. (212) 473-3400. Fax (212) 677-8732. Ruby Lerner, Exec. Dir. The national trade association for independent video and filmmakers, representing their needs and goals to industry, government, and the public. Programs include domestic and foreign festival liaison for independents, screenings and seminars, insurance for members and groups, and information and referral services. Recent activities include monitoring status of independent work on public television, advocacy for cable access, and lobbying for modifications in copyright law. *Dues:* $45 individuals, $75 libraries, $100 nonprofit organizations, $150 business/industry, $25 students. *Publications: The Independent Film and Video Monthly; The AIVF Guide to Film and Video Festivals; The AIVF Guide to Film and Video Distributors; The Next Step: Distributing of Independent Films and Videos; Alternative Visions: Distributing Independent Media in a Home Video World; Directory of Film and Video Production Resources in Latin America and the Caribbean.*

Association of Systematics Collections (ASC). 730 11th St. NW, 2d Floor, Washington, DC 20001. (202) 347-2850. Fax (202) 347-0072. K. Elaine Hoagland, Exec. Dir. Fosters the care, management, and improvement of biological collections and promotes their utilization. Institutional members include private, free-standing museums, botanical gardens, zoos, college and university museums, and public institutions, including state biological surveys, agricultural research centers, the Smithsonian Institution, and the U.S. Fish and Wildlife Service. The ASC also represents affiliate societies, keeps members informed about funding and legislative issues, and provides technical consulting for such subjects as collection permits, care of collections, and taxonomic expertise. *Membership:* 76 institutions, 22 societies, 1,200 newsletter subscribers. *Dues:* Depend on the size of collections. *Publications: ASC Newsletter* (for members and nonmember subscribers, bi-monthly).

Association of Teacher Educators (ATE). Suite ATE, 1900 Association Dr., Reston, VA 22091. (703) 620-3110. Fax (703) 620-9530. Gloria Chernay, Exec. Dir. The ATE serves as a national voice for issues related to preservice, graduate, and inservice teacher education. It also provides opportunities for professional growth and development through its publications and national conferences, workshops, and academies on current issues in teacher education. *Membership:* 3,500 individuals, 500 libraries. *Dues:* $65 regular members, $45 libraries, $20 students and retired. *Publications: Action in Teacher Education* (quarterly); *ATE Newsletter* (bi-mo.); *Education and the Family* (Alleyn and Bacon 1992); *Restructuring the Education of Teachers into the 21st Century* (ATE 1991); *The Handbook of Research on Teacher Education* (Macmillan 1990).

Catholic Library Association (CLA). 461 W. Lancaster Ave., Haverford, PA 19041. (215) 649-5250. Anthony Prete, Exec. Dir.; Maria Ferrante, contact person. Provides educational programs, services, and publications for Catholic libraries and librarians. *Membership:* 1,500. *Dues:* $45 individuals. *Publications: Catholic Library World* (q.); *Catholic Periodical and Literature Index* (q. with annual cumulations).

Center for Advanced Visual Studies/MIT (CAVS). 40 Massachusetts Ave., Cambridge, MA 02139. (617) 253-4415. Fax (617) 253-1660. Otto Piene, Dir. Founded in 1968 by Gyorgy Kepes, CAVS offers a unique situation in which artists explore and realize art work in collaboration with scientists and engineers. Has done significant work on lasers, holography, video, kinetics, environmental art, and sky art.

Center for Instructional Research and Curriculum Evaluation. 1310 S. 6th St., Champaign, IL 61820. (217) 333-3770. Robert E. Stake, Dir. A unit within the College of Education, University of Illinois, the Center is primarily active in conducting curriculum research in the United States, but has been of considerable interest to program evaluation specialists in foreign countries.

*Central Educational Network (CEN). 1400 E. Touhy, Suite 260, Des Plaines, IL 60018-3305. (708) 390-8700. Fax (708) 390-9435. James A. Fellows, Pres. Manages interactive telecommunications network. Provides general audience and instructional television programming and ITV services. *Membership:* PTV stations and educational agencies.

Children's Television International (CTI)/GLAD Productions, Inc. 8000 Forbes Pl., Suite 201, Springfield, VA 22151. (703) 321-8455. Ray Gladfelter, Pres.; Karla Ray, Dir. of Customer Services. An educational organization that develops, produces, and distributes a wide variety of color television programming and television-related materials as a resource to aid children's social, cultural, and intellectual development. Program areas cover language arts, science, social studies, and art for home, school, and college viewing. *Publications:* Teacher's guides that accompany instructional television series and catalogues.

CINE Information. 215 W. 90th St., New York, NY 10024. (212) 877-3999. Barbara Margolis, Exec. Dir. CINE Information is a nonprofit educational organization established to develop sound methods and tools for the more effective use of film by community groups and educational programmers. It produces and distributes materials about film and videotape use and produces films on topics of social and cultural importance. Newest releases include an Academy Award nominee for Best Documentary feature in "Adam Clayton Powell," which was also broadcast on PBS's "The American Experience" series, and American Film Festival winner, "Are We Winning, Mommy? America and the Cold War." "Mommy" was also featured at the Berlin, Toronto, Chicago, and Park City, Utah, Film Festivals. *Publication: In Focus: A Guide to Using Films*, by Linda Blackaby, Dan Georgakas, and Barbara Margolis, a complete step-by-step handbook for film and videotape users, with detailed discussions of how to use film and tape in educational, cultural, and fundraising activities.

Clearinghouse on Development Communication. 1815 N. Fort Myer Dr., 6th Floor, Arlington, VA 22209. (703) 527-5546. Fax (703) 527-4661. Valerie Lamont, Acting Dir. A center for materials and information on applications of communication technology to development problems. Operated by the Institute for International Research and funded by the Bureau for Research and Development of the U.S. Agency for International Development. Visitors and written requests for information are welcome, and an electronic bulletin board, CDCNET, is available to individuals with computer communications software and modems. *Dues:* Subscription, $10. *Publications: Development Communication Report* (q.); other special reports, information packages, project profiles, books, bulletins, and videotapes.

*Close Up Foundation. 44 Canal Center Plaza, Alexandria, VA 22314. (703) 706-3726; (800) 765-3131. Fax (703) 706-0002. Stephen A. Janger, Pres.; Lynn Page Whittaker, Dir. of Publications. A nonprofit, nonpartisan civic education organization promoting informed citizen participation in public policy and community service. Programs reach more than a million participants a year. *Publications: Current Issues*; *The Bill of Rights: A User's Guide*; *Perspectives*; *International Relations*; *The American Economy*; documentary videotapes on domestic and foreign policy issues. Close Up brings 24,000 students and teachers a year to Washington for week-long government studies programs, produces television programs on the C-SPAN cable network for secondary school and home audiences, and conducts the Citizen Bee for high school students and the Civic Achievement Award Program for middle school students.

*Computer-Based Education Research Laboratory (CERL). University of Illinois, 252 Engineering Research Lab, 103 S. Mathews Ave., Urbana, IL 61801. (217) 333-6210. Fax (217) 244-0793. Dr. Edwin L. Goldwasser, Acting Dir. CERL is a research laboratory dedicated to research on and development of systems for the delivery of cost-effective, interactive, computer-based education (CBE). CERL is best known for its PLATO and NovaNET systems, used by colleges and universities, businesses and government installations, and public schools (PLATO originated at the University of Illinois in 1960, NovaNET in 1986). Both of these are large-scale, mainframe-based systems with thousands of users, but CERL has also worked on stand-alone and local-area CBE delivery. NovaNET, the newest development, uses a custom-designed, low-cost mainframe and satellite communications for continent-wide availability. It is capable of simultaneously serving a mix of students, teachers, educational administrators, and courseware developers numbering several thousand. *Publications:* Department and professional journals; publications list available on request.

The Computer Museum. 300 Congress St., Boston, MA 02210. (617) 426-2800. Fax (617) 426-2943. Dr. Oliver Strimpel, Exec. Dir. The world's only computer museum occupies 55,000 square feet in a renovated historic building on Boston's waterfront. Dedicated to inspiring people of all ages and backgrounds about computers, the museum illustrates the evolution, use, and impact of computers from the mammoth machines of the past to state-of-the-art technology via 125 interactive exhibits, including a giant Walk-Through Computer^{TM}, displays, films, and animation; re-creations of vintage computer installations; and the most extensive collection of computers and robots in the world. The museum now exports its most dynamic interactive exhibits to museums and science centers around the globe. *Membership:* 1,400. *Dues:* $35 individuals, $50 family. *Publications: The Computer Museum Annual* (annual journal); *The Computer Museum News* (q. newsletter); Education Group Tour Planner, Educational Activities Kit (in English and Spanish).

*Consortium of College and University Media Centers. l2l Pearson Hall-MRC, Iowa State University, Ames, IA 50011. (515) 294-1811. Fax (515) 294-8089. Don Rieck, Exec. Dir. A professional group of higher education media personnel whose purpose is to improve education and training through the effective use of educational media. Assists educational and training users in business in making films, video, and educational media more accessible. Fosters cooperative planning among university media centers. Gathers and disseminates information on improved procedures and new developments in educational media and media center management. *Membership:* 300. *Dues:* $125/yr. constituents; $35 active; $125 sustaining (commercial); $15 students; $35 associates. *Publications: The Leader* (newsletter to members); *16mm Film Maintenance Manual.*

Copyright Clearance Center, Inc. (CCC). 27 Congress St., Salem, MA 01970. (508) 744-3350. Fax (508) 741-2318 main; (508) 745-9379 for Academic Permissions. Joseph S. Alen, Acting Pres. An organization through which corporations, academic and research libraries, information brokers, government agencies, copyshops, bookstores, and other users of copyrighted information may obtain authorizations and pay royalties for photocopying these materials in excess of exemptions contained in the U.S. Copyright Act of 1976. In addition to offering a Transactional Reporting Service (TRS) and Annual Authorization Service (AAS), which is an annual-license program serving photocopy permissions needs of large U.S. corporations, CCC operates the Academic Permissions Service (APS), a service that provides photocopy authorizations in academic settings, specifically for authorizing anthologies and coursepacks. *Membership:* 2,000 users, over 8,500 foreign and domestic publishers, 1.5 million publications. *Dues:* Vary. *Publications: COPI: Catalog of Publisher Information* (2/yr., $42 issue, $84/yr.); *CopyFacts: The Guide to Rights Holders, Titles, and Fees for the APS* (2/yr., $40 issue, $80/yr.).

*Corporation for Public Broadcasting (CPB). 901 E St. NW, Washington, DC 20004. (202) 879-9800. Donald E. Ledwig, Pres. and CEO. A private, nonprofit corporation authorized by the Public Broadcasting Act of 1967 to develop noncommercial television and radio services for the American people, while insulating public broadcasting from political pressure or influence. CPB supports station operations and funds radio and television programs for national distribution. CPB sets national policy that will most effectively make noncommercial radio and television and other telecommunications services available to all citizens. *Publications:* CPB Report (bi-weekly, 3 yrs. for $25); *Annual Report*; *CPB Public Broadcasting Directory* ($10 plus $2 postage and handling).

*Council for Basic Education. 725 15th St. NW, Washington, DC 20036. (202) 347-4171. A. Graham Down, Exec. Dir. A vocal force advocating a broadly defined curriculum in the liberal arts for all students in elementary and secondary schools. *Membership:* 4,000. *Dues:* $40 members; $25/yr. subscribers. *Publications: Basic Education*; *Perspective* (q., 2 yrs. for $75 members or $45 subscribers); various reports and books.

*Council for Educational Development and Research (CEDaR). 1201 16th St. NW, Suite 305, Washington, DC 20036. (202) 223-1593. Dena G. Stoner, Exec. Dir. Members are educational research and development institutions. Aims to advance the level of programmatic, institutionally based educational research and development and to demonstrate the importance of research and development in improving education. Provides a forum for professional personnel in member institutions. Coordinates national dissemination program. Other activities include research, development, evaluation, dissemination, and technical assistance on educational issues. *Membership:* 14. *Publications: R&D Preview*; *Directory.*

*Council for Exceptional Children (CEC). 1920 Association Dr., Reston, VA 22091. (703) 620-3660. Fax (703) 264-9494. Jeptha Greer, Exec. Dir. A membership organization providing information to teachers, administrators, and others concerned with the education of handicapped and gifted children. Maintains a library and database on literature on special education; prepares books, monographs, digests, films, filmstrips, cassettes, and journals; sponsors annual convention and conferences on special education; provides on-site and regional training on various topics and at varying levels; provides information and assistance to lawmakers on education of the handicapped and gifted; coordinates a political action network on the rights of exceptional persons. *Membership:* 55,000. *Dues:* Professionals, $60-80, depending on state of residence; students, $26-26.50, depending on state of residence. *Publications: Exceptional Children; Teaching Exceptional Children; Exceptional Child Educational Resources;* numerous other professional publications dealing with the education of handicapped and gifted children.

(CEC) Technology and Media Division (TAM). Council for Exceptional Children, 1920 Association Dr., Reston, VA 22091. (703) 620-3660. The Technology and Media Division (TAM) of the Council for Exceptional Children (CEC) encourages the development of new applications, technologies, and media for use as daily living tools by special populations. This information is disseminated through professional meetings, training programs, and publications. TAM members receive four issues annually of the *Journal of Special Education Technology* containing articles on specific technology programs and applications, and five issues of the TAM newsletter, providing news of current research, developments, products, conferences, and special programs information. *Membership:* 1,500. *Dues:* $10 in addition to CEC membership.

*Council of National Library and Information Associations. St. John's University, Library Rm. 322-Grand Central & Utopia Parkways, Jamaica, NY 11439. (718) 990-6735. D. Sherman Clarke, Chair. The council is a forum for discussion of many issues of concern to library and information associations. Current committees at work are the Joint Committee on Association Cooperation and the Ad Hoc Committee on Copyright Implementation. *Membership:* 21 associations. *Dues:* Inquire.

Council on International Non-theatrical Events. 1001 Connecticut Ave. NW, Suite 1016, Washington, DC 20036. (202) 785-1136. Fax (202) 785-4114. Richard Calkins, Exec. Dir. Coordinates the selection and placement of U.S. documentary, television, short subject, and didactic films in more than 200 overseas film festivals annually. A Golden Eagle Certificate is awarded to each professional film considered most suitable to represent the United States in international competition. A CINE Eagle Certificate is awarded to winning adult amateur-, youth-, and university student-made films. Prizes and certificates won at overseas festivals are presented by embassy representatives at an annual awards luncheon. Deadlines for receipt of entry forms are 1 February and 1 August. *Publications: CINE Annual Yearbook of Film and Video Awards; Worldwide Directory of Film and Video Festivals and Events* (annual); *CINE News* (q.).

Education Development Center, Inc. 55 Chapel St., Newton, MA 02160. (617) 969-7100. Fax (617) 244-3436. Janet Whitla, Pres. Seeks to improve education at all levels, in the United States and abroad, through curriculum development, institutional development, and services to the school and the community. Produces filmstrips and videocassettes, primarily in connection with curriculum development and teacher training. *Publications: Annual Report; EDC News* (newsletter, 2/yr.).

Educational Film Library Association. See listing for American Film and Video Association (AFVA).

EPIE Institute (Educational Products Information Exchange). 103 W. Montauk Highway, Hampton Bays, NY 11946. (516) 728-9100. Fax (516) 728-9228. P. Kenneth Komoski, Exec. Dir. Involved primarily in assessing educational materials and providing product descriptions/citations of virtually all educational software. All of EPIE's services, including its Curriculum Alignment Services for Educators, are available to schools and state agencies as well as individuals. *Publications: The Educational Software Selector (T.E.S.S.)* (annual); EPIE's newsletter, *EPIEgram* (9/yr.), is published by Sterling Harbor Press, Box 28, Greenport, NY 11944.

ERIC (Educational Resources Information Center). U.S. Department of Education/OERI, 555 New Jersey Ave. NW, Washington, DC 20208-5720. (202) 219-2289. Fax (202) 219-1817. Robert Stonehill, Dir. ERIC is a nationwide information network that provides access to the English-language education literature. The ERIC system consists of 16 Clearinghouses, 4 adjunct Clearinghouses, and system support components that include the ERIC Processing and Reference Facility, ACCESS ERIC, and the ERIC Document Reproduction Service (EDRS). ERIC actively solicits papers, conference proceedings, literature reviews, and curriculum materials from researchers, practitioners, educational associations and institutions, and federal, state, and local agencies. These materials, along with articles from nearly 800 different journals, are indexed and abstracted for entry into the ERIC database. The ERIC database—the largest education database in the world—now contains almost 800,000 records of documents and journal articles. Users can access the ERIC database online, on CD-ROM, or through print and microfiche indexes. ERIC microfiche collections, which contain the full text of most ERIC documents, are available for public use at nearly 900 locations worldwide. Reprints of ERIC documents, on microfiche or in paper copy, can also be ordered from EDRS. A list of the ERIC Clearinghouses, together with full addresses, telephone numbers, and brief scope notes describing the areas they cover, follows here. *Dues:* None. *Publications: Resources in Education*; *Current Index to Journals in Education*.

ERIC Clearinghouse on Adult, Career, and Vocational Education (CE). Ohio State University, Center on Education and Training for Employment, 1900 Kenny Rd., Columbus, OH 43210-1090. (614) 292-4353; (800) 848-4815. Fax (614) 292-1260. Susan Imel, Dir. All levels and settings of adult and continuing, career, and vocational/technical education. Adult education, from basic literacy training through professional skill upgrading. Career education, including career awareness, career decision making, career development, career change, and experience-based education. Vocational and technical education, including new subprofessional fields, industrial arts, corrections education, employment and training programs, youth employment, work experience programs, education/business partnerships, entrepreneurship, adult retraining, vocational rehabilitation for the handicapped, and workplace literacy.

ERIC Clearinghouse on Assessment and Evaluation (TM). (formerly Tests, Measurement and Evaluation). Catholic University of America, 210 O'Boyle Hall, Washington, DC 20064-4035. (202) 319-5120. Fax (202) 342-5033. Lawrence M. Rudner, Dir. Tests and other measurement devices; methodology of measurement and evaluation; application of tests, measurement, or evaluation in educational projects or programs; research design and methodology in the area of testing and measurement/evaluation; learning theory in general.

ERIC Clearinghouse for Community Colleges (JC). (formerly Junior Colleges). University of California at Los Angeles (UCLA), Math-Sciences Bldg., Rm. 8118, 405 Hilgard Ave., Los Angeles, CA 90024-1564. (310) 825-3931. Fax (310) 206-8095. Arthur M. Cohen, Dir. Development, administration, and evaluation of two-year public and private community and junior colleges, technical institutes, and two-year branch university campuses. Two-year college students, faculty, staff, curricula, programs, support services, libraries, and community services. Linkages between two-year colleges and business/industrial organizations. Articulation of two-year colleges with secondary and four-year postsecondary institutions.

ERIC Clearinghouse on Counseling and Student Services (CG). (formerly Counseling and Personnel Services). University of North Carolina at Greensboro, School of Education, Greensboro, NC 27412-5001. (919) 334-4114. Fax (919) 334-4116. Garry R. Walz, Dir. Preparation, practice, and supervision of counselors at all educational levels and in all settings; theoretical development of counseling and guidance; personnel procedures such as testing and interviewing and the analysis and dissemination of the resultant information; group work and case work; nature of pupil, student, and adult characteristics; personnel workers and their relation to career planning, family consultations, and student orientation activities.

ERIC Clearinghouse on Disabilities and Gifted Education (EC). (formerly Handicapped and Gifted Children). Council for Exceptional Children, 1920 Association Dr., Reston, VA 22091-1589. (703) 264-9474. Fax (703) 264-9494. Bruce Ramirez, Acting Dir. All aspects of the education and development of the handicapped and gifted, including prevention, identification, assessment, intervention, and enrichment, in both special and integrated settings.

ERIC Clearinghouse on Educational Management (EA). University of Oregon, 1787 Agate St., Eugene, OR 97403-5207. (503) 346-5043. (800) 438-8841. Fax (503) 346-2334. Philip K. Piele, Dir. The leadership, management, and structure of public and private educational organizations; practice and theory of administration; preservice and inservice preparation of administrators; tasks and processes of administration; methods and varieties of organization and organizational change; and the social context of educational organizations. Sites, buildings, and equipment for education; planning, financing, constructing, renovating, equipping, maintaining, operating, insuring, utilizing, and evaluating educational facilities.

ERIC Clearinghouse on Elementary and Early Childhood Education (PS). University of Illinois, College of Education, 805 W. Pennsylvania Ave., Urbana, IL 61801-4897. (217) 333-1386. Fax (217) 333-3767. Lilian G. Katz, Dir. The physical, cognitive, social, educational, and cultural development of children from birth through early adolescence; prenatal factors; parental behavior factors; learning theory research and practice related to the development of young children, including the preparation of teachers for this educational level; educational programs and community services for children; and theoretical and philosophical issues pertaining to children's development and education.

ERIC Clearinghouse on Higher Education (HE). George Washington University, One Dupont Cir. NW, Suite 630, Washington, DC 20036-1183. (202) 296-2597. Fax (202) 296-8379. Jonathan D. Fife, Dir. Topics relating to college and university conditions, problems, programs, and students. Curricular and instructional programs and institutional research at the college or university level. Federal programs, professional education (medicine, law, etc.), professional continuing education, collegiate computer-assisted learning and management, graduate education, university extension programs, teaching-learning, legal issues and legislation, planning, governance, finance, evaluation, interinstitutional arrangements, management of institutions of higher education, and business or industry educational programs leading to a degree.

ERIC Clearinghouse on Information & Technology (IR). (formerly Information Resources). Syracuse University, 4-194 Center for Science and Technology, Syracuse, NY 13244-4100. (315) 443-3640. Fax (315) 443-5448. Michael B. Eisenberg, Dir. Educational technology and library and information science at all levels. Instructional design, development, and evaluation are the emphases within educational technology, along with the media of educational communication—computers and microcomputers, telecommunications (cable, broadcast, satellite), audio and video recordings, film, and other audiovisual materials—as they pertain to teaching and learning. Within library and information science, the focus is on the operation and management of information services for education-related organizations. All aspects of information technology related to education are considered within the scope.

ERIC Clearinghouse on Languages and Linguistics (FL). Center for Applied Linguistics, 1118 22d St. NW, Washington, DC 20037-0037. (202) 429-9292. Fax (202) 659-5641. Charles Stansfield, Dir. Languages and language sciences; theoretical and applied linguistics; all areas of foreign language, second language, and linguistics instruction, pedagogy, or methodology; psycholinguistics and the psychology of language learning; cultural and intercultural context of languages; application of linguistics in language teaching; bilingualism and bilingual education; sociolinguistics; study abroad and international exchanges; teacher training and qualifications specific to the teaching of foreign languages and second languages; commonly and uncommonly taught languages, including English as a second language; related curriculum developments and problems.

ERIC Clearinghouse on Reading, English, and Communication (CS). (formerly Reading and Communication Skills). Indiana University, Smith Research Center, Suite 150, 2805 E. 10th St., Bloomington, IN 47408-2698. (812) 855-5847; (800) 759-4723. Fax (812) 855-4220. Carl B. Smith, Dir. Reading, English, and communication skills (verbal and nonverbal), preschool through college, and adults working with their children. Includes family literacy. Research and instructional development in reading, writing, speaking, and listening; identification, diagnosis, and remediation of reading problems; speech communication (including forensics); mass communication; interpersonal and small group interaction; interpretation; rhetorical and communication theory; and theater and drama. Preparation of instructional staff and related personnel in these areas. Includes all aspects of reading behavior, with emphasis on physiology, psychology, and sociology; instructional materials, curricula, tests/measurements, and methodology; and the role of libraries and other agencies in fostering and guiding reading. To obtain list of most recent publications, write to ERIC/CS at preceding address.

ERIC Clearinghouse on Rural Education and Small Schools (RC). Appalachia Educational Laboratory, 1031 Quarrier St., P.O. Box 1348, Charleston, WV 25325-1348. (304) 347-0465; (800) 624-9120. Fax (304) 347-0487. Craig Howley, Dir. Economic, cultural, social, or other factors related to educational programs and practices for rural residents; American Indians/Alaska Natives, Mexican-Americans, and migrants; educational practices and programs in all small schools; outdoor education.

ERIC Clearinghouse for Science, Mathematics, and Environmental Education (SE). Ohio State University, 1929 Kenny Road, Columbus, OH 43210-1080. (614) 292-6717. Fax (614) 292-0263. David L. Haury, Dir. Science, mathematics, environmental, and engineering education at all levels. Within these three broad subject areas, the following topics: development of curriculum and instructional materials; teachers and teacher education; learning theory/outcomes (including the impact of parameters such as interest level, intelligence, values, and concept development upon learning in these fields); educational programs; research and evaluative studies; media applications; computer applications.

ERIC Clearinghouse for Social Studies/Social Science Education (ERIC/ChESS). Indiana University, Social Studies Development Center, Suite 120, 2805 E. Tenth St., Bloomington, IN 47408-2698. (812) 855-3838. Fax (812) 855-0455. John Patrick, Dir. All levels of social studies/social science education; contents and contributions of the social science disciplines (anthropology, economics, geography, civics, sociology, social psychology, political science) and selected humanities disciplines (history, art, music); education as a social science; comparative education (K-12); content and curriculum materials on social topics such as law-related education, ethnic studies, bias and discrimination, aging, adoption, women's equity, and sex education.

ERIC Clearinghouse on Teaching and Teacher Education (SP). (formerly Teacher Education). American Association of Colleges for Teacher Education, One Dupont Cir. NW, Suite 610, Washington, DC 20036-1186. (202) 293-2450. Fax (202) 457-8095. Mary E. Dilworth, Dir. School personnel at all levels; teacher selection and training, preservice and inservice preparation, and retirement; the theory, philosophy, and practice of teaching; curricula and general education not specifically covered by other clearinghouses; all aspects of physical, health, recreation, and dance education.

ERIC Clearinghouse on Urban Education (UD). Teachers College, Columbia University, Institute for Urban and Minority Education, Main Hall, Rm. 303, Box 40, 525 W. 120th St., New York, NY 10027-9998. (212) 678-3433. Fax (212) 678-4048. Erwin Flaxman, Dir. Programs and practices in public, parochial, and private schools in urban areas and the education of particular children and youth of the various racial and ethnic groups in various settings—local, national, and international; the theory and practice of educational equity; urban and minority experiences; and urban and minority social institutions and services.

ACCESS ERIC. Aspen Systems Corp., 1600 Research Blvd., Rockville, MD 20850-3172. 1-800-LET-ERIC [538-3742]. Fax (301) 251-5767. Beverly Swanson, ERIC Project Dir. Toll-free service provides access to the information and services available through the ERIC system. Staff will answer questions as well as refer callers to education sources. ACCESS ERIC also produces several publications and reference and referral databases that provide information about both the ERIC system and current education-related issues and research. *Publications: A Pocket Guide to ERIC; All About ERIC; The ERIC Review*; the Conclusion Brochure series; *Catalog of ERIC Clearinghouse Publications; ERIC Calendar of Education-Related Conferences; ERIC User's Interchange; Directory of ERIC Information Service Centers. Databases*: ERIC Digests Online (EDO); Education-Related Information Centers; ERIC Information Service Providers; ERIC Calendar of Education-Related Conferences. (The databases are available through GTE Education Services on a subscription basis.)

Adjunct ERIC Clearinghouse for United States Japan Studies (ADJ/JS). Indiana University, Social Studies Development Center, 2805 E. 10th St., Suite 120, Bloomington, IN 48408-2373. (812) 855-3838. Fax (812) 855-0455. C. Frederick Risinger, Dir.

Adjunct ERIC Clearinghouse on Chapter 1 (Compensatory Education) (ADJ/Chapter 1). Chapter 1 Technical Assistance Center, PRC Inc., 2601 Fortune Cir. E., One Park Fletcher Bldg., Suite 300-A, Indianapolis, IN 46241-2237. (317) 244-8160; (800) 456-2380. Fax (317) 244-7386. Sheila M. Short, Dir.

Adjunct ERIC Clearinghouse on Consumer Education (ADJ/CN). National Institute for Consumer Education, 207 Rackham Bldg., West Circle Dr., Eastern Michigan University, Ypsilanti, MI 48197-2237. (313) 487-2292. Fax (313) 487-7153. Rosella Bannister, Dir.

Adjunct ERIC Clearinghouse for ESL Literacy Education (ADJ/LE). Center for Applied Linguistics, 1118 22d St. NW, Washington, DC 20037-0037. (202) 429-9292, Ext. 200. Fax (202) 659-5641. Marilyn Gillespie, Dir.

ERIC Document Reproduction Service (EDRS). 7420 Fullerton Rd., Suite 110, Springfield, VA 22153-2852. 1-800-443-ERIC [3742]. Fax (703) 440-1408. Peter M. Dagutis, Dir. Operates the document delivery arm of the ERIC system. Furnishes microfiche and/or paper copies of most ERIC documents. Address purchase orders to the preceding address. Fax order and delivery service available.

ERIC Processing and Reference Facility. 1301 Piccard Dr., Suite 300, Rockville, MD 20850-4305. (301) 258-5500; (800) 799-ERIC (3742). Fax (301) 948-3695. Ted Brandhorst, Dir. A centralized information processing facility serving all components of the ERIC network, under policy direction of Central ERIC. Services provided include: acquisitions, editing, receiving and dispatch, document control and analysis, lexicography, computer processing, file maintenance, database management, and others. Receives and edits abstracts from 16 ERIC Clearinghouses for publication in *Resources in Education* (*RIE*); updates and maintains the *Thesaurus of ERIC Descriptors*. *Publications: Resources in Education; Source Directory; Report Number Index; Clearinghouse Number/ED Number Cross Reference Listing; Title Index; ERIC Processing Manual*; numerous other listings and indexes.

*Far West Laboratory for Educational Research and Development (FWL). 730 Harrison St., San Francisco, CA 94107. (415) 565-3000. Dr. Dean Nafziger, Exec. Dir. Far West Laboratory for Educational Research and Development serves the four-state region of Arizona, California, Nevada, and Utah, working with educators at all levels to plan and carry out school improvements. The mission of FWL is to challenge and enable educational organizations and their communities to create and sustain improved learning and development opportunities for their children, youth, and adults. To accomplish its mission, FWL directs resources toward: advancing knowledge; developing products and programs for teachers and learners; providing assistance to educational agencies; communicating with outside audiences to remain informed and to inform others about the results of research, development, and exemplary practice; and creating an environment in which diverse educational and societal issues can be addressed and resolved. Far West Laboratory maintains a reference library with a complete ERIC microfiche collection and conducts information searches. *Publications:* Books, newsletters; handbooks; guides; research syntheses; reports; training materials. See also Council for Educational Development and Research (CEDaR).

*Federal Communications Commission (FCC). 1919 M St. NW, Washington, DC 20554. (202) 632-7000. Patti Grace Smith, Chief, Consumer Assistance & Small Business Div. An agency that regulates radio, television, telephone, and telegraph operations within the United States. Allocates frequencies and channels for different types of communications activities, issues amateur and commercial operators' licenses, and regulates rates of interstate communication services of many different kinds. *Publications:* Bulletins pertaining to educational broadcasting and general information about FCC-regulated services.

Film Advisory Board (FAB). 1727-1/2 Sycamore, Hollywood, CA 90028. (213) 874-3644. Fax (213) 969-0635. Elayne Blythe, Pres. Previews and evaluates films and film-type presentations in all formats, makes recommendations for improved family entertainment fare, and presents awards of excellence to outstanding motion pictures, television programs, and videos, and for innovations in these industries. Technical awards are also presented, as are awards for outstanding contributions to the entertainment industry and for the most promising newcomers. Awards of excellence are presented for videocassettes; the FAB Award Winner Seal is featured worldwide on many of the family and child videocassettes for Prism, RCA Columbia, Rhino, Turner, Fox, and others. Supplies film list to many national organizations encouraging them to support FAB award-winning products. *Membership:* 450. *Dues:* $40/yr. *Publication: Film Advisory Board Newsletter*, monthly film list distributed to studios, libraries, churches, public relations firms, youth groups, PTA, clubs, and colleges. Now rating home videos with Film Advisory Board (FAB) Rating System, the only official rating system with the MPAA.

Film Arts Foundation (FAF). 346 9th St., 2d Floor, San Francisco, CA 94103. (415) 552-8760. Gail Silva, Dir. Service organization designed to support and promote independent film and video production. Services include low-cost 16mm and Super-8 editing facility, festivals file, resource library, group legal plan, seminars, workshops, annual film and video festival, grants program, monthly publication, work-in-progress screenings, proposal and distribution consultation, nonprofit sponsorship of selected film and video projects, and advocacy for independent film and video. *Membership:* 2,300 plus. *Dues:* $35. *Publication: Release Print.*

*Film/Video Arts, Inc. 817 Broadway, New York, NY 10003. (212) 673-9361. Fax (212) 475-3467. Film/Video Arts is a nonprofit media arts center dedicated to the advancement of emerging and established media artists of diverse backgrounds. F/VA provides support services that include low-cost production equipment and facilities, education and training, exhibition, and grant and employment opportunities. F/VA offers scholarship assistance to women, African-Americans, Latinos, Asians, and Native Americans. *Membership fee*: $40/individuals, $60/nonprofit organizations (Oct. 1-Sept. 30).

*Freedom of Information Center (FOI). 20 Walter William Hall, University of Missouri, Columbia, MO 65211. (314) 882-4856. Kathleen Edwards, Center Mgr. Collects and indexes material on action by government, media, and society affecting the flow of information at international, national, state, and local levels. The Center answers questions on the federal FOI Act, censorship issues, access to government at all levels, privacy, ethics, bar-press guidelines, and First Amendment issues. *Publications:* Back issues of FOI publications available for purchase.

*Government Printing Office (US GPO). North Capitol and H Sts. NW, Washington, DC 20401. (202) 512-2395. Fax (202) 512-2250 for publications and order information. The GPO provides printing and binding services to Congress and the agencies of the federal government distributes and sells government publications through its Superintendent of Documents sales and depository library programs.

Great Plains National ITV Library (GPN). P.O. Box 80669, Lincoln, NE 68501. (402) 472-2007. (800) 228-4630. Fax (402) 472-1785. Lee Rockwell, Dir. Acquires, produces, promotes, and distributes educational video series and singles. Offers more than 100 videotape (videocassette) courses and related teacher utilization materials. Available for purchase or, in some instances, lease. Also distributes instructional videodiscs. *Publications: GPN Educational Video Catalog* (annual); *GPNewsletter* (q.); periodic brochures.

*Health Science Communications Association (HeSCA). 6105 Lindell Blvd., St. Louis, MO 63112. (314) 725-4722. Lionelle Elsesser, Exec. Dir. Draws together people with a wide variety of knowledge, professions, and experience in work toward the common goal of improved instructional design in all areas of the health sciences communications. Recognizes excellence in biocommunications through its media festivals and awards programs. *Membership:* 500. *Dues:* $100 individuals; $145 institutions (1st yr.); $1,000 sustaining; $35 students (without journal); $40 retired members. For additional categories, contact association office. *Publications: Patient Education Sourcebook*; *Feedback* (newsletter); *Journal of Biocommunications*; directory of accredited institutions with programs in biomedical communications.

Hollywood Film Archive. 8344 Melrose Ave., Hollywood, CA 90069. (213) 933-3345. D. Richard Baer, Dir. Archival organization for information about feature films produced worldwide, from the early silents to the present. Offers comprehensive movie reference works for sale, including *Variety Film Reviews* (1907-1990), as well as the Film Superlist series, which provides information both on copyrights and on motion pictures in the public domain, and *Harrison's Reports and Film Reviews* (1919-1962). *Publications:* Reference books.

HOPE Reports. 58 Carverdale Dr., Rochester, NY 14618-4004. (716) 442-1310. Fax (716) 442-1725. Thomas W. Hope, Pres. and Chair. Provides reports for the presentation audiovisual/video communication field, covering statistical and financial status, sales, salaries, trends, and predictions. Also provides calendar scheduling service of national/international events. Makes private surveys and has consulting service. *Publications: Contract Production for the '90s; Video Post-Production; Media Market Trends V; Educational Media Trends through the 1990's; LCD Panels and Projectors; Overhead Projection System; Presentation Slides and Computer Graphics; Educational Media Trends; Producer & Video Post Wages & Salaries; Noncommercial AV Wages & Salaries, II; Corporate Media Salaries, V.*

*Institute for Development of Educational Activities, Inc. (IDEA). 259 Regency Ridge, Dayton, OH 45459. (513) 434-6969. Fax (513) 4345203. Action-oriented research and development organization, originating from the Charles F. Kettering Foundation, established to assist the educational community in bridging the gap that separates research and innovation from actual practice in the schools. Goal is to design and test new responses to improve education and to create arrangements that support local application. Main activities include: developing new and improved processes, systems, and materials; training local facilitators to use the change processes; providing information and services about improved methods and materials. Sponsors an annual fellowship program for administrators and conducts seminars for teachers.

*Institute for Research on Teaching. College of Education, MSU, East Lansing, MI 48824. (517) 353-6413. Penelope Peterson and Jere Brophy, Co-Dirs. Funded primarily by the U.S. Department of Education and Michigan State University; conducts research on the continuing problems of practice encountered by teaching professionals, the teaching of subject matter disciplines in elementary schools (through the Center for the Learning and Teaching of Elementary Subjects), and publishes numerous materials detailing this research. *Publications:* Research series; occasional papers; newsletter; Elementary Subjects Center research series; annual catalog.

*Institute for the Future (IFTF). 2740 Sand Hill Rd., Menlo Park, CA 94025-7020. (415) 854-6322. Fax (415) 854-7850. J. Ian Morrison, Pres. Works with organizations to plan their long-term futures. Helps them to evaluate the external environment and take advantage of the opportunities offered by new technologies. Founded in 1968, IFTF has emerged as a leader in action-oriented research for business, industry, and governments, having worked with more than 300 organizations. Typical projects include environmental scanning, strategic planning assistance, policy analyses, and market outlooks and evaluations for new products and next-generation technologies. The success of the organization is based on several unique strengths, including a pragmatic futures orientation, studies of emerging technologies, networking of ideas and people, and use of scenarios to identify and analyze issues and options. *Publications:* List available from IFTF free of charge.

*Institute of Culture and Communication. East-West Center, 1777 East-West Rd., Honolulu, HI 96848. (808) 944-7666. Larry E. Smith, Interim Dir. A program of the East-West Center, which was established by the U.S. Congress "to promote better relations and understanding among the nations of Asia, the Pacific and the United States through cooperative study, training and research." The Institute is organized around four programs: Multiculturalism; Core Values; Cultural Change; and Culture and Development.

*Institute of International Education. 809 United Nations Plaza, New York, NY 10017. (212) 883-8200. Richard Krasno, Pres. A private, nonprofit organization administering public and private grants to enable U.S. students to study abroad and foreign students to study at universities in this country. *Membership:* 650 U.S. universities. *Publications: Academic Year Abroad; Vacation Study Abroad; Open Doors: Report on International Educational Exchange;*

English Language and Orientation Programs in the United States; numerous publications and directories for foreign nationals interested in study in the United States and for U.S. nationals interested in study abroad.

*International Association for Computer Information Systems (formerly Association for Computer Educators [ACE]). Department of Accounting, University of Wisconsin-Eau Claire, Eau Claire, WI 54702. (715) 836-2952. Dr. Susan Haugen, Treas.; Dr. Thomas Seymour, Pres. Membership for those who teach or have an interest in computers and information systems. *Membership:* 1,000-plus libraries. *Dues:* $35/yr. *Publication: The Journal of Computer Information Systems.*

*International Association of Business Communicators (IABC). One Hallidie Plaza, Suite 600, San Francisco, CA 94102. (415) 433-3400. Fax (415) 362-8762. Norman G. Leaper, Pres. IABC is the worldwide association for the communication and public relations profession. It is founded on the principle that the better an organization communicates with all its audiences, the more successful and effective it will be in meeting its objectives. IABC is dedicated to fostering communication excellence, contributing more effectively to organizations' goals worldwide, and being a model of communication effectiveness. *Membership:* 11,000 plus. *Dues:* $180 in addition to local and regional dues. *Publication: Communication World.*

International Association of School Librarianship (IASL). Box 1486, Kalamazoo, MI 49005. (616) 343-5728. Jean E. Lowrie, Exec. Secy. Seeks to encourage development of school libraries and library programs throughout the world, to promote professional preparation of school librarians and continuing education programs, to achieve collaboration among school libraries of the world, and to facilitate loans and exchanges in the field. *Membership:* 900 plus. *Dues:* $20 personal and institution for North America, Europe, Japan, and Australia, $15 for all other countries; based on membership for associations. *Publications: IASL Newsletter* (q.); *Annual Proceedings*; *Persons to Contact*; *Indicators of Quality for School Library Media Programs*; *Books and Borrowers*; occasional papers.

International Center of Photography (ICP). 1130 Fifth Ave., New York, NY 10128. (212) 860-1777. Fax (212) 360-6490. ICP Midtown, 1133 Avenue of the Americas, New York, NY 10036. (212) 768-4680. Fax (212) 768-4688. Cornell Capa, Dir.; Phyllis Levine, Dir. of Public Information. A comprehensive photographic institution whose exhibitions, publications, collections, and educational programs embrace all aspects of photography from aesthetics to technique; from the 18th century to the present; from master photographers to newly emerging talents; from photojournalism to the avant garde. Changing exhibitions, lectures, seminars, workshops, museum shops, and screening rooms make ICP a complete photographic resource. *Membership:* 7,000. *Dues:* $40 individual membership, $50 double membership, $100 Supporting Patron, $250 Photography Circle, $500 Silver Card Patron, $1,000 Gold Card Patron; corporate memberships available. *Publications: Library of Photography*; *Encyclopedia of Photography—Master Photographs from PFA Collection*; *Man Ray in Fashion*; *Quarterly Program Guide*; *Quarterly Exhibit Schedule.*

International Communication Association. Box 9589, Austin, TX 78766. (512) 454-8299. Fax (512) 454-4221. Robert L. Cox, Exec. Dir. Established to study human communication and to seek better understanding of the process of communication. Engages in systematic studies of communication theories, processes, and skills, and disseminates information. *Membership:* 2,400. *Dues:* $40-$1,450. *Publications: Human Communication Research* (q.); *The Guide to Publishing in Scholarly Communication*; *Communication Theory* (q.); *Journal of Communication* (q.); *Communication Yearbook.*

*International Communications Industries Association (ICIA). 3150 Spring St., Fairfax, VA 22031. (703) 273-7200. Kenton Pattie, Exec. V.P. An international association of media hardware and software producers and manufacturers, dealers, representatives, and others involved with educational, communications, and information activities, services, and products. Maintains close liaison with Congress in matters pertaining to small business media legislation. Annual convention and exhibit, "INFOCOMM International"™ Exposition, each winter brings together more than 10,000 manufacturers, dealers, producers, and equipment users in a show with more than 90,000 square feet of communications products. *Publications: Equipment Directory of Audio-Visual, Computer and Video Products*; *Communications Industries Report*; various market research studies in the video industry.

*International Copyright Information Center (INCINC). c/o Association of American Publishers, 1718 Connecticut Ave. NW, 7th Floor, Washington, DC 20009-1148. (202) 232-3335. Fax (202) 745-0694. Carol A. Risher, Dir. Assists developing nations in their efforts to translate and/or reprint copyrighted works published in the United States.

International Council for Computers in Education (ICCE). See listing for International Society for Technology in Education (ISTE).

International Film and TV Festival of New York. See listing for The New York Festivals.

*International Graphic Arts Education Association (IGAEA). 4615 Forbes Ave., Pittsburgh, PA 15213. (412) 682-5170. Virgil Pufahl, Pres. The president's address is Department of Communication, University of Wisconsin, Platteville, WI 53818. An organization of professionals in graphic arts education and industry, dedicated to promoting effective research and disseminating information concerning graphic arts, graphic communications, and related fields of printing. *Dues:* $15 regular; North America, add $2.00. *Publications: Visual Communications Journal*; *Research and Resource Reports*.

International Information Management Congress (IMC). 1650 38th St., #205W, Boulder, CO 80301. (303) 440-7085. Fax (303) 440-7234. Jack Lacy, Exec. Dir.; Janice Marean, Dir. of Administrative Services. An international trade association for the document imaging industry, the IMC supports education in the information management field through the exchange of information, technical journals and monographs, and conferences and exhibits in different parts of the world. *Membership:* 30 associations, 70 sustaining company members. *Dues:* $120 affiliates; $200 associations; varies for sustaining members. *Publication: IMC Journal* (bi-mo.).

*International Museum of Photography at George Eastman House. 900 East Ave., Rochester, NY 14607. (716) 271-3361. Fax (716) 271-3970. James L. Enyeart, Dir. World-renowned museum of photographic and cinematographic history established to preserve, collect, and exhibit photographic technology and film materials and to understand and appreciate photographic art and imaging science. Services include archives, traveling exhibitions, library regional center for the conservation of photographic materials, and photographic print service. Educational programs, films, symposia, and internship stipends offered. *Dues:* $35 libraries; $45 families; $35 individuals; $25 students or senior citizens; $75 Contributors; $125 Sustainers; $250 Patrons; $500 Benefactors. *Publications: IMAGE*; *Microfiche Index to Collections*; *Newsletter*.

International Society for Technology in Education (ISTE) (formerly International Council for Computers in Education [ICCE]). 1787 Agate St., Eugene, OR 97403-9905. (503) 346-4414. Fax (503) 346-5890. David Moursund, CEO; Maia S. Howes, Exec. Secy. The largest nonprofit professional organization dedicated to the improvement of all levels of schooling through the use of computer-based technology. Technology-using educators from all over the world rely on ISTE for information, inspiration, ideas, and updates on the latest electronic information systems available to the educational community. ISTE is a prominent information center and source of leadership to communicate and collaborate with educational professionals, policymakers, and other organizations worldwide. *Membership:* 12,000 individual members, 75 organizational affiliates, 25 Private Sector Council members. *Dues:* $46 individuals, $215 all-inclusive memberships (U.S.); $1,500 to $5,000, Private Sector Council members. *Publications: The Computing Teacher* (8/yr.); *The Update Newsletter* (7/yr.); *The Journal of Research on Computing in Education* (q.); *The Information Resource Manager (IRM) Quarterly*; guides to instructional uses of computers at the precollege level and in teacher training, about 80 books, and a range of independent study courses that carry graduate-level credit.

International Tape/Disc Association. See listing for ITA.

International Telecommunications Satellite Organization (INTELSAT). 3400 International Dr. NW, Washington, DC 20008. (202) 944-7500. Fax (202) 944-7890. Irving Goldstein, Dir. Gen.; Tony A. Trujillo, Mgr., Public and External Relations. Dedicated to the design, development, construction, establishment, operation, and maintenance of the global, international telecommunications satellite system that currently provides two-thirds of the world's international overseas telecommunications links and virtually all live international television services. *Membership:* 124 countries. *Publications: INTELSAT News* (q.); *INTELSAT* (q.); *Annual Report.*

International Teleconferencing Association (ITCA). 1150 Connecticut Ave. NW, Suite 1050, Washington, DC 20036. (202) 833-2549. Fax (202) 833-1308. Jodi S. Moon, Managing Dir.; Debora A. Schwartz, Mgr., Assoc. Services. Seeks to provide a clearinghouse for the exchange of information amoung users, researchers, and providers in the field of teleconferencing. *Membership:* 1,400. *Dues:* $500 organizational; $100 individual; $250 small business; $1,000 sustaining; $2,000 Gold sustaining; $30 student. *Publications: ITCA Connections Newsletter* (mo.); *Videoconferencing Room Directory*; *Member Directory.*

ITA (formerly International Tape/Disc Association [ITA]). 505 Eighth Ave., New York, NY 10018. (212) 643-0620. Henry Brief, Exec. V.P. An international association providing a forum for the exchange of management-oriented information on global trends and innovations that impact the magnetic and optical media and related industries. *Membership:* 450 corporations. *Dues:* Corporate membership dues. *Publications: ITA Membership Newsletter*; *Seminar Proceedings*; *1991 International Source Directory.*

ITVA (International Television Association). 6311 N. O'Connor Rd., Suite 230, LB51, Irving, TX 75039. (214) 869-1112. Fax (214) 869-2980. Fred M. Wehrli, Exec. Dir. The mission of the International Television Association is to serve the needs and interests of its members, to advance the video profession, and to promote the growth and quality of video and related media. *Membership:* 9,000, 77 commercial member companies. *Dues:* $125 individuals; $350 organizational; $40 students; $1,500 commercial sustaining; $625 commercial associate. *Publications: ITN (International Television News)* (10/yr.); *Membership Directory* (annual).

*Lawrence Hall of Science. University of California, Berkeley, CA 94720. (510) 642-3167. Dr. Marian Diamond, Dir. A center for research and public education. Its Math Education Project (Linda Lipner, Dir.) introduces visitors and teachers to computers through classes, workshops, exhibits, and the publication of software packages. *Publications: Teaching Basic Bit by Bit* (book only); *Creative Play*; *What's in Your Lunch?*; *Micros for Micros: Estimation, Numbers, Words, Music.*

Library of Congress. James Madison Bldg., 101 Independence Ave. SE, Washington, DC 20540. (202) 707-5000. Contact the Public Affairs Officer. The Library of Congress is the major source of research and information for the Congress. In its role as the national library, it catalogs and classifies library materials in some 470 languages, distributes the data in both printed and electronic form, and makes its vast collections available through interlibrary loan and on-site to anyone over high school age. It contains the world's largest television and film archive, acquiring materials through gift, purchase, and copyright deposit. A list of its many publications is available free from Office Systems Services. *Publications:* Listed in *Library of Congress Publications in Print.*

*Lister Hill National Center for Biomedical Communications of the National Library of Medicine. Bldg. 38A, 8600 Rockville Pike, Bethesda, MD 20894. (301) 496-4441. Daniel R. Masys, M.D., Dir. The Center conducts research and development programs in three major categories: computer and information science as applied to the problems of medical libraries, of biomedical research, and health care delivery; biomedical image engineering, including image acquisition, processing, storage retrieval, and communications; and use of new technologies for health professions education. It carries on research in the use of computer-assisted videodisc technology and has a Learning Center for Interactive Technology, which demonstrates new applications for health sciences education.

Magazine Publishers of America (MPA). 575 Lexington Ave., Suite 540, New York, NY 10022. (212) 752-0055. Fax (212) 888-4217. Donald D. Kummerfeld, Pres. MPA is the trade association of the consumer magazine industry. MPA promotes the greater and more effective use of magazine advertising, with ad campaigns in the trade press and in MPA member magazines, presentations to advertisers and their ad agencies, and magazine days in cities around the United States. MPA runs educational seminars, conducts surveys of its members on a variety of topics, represents the magazine industry in Washington, D.C., maintains an extensive library on magazine publishing, and carries on other activities. *Membership:* 230 publishers representing more than 1,200 magazines. *Publications: Newsletter of Consumer Marketing*; *Newsletter of Research*; *Newsletter of International Publishing*; *Magazine*; *Washington Newsletter.*

MECC (Minnesota Educational Computing Corporation). 6160 Summit Dr. N., Minneapolis, MN 55430-4003. (612) 569-1500; (800) 685-MECC. Fax (612) 569-1551. Dale LaFrenz, Pres.; Pat Kallio, Marketing Communications Coord. MECC is the leading producer of K-12 educational software in the United States and an emerging power in the rapidly growing homes market. For the past 18 years, MECC has provided children and young adults with high-quality educational software that helps them develop a lifelong love of learning. More than 80 million MECC products have been sold to homes and schools since MECC was established in 1973. MECC creates learning opportunities that are fun and provides teachers and parents with products that use technology to enhance learning. MECC products take a child-centered approach, celebrating the uniqueness of individual children and cultivating their talents. Its software helps children to combine learning with imagination. In addition to software products, MECC offers instructional management, emerging technology products, and an annual international conference.

Medical Library Association (MLA). 6 N. Michigan Ave., Suite 300, Chicago, IL 60602. (312) 419-9094. Fax (312) 419-8950. Jacqueline Bastille, Pres.; Carla J. Funk, Exec. Dir. MLA is a professional organization of 5,000 individuals and institutions in the health sciences information field, dedicated to fostering medical and allied scientific libraries, promoting professional excellence and leadership of its members, and exchanging medical literature among its members. *Membership:* 3,743 individuals, 1,281 institutions. *Dues:* $105 individuals, $345 sustaining, $24 students; institutional dues depend on periodical subscriptions. *Publications: MLA News* (newsletter, 10/yr.); *Bulletin of the Medical Library Association* (q.); monographs.

*Museum Computer Network, Inc. (MCN). 5001 Baum Blvd., Pittsburgh, PA 15213-1851. (412) 681-1818. Fax (412) 681-5758. Lynn W. Cox, Exec. Dir. As a not-for-profit professional association, membership in MCN means access to professionals committed to using computer technology to achieve the cultural aims of museums. Members include novices and experts, museum professionals, and vendors and consultants, working in application areas from collections management to administrative computing. Activities include an annual conference, educational workshops, advisory services, special projects, and publication of a quarterly newsletter. *Membership dues:* Sponsor $250; vendor $150; institution $100; individual $40. *Publication: Spectra* (newsletter). Subscription to *Spectra* is available to libraries only for $30.

*Museum of Holography. 11 Mercer St., New York, NY 10013. (212) 925-0581. Fax (212) 334-8039. Martha Tomko, Dir. Housed in a landmark cast-iron building, the museum boasts the world's largest collection of holograms (three-dimensional images). Through its extensive exhibition and education programs, the museum shows the work of artists working in the medium and explains how holograms are made, how they work, and how they have become useful tools in art, science, and technology. The museum also maintains a library, a collection of slides and photographs, and an artist-in-residence program. *Publication: Holosphere*.

*Museum of Modern Art, Circulating Film and Video Library. 11 W. 53d St., New York, NY 10019. (212) 708-9530. Fax (212) 708-9531. William Sloan, Libr. Sponsors film study programs and provides film rentals and sales. *Publication: Circulating Film and Video Catalog*.

*Museum of Television and Radio (formerly The Museum of Broadcasting [MB]). 25 W. 52d St., New York, NY 10019. Office (212) 621-6600; Information Tape (212) 621-6800. Fax (212) 621-6700. William S. Paley, Founder; Dr. Robert M. Batscha, Pres. A nonprofit institution with three equally important missions: to collect and preserve radio and television programs; to make these programs available to the public; and to explore and interpret radio and television's heritage through public exhibitions of the collection. The Museum houses a collection of 40,000 radio and television programs, including 10,000 commercials, which reflects more than 70 years of broadcasting history. The fully computerized catalog is used for selecting programs for individual listening and viewing at easy-to-use consoles. Because each program in the Museum's collection is extensively documented, the catalog itself serves as a significant research tool. The Museum also presents major exhibitions and seminars that highlight various aspects of radio and television. Exhibitions focus on topics of social, historical, popular, or artistic interest; seminars feature in-person discussions with writers, producers, directors, actors, and others who have created landmark programming. The Museum has a variety of educational programs for groups of all ages and interests, as well as a visiting scholars program. The Museum is supported by daily contributions, membership fees, and grants by individuals, corporations, foundations, and government agencies. The new museum building opened in September 1991. *Publications:* Exhibition catalogs; screening schedules; flyers.

National Aeronautics and Space Administration (NASA). NASA Headquarters, Code FET, Washington, DC 20546. (202) 358-1540. Fax (202) 358-3048. Dr. Malcolm V. Phelps, Chief, Technology and Evaluation Branch, Education Division. From elementary through postgraduate school, NASA's educational programs are designed to capture students' interests in science, mathematics, and technology at an early age; to channel more students into science, engineering, and technology career paths; and to enhance the knowledge, skills, and experiences of teachers and university faculty. NASA's educational programs include NASA Spacelink (an electronic information system); videoconferences (90-minute interactive staff development videoconferences to be delivered to schools via satellite); NASA Select (informational and educational television programming); and ISY (International Space Year) Videoconferences (two live, interactive videoconferences that provide an opportunity for secondary school students to interact with space scientists and engineers). Additional information is available from the Education Division at NASA Headquarters and counterpart offices at the nine NASA field centers.

National Alliance for Media Arts and Culture (NAMAC). 1212 Broadway, Suite 816, Oakland, CA 94612. (510) 451-2717. Fax (510) 834-3741. Julian Low, Dir. A nonprofit organization dedicated to increasing public understanding of and support for the field of media arts in the United States. Members include media centers, cable access centers, universities, and media artists, as well as other individuals and organizations providing services for production, education, exhibition, distribution, and preservation of video, film, audio, and intermedia. NAMAC's information services are available to the general public, arts and nonarts organizations, businesses, corporations, foundations, government agencies, schools, and universities. *Membership:* 200 organizations, 150 individuals. *Dues:* Institutional ranges from $50 to $250/yr. depending on annual budget; $30/yr. individual. *Publications: Media Arts Information Network*; *NAMAC Directory* (published biennially, available for $25 to nonmembers).

*National Association for Better Broadcasting (NABB). 7918 Naylor Ave., Los Angeles CA 90045. (213) 641-4903. Frank Orme, Pres. Promotes the public interest in broadcasting through the development of greater awareness of the public's rights and responsibilities in broadcasting. *Publications: Better Radio and Television*; *You Own More Than Your Set!*

*National Association for the Education of Young Children (NAEYC). 1834 Connecticut Ave. NW, Washington, DC 20009. (202) 232-8777; (800) 424-2460. Offers professional development opportunities to early childhood educators designed to improve the quality of services to children from birth through age eight, the critical years of development. *Membership:* 70,000 in 390 local and state affiliate groups. *Dues:* $25 regular; $50 comprehensive. *Publications: Young Children* (journal); more than 60 books, posters, videos, and brochures.

National Association for Visually Handicapped (NAVH). 22 W. 21st St., 6th Floor, New York, NY 10010. (212) 889-3141. Lorraine H. Marchi, Founder/Exec. Dir.; Eva Cohan, Asst. to Exec. Dir. (or) 3201 Balboa St., San Francisco, CA 94121. (415) 221-3201. Serves the partially sighted (not totally blind). Offers informational literature for the layperson and the professional, most in large print. Newsletters for adults—*Seeing Clearly*—and for children—*In Focus*—are published at irregular intervals and distributed free throughout the English-speaking world. Maintains a loan library (free) of large-print books. Provides counseling and guidance for the visually impaired and their families and the professionals and paraprofessionals who work with them. *Membership:* 12,000. *Dues:* Basic membership $35 for individuals. *Publications: Visual Aids and Informational Material Catalog*; *Large Print Loan Library*; two newsletters; informational pamphlets on topics ranging from *Diseases of the Macula* to knitting and crochet instructions.

National Association of Broadcasters (NAB). 1771 N St. NW, Washington, DC 20036-2891. (202) 429-5300. Fax (202) 429-5343. Edward O. Fritts, Pres. and CEO. A trade association that represents commercial broadcasters. Encourages development of broadcasting arts and seeks to strengthen and maintain the industry so that it may best serve the public. *Membership:* 7,500 radio and television stations, and associate members. *Dues:* Based on station revenue for radio and on market size for television. *Publications: TV Today*; *RadioWeek*.

*National Association of Business and Educational Radio (NABER). 1501 Duke St., Alexandria, VA 22314. (703) 739-0300; (800) 759-0300. John Sherlock, Dir., Membership/Communications. Represents individuals whose business and professional needs interest them in the uses of TV-shared UHF, and 800 mHz channels for communication purposes. *Membership:* 5,000. *Publications: Business Radio; ShopTalk; TechTalk; SMR Letter; Private Carrier Pages.*

National Association of Secondary School Principals (NASSP). 1904 Association Dr., Reston, VA 22091. (703) 860-0200. Fax (703) 476-5432. Robert Mahaffey, Dir., Publications and Marketing. Provides a national voice for secondary education, supports promising and successful educational practices, conducts research, examines issues, and represents secondary education at the federal level. *Membership:* 40,000. *Publications: NASSP Bulletin; NASSP NewsLeader; Curriculum Report; Legal Memorandum; Schools in the Middle; TIPS for Principals; AP Special; Practitioner and Leadership Magazine.*

National Association of State Boards of Education (NASBE). 1012 Cameron St., Alexandria, VA 22314. (703) 684-4000. Fax (703) 836-2313. Gene Wilhoit, Exec. Dir.; Carolyn Curry, contact person. Studies problems and improves communication among members, exchanges information, provides educational programs and activities, and serves as a liaison with other educators' groups. *Membership:* 650. *Publications: The State Board Connection* (member newsletter, 4/yr.); *Issues in Brief* (4/yr.); guides for policymakers and practitioners; task force reports.

*National Association of State Educational Media Professionals (NASTEMP). New Mexico Department of Education, Education Bldg., Santa Fe, NM 87501-2786. (505) 827-6562. Mary Jane Vinella, Library Media Consultant. The National Association of State Boards of Education is a nonprofit association that represents state and territorial boards of education. Its primary objectives are to strengthen state leadership in education policy making, promote excellence in the education of all students, advocate equality of access to educational opportunity, and assure responsible lay governance of public education. *Membership:* Open to U.S. Department of Education and state and district agencies. *Membership:* 110. *Dues:* \$10. *Publications: Aids to Media Selection for Students and Teachers; Quarterly Newsletter.*

National Association of State Textbook Administrators (NASTA). Division of Textbook Administration, Texas Education Agency, 1701 N. Congress Ave., Austin, TX 78701-1494. (512) 463-9601. Fax (512) 475-3612. Dr. Ira Nell Turman, Pres. NASTA's purposes are (1) to foster a spirit of mutual helpfulness in adoption, purchase, and distribution of textbooks; (2) to arrange for study and review of textbook specifications; (3) to authorize special surveys, tests, and studies; and (4) to initiate action leading to better-quality textbooks. NASTA is not affiliated with any parent organization and has no permanent address. It works with the Association of American Publishers and the Book Manufacturers Institute. Services provided include a working knowledge of text construction, monitoring lowest prices, sharing adoption information, identifying trouble spots, and discussions in the industry. *Membership:* The textbook administrator from each of the states that adopts textbooks at the state level. *Dues:* \$25 individual. *Publication:* Newsletter for members (2/yr.).

*National Audiovisual Center (NAC). National Archives and Records Administration, 8700 Edgeworth Dr., Capitol Heights, MD 20743. (301) 763-1896. Fax (301) 763-6025. George Ziener, Dir. Central information and distribution source for more than 8,000 audiovisual programs produced by or for the U.S. government. Materials are made available for sale or rent on a self-sustaining basis, at the lowest price possible. *Publications: Media Resource Catalog* (1991), listing 600 of the latest and most popular programs, is available free. Also available free are specific subject listings such as science, history, medicine, and safety and health.

*National Cable Television Institute (NCTI). P.O. Box 27277, Denver, CO 80227. (303) 761-8554. Fax (303) 761-8556. Tom Brooksher, Gen. Mgr. Provides educational materials and services for the upgrading of professional competencies of cable television personnel.

National Center for Appropriate Technology (NCAT). P.O. Box 3838, Butte, MT 59702. (406) 494-4572. Fax (406) 494-2905. George Turman, Pres. A nonprofit corporation with a mission to advance the research, development, and widespread adoption of appropriate technologies in the major program areas of energy conservation, sustainable agriculture, affordable housing, environmental protection, and sustainable economic development. NCAT operates national technical assistance services and distributes several how-to and educational publications. *Publications: Connections: A Curriculum in AT for the Fifth and Sixth Grades*; *Energy Education Guidebook*; *Photovoltaics in the Pacific Islands*; others. Free publications catalog is available from NCAT Publications, P.O. Box 4000, Dept. EMTY, Butte, MT 59702.

National Clearinghouse for Bilingual Education (NCBE). 1118 22d St. NW, Washington, DC 20037. (202) 467-0867; (800) 321-NCBE. Joel Gomez, Dir. NCBE is funded by the U.S. Department of Education, Office of Bilingual Education and Minority Languages Affairs, to provide information on the education of limited-English-proficient students to practitioners, administrators, researchers, policymakers, and parents. NCBE collects and disseminates information on print resources, software and courseware, video resources, and organizations. *Publications: FORUM* (bi-monthly newsletter); *Focus* (occasional papers); program information guides.

National Commission on Libraries and Information Science (NCLIS). 1111 18th St. NW, Suite 310, Washington, DC 20036. (202) 254-3100. Fax (202) 254-3111. Peter R. Young, Exec. Dir. A permanent independent agency of the U.S. government charged with advising the executive and legislative branches on national library and information policies and plans. The commission reports directly to the White House and the Congress on the implementation of national policy; conducts studies, surveys, and analyses of the nation's library and information needs; appraises the inadequacies and deficiencies of current resources and services; promotes research and development activities; conducts hearings and issues publications as appropriate; and develops overall plans for meeting national library and information needs and for the coordination of activities at the federal, state, and local levels. *Membership:* 15 commissioners, 14 appointed by the president and confirmed by the Senate; ex-officio, the Librarian of Congress. *Publication: Annual Report.*

*National Council for Accreditation of Teacher Education (NCATE). 2010 Massachusetts Ave. NW, Suite 200, Washington, DC 20036. (202) 466-7496. Fax (202) 296-6620. Arthur E. Wise, Pres. A consortium of professional organizations that establishes standards of quality and accredits professional education units in schools, colleges, and departments of education. Interested in the self-regulation and improvement of standards in the field of teacher education. *Membership:* 520 colleges and universities, 26 educational organizations. *Publications: Standards, Procedures and Policies for the Accreditation of Professional Education Units; Annual List* of accredited programs/units; *Quality Teaching* (newsletter, 3/yr.).

National Council of Teachers of English (NCTE). Commission on Media, 1111 Kenyon Rd., Urbana, IL 61801. (217) 328-3870. Fax (217) 328-9645. Miles Myers, Exec. Dir.; Barbra S. Morris, Commission Dir. An advisory body that identifies key issues in teaching of media. Reviews current projects and recommends new directions and personnel to undertake them, monitors NCTE publications on media, and suggests program ideas for the annual convention.

Membership: 68,000 individual, 125,000 subscribers. *Dues:* $40 individual, $50 institutions. *Publications: English Journal* (8/yr.); *College English* (8/yr.); *Language Arts* (8/yr.); *English Education: Research in the Teaching of English* (q.); *Teaching English in the Two-Year College* (q.).

National Council of the Churches of Christ in the U.S.A. Communication Dept., 475 Riverside Dr., New York, NY 10115. (212) 870-2227. Fax (212) 870-2030. Rev. Dr. J. Martin Bailey, Dir. Ecumenical arena for cooperative work of Protestant and Orthodox denominations and agencies in broadcasting, film, cable, and print media. Offers advocacy to government and industry structures on media services. Services provided include liaison to network television and radio programming; film sales and rentals; distribution of information about syndicated religious programming; syndication of some programming; cable television and emerging technologies information services; news and information regarding work of the National Council of Churches, related denominations, and agencies. Works closely with other faith groups in Interfaith Broadcasting Commission. Online communication via Ecunet/NCCLink. *Membership:* 32 denominations. *Publication: EcuLink.*

*National Education Association (NEA). 1201 16th St. NW, Washington, DC 20036. (202) 833-4000. Kerth Geiger, Pres. The world's largest advocacy organization of teachers, other school employees, and college faculty. Seeks to improve American public education, conducts research on school problems and professional teacher welfare, maintains lobby relationships with the federal government, and provides information to the public about education and educational needs. *Membership:* 2 million. *Dues:* $75 active membership.

*National Endowment for the Arts (NEA). 1100 Pennsylvania Ave. NW, Washington, DC 20506. The NEA is a grant-making agency. For a guide to programs, contact the Public Information Office at (202) 682-5400.

National Endowment for the Humanities (NEH). 1100 Pennsylvania Ave. NW, Rm. 420, Washington, DC 20506. (202) 786-0278. James Dougherty, Asst. Dir., Media Program. Independent federal grant-making agency that supports research and educational programs grounded in the disciplines of the humanities. The Media Program supports film and radio programs in the humanities for public audiences, including children and adults. *Publication: Humanities Projects in Media* (guidelines).

National Federation of Community Broadcasters (NFCB). 666 11th St. NW, Suite 805, Washington, DC 20001. (202) 393-2355. Lynn Chadwick, Pres. NFCB represents its members in public policy development at the national level and provides a wide range of practical services. *Membership:* 70 stations, 100 (assoc.) stations and production groups. *Dues:* Based on income, from $75 to $500 for associations; $400 to $2,500 for participants. *Publications: Legal Handbook*; *Audio Craft* (1989 edition); *Community Radio Monthly*; *The Guide to Political Broadcasting for Public Radio Stations.*

National Film Board of Canada (NFBC). 1251 Avenue of the Americas, New York, NY 10020. (212) 586-5131. Fax (212) 575-2382. John Sirabella, U.S. Marketing Mgr./Nontheatrical Rep. Established in 1939, the NFBC's main objective is to produce and distribute high-quality audiovisual materials for educational, cultural, and social purposes.

*National Film Information Service (NFIS). 8949 Wilshire Blvd., Beverly Hills, CA 90211. (213) 247-3000. Provides an information service on film. All inquiries must be accompanied by SASE.

National Gallery of Art (NGA). Department of Education Resources: Art Information Extension Programs, Washington, DC 20565. (202) 842-6273. Ruth R. Perlin, Head. This department of NGA is responsible for the production and distribution of educational audiovisual programs, including interactive technologies. Materials available (all loaned free to schools, community organizations, and individuals) range from films, videocassettes, and color slide programs to videodiscs. A free catalog of programs is available upon request. Two videodiscs on the Gallery's collection are available for long-term loan. *Publication: Extension Programs Catalogue.*

*National Information Center for Educational Media (NICEM). P.O. Box 40130, Albuquerque, NM 87196. (505) 265-3591; (800) 468-3453. Marjorie M. K. Hlava, Pres. NICEM, in conjunction with the Library of Congress, is a centralized facility that collects, catalogs, and disseminates information about nonbook materials of many different kinds. Its mission is to build and expand the database to provide current and archival information about nonbook educational materials; to apply modern techniques of information dissemination that meet user needs; and to provide a comprehensive, centralized nonbook database used for catalogs, indexes, multimedia publications, special search services, machine-readable tapes, and online access. *Publications:* Indexes to audiovisual educational materials.

National Library of Medicine. 8600 Rockville Pike, Bethesda, MD 20894. (301) 496-6095. Donald A. B. Lindberg, M.D., Dir.; Robert Mehnert, Public Information Officer. Collects, organizes, and distributes literature on biomedicine; seeks to apply modern technology to the flow of biomedical information to health professionals; and supports development of improved medical library resources for the country. Responsible for MEDLINE, SDILINE, CATLINE, SERLINE, CANCERLIT, AVLINE, and TOXLINE. Maintains a collection of 20,000 health science audiovisual materials; supervises the Lister Hill Center for Biomedical Communications and the National Center for Biotechnology Information. Maintains eight regional medical libraries. *Publication: National Library of Medicine News* (newsletter, 6/yr.).

National Press Photographers Association, Inc. (NPPA). 3200 Croasdaile Dr., Suite 306, Durham, NC 27705. (919) 383-7246. Fax (919) 383-7261. Charles Cooper, Exec. Dir. An organization of professional news photographers who participate in and promote photojournalism in publications and through television and film. Sponsors workshops and contests; maintains a tape library and collections of slides in the field. *Membership:* 11,000. *Dues:* $55 professional, $30 student. *Publications: News Photographer*; membership directory; *Best of Photojournalism Books.*

National PTA. 700 N. Rush St., Chicago, IL 60611. (312) 787-0977. Fax (312) 787-8342. Pat Henry, Pres.; Tari Marshall, Dir. of Communications. Advocates for the education, health, safety, and well-being of children and teens. Provides parenting education and leadership training to PTA volunteers. *Membership:* 6.8 million. *Dues:* Varies by local unit. *Sample Publications: PTA Today* (magazine); *What's Happening in Washington* (legislative newsletters); numerous brochures for parents, such as *Help Your Child Get the Most Out of Homework* and *How to Talk to Your Children and Teens about AIDS*. Catalog available.

*National Public Radio (NPR). 2025 M Street NW, Washington, DC 20036. (202) 822-2300. Douglas J. Bennet, Pres. Through member stations in 48 states, Puerto Rico, and the District of Columbia, NPR reaches a broad segment of the population. Its award-winning programming— "All Things Considered," "Morning Edition," "Performance Today," "Car Talk," and "Blues Stage"—has helped build an audience base of more than 13 million weekly listeners. With programs such as "Horizons," "Afropop Worldwide," "Crossroads," and "National Native News," NPR acknowledges the diversity in American society and provides programs that focus on minorities, the elderly, and the disabled. In addition to programming, NPR provides more than 430 member stations with distribution and representation support services.

National Religious Broadcasters (NRB). 7839 Ashton Ave., Manassas, VA 22110. (703) 330-7000. Fax (703) 330-7100. E. Brandt Gustavson, Exec. Dir. NRB essentially has two goals: (1) to ensure that religious broadcasters have access to the radio and television airwaves, and (2) to encourage broadcasters to observe a high standard of excellence in their programming and station management for the clear presentation of the gospel. Holds national and regional conventions. *Membership:* 800 organizational stations, program producers, agencies, and individuals. *Dues:* Based on income. *Publications: Religious Broadcasting Magazine* (mo.); *Annual Directory of Religious Broadcasting*; *Religious Broadcasting Resources Library Brochure*; *Religious Broadcasting Cassette Catalog*.

National School Supply and Equipment Association (NSSEA). 8300 Colesville Rd., Suite 250, Silver Spring, MD 20910. (301) 495-0240. Fax (301) 495-3330. Tim Holt, Exec. V.P. A service organization of 1,200 manufacturers, distributors, retailers, and independent manufacturers' representatives of school supplies, equipment, and instructional materials. Seeks to maintain open communications between manufacturers and dealers in the school market, to find solutions to problems affecting schools, and to encourage the development of new ideas and products for educational progress. *Publications: Tidings*; *Annual Membership Directory*.

*National Science Foundation (NSF). Washington, DC 20550. (202) 357-9498. Primary purposes are to increase the nation's base of scientific knowledge; encourage research in areas that can lead to improvements in economic growth, productivity, and environmental quality; promote international cooperation through science; and develop and help implement science education programs to aid the nation in meeting the challenges of contemporary life. Grants go chiefly to colleges and other research organizations. Applicants should refer to the *NSF Guide to Programs*. Scientific material and media reviews are available to help the public learn about NSF-supported programs.

National Science Teachers Association (NSTA). 1742 Connecticut Ave. NW, Washington, DC 20009. (202) 328-5800. Fax (202) 328-0974. Bill Aldridge, Exec. Dir. An international nonprofit association of science teachers ranging from kindergarten through university level. NSTA conducts one national and three regional conventions and provides numerous programs and services, including awards and scholarships, inservice teacher workshops, professional certification, a major curriculum reform effort, and more. It has position statements on many issues, such as teacher preparation, laboratory science, and the use of animals in the classroom. It is involved in cooperative working relationships in a variety of projects with educational organizations, government agencies, and private industries. *Membership:* 50,000. *Dues:* $50/yr. individual (includes one journal), $50/yr. institutional (includes one journal). *Publications: Science and Children* (8/yr., journal for elementary teachers); *Science Scope* (8/yr., journal for middle-level teachers); *The Science Teacher* (9/yr., for high school teachers); *Journal of College Science Teaching* (6/yr., journal for college teachers); *NSTA Reports* (6/yr., newspaper for K-college teachers); *Quantum* (magazine for physics and math high school students); books (free catalog available).

National Society for Performance and Instruction (NSPI). 1300 L St. NW, Suite 1250, Washington, DC 20005. (202) 408-7969. Fax (202) 408-7972. Paul Tremper, Exec. Dir. NSPI is an international association dedicated to increasing productivity in the workplace through the application of performance and instructional technologies. Founded in 1962, its members are located throughout the United States, Canada, and 30 other countries. The society offers an awards program recognizing excellence in the field. The Annual Conference and Expo are held in the spring. *Membership:* 5,000. *Dues:* $125, active members; $40, students and retirees.

Publications: Performance & Instruction Journal (10/yr.); *Performance Improvement Quarterly*; *News & Notes* (newsletter, 10/yr.); *Annual Membership Directory.*

National Technical Information Service (NTIS). Public Affairs Office, Springfield, VA 22161. (703) 487-4650. Fax (703) 321-8547. NTIS is a self-supporting agency of the U.S. Department of Commerce that actively collects, organizes, and distributes technical information generated by United States and foreign governments in all areas of science and technology. There are 2 million titles in the NTIS permanent archives, some of which date as far back as 1945, with approximately 63,000 new titles added annually. Reprints from the entire collection are available at any time, whether a report dates from 20 years ago or last month. In addition, NTIS provides government-generated computer software and computerized data files, on both tape and diskette, through its Federal Computer Products Center. To keep pace with technology transfer activities, the NTIS Center for the Utilization of Federal Technology licenses federal inventions and makes them available to private industry. In the area of foreign technology, NTIS has recently increased its holdings—up to a third of the reports entering the collection are now from foreign sources. Access to the collection is through a printed catalog, *The Government Reports Announcements & Index*, online, or via CD-ROM of the NTIS Bibliographic Database. Most main commercial online services and optical disk publishers offer access to the NTIS Bibliographic Database. To request a free catalog describing NTIS products and services, contact the NTIS Order Desk at the preceding address and ask for PR827/NCB. *Publication: NTIS Alerts* (covers new research in 167 subject categories and custom combinations; 2/mo. on annual subscription basis).

*National Technology Center (NTC). American Foundation for the Blind, 15 W. 16th St., New York, NY 10011. (212) 620-2080. Evaluations Laboratory: (212) 620-2051. Fax (212) 620-2137. Eliot M. Schreier, Dir. The Center has three components: National Technology Information System, Evaluations Laboratory, and Research and Development Laboratory. Provides a resource for blind and visually impaired persons and professionals in education, rehabilitation, and employment; their families; and rehabilitation professionals, educators, researchers, manufacturers, and employers. The NTC also develops products to enhance education, employment, mobility, and independent living opportunities for blind and visually impaired people worldwide.

National Telemedia Council Inc. (NTC). 120 E. Wilson St., Madison, WI 53703. (608) 257-7712. Fax (608) 257-7714. Dr. Marti Tomas, Pres.; Marieli Rowe, Exec. Dir. The NTC is a national not-for-profit organization dedicated to promoting media literacy, or critical television viewing skills, for children and youth. This is done primarily through work with teachers, parents, and caregivers. NTC activities include the development of the Media Literacy Clearinghouse and Center; the Teacher Idea Exchange (T.I.E.); national conferences, children's film festivals, regional and local workshops, and local study groups; Sponsor Recognition Awards for companies and corporate entities for their support of programs deemed to be outstanding; the Jessie McCanse Award for individual contribution to media literacy. *Dues:* $25 basic membership; $50 contributing; $100 patron. *Publications: Telemedium* (newsletter, q.); *Telemedium UPDATE.*

National University Continuing Education Association (NUCEA). One Dupont Cir. NW, Suite 615, Washington, DC 20036. (202) 659-3130. Fax (202) 785-0374. Robert Comfort, Pres.; Kay J. Kohl, Exec. Dir.; Ruth Futrovsky, Dir. of Pubs.; J. Noah Brown, Dir. of Govt. Relations & Public Affairs. An association of public and private institutions concerned with making continuing education available to all population segments and to promoting excellence in the continuing higher education community. NUCEA has an annual national conference and several professional development seminars throughout the year, and many institutional members offer university and college film rental library services. *Membership:* 400 institutions; 2,000 professionals. *Dues:* Vary according to membership category. *Publications:* Monthly newsletter; quarterly occasional papers; scholarly journal; *Independent Study Catalog; Guide to Certificate Programs at American Colleges and Universities; Conferences and Facilities Directory;* NUCEA-ACE/Macmillan Continuing Higher Education book series; *Lifelong Learning Trends* (a statistical factbook on continuing higher education); *Directory of Black Professionals in Continuing Education;* membership directory; other publications relevant to the field.

*Nebraska Videodisc Design/Production Group (VD-PG). KUON-TV, University of Nebraska, Box 83111, Lincoln, NE 68501. (402) 472-3611. Ron Nugent, Group Dir. A group of designers and producers concerned with the development and production of programs that exploit the unique capabilities of the videodisc. Holds annual symposium and workshops.

*The NETWORK. 300 Brickstone Square, Suite 900, Andover, MA 01810. (508) 470-1080. D. Max McConkey, Dir. A research and service organization providing consultation, training, assistance, and materials to schools, other educational institutions, and private sector firms with educational interests. *Publications: Administering Writing Programs: A Training Package for the Coordination of Writing Programs; The Cumulative Writing Folder; Nutrition Education Curriculum; Sex Equity Curriculum; The Effective Writing Teacher; Eighteen Strategies: An Action Guide to School Improvement; People, Policies and Practices; Examining the Chain of School Improvement,* vols. I-X. See also Council for Educational Development and Research.

Network for Continuing Medical Education (NCME). One Harmon Plaza, 7th Floor, Secaucus, NJ 07094. (201) 867-3550. Fax (201) 867-2491. Jim Disque, Exec. Dir. Produces and distributes videocassettes to hospitals for physicians' continuing education. *Membership:* More than 1,100 hospitals provide NCME programs to their physicians. *Dues:* Subscription fees: VHS-$1,820/yr. Sixty-minute videocassettes are distributed to hospital subscribers twice per month, except during the summer, when one per month is distributed.

The New York Festivals (formerly the International Film and TV Festival of New York). Admin. offices: 780 King St., Chappaqua, NY 10514. (914) 238-4481. Gerald M. Goldberg, Pres. An annual competitive festival for industrial and educational film and video productions, filmstrips and slide programs, multi-image and multimedia presentations, and television programs. Entry fees begin at $100. First entry deadline is August 1.

North American Simulation and Gaming Association (NASAGA). P.O. Box 20590, Indianapolis, IN 46220. (317) 782-1553. John del Regato, Exec. Sec. Provides a forum for the exchange of ideas, information, and resources among persons interested in simulation and games. Assists members in designing, testing, using, and evaluating simulations and/or games and in using these as research tools. Sponsors various conferences. *Membership:* 600. *Dues:* $50 regular, $10 student. *Publication: Simulation and Games* (q.).

Northwest Regional Educational Laboratory (NWREL). 101 SW Main St., Suite 500, Portland, OR 97204. (503) 275-9500. Fax (503) 275-9489. Robert R. Rath, Exec. Dir. Assists education, government, community agencies, and business and labor in bringing about improvement in educational programs and processes by developing and disseminating effective educational products and procedures, including applications of technology. Provides technical assistance and training in educational problem solving. Evaluates effectiveness of educational programs and processes. *Membership:* 817. *Dues:* None. *Publication: Northwest Report* (newsletter).

OCLC Online Computer Library Center, Inc. 6565 Frantz Rd., Dublin, OH 43017-3395. (614) 764-6000. Fax (614) 764-6096. Nita Dean, Mgr., Public Relations. A nonprofit membership organization that engages in computer library service and research and makes available computer-based processes, products, and services for libraries, other educational organizations, and library users. From its facility in Dublin, Ohio, OCLC operates an international computer network that libraries use to catalog books, order custom-printed catalog cards and machine-readable records for local catalogs, arrange interlibrary loans, and maintain location information on library materials. OCLC also provides online and offline reference products and services for the electronic delivery of information. More than 15,000 libraries contribute to and/or use information in the OCLC Online Union Catalog. *Publications: OCLC Newsletter* (6/yr.); *OCLC Reference News* (6/yr.); *Annual Report; Annual Review of Research.*

*Office for International Networks in Education and Development (INET). College of Education, MSU, 238 Erikson, East Lansing, MI 48824-1034. (517) 355-5522. Anne Schneller, Mgr. The INET office makes a number of publications available to development planners and practitioners working on behalf of persons in Africa, Asia, Latin America, and the Middle East. Such materials are distributed for sale or on an exchange basis; that is, the office sends publications in hopes that recipients will give the office further materials, especially those of a "fugitive" nature. Such materials may be in the form of books, working papers, surveys, occasional papers, annual reports, journals, or newsletters that are relevant to education and development. The INET office strongly encourages participants to continue this exchange of publications, which has proved to be so important to low-cost dissemination of information throughout the Third World. INET is interested particularly in matters and materials related to formal and nonformal education for development. *Membership:* Free. *Dues:* None.

*Office of Technology Assessment (OTA). U.S. Congress, Washington, DC 20510-8025. (202) 224-9241. Fax (202) 228-6098. John Gibbons, Dir. Established by Congress to study, report on, and assess the significance and probable impact of new technological developments on U.S. society and to advise Congress on public policy implications and options. Recent assessments focusing on technology and education issues include *Elementary and Secondary Education for Science and Engineering, A Technical Memorandum* (1989); *Higher Education for Science and Engineering, A Background Paper* (1989); *Linking for Learning: A New Course for Education* (1989); *Critical Connections: Communication for the Future* (1990); *Computer Software and Intellectual Property, A Background Paper* (1990). In addition, the assessment, *Power On! New Tools for Teaching & Learning* (1988), includes an interim staff paper on "Trends and Status of Computers in Schools: Use in Chapter 1 Programs and Use with Limited English Proficient Students" (March 1987). The OTA is currently preparing a study of educational assessment tools, to be released early in 1992, and a report on the use of technology to meet adult literacy needs (Winter 1992). *Publications:* For a list, contact the publishing office at (202) 224-8996.

*On-line Audiovisual Catalogers (OLAC). 285 Sharp Rd., Baton Rouge, LA 70815. (504) 342-4938. Bobby Ferguson, Treas. Formed as an outgrowth of the ALA conference, OLAC seeks to permit members to exchange ideas, computer files, and information and to interact with other agencies that influence audiovisual cataloging practices. *Membership:* 725. *Dues:* Available for single or multiple years, ranges from $10 to $27 individual, $16 to $45 institutional. *Publication: OLAC Newsletter.*

Oral History Association. 1093 Broxton Ave, No. 720, Los Angeles, CA 90024. (310) 825-0597. Fax (310) 206-1864. Richard Candida Smith, Exec. Sec. Seeks to develop the use of oral history as primary source material and to disseminate oral history materials among scholars. *Membership:* 1,400. *Dues:* $50 individual, $25 student, $75 contributing, $500 life; $75 institution, $120 sponsoring institution; $50 library (nonvoting). *Publications: Oral*

History Association Newsletter (q.); *Oral History Review*; *Oral History Evaluation Guidelines*; *Annual Report and Membership Directory*; *Oral History and the Law*; *Oral History in the Secondary School Classroom*; *Using Oral History in Community History Projects*; *Oral History Evaluation Guidelines.*

Pacific Film Archive (PFA). University Art Museum, 2625 Durant Ave., Berkeley, CA 94720. (510) 642-1437 (library); (510) 642-1412 (general). Fax (510) 642-4889. Edith Kramer, Dir. and Curator of Film; Nancy Goldman, Head, PFA Library and Film Study Center. Sponsors the exhibition, study, and preservation of classic, international, documentary, animated, and avant-garde films. Provides on-site research screenings of films in its collection of over 6,000 titles. Provides access to its collections of books, periodicals, stills, and posters (all materials are noncirculating). Offers UAM members reference and research services to locate film and video distributors, credits, stock footage, etc. *Membership:* Through parent organization, the University Art Museum. *Dues:* $35 individual and nonprofit departments of institutions. *Publications: UAM/PFA Calendar* (6/yr.).

*PCR: Films and Video in the Behavioral Sciences. Special Services Bldg., Pennsylvania State University, University Park, PA 16802. (814) 863-3102; purchasing info, (800) 826-0132. Fax (814) 863-2574. Thomas McKenna, Mng. Ed. Collects and makes available to professionals 16mm films and video in the behavioral sciences judged to be useful for university teaching and research. A free catalog of the films in PCR is available. The PCR catalog now contains some 1,400 films in the behavioral sciences (psychology, psychiatry, anthropology, animal behavior, sociology, teaching and learning, and folklife). Some 7,000 professionals now use PCR services. Films and tapes are available on loan for a rental charge. Many films may also be purchased. Films may be submitted for international distribution. Contact the managing editor through PCR.

*Photographic Society of America (PSA). 3000 United Founders Blvd., Suite 103, Oklahoma City, OK 73102. (405) 843-1437. Terry S. Stull, Operations Mgr. A nonprofit organization for the development of the arts and sciences of photography and for the furtherance of public appreciation of photographic skills. Its members, largely amateurs, consist of individuals, camera clubs, and other photographic organizations. Divisions include color slide, motion picture, nature, photojournalism, travel, pictorial print, stereo, and techniques. Sponsors national, regional, and local meetings, clinics, and contests. Request dues information from preceding address. *Publication: PSA Journal.*

Professors of Instructional Design and Technology (PIDT). Center for Media and Teaching Resources, Indiana University, Bloomington, IN 47405-5901. (812) 855-2854. Fax (812) 855-8404. Dr. Thomas M. Schwen, contact person. An organization designed to encourage and facilitate the exchange of information among members of the instructional design and technology academic and corporate communities. Also serves to promote excellence in academic programs in instructional design and technology and to encourage research and inquiry that will benefit the field while providing leadership in the public and private sectors in its application and practice. Membership consists of faculty employed in higher education institutions whose primary responsibilities are teaching and research in this area; their corporate counterparts; and other persons interested in the goals and activities of the PIDT. *Membership:* 300. *Dues:* None.

*Project in Distance Education. *One key component of the OAS Multinational Project on Secondary and Higher Education.* Organization of American States, Department of Educational Affairs, 1889 F St. NW, Washington, DC 20006. (202) 458-3309. Arturo Garzon, contact person. Promotes development of distance education in Latin America and Caribbean countries through technical cooperation, planning, human resource and institution building, and research. Main projects in Argentina, Brazil, Colombia, Costa Rica, El Salvador, and Panama.

*Project in Educational Technology. *One key component of the OAS Multinational Project on Secondary and Higher Education.* Organization of American States, Department of Educational Affairs, 1889 F St. NW, Washington, DC 20006. (202) 458-3309. Arturo Garzon, contact person. Maintains support, information, and personnel exchanges among educational technology centers in Brazil, Argentina, and Chile, with tie-ins to other Latin American countries. Emphasizes development of human resources through a variety of programs, seminars, short courses, on-site training, and technical cooperation. Also disseminates information through its journal. *Publication: Revista de Tecnologia Educativa.*

*Public Broadcasting Service (PBS). 1320 Braddock Pl., Alexandria, VA 22314. (703) 739-5000. Bruce Christensen, Pres. Serves as a distributor of national public television programming, obtaining all programs from the stations or independent producers; PBS is not a production facility. Owned and operated by the licensees through annual membership fees. Funding for technical distribution facilities in part by the Corporation for Public Broadcasting. PBS services include national promotion, program acquisition and scheduling, legal services, development and fundraising support, engineering and technical studies, and research. Of special interest are the Adult Learning Service, which offers telecourses through college, public television station partnerships, and PBS VIDEO, which offers PBS programs for rent/sale to educational institutions. PBS is governed by a board of directors elected by licensees for three-year terms. *Membership:* 172 licensees; 337 stations.

PBS Adult Learning Service (ALS). 1320 Braddock Pl., Alexandria, VA 22314-1698. (800) 257-2578. Fax (703) 739-8495. Will Philipp, Dir. Contact ALS Customer Service. The mission of ALS is to help colleges, universities, and public television stations increase learning opportunities for distance learners; enrich classroom instruction; update faculty; train administrators, management, and staff; and provide other educational services for local communities. A pioneer in the widespread use of video and print packages incorporated into curricula and offered for credit by local colleges, ALS began broadcasting telecourses in 1981. Since that time, over 2 million students have earned college credit through telecourses offered in partnership with more than half of the nation's colleges and universities. In 1988, ALS established the Adult Learning Satellite Service (ALSS) to provide colleges, universities, businesses, hospitals, and other organizations with a broad range of educational programming via direct satellite. *Membership:* 400-plus colleges, universities, hospitals, government agencies, and Fortune 500 businesses are now ALSS Associates. Organizations that are not Associates can still acquire ALS programming, but at higher fees. *Dues:* $1,500/yr.; multisite and consortia rates are available. *Publications: ALSS Programming Line-Up* (catalog of available programming, 3/yr.); *The Agenda* (news magazine about issues of interest to distance learning and adult learning administrators).

*PBS ENCORE. 1320 Braddock Pl., Alexandria, VA 22314. (703) 739-5225. Michael Patterson, Mgr. Distributes PBS programs with extant broadcast rights to public television stations. *Publications: PBS Encore Catalog; Monthly News & Update Memo.*

PBS VIDEO. 1320 Braddock Pl., Alexandria, VA 22314. (703) 739-5157; (800) 424-7963. Fax (703) 739-5269. Jon Cecil, Dir., PBS VIDEO Marketing. Markets and distributes PBS television programs for sale on videocassette to colleges, public libraries, schools, governments, and other organizations and institutions. *Publications: PBS VIDEO Catalog* and its supplement; *PBS VIDEO Check It Out; PBS Video News; PBS VIDEO Visions.*

Puppeteers of America. 5 Cricklewood Path, Pasadena, CA 91107. (818) 797-5748. Gayle Schulter, Membership Chair. Founded in 1937 to promote and develop the art of puppetry. It has a large collection of films and videotapes for rent in its audiovisual library and offers books, plays, and related items from the Puppetry Store. Puppeteers is a national resource center that offers workshops, exhibits, a puppetry exchange, and regional festivals. *Dues:* Various classes of membership, which range from $15 to $40. *Publications: Puppeteering Journal* (annual directory); bi-monthly newsletter; quarterly journals.

*Radio Free Europe/Radio Liberty (RFE-RL, Inc.). 1201 Connecticut Ave. NW, Washington DC 20036. (202) 457-6900. An independent radio broadcast service funded by federal grants, which broadcasts to the nations of the former Soviet Union; Bulgaria, Czechoslovakia, Hungary, Poland, and Romania; the Baltic States; and Afghanistan.

*Recording for the Blind. 20 Roszel Rd., Princeton, NJ 08540. (609) 452-0606. Supported by volunteers and contributions from individuals, corporations, and foundations. Supplies free recordings of educational books for visually, perceptually, and physically disabled students and professionals.

*Recording Industry Association of America, Inc. (RIAA). 1020 19th St. NW, Suite 200, Washington, DC 20036. (202) 775-0101. Jason S. Berman, Pres. Compiles and disseminates U.S. industry shipment statistics by units and wholesale/retail dollar equivalents; establishes industry technical standards; conducts audits for certification of gold and platinum records and video awards; acts as the public information arm on behalf of the U.S. recording industry; provides antipiracy intelligence to law enforcement agencies; presents an RIAA cultural award for contributions to cultural activities in the United States; and acts as a resource center for recording industry research projects. *Membership:* 50 sound recording manufacturers. *Publications: Statistical Report*; *Industry Sourcebook*; newsletter; press releases.

Smithsonian Institution. c/o Smithsonian Information, Smithsonian Institution, Washington, DC 20560. (202) 357-2700. Robert McCormick Adams, Secy. An independent trust instrumentality of the United States that conducts scientific, cultural, and scholarly research; administers the national collections; and performs other educational public service functions, all supported by Congress, trusts, gifts, and grants. Includes 15 museums, including the National Museum of Natural History, the National Museum of American History, and the National Air and Space Museum. Museums are free and open daily except December 25. The Smithsonian Institution Traveling Exhibition Service (SITES) organizes exhibitions on art, history, and science and circulates them across the country and abroad. *Membership:* Smithsonian Associates (Resident and National Air and Space). *Dues:* Vary. *Publications: Smithsonian*; *Air & Space/Smithsonian*.

*Social Science Education Consortium (SSEC). 3300 Mitchell Ln., Suite 240, Boulder, CO 80301-2272. (303) 492-8154. James R. Giese, Exec. Dir. The major goal of SSEC is to improve social studies instruction at all levels—elementary, secondary, and college. The consortium disseminates information about social studies materials, instructional methods, and trends. It assists educators in identifying, selecting, and using new ideas and methods in social studies and provides a forum for social scientists and educators to exchange ideas and views. A free catalog of publications and services is available on request. *Membership:* 140.

Society for Applied Learning Technology (SALT). 50 Culpeper St., Warrenton, VA 22186. (703) 347-0055. Raymond G. Fox, Pres. Seeks to advance the development of highest standards and practices in the application of technology to learning, to foster wide dissemination of understanding and knowledge in actual and potential uses of technology in learning, and to provide an effective educational channel among scientists, managers, and users of training and learning technology. *Membership:* 800. *Dues:* $45. *Publications: Journal of Educational Technology Systems*; *Journal of Interactive Instructional Development*; *Journal of Medical Education Technologies*. Send for list of books.

Society for Computer Simulation (SCS). P.O. Box 17900, San Diego, CA 92177-7900. (619) 277-3888. Fax (619) 277-3930. Chip G. Stockton, Exec. Dir. Founded in 1952, SCS is a professional-level technical society devoted to the art and science of modeling and simulation. Its purpose is to advance the understanding, appreciation, and use of all types of computer models for studying the behavior of actual or hypothesized systems of all kinds. Sponsors standards and local, regional, and national technical meetings and conferences, such as Eastern & Western Simulation Multiconferences, Summer Computer Simulation Conference, Winter Simulation Conference, International Simulation Technology Conference (SIMTEC), National Educational Computing Conference (NECC), and others. *Membership:* 1,900. *Dues:* $50. *Publications: Simulation* (mo.); Simulation series (q.); *Transactions of SCS* (q.). Additional office in Ghent, Belgium.

Society for Imaging Science and Technology (IS&T) (formerly Society of Photographic Engineering). 7003 Kilworth Ln., Springfield, VA 22151. (703) 642-9090. Fax (703) 642-9094. Calva Lotridge, Exec. Dir. Seeks to advance the science and engineering of imaging materials and equipment and to develop means for applying and using imaging techniques in all branches of engineering and science. *Membership:* 3,000; 17 chapters. *Publication: Journal of Imaging Science and Technology.*

*Society for Photographic Education (SPE). Campus Box 318, University of Colorado, Boulder, CO 80309. (303) 492-0588. Judith Thorpe, Exec. Dir. An association of college and university teachers of photography, museum photographic curators, writers, and publishers. Promotes higher standards of photographic education. *Membership:* 1,700. *Dues:* $50. *Publications: Exposure*; newsletter.

Society of Cable Television Engineers (SCTE). 669 Exton Commons, Exton, PA 19341. (215) 363-6888. William W. Riker, Exec. V.P. SCTE is dedicated to the technical training and further education of members. A nonprofit membership organization for persons engaged in engineering, construction, installation, technical direction, management, or administration of cable television and broadband communication technologies. Also eligible for membership are students in communications, educators, government and regulatory agency employees, and affiliated trade associations. *Membership:* 9,000. *Dues:* $40/yr. *Publication: The Interval.*

Society of Motion Picture and Television Engineers (SMPTE). 595 W. Hartsdale Ave., White Plains, NY 10607-1824. (914) 761-1100. Fax (914) 761-3115. Lynette Robinson, Exec. Dir. Fosters the advancement of engineering and technical aspects of motion pictures, television, and allied arts and sciences; disseminates scientific information in these areas; and sponsors lectures, exhibitions, classes, and conferences. Open to those with clearly defined interest in the field. *Membership:* 9,500. *Dues:* $65. *Publications:* Booklets and reports related to nonbook media, such as *SMPTE Journal*; *Special Effects in Motion Pictures*; test films.

*Society of Photo Technologists (SPT). 6535 S. Dayton, Suite 2000, Englewood, CO 80111. (303) 799-0667. Karen A. Hone, contact person. An organization of photographic equipment repair technicians, which improves and maintains communications between manufacturers and independent repair technicians. *Membership:* 1,000. *Dues:* $60-$250. *Publications: SPT Journal*; *SPT Parts and Services Directory*; *SPT Newsletter*; *SPT Manuals—Training and Manufacturer's Tours*.

Society of Photographic Engineering. See listing for Society for Imaging Science and Technology (IS&T).

*SOFTSWAP. P.O. Box 271704, Concord, CA 94527-1704. (415) 685-7289. Hal Gibson, contact person. SOFTSWAP is an inexpensive yet high-quality library of many teacher-developed and commercial educational programs for use in Apple, IBM, and MAC computers. These copyrighted programs are organized onto disks that are sold for a nominal charge, with permission to copy. *Publications:* Catalog; newsletter.

Special Libraries Association (SLA). 1700 18th St. NW, Washington, DC 20009-2508. (202) 234-4700. Fax (202) 265-9317. David R. Bender, Exec. Dir. SLA is an international professional organization of more than 13,000 librarians, information managers, and brokers serving business, research, government, universities, media, museums, and institutions that use or produce specialized information. Founded in 1909, the goal of the Association is to advance the leadership role of special librarians in the information society. SLA encourages its members to increase their professional competencies and performance by offering continuing education courses, workshops, and middle management and executive management courses. *Membership:* 13,000 plus. *Publications: SpeciaList* (mo. newsletter); *Special Libraries* (q.); bibliographic aids in library and information services.

SpecialNet. Part of the GTE Education Service Network. 1090 Vermont Ave. NW, Suite 800, Washington, DC 20005. (202) 408-7021; (800) 659-3000. Fax (202) 628-8216. Brenda Jacobs, contact person. A computerized, fee-charging information database emphasizing special education resources.

Speech Communication Association (SCA). 5105 Backlick Rd., Bldg. E, Annandale, VA 22003. (703) 750-0533. James L. Gaudino, Exec. Dir. A voluntary society organized to promote study, criticism, research, teaching, and application of principles of communication, particularly of speech communication. *Membership:* 7,000. *Dues:* $75. *Publications: Spectra Newsletter* (mo.); *Quarterly Journal of Speech*; *Communication Monographs*; *Communication Education*; *Critical Studies in Mass Communication*; *Speech Communication Teacher*; *Index to Journals in Communication Studies through 1985*; *Speech Communication Directory of SCA and the Regional Speech Communication Organizations* (CSSA, ECA, SSCA, WSCA). For additional publications, request brochure.

Superintendent of Documents. U.S. Government Printing Office, Washington, DC 20402. (202) 783-3238. Fax (202) 512-2250. Functions as the principal sales agency for U.S. government publications. Has over 20,000 titles in its active sales inventory. For information on the scope of its publications, write for the free Subject Bibliography index listing of over 240 subject bibliographies on specific topics. Of particular interest are SB 258, *Grants and Awards*; SB 114, *Directories and Lists of Persons and Organizations*; SB 73, *Motion Pictures, Films and Audiovisual Information*; SB 207, *Small Business*; SB 85, *Financial Aid for Students*.

Teachers and Writers Collaborative (T&W). 5 Union Square W., New York, NY 10003. (212) 691-6590. Nancy Larson Shapiro, Dir. Sends writers and other artists into New York public schools to conduct long-term projects with classroom teachers and students and publishes materials on how to teach creative writing based on these workshops. *Dues:* $35/yr. basic membership. *Publications: Teachers & Writers* (magazine); *The T&W Guide to Walt Whitman; Playmaking; Blazing Pencils; The List Poem; The Whole Word Catalogue*, vols. 1 & 2; *Personal Fiction Writing; The Writing Workshop*, vols. 1 & 2; *The T&W Handbook of Poetic Forms; The Art of Science Writing; Like It Was: A Complete Guide to Writing Oral History; Origins; Moving Windows: Evaluating the Poetry Children Write; Poetic Forms: 10 Audio Programs; Acrostic* and *Pantoum* (software packages). Free publications catalog available.

*Telecommunications Research and Action Center (TRAC). Box 12038, Washington, DC 20005. (202) 462-2520. Samuel Simon, counsel. Seeks to educate telecommunications consumers, to improve broadcasting, and to support local and national media reform groups and movements. *Dues:* $25/yr. *Publications: After Divestiture: What the AT&T Settlement Means for Business and Residential Telephone Service; Citizens' Media Directory; A Citizens' Primer on the Fairness Doctrine; Phonewriting: A Consumer's Guide to the New World of Electronic Information Services.*

Theater Library Association (TLA). 111 Amsterdam Ave., Rm. 513, New York, NY 10023. (212) 870-1670. Richard M. Buck, Secy./Treas. Seeks to further the interests of collecting, preserving, and using theater, cinema, and performing arts materials in libraries, museums, and private collections. *Membership:* 500. *Dues:* $20 individual, $25 institutional. *Publications: Broadside* (q.); *Performing Arts Resources* (membership annual).

Training Media Association. 198 Thomas Johnson Dr., Suite 206, Frederick, MD 21702. (301) 662-4268. Robert A. Gehrke, Exec. Dir. An organization dedicated to the protection of film and videotape copyright and copyright education. *Membership:* 75. *Dues:* Based on number of employees. *Publication: The Monthly.*

*Training Modules for Trainers (TMT). School of Education, University of Michigan, Ann Arbor, MI 48109. (313) 763-4668. Dr. Carl F. Berger, Dir. Funded by the Michigan Department of Education, the TMT Project was conceived to provide materials for use by trainers in addressing the computing needs of the educational community. The materials consist of a set of modules, each containing an overview, goals, training leader prerequisites, competency list, issues narrative, references, activities, blackline masters, and a feedback form. In addition, there is a videotape and set of slides available to supplement certain modules. Module topics include training methods, district planning, instructional methods, applications concepts, software evaluation, hardware configuration, basic technical skills, instructional management, software design, computers in the curriculum, computer-mediated communication, administrative uses, future images, computers and media services, emerging technology, artificial intelligence, CD-ROM, distance education, and videodiscs. *Publications: Training Modules for Trainers: A Resource for Training Leaders in the Educational Use of Computers* (set of 19).

United Nations Department of Public Information, Dissemination Division. United Nations, Rm. S-1037 A, New York, NY 10017. (212) 963-6835. Fax (212) 963-6914. Chief, *Information Dissemination Service*, Rm. S-0260. (212) 963-6824. Fax (212) 963-4642. *Film, Video and Radio Distribution*, Rm. S-0805. (212) 963-6982. Fax (212) 963-6869. *Print and Electronic Materials Distribution*, Rm. S-0260. (212) 963-1258. Fax (212) 963-4642. Vadim Perfiliev, Dir. The Department of Public Information produces and distributes films, radio, video, still pictures, charts, posters, and various publications on the United Nations and its activities. Distribution is worldwide and is done in part through a network of United Nations information centers, as well as via distributors and direct from U.N. Headquarters in New

York. Information products are provided in a number of different languages, mainly in the six official U.N. languages: Arabic, Chinese, English, French, Russian, and Spanish.

University Film and Video Association (UFVA). c/o Loyola Marymount University, Communication Arts Department, Los Angeles, CA 90045. (310) 338-3033. Fax (310) 338-3030. Donald J. Zirpola, Pres. Members are persons involved in the arts and sciences of film and video. Promotes film and video production in educational institutions, fosters study of world cinema and video in scholarly resource centers, and serves as central source of information on film/video instruction, festivals, grants, jobs, production, and research. *Membership:* Approx. 800. *Dues:* Individuals $35; students $15; institutions $75; commercial firms $150. *Publications: Journal of Film and Video; UFVA Digest;* membership directory.

*Women in Film (WIF). 6464 Sunset Blvd., No. 900, Hollywood, CA 90028. (213) 463-6040. Marcy Kelly, Pres. For women in film and television, a communications and support network, an education and advocacy resource, and a showcase for outstanding work being done by women directors, producers, and writers. The mission of Women in Film is to advance the employment, position, and depiction of women. WIF annually produces the Women in Film Festival (four days of premiere, documentary, video, and animation screenings, awards in 11 categories, special events and seminars); the Crystal Awards (recognizing contributions in film and television that promote the organization's mission); a program of film-finishing grants and scholarships for women through the Women in Film Foundation; a series of workshops on subjects related to improving the image and increasing the participation of women in the industry. *Membership criteria:* Three years' professional experience in film and television. *Dues:* $125/yr. *Publication: Newsletter* (mo.).

World Future Society (WFS). 4916 St. Elmo Ave., Bethesda, MD 20814-6089. (301) 656-8274. Edward Cornish, Pres. Organization of individuals interested in the study of future trends and possibilities. *Membership:* 30,000. *Dues:* For information, please write to preceding address. *Publications: The Futurist: A Journal of Forecasts, Trends and Ideas About the Future; Futures Research Quarterly; Future Survey.* The society's bookstore offers audio- and videotapes, books, and other items.

Canada

This section on Canada includes information on 11 Canadian organizations whose principal interests lie in the general fields of education, educational media, instructional technology, and library and information science. Organizations listed in the 1992 *EMTY* were contacted for updated information and changes have been made accordingly. If no response was received, the entry for 1992 is repeated and indicated by an asterisk.

ACCESS NETWORK. 16930 114th Ave., Edmonton AB T5M 3S2, Canada. (403) 451-7272. Fax (403) 452-7233. Peter L. Senchuk, Pres. and CEO; Jean Campbell, Gen. Mgr. (Acting), Educational Services; Malcolm Knox, Gen. Mgr., Television; Don Thomas, Gen. Mgr., ACCESS NETWORK-CKUA Radio. ACCESS NETWORK is the registered trade name of the Alberta Educational Communications Corporation, which was established October 17, 1973, to consolidate and upgrade a variety of educational media services developing at that time within the province. ACCESS NETWORK acquires, develops, produces, and distributes television and radio programs, microcomputer courseware, multimedia kits, and related printed support materials for educational purposes. In 1985, the Corporation launched a province-wide educational television service, which is available by cable, satellite, and off-air transmitters to 82 percent of Alberta's population. ACCESS NETWORKCKUA AM/FM broadcasts through a province-wide AM and FM radio network. Intended primarily for use in Alberta classrooms, ACCESS NETWORK productions are now available for national and international distribution.

Association for Media and Technology in Education in Canada (AMTEC). Instructional Technology Centre, University of Alberta, Faculty of Education, B-117 Education Centre, Edmonton, AB T6G 2G5, Canada. David Mappin, Pres. Promotes applications of educational technology in improving education and the public welfare. Fosters cooperation and interaction; seeks to improve professional qualifications of media practitioners; organizes and conducts media and technology meetings, seminars, and annual conferences; stimulates and publishes research in media and technology. *Membership: 550. Publications: Canadian Journal of Educational Communication* (q.); *Media News* (q.); *Membership Directory* (with membership).

*Canadian Association of Broadcasters/Association canadienne des radiodiffusers (CAB/ACR). Box 627, Station B, Ottawa, ON KIP 5S2, Canada. (613) 2334035. Fax (613) 2336961. A nonprofit trade association representing the majority of Canada's local-serving, advertising-supported radio and television stations.

*Canadian Book Publishers' Council (CBPC). 250 Merton St., Suite 203, Toronto, ON M4S 1B1, Canada. (416) 322-7011, (416) 322-6999. Jacqueline Hushion, Exec. Dir. CBPC members publish and distribute an extensive list of Canadian and imported materials to schools, universities, bookstores, and libraries. CBPC provides exhibits throughout the year and works through a number of subcommittees and groups within the organization to promote effective book publishing. *Membership:* 40 companies, educational institutions, or government agencies that publish books as an important facet of their work.

Canadian Broadcasting Corporation (CBC). 1500 Bronson Ave., Box 8478, Ottawa, ON K1G 3J5, Canada. (613) 724-1200. The CBC is a publicly owned corporation established in 1936 by an Act of the Canadian Parliament to provide a national broadcasting service in Canada in the two official languages. The CBC is financed mainly by public funds voted annually by Parliament.

*Canadian Education Association/Association canadienne d'education (CEA). 252 Bloor St. W., Suite 8-200, Toronto, ON M5S 1V5, Canada. (416) 924-7721. Robert E. Blair, Exec. Dir. The Canadian equivalent of the U.S. National Education Association. *Publications: CEA Handbook; Education Canada; CEA Newsletter; An Overview of Canadian Education; Women and Men in Education: A National Survey of Gender Distribution in School Systems; Marketing the School System; School Board Leave Policies; Dollars and Sense: How School Boards Save Money; Evaluation for Excellence: The Price of Quality; The Public Finance of Elementary and Secondary Education in Canada; Student Transportation in Canada: Facts and Figures; Federal Involvement in Public Education; Canada and Citizenship Education.*

Canadian Film Institute (CFI). 2 Daly, Ottawa, ON KIN 6E2, Canada. (613) 232-6727. Fax (613) 232-6315. Serge Losique, Exec. Dir. Established in 1935, the Institute promotes the study of film and television as cultural and educational forces in Canada. It distributes over 6,000 films and videos on the sciences and the visual and performing arts through the Canadian Film Institute Film Library. *Publications: The Guide to Film, Television, and Communications Studies in Canada 1989-* (bilingual); Canadian Film series (monographs); *Northern Lights* (programmer's guide to the Festival of Festivals Retrospective); *Switching on to the Environment* (critical guide).

*Canadian Library Association. 200 Elgin St., Suite 602, Ottawa, ON K2P IL5, Canada. Marnie Swanson, Pres.; Margaret Andrewes, Pres.-Elect (officers change July 1992); Karen Adams, Exec. Dir.

Canadian Museums Association/Association des musées canadiens (CMA/AMC). 280 Metcalfe St., Suite 400, Ottawa, ON K2P 1R7, Canada. (613) 233-5653. Fax (613) 233-5438. John G. McAvity, Exec. Dir. Seeks to advance public museum service in Canada. *Membership:* 2,000. *Publications: Museogramme* (mo. newsletter); *Muse* (q. journal); *Directory of Canadian Museums* (listing all museums in Canada plus information on government departments, agencies, and provincial and regional museum associations). CMA offers a correspondence course that serves as an introduction to museum operations and philosophy through selected readings.

*National Film Board of Canada (NFBC). 1251 Avenue of the Americas, New York, NY 10020. (212) 586-5131. John Sirabella, Nontheatrical Rep. Established in 1939, the NFBC's main objective is to produce and distribute high-quality audiovisual materials for educational, cultural, and social purposes. *Publication: U.S. Film Resource Guide.*

Ontario Film Association, Inc. 3-1750 The Queensway, Suite 1341, Etobicoke, ON M9C 5H5, Canada. A nonprofit organization whose primary objective is to promote the sharing of ideas and information about film and video through seminars, workshops, screenings, and publications. Sponsors the annual Grierson Documentary Seminar on film and video subjects and the Annual Showcase of film and video, a marketplace for buyers. *Publication: Visual Media/Visuels Miedias.*

Part Seven
Graduate Programs

Doctoral Programs in Instructional Technology

This directory presents information on 62 doctoral (Ph.D. and Ed.D.) programs in instructional technology, educational communications/technology, media services, and closely allied programs throughout the United States and the District of Columbia. Notification of the closing of one program is also included. Information in this section for 30 of the programs was obtained from, and updated by, the institutional deans, chairs, or their representatives, in response to an inquiry questionnaire mailed to them during the fall of 1992. Updated information was requested with the proviso that, if no reply was received, the information from the 1992 edition would be used to ensure that the program would be represented in the listing. In 30 cases, the information given is from the 1992 edition; programs for which the information was current in 1992 are indicated by one asterisk (*), and those from whom no response has been received for two or more years are indicated by two asterisks (**).

Entries provide the following data: (1) name and address of the institution; (2) chairperson or other individual in charge of the doctoral program; (3) types of degrees offered and specializations, including information on positions for which candidates are prepared; (4) special features of the degree program; (5) admission requirements, including minimal grade point average; (6) number of full-time and part-time faculty; (7) number of full-time and part-time students; (8) types of financial assistance available; and (9) the number of doctoral degrees awarded during the period between 1 July 1991 and 31 December 1992.

Directors of advanced professional programs for instructional technology/media specialists should find this information useful as a means of comparing their own offerings and requirements with those of institutions offering comparable programs. This listing should also assist individuals seeking a school at which to pursue advanced graduate studies in locating institutions that best suit their interests and requirements.

Additional information on the programs listed, including instructions on applying for admission, may be obtained by contacting individual program coordinators. General or graduate catalogs usually are furnished for a minimal charge; specific program information normally is sent at no charge.

In endeavoring to provide complete listings, we are greatly indebted to those individuals who responded to our requests for information. Although considerable effort has been expended to ensure completeness of the listings, there may be institutions within the United States or its territories that now have programs or that have been omitted. Readers are encouraged to furnish new information to the publisher who, in turn, will follow up for the next edition of *EMTY*.

Institutions in this section are listed alphabetically by state.

ALABAMA

University of Alabama. School of Library and Information Studies, The University of Alabama, Box 87052, Tuscaloosa, AL 35487-0252. (205) 348-1523. Fax (205) 348-3746. J. Gordon Coleman, Jr., Asst. Dean and Assoc. Prof., Doctoral Program, School of Library and Information Studies. *Specializations:* Ph.D. in Librarianship with specializations in library management, information studies, youth services, library media studies, historical studies. *Features:* Program is designed to fit the needs of the student using the resources of the entire university. Students may prepare for careers in teaching and research in colleges and universities or for innovative practice in the profession. *Admission Requirements:* Master's in library science, instructional technology, or equivalent; Miller Analogies score of 55 or GRE score of 1,650; 3.5 graduate GPA. *Faculty:* 10 full-time; 1 part-time. *Students:* 5 full-time; 14 part-time. *Financial Assistance:* Fellowships, assistantships, scholarships. *Doctorates Awarded 1991-92:* 2 (relatively new program).

ARIZONA

**Arizona State University. College of Education, Tempe, AZ 85287-0611. (602) 965-7485. Fax (602) 965-9144. Howard Sullivan, Prof., Div. of Psychology in Education, College of Education. *Specializations:* School offers program of study leading to the Ph.D. degree in Educational Technology. Primary content focus is on instructional design and development, with strong research emphasis. Students may complement this focus with concentrated work in such areas as instructional media, computer-based education, training, etc. Preparation is for work as university faculty and instructional designers and trainers in business, industry, the military, and higher education. *Features:* Instructional development internships in higher education or in business, industry, and the military. *Admission Requirements:* Three months prior to enrollment: all university application forms, two transcripts from each institution in which previous academic work has been completed, three letters of reference, a score report for either the Miller Analogies Test (65 or higher) or the GRE (1,200 or higher verbal plus quantitative), statement of professional goals, and undergraduate GPA of 3.0 or better. *Faculty:* 3 full-time. *Students:* 12 full-time; 12 part-time. *Financial Assistance:* Graduate assistantships; summer assistantship opportunities; fellowships; scholarships; loans administered through the university financial aid office. *Doctorates Awarded 1989-90:* 2.

CALIFORNIA

**United States International University. School of Education, San Diego, CA 92131. (619) 693-4595. *Specializations:* The Ed.D. program is designed to attract students interested in a variety of emphases: computer literacy, teaching with or about computers, computer program coordination, instructional systems development, distance education, and microcomputer management. Prepares individuals to serve in a variety of positions: school district coordinators for instructional computing, specialists in designing learning strategies and training programs, university directors of learning resources, and change agents in industry and the military having teaching or training as a primary concern. *Features:* Program involves required core courses in human behavior and futuristics; concentration courses in leadership, cognitive theory, global education, statistics; and elective specialization courses, including computer literacy, problem solving, microcomputer programming, microcomputer applications, issues in computer education, curriculum theory and design, and instructional systems development. The development of independent microcomputer use skills is emphasized. *Admission Requirements:* Admission to graduate program recommended by committee of faculty to the Dean of the School of Education. Evaluation of GRE or Miller Analogies Test score(s), candidate's vita, three letters of recommendation, statement of purpose for study, and final committee interview. *Faculty:* 15 full-time; 5 part-time. *Students:* 40 full-time; 10 part-time. *Financial Assistance:* A limited number of graduate assistantships offered in conjunction with research and development work undertaken at the university. *Doctorates Awarded 1987-88:* 8.

*University of California at Berkeley. School of Library and Information Studies, Berkeley, CA 94720. Robert Harlan, Prof., Coord., School of Library and Information Studies. *Specializations:* School offers the Ph.D. degree in library and information studies. *Features:* Ph.D. requires original piece of research revealing high critical ability and powers of imagination and synthesis. The program stresses the need for familiarity with information processing technology, educational technology, database management systems, etc. *Admission Requirements:* Contingent upon admission to graduate standing, including graduation from an accredited master's degree program with at least a B average. *Faculty:* 12 full-time. *Students:* Approx. 34. *Financial Assistance:* Scholarships, fellowships, assistantships (research and teaching), and readerships. *Doctorates Awarded 1990-91:* 2.

*University of California at Los Angeles. Department of Education, Los Angeles, CA 90024-1521. (310) 825-6608. Fax (310) 206-6293. Aimee Dorr, Prof. of Education, Learning and Instruction Specialization, Div. of Educational Psychology, Dept. of Education. *Specializations:* Offers Ph.D. and Ed.D. programs. Ph.D. program prepares graduates for research, teaching educational technology, and consultancies in the development of instructional materials. Ed.D. program prepares graduates for leadership roles in the development of instructional materials and educational technologies. *Features:* The program addresses the design and utilization principles and processes underlying all effective applications of instructional technologies and their products. Television, microcomputer-based, and multimedia systems are encouraged. *Admission Requirements:* Superior academic record, combined GRE score of 1,000 or better. For the Ed.D. program, two or more years of relevant field experience is desirable. *Faculty:* 2 full-time; 6 part-time. *Students:* 10 full-time. *Financial Assistance:* Includes fellowships, tuition remission, and some paid research and teaching assistantships. *Doctorates Awarded 1990-91:* 0.

University of Southern California. School of Education, Los Angeles, CA 90089-0031. (213) 740-3476. Fax (213) 746-8142. Edward J. Kazlauskas, Assoc. Prof., Prog. Chair, Instructional Technology. *Specializations:* M.A., Ph.D., Ed.D. to prepare individuals to teach instructional technology; manage educational media/training programs in business or industry, research and development organizations, and higher educational institutions; perform research in instructional technology and media; and deal with computer-driven technology. *Features:* Special emphasis upon instructional design, systems analysis, and computer-based training. *Admission Requirements:* A bachelor's degree and satisfactory performance (combined score of 1,000) on the GRE aptitude test. *Faculty:* 5 full-time; 1 part-time. *Students:* 10 full-time; 22 part-time. *Financial Assistance:* Part-time work available (instructional technology-related) in the Los Angeles area and on the university campus.

COLORADO

University of Colorado at Denver. School of Education, Campus Box 106, P.O. Box 173364, Denver, CO 80217-3364. (303) 556-4881. Fax (303) 556-4822. David H. Jonassen, Prof., Chair of Instructional Technology Program, School of Education. *Specializations:* Ph.D. in instructional technology, in instructional development, and/or instructional computing for use in business/industry and higher education. *Features:* Courses in management and consulting, emphasizing instructional development, interactive video technologies, evaluation, and internship opportunities in a variety of agencies. *Admission Requirements:* Satisfactory GPA, GRE, writing/publication background, letters of recommendation, transcripts, and application form.

Faculty: 5-1/2 full-time; 4 part-time. *Students:* 12 part-time; 3 full-time. *Financial Assistance:* Corporate internships are available. *Doctorates Awarded 1991-92:* 0 (relatively new program).

*University of Northern Colorado. College of Education, Greeley, CO 80639. (303) 351-2687. Fax (303) 351-2377. Edward P. Caffarella, Prof., Chair, Educational Technology, College of Education. *Specializations:* Ph.D. in Educational Technology with emphasis areas in instructional development/design, interactive technology, and technology integration. *Features:* Graduates are prepared for careers as instructional technologists, course designers, trainers, instructional developers, media specialists, and human resource managers. *Admission Requirements:* GPA of 3.2, three letters of recommendation, congruency between applicant's statement of career goals and program goals, GRE combined test score of 1,650, and interview with faculty. *Faculty:* 6 full-time; 2 part-time. *Students:* 28 doctoral, 48 M.A., 15 graduate certification. *Financial Assistance:* A limited number of Colorado Fellowships are available for fulltime incoming students; graduate and teaching assistantships are available for full-time students. *Doctorates Awarded 1990-91:* 3.

CONNECTICUT

*University of Connecticut. Storrs, CT 06269-2001. (203) 486-2530. Fax 486-1766. Phillip Sleeman, Dir., University Center for Instructional Media and Technology, and Prof. of Education. *Specializations:* Ph.D. degree program involving advanced instructional media and technology to prepare individuals for instructional technology positions of major responsibility in universities, colleges, community colleges, large school systems, state departments of education, government, industry, and other educational and media organizations of national scope. *Features:* The program seeks an optimum mix of competencies involved in solving instructional media and technology problems, with competencies in several fields of professional education (psychological foundations, social foundations, research and evaluation, business administration, curriculum and supervision, instructional media and technology, interactive video, computers, videodiscs, teleconferencing, computer graphics, and data processing). *Admission Requirements:* Admission to graduate school; undergraduate GPA above 3.0; filing of Miller Analogies Test; evidence of scholarly attainments, interests, and potential for growth; strength and validity of career motive; previous significant experience in the instructional media field; and at least five years of highly successful teaching experience (of which one or more years of administrative or supervisory experience would be desirable). *Faculty:* 2 full-time; 4 part-time. *Students:* Data not available. *Financial Assistance:* A number of graduate assistantships, predoctoral fellowships, research fellowships, and federal and minority fellowships available competitively. *Doctorates Awarded 1990-91:* 4.

FLORIDA

Florida State University. Instructional Systems Program, Department of Educational Research, College of Education, 305 Stone Bldg., Tallahassee, FL 32306. (904) 644-8785. Fax (904) 644-8776. Walter Dick, Prof. and Program Leader. *Specializations:* Ph.D. degree in instructional systems with specializations for persons planning to work in academia, business, industry, government, or military. *Features:* Core courses include systems and materials development, analysis of media, project management, psychological foundations, current trends in instructional design, and research and statistics. Internships are also required. *Admission Requirements:* Total score of 1,000 on the verbal and quantitative sections of the GRE, or a GPA of 3.0 for the last two years of undergraduate study; international students, TOEFL score of 550. *Faculty:* 6 full-time; 5 part-time. *Students:* 46 (mostly full-time).

Financial Assistance: Some graduate research assistantships on faculty grants and contracts; university fellowships. *Doctorates Awarded 1991-92:* 5.

*Nova University. Center for Computer and Information Sciences, 3301 College Ave., Fort Lauderdale, FL 33314. (800) 541-6682, ext. 1984; (305) 475-7563. Fax (305) 476-1982. Dr. Edward Simco, Dean, Center for Computer and Information Sciences. *Specializations:* Sc.D. in the areas of Information Systems, Information Science, and Training and Learning; Ed.D. in Computer Education. *Features:* Minimal residency requirements; three-year program; course requirements are completed using online interaction, institutes, regional symposia, audiobridge, videotapes, and ECs (Electronic Classroom sessions). Current students are located throughout the country and world. *Admission Requirements:* Master's degree from an accredited university, appropriate work experience and related credentials, and demonstrated computer literacy. *Faculty:* 10 full-time. *Students:* Full-time in each of the following programs: Computer Education, 116; Training and Learning, 30; Information Systems, 115; Information Science, 29; total 290. *Financial Assistance:* Guaranteed student loan program. *Doctorates Awarded 1990-91:* 17.

University of Florida. College of Education, Gainesville, FL 32611. (904) 392-0705, ext. 600; (904) 392-0705. Fax (904) 392-7159. Lee Mullally, Assoc. Prof., Chair, Educational Media and Instructional Design Program, College of Education. *Specializations:* Ph.D. and Ed.D. programs that stress theory, research, training, teaching, evaluation, and instructional development. *Admission Requirements:* A composite score of at least 1,100 on the GRE, an undergraduate GPA of 3.0 minimum and a graduate GPA of 3.5 minimum, and three letters of recommendation. *Faculty:* 2 full-time. *Students:* 16 full- and part-time. *Financial Assistance:* A few scholarships through the Graduate School. *Doctorates Awarded l991-92:* 1.

GEORGIA

Georgia State University. College of Education, Atlanta, GA 30303-3083. (404) 651-2510. Fax (404) 651-2546. Francis D. Atkinson, Coord., Instructional Technology Programs, Dept. of Curriculum and Instruction. *Specializations:* Ph.D. in Instructional Technology. *Admission Requirements:* Three letters of recommendation, handwritten and autobiographical sketch, admission tests, and acceptance by department. *Faculty:* 2 full-time; 6 part-time. *Students:* 3 full-time; 12 part-time. *Financial Assistance:* Assistantships, paid internships, student loans and grants. *Doctorates Awarded l991-92:* 0.

*University of Georgia. College of Education, 607 Aderhold Hall, Athens, GA 30602. (404) 542-3810. Fax (404) 542-2321. Murray H. Tillman, Chair, Dept. of Instructional Technology. *Specializations:* M.Ed, Ed.S., and Ed.D. for leadership positions as specialists in instructional design and development. The program offers advanced study for individuals with previous preparation in instructional media and technology, as well as a preparation for personnel in other professional fields requiring a specialty in instructional systems/instructional technology. Representative career fields for graduates include designing/developing/evaluating new courses, tutorial programs, and instructional materials in a number of different settings; military/industrial training; medical/dental/nursing professional schools; allied health agencies; teacher education/staff development centers; state/local school systems; higher education/teaching/research; and publishers/producers of instructional products (textbooks, workbooks, films, etc.). *Features:* Minor areas of study available in a variety of other departments. Personalized programs are planned around a common core of courses; practica, internships, and/or clinical experiences. Research activities include special assignments, applied projects, and task forces, as well as thesis and dissertation studies. *Admission Requirements:* Application to graduate school, satisfactory GRE score, other criteria as outlined in

Graduate School Bulletin. *Faculty:* 10 full-time. *Students:* 21 full-time. *Financial Assistance:* Graduate assistantships available. *Doctorates Awarded 1990-91:* 4.

ILLINOIS

Northern Illinois University. College of Education, DeKalb, IL 60115. (815) 753-0464. Fax (815) 753-9388. Dr. Gary L. McConeghy, Chair, Instructional Technology, College of Education—LEPS. *Specializations:* Ed.D. in Instructional Technology, emphasizing instructional design and development, computer education, media administration, production, and preparation for careers in business, industry, and higher education. *Features:* Considerable flexibility in course selection, including advanced seminars, internships, individual study, and research. Program is highly individualized. A total of 60 courses offered by several departments, including Library Science, Radio/Television/Film, Art, Journalism, Educational Psychology, and Research and Evaluation. *Admission Requirements:* 2.75 undergraduate GPA, 3.5 M.S. GPA; combined score of 1,000 on GRE; a writing sample; and three references. *Faculty:* 5 full-time; 5 part-time. *Students:* 66 part-time. *Financial Assistance:* Assistantships available at times in various departments. *Doctorates Awarded 1991-92:* 2.

Southern Illinois University. School of Education, Box 1049, Edwardsville, IL 62026. (618) 692-2328. Fax (618) 692-3359. William P. Ahlbrand, Assoc. Dean and Ed.D. Program Dir. *Specializations:* Ed.D. (all-school degree) in instructional processes emphasizing theory and research, teaching, evaluation, and instructional systems design and development. Doctoral graduates are employed in public school systems and universities, generally in the Midwest. *Admission Requirements:* GRE verbal and quantitative composite of 1020, master's GPA of B+; usually admit only 10 students per year. *Faculty:* 8 full-time. *Students:* 4 full- and part-time. *Financial Assistance:* Doctoral assistantships and Graduate School fellowships. *Doctorates Awarded 1991-92:* 6.

Southern Illinois University at Carbondale. College of Education, Carbondale, IL 62901-4610. (618) 536-2441. Fax (618) 453-1646. Billy G. Dixon, Prof., Chair, Dept. of Curriculum and Instruction, College of Education. *Specializations:* Ph.D. in education including specialization in instructional technology. *Features:* All specializations are oriented to multiple education settings. *Admission Requirements:* 3.25 GPA or better; Miller Analogies Test or GRE score; letters of recommendation; and a writing sample. *Faculty:* 5 full-time; 5 part-time. *Students:* 23. *Financial Assistance:* Six graduate scholarships available, as well as a university fellowship program. *Doctorates Awarded 1991-92:* 3.

University of Illinois at Urbana-Champaign. College of Education, Champaign, IL 61820. (217) 244-3391. Fax (217) 244-4572. J. Richard Dennis, Assoc. Prof., Dept. of Curriculum and Instruction, College of Education. *Specializations:* Ph.D., Ed.D. programs (including advanced certificate program) with emphasis in the following areas: preparation of university research faculty, materials/training designers, computer resources managers, and continuing professional teacher training. *Features:* Programs designed to accommodate individuals with diverse background preparations. *Admission Requirements:* Master's degree, 4.0 out of 5.0 GPA, GRE at least 50th percentile in two of Verbal, Quantitative, and Analytic; a sample of scholarly writing in English; TOEFL scores, including scores on Test of Written English and Test of Spoken English for non-English-speaking students. *Faculty:* 8 full- and part-time. *Students:* 15 full and parttime. *Financial Assistance:* Fellowships for very highly academically talented; assistantships for 30-40 percent; some tuition fee waivers. *Doctorates Awarded 1991-92:* 4.

University of Illinois at Urbana-Champaign. Department of Educational Psychology, 220 A Ed., 1310 S. 6th St., Champaign, IL 61820. Charles K. West, Prof., Div. of Learning and Instruction, Dept. of Educational Psychology. *Specializations:* Ph.D. in educational psychology with emphasis in educational computing. *Features:* Individually tailored program. Strongly research-oriented with emphasis on applications of cognitive science to instruction. *Admission Requirements:* Flexible: good academic record, high GRE scores, and strong letters of recommendation. *Faculty:* 17. *Students:* 36. *Financial Assistance:* Scholarships, research assistantships, and teaching assistantships available. *Doctorates Awarded 1991-92:* 6.

INDIANA

**Indiana University. School of Education, Bloomington, IN 47405. (812) 855-1791. Fax (812) 855-3044. Charles Reigeluth, Prof., Chair, Dept. of Instructional Systems Technology, School of Education. *Specializations:* Offers Ph.D. and Ed.D. degrees. *Features:* Three major emphasis areas—instructional design and development, message design and production, and organizational change. Students draw on all areas when planning their academic programs. Virtually all students are full-time residents. Many opportunities for students to combine practice with study by working in the AV center and other appropriate agencies on and off campus. *Admission Requirements:* Satisfactory GPA, verbal, quantitative, and analytical sections of the GRE. *Faculty:* 10 full-time equivalent. *Students:* Approximately 100 doctoral students, 83 master's students. *Financial Assistance:* Graduate assistantships, associate instructorships, fellowships, scholarships, and fee remissions. *Doctorates Awarded 1988-89:* 8.

Purdue University. School of Education, W. Lafayette, IN 47907-1442. (317) 494-5673. Fax (317) 494-0587. James D. Russell, Prof. of Educational Computing and Instructional Development, Dept. of Curriculum and Instruction. *Specializations:* Ph.D. programs in instructional research and development or educational computing. *Admission Requirements:* GPA of 3.0 or better, three recommendations, scores totaling 1,000 or more on the GRE, statement of personal goals. *Faculty:* 6 full-time. *Students:* 9 full-time; 24 part-time. *Financial Assistance:* Assistantships and fellowships. *Doctorates Awarded 1991-92:* 9.

IOWA

Iowa State University. College of Education, Ames, IA 50011. (515) 294-6840. Fax (515) 294-9284. Michael Simonson, Prof., Curriculum and Instruction Dept., College of Education. *Specializations:* Ph.D. in education with emphasis in curriculum and instructional technology. *Features:* Practicum experiences related to professional objectives, supervised study and research projects tied to long-term studies within the program, development and implementation of new techniques, teaching strategies, and operational procedures in instructional resources centers and four computer labs. *Admission Requirements:* Top half of undergraduate class, autobiography, three letters of recommendation, GRE general test scores. *Faculty:* 3 full-time; 3 part-time. *Students:* 21 full-time; 20 part-time. *Financial Assistance:* 10 assistantships. *Doctorates Awarded 1991-92:* 5.

*University of Iowa. College of Education, Iowa City, IA 52242. (319) 335-5577. Fax (319) 335-5386. Leonard S. Feldt, Prof., Psychological and Quantitative Foundations, College of Education. *Specializations:* Computer applications, instructional development, training and human resource development. *Features:* Flexibility in planning to fit individual needs, backgrounds, and career goals. The program is interdisciplinary, involving courses within divisions of the College of Education, as well as in the schools of Business, Library Science, Radio and Television, Linguistics, and Psychology. *Admission Requirements:* A composite score of at least 1,000 on GRE (verbal and quantitative) and a 3.2 GPA on all previous graduate work for regular admission. (Conditional admission may be granted.) Teaching or relevant experience may be helpful. *Faculty:* 4 fulltime; 3 parttime. *Students:* 40 full- and part-time. *Financial Assistance:* Special assistantships (in the College of Education) for which students in any College of Education program may compete. Application deadlines for the special assistantships is 1 February. *Doctorates Awarded 1990-91:* 6.

KANSAS

Kansas State University. College of Education, Manhattan, KS 66506-5301. (913) 532-5556. Fax (913) 532-7304. Jackson Byars, Prof., Dept. of Educational Media and Technology, College of Education. *Specializations:* Ph.D. and Ed.D. program. This program is offered on a semester basis and requires 90 credit hours, including 60 in media and technology, one year of residency, and a dissertation. *Faculty:* 4, 0, 6. *Students:* 26. *Financial Assistance:* Data not available. *Doctorates Awarded 1987-88:* 8.

University of Kansas. Instructional Technology Center, Lawrence, KS 66045. (913) 864-3057. Ronald Aust, Asst. Prof., Curriculum and Instruction, Dir., Instructional Technology Center. *Specializations:* Ph.D., Ed.D., and Ed.S., and M.S. to prepare instructional technologists to serve in leadership roles in a variety of educational settings. Emphasis is on the use of research-based data to guide decision making in the various roles required of instructional technologists. Special attention is given to the principles of and procedures for designing instruction with computers, video, interactive video, and distance-learning applications. *Features:* The Instructional Technology Center provides a laboratory setting to assist in research projects and in the acquisition of production, instructional development, and media management skills. The department's microcomputer laboratories provide access to current equipment and software. Students are encouraged to work with faculty on appropriate projects. In addition to a common core, flexibility is built into the program so students may pursue their own interests. *Admission Requirements:* Regular admission, 3.5 GPA and 900 GRE; Provisional, 3.25 GPA and 900 GRE or 3.5 GPA with less than 900 GRE. *Faculty:* 3. *Students:* 5 full-time; 12 part-time. *Financial Assistance:* 4 graduate teaching assistantships (apply by 1 March). *Doctorates Awarded 1988-89:* 3.

KENTUCKY

University of Kentucky. College of Education, Lexington, KY 40506. (606) 257-4661. Gary Anglin, Assoc. Prof., Dept. of Curriculum and Instruction, College of Education. *Specializations:* Ed.D. program emphasizing instructional design/instructional technology, research, and teaching. *Features:* Data not available. *Admission Requirements:* A minimum composite score (verbal and quantitative) of 1,000 on the GRE, minimum undergraduate GPA of 2.5, minimum graduate GPA of 3.4. Concurrent applications to the graduate school and department are required, including letters of recommendation. *Faculty:* 2 full-time. *Students:* 12. *Financial Assistance:* A limited number of teaching associateships and research assistantships are awarded on a competitive basis. Applicants for available minority fellowships are encouraged. *Financial Assistance:* Package includes tuition remission. *Doctorates Awarded 1988-89:* 0.

MARYLAND

**The Johns Hopkins University. School of Continuing Studies, Baltimore, MD 21218. (301) 338-8273. Fax (301) 338-8424. Diane Tobin, Coord., Div. of Education, School of Continuing Studies. *Specializations:* Ed.D. in human communications and its disorders—a dual-major degree in technology and one of the following areas: mild-moderate handicapped and severely/profoundly handicapped. The program requires 99 semester hours beyond the baccalaureate, including 12 hours of dissertation research and 27 hours in computers and related rehabilitation educational technology. (A master's level program is also offered.) *Features:* Computer courses, including but not limited to assistive technology, authoring programs and systems, LOGO, interactive videodisc, hardware and adaptive devices, software selection/evaluation, expert systems, robotics, networking, and computerized information and data management in special education. Internships and practicum opportunities in special education and rehabilitation settings. *Admission Requirements:* Master's or doctorate from an accredited institution. *Faculty:* 3 full-time; 12 part-time. *Students:* 30 full- and part-time. *Financial Assistance:* Data not available. *Doctorates Awarded 1989-90:* 1.

University of Maryland. College of Library and Information Services, College Park, MD 20742-4345. (301) 405-2038. Fax (301) 314-9145. Diane Barlow, Dir., Student Services, College of Library and Information Services. *Specializations:* Ph.D. in Library Science and Educational Technology/Instructional Communication. *Features:* Program is broadly conceived and interdisciplinary in nature, using the resources of the entire campus. The student and the advisor design a program of study and research to fit the student's background, interests, and professional objectives. Students prepare for careers in teaching and research in information science and librarianship and elect concentrations including educational technology/instructional communication. *Admission Requirements:* Baccalaureate degree (the majority enter with master's degrees in library science, educational technology, or other relevant disciplines), GRE general tests, three letters of recommendation, and a statement of purpose. Interviews required when feasible. *Faculty:* 15 full-time; 16 part-time. *Students:* 20 full-time. *Financial Assistance:* Some fellowships starting at $8,800, with remission of tuition; some assistantships also available. *Doctorates Awarded 1991-92:* 0.

MASSACHUSETTS

Boston University. School of Education, 605 Commonwealth Ave., Boston, MA 02215. (617) 353-3519. Fax (617) 353-3924. Gaylen B. Kelley, Prof., Chair, Program in Educational Media and Technology, School of Education. *Specializations:* Ed.D. specializing in instructional design/development for developing and teaching academic programs in instructional technology in community colleges and universities; or specialization in such application areas as business and industrial training, biomedical communication, or international development projects. Program specializations in instructional development, media production and design, and instructional facilities design for media and technology. Students participate in mandatory research sequence and may elect courses in other university schools and colleges. *Features:* Doctoral students have a great deal of flexibility in program planning and are encouraged to plan programs that build on prior education and experience that lead to specific career goals; there is strong faculty participation in this process. *Admission Requirements:* Three letters of recommendation, Miller Analogies Test or GRE test score(s), undergraduate and graduate transcripts, completed application form with statement of goals. Minimum GPA is 2.7 with Miller Analogies Test score of 50. *Faculty:* 1 full-time; 3 associates; 7 part-time. *Students:* 12 full-time; 65 part-time. *Financial Assistance:* Some assistantships and fellowships. *Doctorates Awarded 1991-92:* 11.

MICHIGAN

**Michigan State University. College of Education, East Lansing, MI 48824. (517) 355-8538. Fax (517) 354-6393. Leighton A. Price, Prof., Coord. of the Educational Systems Development Program in the Dept. of Counseling, Educational Psychology and Special Education. *Specializations:* Ph.D. and Ed.D. to prepare individuals to improve the quality and effectiveness of instructional delivery systems, to improve learning at all educational and training levels, and to serve as instructional developers and highly qualified training personnel. Emphasis is given to systems design and analysis, to selection and evaluation of instructional computing and other educational technologies, to design and validation of instructional materials, and to research on attributes of teaching strategies and supporting technologies. *Features:* Individually designed doctoral programs, guided field experience in instructional design projects, and cognitive work in areas such as communication, higher education, or instructional resource management. *Admission Requirements:* Master's degree with an acceptable academic record, transcripts, teaching credentials (preferred), three letters of recommendation, acceptable verbal and quantitative GRE scores, statement describing professional goals and ways that the doctoral program may contribute to achievement, and a personal interview. *Faculty:* 9 full-time; 1 part-time. *Students:* 15 Ph.D. candidates. *Financial Assistance:* Some fellowship and graduate assistantship opportunities in instructional development and technology. *Doctorates Awarded 1987-88:* 3.

**University of Michigan. Department of Educational Studies. Ann Arbor, MI 48109-1259. (313) 747-0612. Fax (313) 763-1229. Patricia Baggett, Assoc. Prof., Chair, Computers and Education. *Specializations:* M.A., Ed.D., and joint M.A. and Ph.D. with the Computer Science Department. *Faculty:* 2 full-time; several partial appointments. *Students:* Approx. 15.

*Wayne State University. College of Education, Detroit, MI 48202. (313) 577-1728. Fax (313) 577-3606. Rita C. Richey, Prof., Program Coord., Instructional Technology Programs, Div. of Administrative and Organizational Studies, College of Education. *Specializations:* Ed.D. and Ph.D. programs to prepare individuals for leadership in business, industry, health care, and the K-12 school setting as instructional development specialists; media or learning resources managers or consultants; specialists in instructional video; and computer-assisted specialists. *Features:* Guided field experience and participation in instructional development activities in business and industry. *Admission Requirements:* Master's, GPA of 3.5, GRE, and Miller Analogies Test, strong professional recommendations, and an interview. *Faculty:* 3 full-time; 5 part-time. *Students:* 135 full- and part-time. *Financial Assistance:* Contract industrial internships, university scholarships. *Doctorates Awarded 1990-91:* 15.

MINNESOTA

University of Minnesota. College of Education, Minneapolis, MN 55455. (612) 624-2034. Fax (612) 626-7496. Gregory C. Sales, Assoc. Prof., Curriculum and Instructional Systems, College of Education. *Specializations:* Ph.D. in Education is offered through the graduate school. Areas of study include instructional design and technology, computer-based instruction, and instruction research. *Features:* Internships and special field experiences. *Admission Requirements:* 3.0 GPA, Miller Analogies Test 60 or higher, GRE (required as of 9/93). *Faculty:* 2.5 full-time; 1 part-time. *Students:* 115 full- and part-time. *Financial Assistance:* Determined on an individual basis. *Doctorates Awarded 1991-92:* 4.

MISSOURI

**University of Missouri-Columbia. College of Education, Columbia, MO 65211. (314) 882-3832. Fax (314) 882-5071. John F. Wedman, Assoc. Prof., Educational Technology Program, Curriculum and Instruction Dept., College of Education. *Specializations:* Ph.D. and Ed.D. programs to prepare individuals for positions in higher education and instructional development positions in both industry and the military. *Features:* Program deals with educational computing, instructional design, and media development. Support areas, such as communications and management, are integrated with educational technology courses to form a degree plan that is both focused and broad-based. An internship experience, in a setting consistent with the career goals of the student, is also included. *Admission Requirements:* Graduate GPA above 3.5 and a combined score of 1,350 or better on the GRE or a graduate GPA of 3.2 and a combined score of 1,500 or better on the GRE. Minimum of two years of appropriate professional experience, letters of recommendation, and statement of purpose. A TOEFL score of 550 or better is required for students whose native language is not English. *Faculty:* 3 full-time; 3 part-time, plus selected faculty in interdisciplinary fields. *Students:* 14 students are currently active in the doctoral program. *Financial Assistance:* Scholarships and fellowships, ranging from $200 to $8,000, available from several sources. Teaching and research assistantships available to qualifed individuals. Special financial support available for minority and foreign national students. *Doctorates Awarded 1989-90:* 2.

NEBRASKA

University of Nebraska. Teachers College, Lincoln, NE 68588-0515. (402) 472-2018. Fax (402) 472-8317. E-mail: dbrooks@unlinfo.unl.edu. David Brooks, Prof., Coord., Teachers College. *Specializations and Features:* Ph.D. and Ed.D. programs are in administration, curriculum, and instruction with an emphasis in instructional technology (IT). Students in these programs demonstrate competencies for professions in instructional design, research in IT, and training by developing appropriate portfolios. Within the context of a balanced graduate experience in IT, extensive experiences in the use of CD-ROM technologies are possible. *Admission Requirements:* Admission standards are set by the graduate college. *Faculty:* 3 full-time faculty teach in the IT program; 5 are involved in CD-ROM design and production. *Financial Assistance:* Scholarship and externally based funding support available. *Doctorates Awarded 1991-92:* 1.

NEW JERSEY

Rutgers-The State University of New Jersey. The Graduate School, New Brunswick, NJ 08903. (908) 932-7447. Fax (908) 932-6916. Brent D. Ruben, Prof., Dir., Ph.D. Program in Communication, Information and Library Studies, The Graduate School. *Specializations:* Ph.D. programs in communication; information and communication in management and organizational processes; information systems, structures, and users; information and communication policy and technology; and library and information services. *Features:* Program provides doctoral-level coursework for students seeking theoretical and research skills for scholarly and professional leadership in the information and communication fields. *Admission Requirements:* Typically, students should have completed a master's degree in information studies, communication, library science, or related field. The undergraduate GPA should be 3.0 or better. The GRE is required; TOEFL is also required for foreign applicants whose native language is not English. *Faculty:* 42 full- and part-time. *Students:* 96 full- and part-time. *Financial Assistance:* Assistantships and Title II-B fellowships. *Doctorates Awarded 1991-92:* 5.

NEW YORK

**Columbia University. Teachers College, New York, NY 10027. (212) 678-3344. Fax (212) 678-4048. John B. Black, Prof. and Chair. *Specializations:* Ed.D. for individuals seeking careers in instructional technology; programs in instructional technology (in a department that also includes communication and computing in education). *Features:* Part-time employment is available and encouraged as part of the coursework of 90 semester hours (in addition to the dissertation). Programs are individually planned, interdisciplinary, and based on prior and present interests and anticipated future developments in instructional technology. Up to 45 credits of relevant coursework may be transferred. *Admission Requirements:* A record of outstanding capability, potential for leadership and creativity as indicated from academic records, recommendations, score on the GRE, statement of express interest and future plans. *Faculty:* 5 full-time; 2 part-time. *Students:* 12 full-time; 32 part-time. *Financial Assistance:* Limited scholarships (applications must be received before 1 January for the following September semester) and work-study financial aid for qualified applicants. *Doctorates Awarded 1987-88:* 3.

New York University. School of Education, New York, NY 10003. (212) 998-5177. Fax (212) 995-4041. Francine Shuchat Shaw, Assoc. Prof., Dir., Educational Communication and Technology Program; Donald T. Payne, Assoc. Prof., Doctoral Advisor, Educational Communication and Technology Program, 239 Greene St., Suite 300, School of Education. *Specializations:* Ph.D., Ed.D. in education for the preparation of individuals to perform as instructional media designers, developers, and producers in education, business and industry, health and medicine, community services, government, and other fields; to coordinate media communications programs in educational television centers, museums, schools, corporations, health and medicine, and community organizations; to serve as directors and supervisors in audiovisual programs in all settings listed; and to teach in educational communications and instructional technology programs in higher education. *Features:* Emphasizes theoretical foundations, in particular a cognitive perspective of learning and instruction and their implications for designing media-based learning environments; participation in special research and production projects in multi-image, television, microcomputers, and computer-based interactive multimedia systems. *Admission Requirements:* Combined score of 1,000 minimum on GRE, interview related to academic and/or professional preparation and career goals. *Faculty:* 2 full-time; 10 part-time. *Students:* 15 full-time; 35 part-time. *Financial Assistance:* Several graduate and research assistantships and some financial aid and work-study programs. *Doctorates Awarded 1991-92:* 3.

State University of New York at Buffalo. Graduate School of Education, Buffalo, NY 14214. (716) 636-3164. Fax (716) 645-2481. Taher A. Razik, Prof. of Education, Dept. of Educational Organization, Administration and Policy, 480 Baldy Hall. *Specializations:* Ph.D., Ed.D., and Ed.M. in instructional design systems and management. Emphasis is on the systems approach, communication, and computer-assisted instruction and model building, with a specific focus on the efficient implementation of media in instruction. *Features:* The program is geared to instructional development, systems analysis, systems design and management in educational and noneducational organizations; research is oriented to the analysis of communication and information theory. Laboratories are available to facilitate student and faculty research projects in educational and/or training settings. Specifically, the knowledges and skills are categorized as follows: planning and designing; delivery systems and managing; and evaluating. *Admission Requirements:* Satisfactory scores on the Miller Analogies Test and/or GRE, minimum 3.0 GPA, sample of student writing, and personal interview. *Faculty:* 3 full-time; 3 part-time. *Students:* 25 full- and part-time. *Financial Assistance:* Some graduate assistantships and various fellowships (apply by March 10). *Doctorates Awarded 1991-92:* 3.

Syracuse University. School of Education, Syracuse, NY 13244-2340. (315) 443-3703. Fax (315) 443-5732. Philip L. Doughty, Prof., Chair, Instructional Design, Development, and Evaluation Program, School of Education. *Specializations:* Ph.D. and Ed.D. degree programs for instructional design of programs and materials, educational evaluation, human issues in instructional development, media production (including computers and videodisc), and educational research and theory (learning theory, application of theory, and educational and media research). Graduates are prepared to serve as curriculum developers, instructional developers, program and product evaluators, researchers, resource center administrators, communications coordinators, trainers in human resource development, and higher education instructors. *Features:* Field work and internships, special topics and special issues seminar, student- and faculty-initiated minicourses, seminars and guest lecturers, faculty-student formulation of department policies, and multiple international perspectives. *Admission Requirements:* A master's degree from an accredited institution and GRE (V, Q & A) scores. *Faculty:* 5 full-time; 4 part-time. *Students:* 39 full-time; 37 part-time. *Financial Assistance:* Some fellowships, scholarships, and graduate assistantships entailing either research or administrative duties in instructional technology. *Doctorates Awarded 1991-92:* 4.

OHIO

*Kent State University. Instructional Technology Program, White Hall 405, KSU, Kent, OH 44242. (216) 672-2294. Fax (216) 672-3407. Dr. David Dalton, Prog. Coord. *Specializations:* Ph.D. in educational psychology with courses in research methods, new technologies, instructional design, production, and evaluation of media programming, change strategies, etc. *Features:* Program encourages students to take elective courses in relevant departments in the College of Education and across the university (for example, in communications, psychology, technology, etc.). *Admission Requirements:* Obtain a doctoral program application packet from the Graduate School of Education, White Hall 306. Send two completed copies of the application, a $10 application fee, transcripts, five letters of recommendation (at least two from previous instructors), score on one of the following: Miller Analogies Test, Terman Concept Mastery Test, or GRE. *Faculty:* 4. *Financial Assistance:* Graduate assistantships and teaching assistantships available. *Graduates:* A few each year.

The Ohio State University. College of Education, Columbus, OH 43210. (614) 292-4872. Fax (614) 292-7900. Marjorie Cambre, Assoc. Prof., Instructional Design and Technology Program, College of Education. *Specializations:* Ph.D. in Instructional and Interactive Technologies, within the program area of Instructional Design and Technology, for the preparation of individuals to perform research and to teach in higher education, administer comprehensive media services, or engage in research, production, and development of leadership functions in higher education and related educational agencies. *Features:* Interdisciplinary work in other departments (journalism, communications, radio and television, computer and information science); individual design of doctoral programs according to candidate's background, experience, and goals; and internships provided on campus in business and industry and in schools; integrated school media laboratory, microcomputer, and videodisc laboratories. *Admission Requirements:* Admission to graduate school and specific program area in the College of Education, GRE general test (Ph.D. only), minimum 2.7 GPA, and satisfactory academic and professional recommendations. *Faculty:* 6 full-time; 1 part-time. *Students:* 20 full-time, 7 part-time. *Financial Assistance:* Some assistantships. *Doctorates Awarded 1991-92:* 5.

The Ohio State University. College of the Arts, Department of Art Education, 340 Hopkins Hall, 128 North Oval Mall, Columbus, OH 43210. (614) 292-0259. Fax (614) 292-4401. Dr. Tony Scott, Prog. Coord., Program in Electronic Media in Art Education. *Specializations:* Ph.D. in Art Education with specialization in the teaching and learning of computer graphics and computer-mediated art; multimedia production and its curricular implications; electronic networking in the arts; multicultural aspects of computing; hypermedia applications for teaching and art education research; and the application of computing to arts administration, galleries, and museums. *Features:* Students with previous experience in computing in the arts or art education will be eligible for consideration for membership in The Advanced Computing Center for the Arts and Design (ACCAD), an interdisciplinary research center within the College of the Arts. The program will also be closely linked with The Wexner Center for the Arts on the Ohio State campus. Students may study the application of computing to art education in concert with one of the other specialties offered by the Department of Art Education: Studies in the teaching of art criticism, art history and aesthetics; multicultural and cross-cultural approaches to art education; classroom-based research in art education; the professional development of art teachers, and arts administration. *Faculty:* 2 full-time in specialty; 14 in department. *Students:* 12 full-time. *Financial Assistance:* Graduate teaching associate positions that carry tuition and fee waivers and pay a monthly stipend; various fellowship programs for applicants with high GRE scores. *Doctorates Awarded 1991-92:* 0 (new program).

University of Toledo. College of Education and Allied Professions, Toledo, OH 43606-3390. (419) 537-3846. Fax (419) 537-3853. Amos C. Patterson, Prof., Dir. of Academic Programs, College of Education and Allied Professions. *Specializations:* Ph.D. and Ed.D. *Features:* Research and theory in the areas of instructional design, development, evaluation, computers, video, and training and human resources development. Emphasis is in the empirical study of systematic processes in instructional technology. Residency requirement of one year or three full-time summer quarters, depending on Ph.D. or Ed.D. option. Option of one or two minor areas of study to be included in total program hours. *Admission Requirements:* GRE score of 1,000, combined totals, Miller Analogies Test at or above 50th percentile, three letters of recommendation, official transcripts of undergraduate and graduate work, and autobiographical details. *Faculty:* 7 full-time, 2 part-time. *Students:* 13 full-time; 14 part-time. *Financial Assistance:* Graduate assistantships for research and teaching, Board of Trustee scholarships and grants (tuition only). *Doctorates Awarded 1991-92:* 7.

OKLAHOMA

*Oklahoma State University. College of Education, Stillwater, OK 74078. (405) 744-7125. Fax (405) 744-7713. Bruce Petty, Coord., Dept. of Curriculum and Instruction, College of Education. *Specializations:* M.S. and Ed.D. programs in educational technology: microcomputers, media management/administration, materials production, utilization/application, theory and research, selection, college teaching, evaluation, instructional systems design, instructional development, curriculum foundations, and learning theory. *Admission Requirements:* Minimum of 3.0 GPA on undergraduate work (master's), Miller Analogies Test, and minimum of one year teaching experience (doctorate). *Faculty:* 2 full-time; 2 part-time. *Students:* 14 full-time, 18 part-time M.S. candidates; 8 full-time, 12 part-time Ed.D. candidates. *Financial Assistance:* 8 graduate assistantships. *Doctorates Awarded 1990-91:* 1.

University of Oklahoma. Department of Educational Psychology, 820 Van Vleet Oval, Norman, OK 73019-0260. (405) 325-5974. Fax (405) 325-3242. Raymond B. Miller, Prog. Area Coord., Dept. of Educational Psychology. *Specializations:* Ph.D. in instructional psychology and technology. *Features:* The program is built around a core of learning and cognition, instructional design, and research methods. Students' programs are tailored to their professional goals within the areas of emphasis within instructional psychology and technology, e.g., instructional design, computer applications, management of technology programs. *Admission Requirements:* A minimum of 3.25 GPA in all graduate work or 3.0 in the last 60 hours of undergraduate work, GRE scores, three letters of recommendation. *Faculty:* 10 full-time; 2 part-time. *Financial Assistance:* Assistantships, out-of-state fee waivers, graduate scholarships (both general and targeted minorities). *Doctorates Awarded 1991-92:* 1.

OREGON

University of Oregon. Division of Teacher Education, Eugene, OR 97401. This program was closed August 30, 1992, because of statewide budget cuts in higher education.

PENNSYLVANIA

Pennsylvania State University. 270 Chambers Bldg., University Park, PA 16802. (814) 865-0473. Fax (814) 865-3315. D. W. Johnson, Prof. in Charge. *Specializations:* Ph.D. and Ed.D. in instructional systems design, development, management, evaluation, and research in instructional endeavors within business, industrial, medical, health, religious, higher education, and public school settings. Present research emphases are on instructional development, dissemination, implementation, and management; interactive video; computer-based education; and visual learning. *Features:* A common thread throughout all programs is that candidates have basic competencies in the understanding of human learning; curriculum; instructional design, development, and evaluation; and research procedures. Practical experience is available in mediated independent learning, research, instructional development, computer-based education, and dissemination projects. *Admission Requirements:* GRE or Miller Analogies Test, TOEFL, transcript, two letters of recommendation. *Faculty:* 6 full-time; 2 affiliates; 2 part-time. *Students:* Approx. 260 full- and part-time. *Financial Assistance:* Some assistantships, graduate fellowships, student aid loans. *Doctorates Awarded 1991-92:* 10.

**Temple University. College of Educational Media Program, College of Education, Department of Curriculum, Instruction and Technology, Philadelphia, PA 19122. (215) 787-6001. Elton Robertson, Prof., Dept. of Educational Media. *Specializations:* Ed.D. in Curriculum, Instruction, and Technology with emphasis in educational media for proficiency in employing instructional technology to enhance learning and teaching at elementary, secondary, and university levels, as well as in industrial training situations. *Features:* The program is designed to take into account the candidate's personal and professional goals. Practical experience is provided for those wishing to (1) teach media-related courses, (2) apply the newer interactive technology to enhance the instructional development process, and (3) function in various administrative roles in support of learning resource and instructional resource centers. *Admission Requirements:* Bachelor's degree, master's degree, or 24 credits in educational media, admission to the graduate school, media experience, and a satisfactory interview with the faculty. *Faculty:* 2 full-time. *Students:* 3 full-time; 27 part-time. *Financial Assistance:* 4 departmental assistantships, fellowships. *Doctorates Awarded 1989-90:* 4.

*University of Pittsburgh. School of Education, Pittsburgh, PA 15260. (412) 612-7254. Fax (412) 648-5911. Barbara Seels, Assoc. Prof., Prog. Coord., Program in Instructional Design and Technology, Dept. of Instruction and Learning, School of Education. *Specializations:* Ed.D. and M.Ed. programs for the preparation of instructional technologists with skills in designing, developing, using, evaluating, and managing processes and resources for learning. Certification option for instructional technologists available. *Features:* Program prepares people for positions in which they can effect educational change through instructional technology. Program includes three competency areas: instructional design, technological delivery systems, and communications research. *Admissions Requirements:* Submission of written statement of applicant's professional goals, three letters of recommendation, demonstration of English proficiency, satisfactory GPA, sample of professional writing, GRE, and personal interviews. *Faculty:* 3 ful-ltime. *Students:* 20 full-time, 40 part-time. *Financial Assistance:* Tuition scholarships and assistantships may be available. *Doctorates Awarded 1990-91:* 11.

TENNESSEE

*Memphis State University. College of Education, Memphis, TN 38152. (901) 678-2365. Fax (901) 678-4778. Thomas Rakes, Prof., Chair, Dept. of Curriculum and Instruction. *Specializations:* Ed.D. offered in instructional design with career emphasis in schools, health care, and business and industry. *Features:* Internship, special projects, and research opportunities. *Admission Requirements:* Master's degree or equivalent and acceptable GRE scores. *Faculty:* 3 full-time; 2 part-time. *Students:* Data not available. *Financial Assistance:* Assistantships. *Doctorates Awarded 1990-91:* 5.

University of Tennessee. College of Education, Department of Curriculum and Instruction, Knoxville, TN 37996-3400. Dr. Al Grant, Coord., Instructional Media and Technology Program. *Specializations:* M.S. in Ed. and Ed.S. in the Department of Curriculum and Instruction, concentration in Instructional Media and Technology; Ph.D., College of Education, concentration in Instructional Media and Technology, Ed.D. in Curriculum and Instruction, concentration in Instructional Media and Technology. *Features:* Coursework in media management, advanced software production, utilization, research, theory, psychology, instructional computing, television, and instructional development. Coursework will also meet the requirements for state certification as Instructional Materials Supervisor in the public schools of Tennessee. *Admission Requirements:* Send for the Graduate Catalog, The University of Tennessee. *Media Faculty:* 1 full-time, with additional assistance from Curriculum and Instruction and university faculty. *Doctorates Awarded 1991-92:* 0.

TEXAS

*East Texas State University. Department of Secondary and Higher Education, Commerce, TX 75429. (903) 886-5504. Fax (903) 886-5039. Ron Johnson, Coord, Dept. of Secondary and Higher Education. *Specializations:* Ed.D. is offered for individuals interested in emphasizing educational technology within the broad area of supervision, curriculum, and instruction; master's degree with majors in educational technology or library science is offered. Programs are designed to prepare professionals in instructional design, production of instructional materials, and teaching and leadership in public schools and higher education. *Features:* Programs are designed to meet professional goals of individuals. Opportunities are provided for practical applications through internships, practicums, and assistantships. *Admission Requirements:* Satisfactory GPA and GRE score, evidence of literary and expository skills and aptitudes, and recommendations. *Faculty:* 8 full-time; 2 part-time.

Texas A&M University. College of Education, College Station, TX 77843. (409) 845-7276. Fax (409) 845-9663. Ronald D. Zellner, Assoc. Prof., Coord., Educational Technology Program, College of Education. *Specializations:* Ph.D. and Ed.D. programs to prepare individuals to teach college and university courses in educational technology, manage learning resource centers, and apply educational technology skills and knowledge in various settings related to communication and instructional processes in higher education, public education, business and industry, and public and private agencies. *Features:* The doctoral programs are flexible and interdisciplinary; degrees are established and granted in conjunction with the Department of Curriculum and Instruction and other departments in the College of Education; specialization areas include computer applications (CAI, CMI, interactive video), media, and video production; program provides laboratories, equipment, and a PBS television station. *Admission Requirements:* GPA 3.0, GRE 800. *Faculty:* 4 full-time; 1 part-time. *Students:* 4 full-time; 1 part-time. *Financial Assistance:* Several teaching assistantships. *Doctorates Awarded 1991-92:* 1.

The University of Texas. College of Education, Austin, TX 78712. (512) 471-5211. Fax (512) 471-4607. DeLayne Hudspeth, Assoc. Prof., Area Coord., Instructional Technology, Dept. of Curriculum and Instruction, College of Education. *Specializations:* Ph.D. program emphasizes research, design, and development of instructional systems and communications technology. *Features:* The program is interdisciplinary in nature, although certain competencies are required of all students. Programs of study and dissertation research are based on individual needs and career goals. Learning resources include a model LRC, computer labs and class-rooms, a color television studio, interactive multimedia lab, and access to a photo and graphics lab. *Admission Requirements:* Minimum 3.0 GPA and a score of at least 1,100 on the GRE. *Faculty:* 4 full-time; 3 part-time. Many courses are offered cooperatively by other departments, including Radio-TV Film, Computer Science, and Educational Psychology. *Students:* 31. *Financial Assistance:* Assistantships are available in planning and developing instructional materials, teaching undergraduate computer literacy, and assisting with research in instructional technology; there are also some paid internships. *Doctorates Awarded 1991-92:* 8.

UTAH

*Brigham Young University. Department of Instructional Science, Provo, UT 84602. (801) 378-5097. Fax (801) 378-4017. Paul F. Merrill, Prof., Chair. *Specializations:* M.S. and Ph.D. degrees are offered in instructional science and technology. In the M.S. program, students may specialize in instructional design and production, computers in education, or research and evaluation. In the Ph.D. program, students may specialize in instructional design, instructional psychology, or research and evaluation. *Features:* Course offerings include principles of learning, instructional design, assessing learning outcomes, evaluation in education, empirical inquiry in education, project and instructional resource management, quantitative reasoning, microcomputer materials production, naturalistic inquiry, and more. Students are required to participate in internships and projects related to development, evaluation, measurement, and research. *Admission Requirements:* For further information, write to Dr. Paul F. Merrill at the preceding address. *Faculty:* 10 full-time. *Students:* 20 M.S., 40 Ph.D. *Doctorates Awarded 1989-90:* 6.

Utah State University. College of Education, Logan, UT 84322-2830. (801) 750-2694. Fax (801) 750-2693. Don C. Smellie, Prof., Chair, Dept. of Instructional Technology, College of Education. *Specializations:* Ph.D. in Educational Technology. Offered for individuals seeking to become professionally involved in instructional development in corporate education, public schools, community colleges, and universities. Teaching and research in higher education is another career avenue for graduates of the program. *Features:* The doctoral program is built on a strong master's and specialist's program in instructional technology. All doctoral students complete a core with the remainder of the course selection individualized, based upon career goals. *Admission Requirements:* 3.0 GPA, successful teaching experience or its equivalent, a combined verbal and quantitative score of 1,100 on the GRE, written recommendations, and a personal interview. *Faculty:* 9 full-time; 7 part-time. *Students:* 120 M.S./M.Ed. candidates; 5 Ed.S. candidates; 24 Ph.D. candidates. *Financial Assistance:* Approximately 18 to 26 assistantships (apply by June 1). *Doctorates Awarded 1991-92:* 3.

VIRGINIA

*University of Virginia. Curry School of Education, Charlottesville, VA 22903. (804) 924-7471. Fax (804) 924-0747. John B. Bunch, Assoc. Prof. of Education, Dept. of Educational Studies, School of Education. *Specializations:* Ed.D. or Ph.D. program for well-qualified students seeking professional training in the design, production, and evaluation of instructional programs and materials in school or nonschool settings. Students may also work with faculty to conduct research on the effective uses of technology for instruction or information exchange. Graduates are placed as instructional developers or media specialists in education, as training developers in business, industry, or government agencies, or as university faculty. *Features:* A relatively small program that enables the department to tailor programs to the needs and goals of individual students (including options of minor area concentrations in other professional schools). Specializations are available in interactive technologies (a multimedia approach employing computer, compact disc, and videodisc-based materials), or media production (including video and photography). *Admission Requirements:* Satisfactory performance on GRE, written recommendations, and a personal interview. *Faculty:* 3 full-time. *Students:* 15 full-time; 25 part-time. *Financial Assistance:* A number of graduate assistantships are available as well as a limited number of fellowships (application must be made prior to April 1). *Doctorates Awarded 1990-91:* 4.

Virginia Polytechnic Institute and State University. College of Education, Blacksburg, VA 24061-0313. (703) 231-5598. Fax (703) 231-3717. Thomas M. Sherman, Prog. Area Leader, Instructional Systems Development, Curriculum and Instruction. *Specializations:* Ed.D. and Ph.D. in Instructional Technology. Preparation for education, business, and industry. *Features:* Areas of emphasis are instructional design, educational computing, evaluation, and media management. Facilities include 70 computer lab microcomputers (IBM, Macintosh), interactive video, speech synthesis, and telecommunications. *Admission Requirements:* 3.3 GPA for master's degree, interview, three letters of recommendation, transcripts of previous academic work. *Faculty:* 8 full-time; 5 part-time. *Students:* 10 full-time; 8 part-time. *Financial Assistance:* 10 assistantships, tuition scholarships, and contracts with other agencies. *Doctorates Awarded 1991-92:* 1.

WASHINGTON

**University of Washington. College of Education, Seattle, WA 98195. (206) 543-1877. Fax (206) 543-8439. William D. Winn, Prof. of Education, College of Education. *Specializations:* Ph.D. and Ed.D. for individuals in business, industry, higher education, public schools, and organizations concerned with education or communication (broadly defined). *Features:* Emphasis on instructional design as a process of making decisions about the shape of instruction; additional focus on research and development in such areas as message design (especially graphics and diagrams); electronic information systems; interactive instruction via videodisc, videotex, and computers. *Admission Requirements:* GRE scores, letters of reference, transcripts, personal statement, master's degree or equivalent in field appropriate to the specialization, 3.5 GPA in master's program, two years of successful professional experience and/or experience related to program goals. *Faculty:* 2 full-time; 3 part-time. *Students:* 12 full-time; 32 part-time. *Financial Assistance:* Assistantships awarded competitively and on basis of program needs; other assistantships available depending on grant activity in any given year. *Doctorates Awarded 1989-90:* 3.

WEST VIRGINIA

West Virginia University. College of Human Resources and Education, Morgantown, WV 26506. (304) 293-3803. Fax (304) 293-7300. David McCrory Prof., Chair; George Maughan, Coord., Technology Education, Communication and Information Systems Sequence of Study. *Specializations:* M.A. and Ed.D. degree programs in history of technical development, research, college teaching, instructional systems design, instructional development, and communication and information systems. *Admission Requirements:* GRE and Miller Analogies Test, minimum GPA 3.0. *Faculty:* 4 full-time; 2 part-time. *Students:* 10 full-time; 6 part-time. *Financial Assistance:* Two teaching assistantships, three research assistantships. *Doctorates Awarded 1991-92:* 3.

WISCONSIN

*University of Wisconsin-Madison. School of Education, Madison, WI 53706. (608) 263-4670. Michael Streibel, Prof., Dept. of Curriculum and Instruction, School of Education. *Specializations:* Ph.D. programs to prepare college and university faculty. *Features:* The program is coordinated with media operations of the university. Traditional instructional technology courses are processed through a social, cultural, and historical frame of reference. Current curriculum emphasizes communication, perception, and cognitive theories, critical cultural studies, and theories of textual analysis and instructional development. Strength in small-format video production and computers. *Admission Requirements:* Previous experience in instructional technology preferred, previous teaching experience, minimum 2.75 GPA on all undergraduate work completed, acceptable scores on either Miller Analogies Test or GRE, and a minimum 3.0 GPA on all graduate work. (Note: Exceptions may be made on some of these requirements if all others are acceptable.) *Faculty:* 3 full-time; 1 part-time. *Students:* 21 Ph.D.; 27 M.S. *Financial Assistance:* A few stipends of approximately $1,000 a month for 20 hours of work per week; other media jobs are also available.

WYOMING

*University of Wyoming. College of Education, Box 3374, Laramie, WY 82071. (307) 766-3896. Fax (307) 766-6668. Patricia McClurg, Prog. Area Coord., Instructional Technology. *Specializations:* The College of Education offers both the Ed.D. and the Ph.D. programs. Students select areas of specialization and Instructional Technology is one option. *Faculty:* 6 full-time. *Doctorates Awarded 1989-90:* 0. For additional information, contact Dr. Patricia McClurg and see the university's master's degree programs.

Master's Degree and Six-Year Programs
in Instructional Technology

During the fall semester of 1992, an inquiry-questionnaire was sent to the program chairs or their representatives for the 192 programs listed in this yearbook. Responses were received from 82 of the programs. Information provided for 30 additional programs was updated in the 1992 edition of *EMTY*; data for the remaining 80 programs were last updated in 1991. Those programs for which the information is not current are indicated by an asterisk (*) before the name of the institution, and data that appeared in the 1992 edition are provided so that the program can be represented in this edition.

Each entry in the directory contains as much of the following information as is available: (1) name and mailing address of the institution; (2) name, academic rank, and title of program head; (3) name of the administrative unit offering the program; (4) minimum degree requirements; (5) number of full-time and part-time faculty; and (6) number of students who graduated with master's degrees from the program during the one-year period between 1 July 1991 and 30 June 1992. The availability of six-year specialist/certificate programs in instructional technology and related media is indicated where appropriate following the description of the master's program.

Several institutions appear in both this list and the list of graduate programs in educational computing, either because their computer technology programs are offered separately from the educational/instructional technology programs, or because they are separate components of the overall educational technology program.

To ensure completeness of this directory, considerable effort has been expended. However, readers who know of either new programs or omissions are encouraged to provide information to the publisher who, in turn, will follow up on them for the next edition of *EMTY*. Information on any programs that have been discontinued would also be most welcome.

Individuals who are interested in any of these graduate programs are encouraged to make direct contact with the head of the program to obtain the most recent information available.

Institutions in this section are arranged alphabetically by state.

ALABAMA

Alabama State University. Library Education Media, School of Education, P.O. Box 271, Montgomery, AL 36195. (205) 293-4107. Fax (205) 262-0474. Katie R. Bell, Ph.D. Coord., Library Education Media, School of Education. *Specializations:* M.Ed., AA Certification, and Ed.S., preparation for K-12 school media programs. *Degree Requirements:* 36 semester hours; thesis required for Ed.S.; 300-clock-hour practicum (100 each in elementary, high school, and other library settings); research project required for M.Ed. and AA Certification. *Faculty:* 2 full-time; 3 part-time. *Students:* 1 full-time; 21 part-time. *Financial Assistance:* Assistantships available for full-time students. *Master's Degrees Awarded 1 July 1991-30 June 1992:* 4. An advanced certificate program is available (see Specializations).

*Auburn University. Educational Foundations, Leadership, and Technology, Auburn, AL 36849. Fax (205) 844-5785. Jeffrey Gorrell, Prof., Dept. Head. *Degree Requirements:* 48 quarter hours including 36 in media. *Faculty:* 24, 14, 10. *Graduates:* 4. The school also offers a six-year specialist degree program in instructional technology.

Jacksonville State University. Instructional Media Division, Jacksonville, AL 36265. (205) 782-5011. Martha Merrill, Coord., Dept. of Educational Resources, Instructional Media Div. *Specializations:* M.S. in Education with emphasis on instructional media. *Minimum Degree Requirements:* 33 semester hours including 18 in media; thesis optional. *Faculty:* 2 full- and part-time. *Students:* 30 full- and part-time. *Master's Degrees Awarded 1 July 1991-30 June 1992:* 5.

University of Alabama. School of Library and Information Studies, Tuscaloosa, AL 35487-0252. (205) 348-4610. Fax (205) 348-3746. Philip M. Turner, Prof., Dean. *Specializations:* M.L.S., Ed.S., M.F.A., Ph.D. *Minimum Degree Requirements:* M.L.S., 36 semester hours, no thesis; Ed.S., 30 semester hours, no thesis; M.F.A., 48 semester hours, creative project; Ph.D., 48 semester hours, dissertation. *Faculty:* 11 full-time; 3 part-time. *Students:* 120 full-time; 100 part-time. *Financial Assistance:* 21 graduate assistantships. *Master's Degrees Awarded 1 July 1991-30 June 1992:* 75. The school also offers a six-year specialist degree program in instructional technology.

University of South Alabama. College of Education, 307 University Blvd., Mobile, AL 36688. (205) 460-6201. Fax (205) 460-7830. Richard L. Daughenbaugh, Prof., Dept. of Behavioral Studies and Educational Technology, College of Education. *Specializations:* M.Ed. program in Educational Media for state school library media certification; M.S. program in Instructional Design for employment in business, industry, the military, etc.; the Ed.S. in Educational Media leads to higher certification in library media. *Minimum Degree Requirements:* 58 quarter hours including 42 in media; thesis optional. *Faculty:* 3 full- and part-time. *Students:* 51 full- and part-time. *Financial Assistance:* Assistantships. *Master's Degrees Awarded 1 July 1991-30 June 1992:* 6. The school also offers a six-year specialist degree program in Instructional Technology for the improvement of teaching.

ARIZONA

Arizona State University. Educational Media and Computers, Education, FMC Payne 146, Tempe, AZ 85287-0111. (602) 965-7192. Fax (602) 965-8887. Gary G. Bitter, Coord., Educational Media and Computers. *Specialization:* Master's degree. *Minimum Degree Requirements:* 33 semester hours, including 21 hours educational media and computers, 9 hours education, 3 hours outside program, 3-hour practicum/internship required, comprehensive exam required. *Faculty:* 7 full-time. *Students:* 87 full-time; 69 part-time. *Financial Assistance:* Assistantships. *Master's Degrees Awarded 1 July 1991-30 June 1992:* 23.

*Arizona State University. Learning and Technology, 322 Payne, Tempe, AZ 85287-0611. (602) 965-4963. Vernon S. Gerlach, Prof., Coord., Learning and Technology, Div. of Psychology in Education. *Specializations:* M.A., M.Ed. *Minimum Degree Requirements:* 30 semester hours; comprehensive exam required; thesis optional. *Faculty:* 3 full-time. *Master's Degrees Awarded:* 26.

*University of Arizona. Graduate Library School, 1515 E. First St., Tucson, AZ 85719. (602) 621-3565. Fax (602) 621-3279. C.D. Hurt, Prof. and Dir., Graduate Library School. *Specialization:* Master's degree. *Minimum Degree Requirements:* 38 graduate semester hours including 12 hours of core courses and a computer proficiency requirement; comprehensive required. *Faculty:* 9. *Master's Degrees Awarded 1989 Calendar Year:* 94.

ARKANSAS

Arkansas Tech University. Department of Instructional Technology, Russellville, AR 72801. (501) 968-0434. Fax (501) 968-9811. Connie Zimmer, Asst. Prof. of Secondary Education. *Specializations:* M.Ed. in Instructional Technology, six-year program. *Features:* Program includes Library Media Education, Training Program, Media Production, and Computer Education. *Minimum Degree Requirements:* 36 credit hours for M.Ed., thesis optional, practicum available. *Faculty:* 1 full-time, 3 part-time. *Students:* 50 part-time. *Financial Assistance:* Graduate assistantships available. *Master's Degrees Awarded 1 July 1991-30 June 1992:* 8.

*University of Arkansas. College of Education 350, Fayetteville, AR 72701. Jacqueline O'Dell, Prog. Coord. for Educational Technology. *Specialization:* M.S. in Education. *Minimum Degree Requirements:* 33 credit hours, 18 in educational technology. *Faculty:* 3 full-time; 2 part-time. *Master's Degrees Awarded 1989-90:* 20.

University of Central Arkansas. Library Science Department, Campus Box 4918, Conway, AR 72035. (501) 450-5463. Fax (501) 450-5468. Selvin W. Royal, Prof., Chair, Applied Academic Technologies. *Specializations:* M.S. Educational Media/Library Science: Track 1—School Library Media, Track 2—Public Information Agencies, Track 3—Media Information Studies. *Minimum Degree Requirements:* 36 semester hours, optional thesis, practicum (for Track 1), professional research paper. *Faculty:* 5 full-time; 3 part-time. *Students:* 8 full-time; 25 part-time. *Financial Assistance:* 3 to 4 graduate assistantships each year. *Master's Degrees Awarded 1 July 1991-30 June 1992:* 18. Advanced certificate program is available for Track 1 to a Master's School Library Media Specialist.

CALIFORNIA

California State University-Chico. College of Communication and Education, Chico, CA 95929-0504. (916) 898-5367. Fax (916) 898-4345. John Ittelson, Prof., Advisor, Instructional Technology Prog. *Specializations:* M.A. in Information and Communication Studies, Instructional Technology. *Minimum Degree Requirements:* 30 semester hours; thesis or project required. *Faculty:* 3 full-time. *Students:* 10 full-time. *Master's Degrees Awarded 1 July 1991-30 June 1992:* 5.

California State University-Dominguez Hills. School of Education, Carson, CA 90747. (310) 516-3524. Fax (310) 516-3518. Peter Desberg, Prof., Coord., Computer-Based Education Program. *Specializations:* M.A., Certificate in Computer-Based Education. *Minimum Degree Requirements:* 30 semester hours including a master's project; 15 hours for the certificate. *Faculty:* 4 full-time. *Students:* 90 full-time and part-time. *Master's Degrees Awarded 1 July 1991-30 June 1992:* 15. An advanced certificate program is available.

*California State University-Long Beach. Instructional Media, Long Beach, CA 90840. (213) 985-4966. Fax (213) 985-1753. Richard J. Johnson, Prof., Chair, Dept. of Instructional Systems Technology. *Specialization:* Master's degree. *Minimum Degree Requirements:* 30 semester hours including 21 in media; thesis optional. *Faculty:* 6 full-time; 4 part-time. *Master's Degrees Awarded 1989-90:* 19.

*California State University-Los Angeles. School of Education, Los Angeles, CA 90032-8143. (213) 343-4346; (213) 343-4330. Fax (213) 343-4318. James H. Wiebe, Prof., Div. of Educational Foundations, School of Education. *Specialization:* M.A. *Minimum Degree Requirements:* 45 quarter hours including 33 in media, including 2 options in the M.A. degree program: (1) computer education, and (2) instructional media and design. *Admission Requirements:* B.A. or B.S., 2.75 GPA, GRE not required. *Faculty:* 6 full-time. *Students:* 30. *Financial Assistance*: Contact Student Financial Services Office at (213) 343-3240 for information. *Master's Degrees Awarded:* 25.

California State University-Northridge. Department of Radio-TV-Film, 18111 Nordhoff St., Northridge, CA 91330. Lili Berks, Grad. Coord., LSUN, Dept. of Radio-Television-Film. *Specializations:* M.A. with emphasis in Screenwriting or Film/TV Theory and Criticism; M.A. in Corporate Educational Media; M.A. in Media Management. *Minimum Degree Requirements:* 30 semester hours, thesis/project for screenwriting, comprehensive exam or thesis option for theory/criticism. *Faculty:* 12 full- and part-time. *Students:* 30 full- and part-time. *Master's Degrees Awarded 1 July 1991-30 June 1992:* 4.

California State University-San Bernardino. Television Center, San Bernardino, CA 92407. (714) 880-5619. Fax (714) 880-7001. Susan Cooper, Coord. *Specializations:* M.A. in Education, option Instructional Technology. *Minimum Degree Requirements:* 48 quarter hours including 28 in media/computers; 12 in education; plus 4 hours in graphics and telecommunications and 4 hours in interactive multimedia. Elective in information systems advised. Project for MA required. *Faculty:* 4 full-time; 1 part-time. *Students:* 35 part-time. *Master's Degrees Awarded 1 July 1991-30 June 1992:* 8. Advanced certificate programs in Computer Technology and in Educational Technology are available.

*National University. School of Education, Vista, CA 92083. (619) 945-6430. Fax (619) 945-6398. James R. Brown, Dir., Dept. of Instructional Technology, School of Education. *Specialization:* Master's degree. *Minimum Degree Requirements:* The equivalent of 60 quarter hours with media courses tailored to meet student needs; thesis required. *Faculty:* 1 full-time. *Master's Degrees Awarded 1989-90:* 37.

*Pepperdine University. Graduate School of Education and Psychology, 400 Corporate Pointe, Culver City, CA 90230. (213) 568-5600. Fax (213) 568-5727. Dr. Robert C. Paull, Chair, M.A. in Education with Concentration in Educational Technology; Terence R. Cannings, Ed.D., Dir., M.S. in School Administration with Concentration in Educational Technology. *Specializations:* M.A. in Education with Concentration in Educational Technology; M.S. in School Administration with Concentration in Educational Technology. *Features:* Programs can be completed in 12-18 months; evening and weekend classes. *Admission Requirements:* 3.0 GPA in undergraduate major; 2.5 cumulative GRE waived with 3.0 GPA; two letters of recommendation. *Faculty:* 4 full-time; 2 part-time. *Students:* Approximately 25 students per year enroll in this concentration; 50 percent full-time, 50 percent part-time. *Financial Assistance:* University, state, and federal financial aid available. *Master's Degrees Awarded 1991:* 20.

*San Diego State University. Educational Technology, San Diego, CA 92182-0311. (619) 594-6718. Patrick Harrison, Prof., Chair, Dept. of Educational Technology. *Specialization:* Master's degree. *Minimum Degree Requirements:* 30 semester hours including 27 in educational technology, instructional design, and training. *Faculty:* 6 full-time. *Master's Degrees Awarded 1989-90:* 50.

San Francisco State University. School of Education, Department of Instructional Technologies, 1600 Holloway Ave., San Francisco, CA 94132. (415) 338-1509. Fax (415) 338-7019. Eugene Michaels, Chair & Prof. *Specializations:* Master's degree with emphasis on Training and Designing Development, Instructional Computing, and Instructional and Interactive Video. *Minimum Degree Requirements:* 30 semester hours, field study thesis or project required. *Faculty:* 3 full-time; 4-7 part-time. *Students:* 160. *Master's Degrees Awarded 1 July 1991-30 June 1992:* 30. The school also offers an 18-unit Graduate Certificate in Training Systems Development, which can be incorporated into the master's program.

San Jose State University. Instructional Technology Program, School of Education, San Jose, CA 95192-0076. (408) 924-3620. Fax (408) 924-3713. Robert Stephens, Assoc. Prof., Chair, Instructional Technology Program, Educational Leadership and Development Div. *Minimum Degree Requirements:* 30 semester hours including 24 in instructional technology, 6 elective from outside program; competency exams in word processing, database management, and spreadsheets. *Faculty:* 7 full-time; 5 part-time. *Students:* 10 full-time; 300 part-time. *Master's Degrees Awarded 1 July 1991-30 June 1992:* 32. A cooperative doctorate (Ed.D.) with the University of California was scheduled to begin in January 1993.

*United States International University. School of Education, San Diego, CA 92131. (714) 271-4300. Dr. Maria T. Fernandez-Wilson, Acting Prog. Coord. and Asst. Prof., School of Education. *Specialization:* M.A. in Computer Education. *Features:* Tailored to meet computer literacy, problem solving, software applications, curriculum development, and integrating microcomputers into instructional needs of classroom teachers, curriculum coordinators, and district-level specialists from the United States and a number of international countries. (International Summer 3-3-3 Master's Program available for candidates who wish to study abroad for one or two summers with a one-course-per-quarter load during the academic year.) *Minimum Degree Requirements:* 45 quarter hours and 9 courses. *Faculty:* 12 full-time. *Master's Degrees Awarded:* 34.

*University of California-Berkeley. School of Library and Information Studies, Berkeley, CA 94720. Charlotte Nolan, Assoc. Dean, Library and Information Studies, School of Library and Information Studies. *Specialization:* Master's degree. *Minimum Degree Requirements:* 28 semester hours in library science, computer science, and related. *Faculty:* 12, 6, 2. *Master's Degrees Awarded:* 91. The school also offers a six-year specialist degree certificate program.

*University of California-Los Angeles. Graduate School of Education, Los Angeles, CA 90024-1521. (310) 825-8326; (310) 825-1838. Fax (310) 206-6293. Aimee Dorr, Prof., Learning and Instruction Specialization, Div. of Educational Psychology, Graduate School of Education. *Specialization:* M.A. only. *Minimum Degree Requirements:* 36 quarter hours with emphasis on all media of communication and instruction. *Faculty:* 4 full-time; 2 part-time. *Master's Degrees Awarded 1990-91:* 3.

*University of California-Santa Barbara. Department of Education, Santa Barbara, CA 93106. (805) 893-3102. Willis D. Copeland, Prof., Program Leader, Instruction, Dept. of Education. *Specialization:* Master's degree. *Minimum Degree Requirements:* 40 quarter hours including 28 required and 12 elective; thesis required. *Faculty:* 1 full-time, 2 part-time. *Master's Degrees Awarded 1989-90:* 16.

University of Southern California. Instructional Technology, Division of Curriculum and Instruction, Los Angeles, CA 90007-0031. (213) 740-3476. Fax (213) 746-8142. Ed Kazlawskas, Prof., Chair, Dept. of Curriculum and Teaching, School of Education. *Specialization:* Master's degree. *Minimum Degree Requirements:* 31 semester hours including 12 hours in media; thesis optional. *Faculty:* 5 full-time; 1 part-time. *Students:* 2 full-time; 8 part-time. *Master's Degrees Awarded 1 July 1991-30 June 1992:* 6.

COLORADO

University of Colorado-Denver. Instructional Technology Program, School of Education, Denver, CO 80217-3364. (303) 556-4881. Fax (303) 556-4822. David H. Jonassen, Prof. and Chair, Instructional Technology Program, School of Education. *Specialization:* Master's degree. *Minimum Degree Requirements:* For several tracks, including instructional computing, corporate training and development, library/media and instructional technology, 36 semester hours including comprehensive; project or internship required. *Faculty:* 9 full-time; 1 part-time. *Master's Degrees Awarded:* 38.

University of Northern Colorado. College of Education, Greeley, CO 80639. (303) 351-2687. Fax (303) 351-2377. Edward F. Caffarella, Prof., College of Education. *Specializations:* M.A. in Educational Technology; M.A. in Educational Media. *Minimum Degree Requirements:* 36 semester hours; comprehensive exam. *Faculty:* 5 full-time; 2 part-time. *Students:* 4 full-time; 68 part-time. *Financial Assistance:* Graduate assistantships and loans. *Master's Degrees Awarded 1 July 1991-30 June 1992:* 14. Ph.D. program is also offered.

CONNECTICUT

*Central Connecticut State University. Department of Educational Technology and Media, New Britain, CT 06050. (203) 827-7671. Mary Ann Pellerin, Assoc. Prof., Chair, Dept. of Educational Technology and Media. *Specializations:* M.S. degree; Certification for Library Media Specialists; Elementary Education with Specialization in Educational Technology. *Minimum Degree Requirements:* 33-36 semester hours, of which the number taken in media varies. *Faculty:* 2 full-time; 6 part-time. *Degrees Awarded 1989-90:* 3m, 6w, M.S.; 2m, 4w, Certified Library Media Specialists; 2w, Elementary Education with Specialization in Educational Technology; 1w, M.S. without certification. The school offers fifth- and sixth-year planned programs in educational media.

Fairfield University. Graduate School of Education and Allied Professions, Fairfield, CT 06430. (203) 254-4000, ext. 2697. Fax (203) 254-4087. Dr. Ibrahim M. Hefzallah, Prof., Co-Dir. of Media/Educational Technology Program; Dr. John Schurdak, Assoc. Prof., Co-Dir., Computers in Education/Educational Technology Program. *Specializations:* M.A. in Media/Educational Technology (includes instructional development, television production, or a customized course of study); Computers in Education. *Minimum Degree Requirements:* 33 semester hours and comprehensive exam; C.A.S., 30 credits beyond the M.A. and research project at the end. *Faculty:* 2 full-time; 9 part-time. *Students:* 60 part-time. *Financial Assistance:* Work study, graduate assistantships. *Master's Degrees Awarded 1 July 1991-30 June 1992:* 10. A Certificate of Advanced Studies in Media/Educational Technology is available, which includes instructional development, television production, and media management; customized course of study also available.

Southern Connecticut State University. School of Library Science and Instructional Technology, 501 Crescent St., New Haven, CT 06515. (203) 397-4530. Fax (203) 397-4677. Nancy Disbrow, Chair, School of Library Science and Instructional Technology. *Specializations:* M.S. in Instructional Technology; Sixth-Year Professional Diploma Library-Information Studies (student may select area of specialization in instructional technology). *Minimum Degree Requirements:* For instructional technology only, 30 semester hours including 21 in media with comprehensive examination; 36 hours without examination. For sixth year: 30 credit hours with 6 credit hours of core requirements, 9-15 credit hours in specialization. *Faculty:* 1 full-time; 3 part-time. *Students:* 37 full- and part-time in M.S./IT program. *Financial Assistance:* Graduate assistantship: salary $1,800 per semester; assistants pay tuition and a general university fee sufficient to defray cost of student accident insurance. *Master's Degrees Awarded 1 July 1991-30 June 1992:* 6. The school also offers a Professional Diploma in Library Information Studies; students may select instructional technology as area of specialization.

DISTRICT OF COLUMBIA

Gallaudet University. School of Education, 800 Florida Ave. NE, Washington, DC 20002-3625. (202) 651-5536 (voice or TDD). Ronald E. Nomeland, Prof., Chair, Dept. of Educational Technology. *Specializations:* M.S. in Special Education/Deafness with specialization in Educational Computing, Instructional Design, and Media Product Development. *Features:* Combines educational technology skills with study in special education and deafness to prepare graduates for positions in programs serving deaf and other handicapped learners as well as in regular education programs, or in government and industry. *Minimum Degree Requirements:* 36 semester hours, including 26 in educational media and a comprehensive exam; optional practicum. *Faculty:* 3 full-time; 1 part-time. *Students:* 9 full-time; 4 part-time. *Financial Assistance:* Partial tuition waiver; graduate assistantships. *Master's Degrees Awarded 1 July 1991-30 June 1992:* 4.

*Howard University. School of Education, 2400 Sixth St. NW, Washington, DC 20059. (202) 806-2500. John W. Greene. Prof., Chair, Dept. of Educational Leadership and Community Services, School of Education, and Coord., Educational Technology Prog. *Specializations:* M.Ed., M.A. *Minimum Degree Requirements:* 36 semester hours for M.Ed., including introduction to educational technology; computer-assisted instruction; individualized instruction; and instructional systems development; thesis required for M.A. degree. *Faculty:* 3, 3, 5. *Master's Degrees Awarded:* 13. The school also offers a certificate of advanced graduate study usually totalling 30 credit hours, of which 12-20 hours are in educational technology.

*University of the District of Columbia (UDC). College of Education and Human Ecology, 800 Mount Vernon Pl. NW, Washington, DC 20747. (202) 727-2756. Leo Pickett, Assoc. Prof. and Chair, Dept. of Media/Library and Instructional Systems, College of Education and Human Ecology. *Specializations:* M.S. in Instructional Systems; M.S. in Library and Information Science. *Minimum Degree Requirements:* 30 semester hours of required courses and 6 hours of electives. *Faculty:* 5 full-time; 2 part-time. *Master's Degrees Awarded 1989-90:* 21.

FLORIDA

Barry University. School of Education, 11300 Northeast Second Ave., Miami Shores, FL 33161. (305) 899-3608. Fax (305) 899-3630. Sister Evelyn Piche, Dean, School of Education; Joel S. Levine, Prof. and Dir. of Computer Education Programs. *Specializations:* Master's degree and Education Specialist degree in Computer Science Education and Computer Applications in Education. *Minimum Degree Requirements:* Master's degree—36 semester credit hours including directed research; Education Specialist degree, 36 semester hours including directed research and seminar on Computer-Based Technology in Education. *Faculty:* 4 full-time; 6 part-time. *Students:* 5 full-time; 5 part-time. *Financial Assistance:* Assistantships, discounts to educators. *Master's Degrees Awarded 1 July 1991-30 June 1992:* 30.

*Florida Atlantic University. College of Education, Boca Raton, FL 33431. (407) 367-3602. Dan Kauffman, Prof., Cognitive Science and Artificial Intelligence, College of Education. *Specialization:* Master's degree. *Minimum Degree Requirements:* 33 semester hours with emphasis on cognitive science and educational technology; thesis optional but recommended. Graduates must demonstrate competence in learning theory, research methodology, future technologies, hypertext/hypermedia, computer applications, chaos theory, and two computer languages. *Faculty:* 2 full-time; 1 part-time. *Master's Degrees Awarded:* 8.

Florida State University. Department of Educational Research, College of Education, Stone Bldg., Tallahassee, FL 32306. (904) 644-8785. Fax (904) 644-8776. Dr. Walter Dick, Prof. and Prog. Leader, Instructional Systems Prog. *Specialization:* M.S. in Instructional Systems. *Minimum Degree Requirements:* 36 semester hours; 2-4-hour internship required; written comprehensive exam. *Faculty:* 6 full-time; 5 part-time. *Students:* 44, most of them full-time. *Financial Assistance:* Some graduate research assistantships on faculty grants and contracts; university fellowships for high GRE students. *Master's Degrees Awarded 1 July 1991-30 June 1992:* 17. A specialist degree program is currently being developed.

*Jacksonville University. Division of Education, Jacksonville, FL 32211. (904) 744-3950. Fax (904) 744-0101. Daryle C. May, Prof. and Dir. of Teaching Prog. in Computer Education, Div. of Education. *Specialization:* Master's degree. *Minimum Degree Requirements:* 36 semester hours, including 18 in computer-related major. *Faculty:* 7 full-time. *Master's Degrees Awarded 1989-90:* 17.

*Nova University. Center for Advancement of Education, 3301 College Ave., Fort Lauderdale, FL 33314. (800) 541-NOVA. Fax (305) 370-5698. Donald Stanier, Dir., the GEM Programs. *Specializations:* M.S. and Ed.S. in Educational Media. Master's degree program based on modules. *Minimum Degree Requirements:* 39 credit hours all in media; practicum required instead of thesis. *Faculty:* Information not available. *Master's Degrees Awarded 1989-90:* 25.

University of Central Florida. College of Education, Orlando, FL 32816. (407) 275-2153. Fax (407) 823-5135. Richard Cornell, Instructional Systems; Donna Baumbach, Educational Media, Dept. of Educational Services, Educational Media/Instructional Technology Programs, College of Education. *Specializations:* M.A. in Instructional Systems; M.Ed. in Educational Media. *Minimum Degree Requirements:* 36-45 semester hours; practicum required in both programs; thesis, project, or additional coursework required. *Students:* 10 full-time; 108 part-time. *Faculty:* 32 full-time; 5 part-time. *Financial Assistance:* Graduate assistantships in department and college. *Master's Degrees Awarded 1 July 1991-30 June 1992:* 30. A doctorate in C&I with an emphasis in Instructional Technology is also offered.

University of Florida. Educational Media and Instructional Design, Gainesville, FL 32611. (904) 392-0705. Lee J. Mullally, Assoc. Prof. and Prog. Leader, Educational Media and Instructional Design. *Specialization:* Master's degree. *Minimum Degree Requirements:* 36 semester hours including 24 in educational media and instructional design; thesis optional. *Faculty:* 2 full-time. *Students:* 24 full- and part-time. *Master's Degrees Awarded 1 July 1991-30 June 1992:* 2. The Education Specialist Program is an advanced degree program and has the same requirements for admission as the Ph.D. and Ed.D. programs.

*University of Miami. School of Education and Allied Professions, Coral Gables, FL 33124. (305) 284-3005. Fax (305) 284-3023. Charles E. Hannemann, Assoc. Prof., Area Coord. for Educational Technology, Dept. of Teaching and Learning, School of Education. *Specializations:* M.S.Ed. in Organizational Training; M.S.Ed. in Instructional Design. *Minimum Degree Requirements:* 30 semester hours, including 12 hours in media, for M.S.Ed. in Organizational Training; 30 credit hours, including 15 hours in media, for M.S.Ed. in Instructional Design; comprehensive written exam required. *Faculty:* 2 full-time. *Master's Degrees Awarded 1989-90:* 11.

*University of South Florida. School of Library and Information Science, Tampa, FL 33620. (813) 974-3520. Fax (813) 974-3826. John McCrossan, Prof., Dir., School of Library and Information Science. *Specialization:* Master's degree. *Minimum Degree Requirements:* 36 semester hours, thesis optional. *Faculty:* 9 full-time; 1 part-time. *Master's Degrees Awarded 1989-90:* 79. The sixth-year specialist program allows students to specialize in areas such as services for special clientele and library management.

GEORGIA

*Georgia Southern University. School of Education, Statesboro, GA 30460. (912) 681-5203. Jack A. Bennett, Assoc. Prof., Dept. of Educational Leadership, Technology, and Research. *Specialization:* M.Ed. *Minimum Degree Requirements:* 60 quarter credit hours, including a varying number of hours of media for individual students. *Faculty:* 3 full-time. *Master's Degrees Awarded 1989-90:* 6. The school also offers a six-year specialist degree program.

Georgia State University. College of Education, Atlanta, GA 30303-3083. (404) 651-2510. Fax (404) 651-2546. Francis T. Atkinson, Coord., Instructional Technology Programs, Dept. of Curriculum and Instruction, School of Education. *Specialization:* M.S. in Instructional Technology. *Minimum Degree Requirements:* 60 quarter hours; comprehensive exam; internship required. *Faculty:* 2 full-time; 6 part-time. *Students:* 10 full-time; 65 part-time. *Financial Assistance:* Assistantships, paid internships, student loans and grants. *Master's Degrees Awarded 1 July 1991-30 June 1992:* 6. An advanced certificate program in Library/Media is available.

University of Georgia. College of Education, 607 Aderhold Hall, Athens, GA 30602. (404) 542-3810. Fax (404) 542-2321. Murray H. Tillman, Prof., Chair, Dept. of Instructional Technology, College of Education. *Specializations:* Master's degree in Instructional Technology; master's degree in Computer-Based Education. *Minimum Degree Requirements:* 60 or more quarter hours in each master's degree; both have an oral examination. *Faculty:* 10 full-time. *Students:* 20 full-time; 45 part-time. *Financial Assistance:* Limited assistance. *Master's Degrees Awarded:* 9 Computer-Based Education; 12 Instructional Technology. The school also offers a 45-hour, six-year specialist degree program in instructional technology and a doctoral program.

*Valdosta State College. School of Education, 1500 N. Patterson St., Valdosta, GA 31698. (912) 333-5927. Fax (912) 333-7408. Catherine Price, Assoc. Prof., Dept. of Instructional Technology. *Specialization:* Master's degree. *Minimum Degree Requirements:* 65 quarter credits. *Faculty:* 3 full-time; 2 part-time.

West Georgia College. Department of Media Education, Education Center, Carrollton, GA 30118. (404) 836-6558. Fax (404) 836-6729. Price Michael, Prof., Chair, Media Education Dept. *Specializations:* M.Ed. with specialization in Media and add-on certification for students with master's degrees in other disciplines. *Minimum Degree Requirements:* 60 quarter hours minimum, including practicum. Additional hours may be required for state certification. *Faculty:* 3 full-time. *Students:* 126 full-time; 3 part-time. *Financial Assistance:* One graduate assistantship for each department. *Master's Degrees Awarded 1 July 1991-30 June 1992:* 9. The school also offers a six-year specialist degree program.

HAWAII

University of Hawaii-Manoa. Educational Technology Department, 1776 University Ave., Honolulu, HI 96822. (808) 956-7671. Fax (808) 956-3905. Geoffrey Z. Kucera, Prof., Chair, Educational Technology Dept. *Specializations:* M.Ed. in Educational Technology with specialization in Instructional Development and in Computer Technology. *Minimum Degree Requirements:* 39 semester hours (27 in educational technology, 3 in practicum, 3 in internship, 6 in electives), thesis and non-thesis available. *Faculty:* 5 full-time; 2 part-time. *Students:* 4 full-time; 12 part-time. *Financial Assistance:* Consideration given to meritorious second-year students for tuition waivers and scholarship applications. *Master's Degrees Awarded 1 July 1991-30 June 1992:* 4.

IDAHO

*Boise State University. College of Technology, Boise, ID 83725. (208) 385-1312. Fax (208) 385-1856. Mark E. Eisley, Dir., Instructional/Performance Technology Prog., College of Technology. *Specialization:* Master's degree. *Minimum Degree Requirements:* 33 semester hours in instructional/performance technology and related coursework; project or thesis required (included in 33 credit hours). Program is also delivered through computer-mediated conferencing to students located anywhere in North America. *Faculty:* 2 full-time; 5 part-time. *Master's Degrees Awarded 1989-90:* 8.

ILLINOIS

*Chicago State University. Department of Library Science and Communications Media, Chicago, IL 60628. (312) 995-2278. Harry Liebler, Prof., Chair, Dept. of Library Science and Communications Media. *Specialization:* Master's degree. *Minimum Degree Requirements:* 36 semester hours; thesis optional. *Faculty:* 4 full-time. *Master's Degrees Awarded 1989-90:* 48.

*Eastern Illinois University. Buzzard Bldg., Rm. 213, Charleston, IL 61920. (213) 581-5931. John T. North, Prof., Chair, Dept. of Information Services and Technology. *Specialization:* Master's degree. *Minimum Degree Requirements:* 32 semester hours, including 24 in library/media; thesis optional. *Faculty:* 3 full-time; 1 part-time. *Master's Degrees Awarded 1989-90:* 10.

*Governors State University. College of Arts and Sciences, University Park, IL 60466. (708) 534-5000, ext. 2432. Fax (708) 534-0054. Michael Stelnicki, Prof., Instructional and Training Technology, College of Arts and Sciences. *Specializations:* M.A. in Communication with I and IT major. *Features:* Emphasizes three professional areas—Instructional Design, Performance Analysis, and Design Logistics. *Minimum Degree Requirements:* 36 credit hours (trimester), all in instructional and performance technology. *Faculty:* 2 full-time; 1 part-time. *Students:* 4 full-time; 32 part-time. *Master's Degrees Awarded 1990-91:* 12.

*Illinois State University. Department of Communication, Normal, IL 61761. Vincent Hazelton, Prof., Chair, Dept. of Communication Prog. *Minimum Degree Requirements:* 32 semester hours, including 18 in media; thesis optional. Faculty: 2. *Master's Degrees Awarded 1989-90:* 10.

Northeastern Illinois University. 5500 N. St. Louis, Chicago, IL 60625. (312) 794-2958. Fax (312) 794-6243. Christine C. Swarm, Prof., Coord. of Instructional Media Program. *Specializations:* Master's degrees with Educational Computer area of concentration or School Media Center online courses. *Faculty:* 2 full-time; 1.5 part-time. *Students:* 42 part-time. *Master's Degrees Awarded 1 July 1991-30 June 1992:* 22.

Northern Illinois University. Instructional Technology Faculty, LEPS Department, DeKalb, IL 60115. (815) 753-0464. Fax (815) 753-9388. Dr. Gary L. McConeghy, Chair, Instructional Technology. *Specializations:* M.S.Ed. in Instructional Technology with specializations in Instructional Design, Microcomputers, or Media Administration. *Minimum Degree Requirements:* 39 semester hours, practicum and internship highly recommended. *Faculty:* 5 full-time; 5 part-time. *Students:* 106 part-time. *Financial Assistance:* Assistantships available at times in various departments. *Master's Degrees Awarded 1 July 1991-30 June 1992:* 21.

Rosary College. Graduate School of Library and Information Science, River Forest, IL 60305. (708) 524-6850. Fax (708) 366-5360. Michael E. D. Koenig, Dean. *Specialization:* Master of Arts in Library Science. *Minimum Degree Requirements:* 36 semester hours, 4 core courses (3 hours each), 8 electives. *Faculty:* 11 full-time; 16 part-time. *Students:* 399 (183 FTE). *Financial Assistance:* Yes. *Master's Degrees Awarded 1 July 1991-30 June 1992:* 140. The school also offers certificate programs in Law Librarianship, Library Administration, and Technical Services, and several joint-degree programs.

Southern Illinois University at Carbondale. College of Education, Carbondale, IL 62901-4610. (618) 536-2441. Fax (618) 453-1646. Billy G. Dixon, Chair, Dept. of Curriculum and Instruction. *Specializations:* M.S. in Education; specializations in Instructional Development and Computer-Based Instruction. *Features:* The ID program emphasizes nonschool (primarily corporate) learning environments. *Minimum Degree Requirements:* 32 semester hours plus thesis or 36 credit hours without thesis. *Faculty:* 6 full-time; 4 part-time. *Students:* 30 full-time; 45 part-time. *Financial Assistance:* Some graduate assistantships and scholarships available to qualified students. *Master's Degrees Awarded 1 July 1991-30 June 1992:* 11.

*Southern Illinois University at Edwardsville. Instructional Technology Program, School of Education, Edwardsville, IL 62026-1125. (618) 692-3277. Charles Nelson, Coord., Dept. of Educational Leadership Program. *Specialization:* Master's degree. *Minimum Degree Requirements:* 52 quarter hours, including 36 in instructional technology; thesis optional. *Faculty:* 6 part-time. *Master's Degrees Awarded 1989-90:* 29.

University of Illinois at Urbana-Champaign. College of Education, Champaign, IL 61820. (217) 244-3391. Fax (217) 244-4572. J. Richard Dennis, Assoc. Prof., Dept. of Curriculum and Instruction, College of Education. *Specialization:* Master's degree. *Minimum Degree Requirements:* 32 semester hours with emphasis on Theory and Design of Interactive Instructional Systems, Educational Psychology, and Educational Policy Studies. *Faculty:* 15. *Students:* 20. *Financial Assistance:* Fellowships for very highly academically talented; assistantships for about 10-15 percent; some tuition waivers. *Master's Degrees Awarded 1 July 1991-30 June 1992:* 12. The school also offers a six-year specialist degree program in Instructional Technology.

University of Illinois at Urbana-Champaign. Department of Educational Psychology, Champaign, IL 61820. (217) 333-2245. Fax (217) 244-7620. Charles K. West, Prof., Div. of Learning and Instruction, Dept. of Educational Psychology. *Specializations:* M.A., M.Ed. *Minimum Degree Requirements:* 8 units of credit, at least 3 of which must be in 400-level courses, 2 in the major field (graduate courses are offered for 1 or 1/2 unit each); thesis required. *Faculty:* 17. *Students:* 9.

*Western Illinois University. Department of Media and Educational Technology, Macomb, IL 61455. (309) 295-1414. Don Crawford, Prof., Chair, Dept. of Media and Educational Technology (offered in cooperation with Department of Educational Administration). *Specialization:* Master's degree. *Minimum Degree Requirements:* 32-36 semester hours, including 18 in media; thesis optional. *Faculty:* 10, 5. Note: Faculty includes individuals also teaching undergraduate courses (our basic mission). We offer graduate courses in library/media and educational computing for support in other programs. *Master's Degrees Awarded 1989-90:* 6.

INDIANA

Indiana State University. Media Technology, Terre Haute, IN 47809. (812) 237-2937. Fax (812) 237-4348. James E. Thompson, Prof., Chair, Dept. of Educational Foundations and Media Technology. *Specializations:* Master's degree; six-year Specialist Degree program in Instructional Technology. *Minimum Degree Requirements:* 32 semester hours, including 18 in media; thesis optional. *Faculty:* 5 full-time. *Students:* 15 full-time; 10 part-time. *Financial Assistance:* Assistantships, fellowships. *Master's Degrees Awarded 1 July 1991-30 June 1992:* 13.

*Indiana University. School of Education, Bloomington, IN 47405. (812) 855-1791. Fax (812) 855-3044. Charles Reigeluth, Chair and Prof., Dept. of Instructional Systems Technology. *Specializations:* M.S. in Educational Media; Post-Masters, Non-Degree Program in Instructional Supervision, School Media Services; Educational Specialist in Curriculum and Instruction, Educational Media. *Minimum Degree Requirements:* 32 semester hours, including 18 in media; thesis optional. *Faculty:* 7 full-time; 10 part-time. *Students:* 83. *Financial Assistance:* Assistantships and scholarship. *Master's Degrees Awarded 1989-90:* 12. A sixth-year program is available.

Purdue University. School of Education, W. Lafayette, IN 47907-1442. (317) 494-5673. Fax (317) 494-0587. James Russell, Prof., Educational Computing and Instructional Development, Dept. of Curriculum and Instruction. *Specializations:* Master's degree, Educational Specialist, and Ph.D. in Instructional Research and Development or Educational Computing. *Minimum Degree Requirements:* 30 semester hours of coursework and a research project; thesis or non-thesis option; practicum is strongly encouraged. *Faculty:* 6 full-time. *Students:* 12 full-time; 22 part-time. *Financial Assistance:* Assistantships and fellowships. *Master's Degrees*

Awarded 1 July 1991-30 June 1992: 18. The school also offers a six-year Specialist Degree program in Instructional Technology and related fields with emphasis in instructional research and development.

*Purdue University-Calumet. Department of Education, Hammond, IN 46323. (219) 989-2360. John R. Billard, Assoc. Prof., Coord., Educational Media Prog., Dept. of Education. *Specialization:* Master's degree. *Minimum Degree Requirements:* 33 credit hours, including 24 in media; thesis optional. *Faculty:* 2, 2, 2. *Graduates 1989-90:* 3m, 5w.

IOWA

Iowa State University. College of Education, Ames, IA 50011. (515) 294-6840. Fax (515) 294-9284. Michael Simonson and Roger Volker, Profs. and Coords., Curriculum and Instructional Technology (including media and computers). *Specializations:* M.S. and M.Ed. in Curriculum and Instructional Technology. *Minimum Degree Requirements:* 30 semester hours; thesis required. *Faculty:* 3 full-time; 3 part-time. *Students:* 20 full-time; 20 part-time. *Financial Assistance:* 10 assistantships available. *Master's Degrees Awarded 1 July 1991-30 June 1992:* 10.

*Tri-College Department of Education (a consortium of Clarke College, the University of Dubuque, and Lorcas College). Clarke College, 2000 University, Dubuque, IA 52001. (319) 588-6300. Fax (319) 588-6789. Judith Decker, Prof., Coord. *Specialization:* Master's degree. *Minimum Degree Requirements:* 20-22 semester hours in computers, 9 hours in education, and 2-7 of electives. *Faculty:* 3 part-time. *Master's Degrees Awarded 1989-90:* 4.

*University of Iowa. College of Education, Iowa City, IA 52242. Leonard S. Feldt, Prof., Chair, Psychological and Quantitative Foundations. *Specialization:* Master's degree. *Minimum Degree Requirements:* 35 semester hours with or without thesis. *Faculty:* 4 full-time; 3 part-time. *Students:* 75 full- and part-time; number of degree candidates will be held constant for next two years. *Master's Degrees Awarded 1990-91:* 20.

*University of Northern Iowa. Department of Curriculum and Instruction, Cedar Falls, IA 50614. (319) 273-2309. Fax (319) 273-2917. Robert R. Hardman, Prof. and Dir., Educational Media. *Specializations:* Master's degrees in Educational Media, Communications and Training Technology, and Computer Applications in Education. *Minimum Degree Requirements:* For the Educational Media degree, 38 semester hours, including 34 in media; thesis optional. For the Communications and Training Technology degree, 38 credit hours, including 32 in media; thesis optional. For the Computer Applications in Education degree, 30 credit hours, including 18 in computers; thesis optional. *Faculty:* 3 full-time; 6 part-time. *Master's Degrees Awarded:* 4 in Educational Media; 14 in Communications and Training Technology.

KANSAS

Emporia State University. School of Library and Information Management, Emporia, KS 66801. (316) 343-5203. Martha L. Hale, Dean, School of Library and Information Management. *Specialization:* Master's of Library Science (ALA accredited program). *Features:* The program is also available in Colorado and other out-of-state sites. Video courses are being developed. *Minimum Degree Requirements:* 42 semester hours, comprehensive examination. *Faculty:* 12 full-time; 30 part-time. *Students:* Approx. 60 full-time; approx. 500 part-time in all sites. *Master's Degrees Awarded 1 July 1991-30 June 1992:* 157. The school also offers a

School Library Certification program, which includes 27 hours of the MLS program plus technologies mainstreamed into other courses.

*Kansas State University. College of Education, Manhattan, KS 66502. (913) 532-5551. Fax (913) 532-7304. John A. Hortin, Prof., Dept. of Curriculum and Instruction. *Specialization:* Master's degree. *Minimum Degree Requirements:* 30 semester hours, including 21 in media; thesis optional. *Faculty:* 4 full-time. *Master's Degrees Awarded 1989-90:* 31. The school also offers a supervisory certification program in Instructional Technology.

*University of Kansas. School of Education, Lawrence, KS 66045. (913) 864-3057. Fax (913) 864-3566. Ronald Aust, Asst. Prof., Dir., Instructional Technology Center. *Specialization:* Master's degree. *Minimum Degree Requirements:* 30 credit hours, including 10 in media; thesis optional. *Faculty:* 2 full-time; 3 part-time. *Master's Degrees Awarded 1989-90:* 5.

KENTUCKY

*University of Kentucky. College of Education, Lexington, KY 40506. (606) 257-5972. Gary Anglin, Assoc. Prof., Instructional Design, Dept. of Curriculum and Instruction, College of Education. *Specialization:* Master's degree in Instructional Technology. *Minimum Degree Requirements:* 36 semester hours, including 24 in instructional design and technology; no thesis required. *Faculty:* 2 full-time. *Master's Degrees Awarded 1989-90:* 26. The school also offers six-year specialist and doctoral degree programs in Instructional Technology.

*University of Louisville. School of Education, Louisville, KY 40292. (502) 588-5555. Carolyn Rude-Parkins, Occupational Education. *Specialization:* M.Ed., Occupational Education with Instructional Technology Concentration. *Minimum Degree Requirements:* 30 semester hours; thesis optional. *Faculty:* 5 professors in three departments contribute to this concentration. *Master's Degrees Awarded:* 4. Note: Media utilization instruction is mainstreamed within education courses. The collaborative Technology Project with Jefferson County Public Schools supports courses in computer technology applications.

*Western Kentucky University. Department of Teacher Education, Bowling Green, KY 42101. (502) 745-3446. Fax (502) 745-6474. Robert C. Smith, Assoc. Prof., LME Coord. *Specialization:* Master's degree. *Minimum Degree Requirements:* 33 semester hours, including 21 in media; thesis optional. *Faculty:* 5 full-time; 2 part-time. *Master's Degrees Awarded 1989-90:* 9.

LOUISIANA

Louisiana State University. School of Library and Information Science, Baton Rouge, LA 70803. (504) 388-3158. Fax (504) 388-1465. Bert R. Boyce, Dean, Prof., School of Library and Information Science. *Specializations:* M.L.I.S., C.L.I.S. (post-master's certificate), Louisiana School Library Certification. *Minimum Degree Requirements:* M.L.I.S., 37 hours; comprehensive examination; one semester full-time residence; completion of degree program in five years. *Faculty:* 11 full-time. *Students:* 82 full-time; 78 part-time. *Financial Assistance:* A large number of graduate assistantships are available to qualified students. *Master's Degrees Awarded 1 July 1991-30 June 1992:* 92. An advanced certificate program is available.

McNeese State University. Department of Administration and Educational Technology, Lake Charles, LA 70609-1815. (318) 475-5421. Fax (318) 475-5467. Virgie M. Dronet. *Specialization:* M.Ed. in Educational Technology. *Minimum Degree Requirements:* 30 semester hours. *Faculty:* 2 full-time; 4 part-time. *Students:* 32 full-time. *Financial Assistance:* 4 graduate assistantships per year. *Master's Degrees Awarded 1 July 1992-30 June 1992:* 17. Advanced certificate programs in Computer Literacy and Computer Education are offered; both are state certificates.

*Northeast Louisiana University. College of Education, 700 University Ave., Monroe, LA 71209. (318) 357-3133. Bill L. Perry, Dir., Ed. Media, Dept. of Administration and Supervision. *Specialization:* Master's degree. *Minimum Degree Requirements:* 36 semester credits. *Faculty:* 2 full-time.

*Southern University. College of Arts and Humanities, Baton Rouge, LA 70813. (504) 771-4500. Henry Wiggins, Prof., Chair, Dept. of Mass Communications. *Specialization:* Master's degree. *Minimum Degree Requirements:* 30 credit hours, including 21 in mass communications and instructional technology; thesis optional. *Faculty:* 11 full- and part-time. *Master's Degrees Awarded 1989-90:* 32.

MARYLAND

*The Johns Hopkins University. Division of Education, Baltimore, MD 21218. (301) 338-8273. Fax (301) 338-8424. Dianne Tobin, Coord., M.S. Technology for Educators, Ed.D. Technology for Special Education, Div. of Education. *Specialization:* Master's degree. *Minimum Degree Requirements:* 33 semester hours, 8 required courses in computer-related technology and media, with remaining courses being electives in several broad areas. *Faculty:* 2 full-time; 8 part-time. *Master's Degrees Awarded 1990:* 20.

*Towson State University. College of Education, Baltimore, MD 21204. (301) 830-2576. Paul E. Jones, Assoc. Prof., Instructional Technology Prog., General Education Dept. *Specializations:* Master's degrees with concentrations available in Instructional Development and School Library Media. *Faculty:* 5 full-time. *Master's Degrees Awarded:* 7.

*University of Maryland. College of Library and Information Services, College Park, MD 20742. (301) 454-5441. Claude E. Walston, Dean and Prof. *Specialization:* Master's degree. *Minimum Degree Requirements:* 36 semester hours, including majors in library media; no thesis required. *Faculty:* 15 full-time; 13 part-time. *Master's Degrees Awarded 1989-90:* 24.

University of Maryland, Baltimore County (UMBC). Department of Education, 5408 Wilkens Ave., Baltimore, MD 21228. (410) 455-2382. Fax (410) 455-3986. Dr. Diane M. Lee, Coord. Grad. Progs. in Education. *Specializations:* Master's degrees in School Instructional Systems, Post-Baccalaureated Teacher Certification, English as a Second Language, Training in Business and Industry. *Minimum Degree Requirements:* 36 semester hours, including 18 in systems development for each program; an internship is required. *Faculty:* 7 full-time; 9 part-time. *Students:* 56 full-time; 196 part-time. *Master's Degrees Awarded 1 July 1991-30 June 1992:* 58. An advanced certificate program is available.

Western Maryland College. Department of Education, Main St., Westminster, MD 21157. (301) 857-2507. Paula K. Montgomery, Asst. Prof., Coord., Media/Library Science, Dept. of Education. *Specializations:* M.S. in Media/Library Science; Educational Media Generalist, Level II. *Minimum Degree Requirements:* 34 credit hours, including 19 in media and 6 in education; comprehensive examination. *Faculty:* 1 full-time; 7 part-time. *Students:* 120 full- and part-time. *Master's Degrees Awarded 1 July 1991-30 June 1992:* 15.

MASSACHUSETTS

*Boston College. Department of Education, McGuinn 531, Chestnut Hill, MA 02167. (617) 353-3519. Fax (617) 353-3924. Walter M. Haney, Assoc. Prof., Dir., Educational Technology Prog., 523 McGuinn Hall, Dept. of Education, Graduate School of Arts and Sciences. *Specialization:* Master's degree in Educational Media. *Minimum Degree Requirements:* 36 semester hours, including 30 in media; practicum; thesis optional. *Faculty:* 8 full-time. *Master's Degrees Awarded 1989-90:* 9. The school also offers a Certificate of Advanced Education Studies degree (30 credit hours) beyond M.Ed. and a special fifth-year M.Ed. program in Instructional Technology for Boston College undergraduates.

*Boston University. School of Education, 605 Commonwealth Ave., Boston, MA 02215. (617) 353-3519. Gaylen B. Kelley, Prof., Prog. Dir. of Educational Media and Technology, Div. of Instructional Development. *Specialization:* Master's degree. *Minimum Degree Requirements:* 32 semester hours; thesis optional. *Faculty:* 4 full-time; 10 part-time. *Master's Degrees Awarded 1989-90:* 13. The school also offers a six-year specialist degree program Certificate of Advanced Graduate Specialization (C.A.G.S.) in Instructional Technology and a corporate training program.

*Bridgewater State College. Department of Media and Librarianship, Bridgewater, MA 02324. (508) 697-1370. Alan Lander, Prof., Chair, Dept. of Media and Librarianship. *Specialization:* Master's degree. *Minimum Degree Requirements:* 33 semester hours, including 27 in media; thesis optional. *Faculty:* 4 full-time. *Master's Degrees Awarded 1989-90:* 9. The school also offers a unified Media Specialist Certification program that provides preparation and background in both print and nonprint resources and services.

*Fitchburg State College. Communications/Media Department, Fitchburg, MA 01420. (508) 345-2151, ext. 3260; (508) 343-8603. Lee DeNike, David Ryder, Profs., Communications/Media Dept. *Specialization:* M.S. in Communications/Media Management. *Minimum Degree Requirements:* 36 semester hours in communications/media management, including a required thesis. *Faculty:* 5. *Master's Degrees Awarded:* 8.

Harvard University. Graduate School of Education, Appian Way, Cambridge, MA 02138. (617) 495-9373. Fax (617) 495-9268. Gerry Lesser, Prof., Chair; Yesha Sivan, Coord., Technology in Education. *Specialization:* M.Ed. in Technology in Education. *Features:* The TIE program is a concentration within the Human Development and Psychology Department. Students focus on the interaction between technology (computers, television, etc.) and education (at any level). The program is designed to provide both a sound theoretical foundation and practical experience in areas related to effective use of educational technologies, with emphasis on educational design and research issues rather than technical production skills. *Minimum Degree Requirements:* Students must complete 8 courses per year: 1 core course, 3 technology-related courses, 2 human development courses, 2 electives. *Faculty:* 1 full-time, 7 part-time. *Students:* Approx. 30. *Financial Assistance:* Within the school's policy. *Master's Degrees Awarded 1 July 1991-30 June 1992:* 30. An advanced certificate program is available.

Simmons College. Graduate School of Library and Information Science, 300 The Fenway, Boston, MA 02115-5898. (617) 738-2264. Fax (617) 738-2099. Robert D. Stueart, Dean; Dr. James C. Baughman, Dir., Unified Media Specialist Prog. *Specializations:* M.S., specialist preparation for Unified Media Specialist Joint Degree (for Teacher Certification) with Education Department. *Features:* The program prepares individuals for a variety of careers—technology/media emphasis being only one. There are special programs for Unified Media Specialist and Archives Management with strengths in information science/systems, media management, etc. *Minimum Degree Requirements:* 36 semester hours; practicum/internship required for UMS; research projects, independent studies possible. *Faculty:* 13.5 full-time; 12 part-time. *Students:* 60 full-time; 335 part-time. *Financial Assistance:* Grants and scholarships are available. *Master's Degrees Awarded 1 July 1991-30 June 1992:* 181. A Doctor of Arts in Administration is also offered.

University of Massachusetts-Boston. School of Education, Harbor Campus, Boston, MA 02125. (617) 287-7622 or 287-5980. Fax (617) 265-7173. Canice McGarry, Instructional Design Prog. *Specialization:* M.Ed. in Instructional Design. *Minimum Degree Requirements:* 36 semester hours, thesis or project required. *Faculty:* 1 full-time; 9 part-time. *Students:* 85 part-time. *Financial Assistance:* Graduate assistantships providing tuition plus stipend. *Master's Degrees Awarded 1 July 1991-30 June 1992:* 27.

MICHIGAN

*Eastern Michigan University. Teacher Education Department, Ypsilanti, MI 48197. (313) 487-3260. Dr. Bert Greene, Prof., Coord., Educational Technology Concentration, Teacher Education Dept. *Specialization:* Master's degree in Educational Technology. *Minimum Degree Requirements:* 30 semester hours, including 18 in educational technology. *Faculty:* 8 full-time. *Master's Degrees Awarded 1989-90:* 15.

*Michigan State University. College of Education, East Lansing, MI 48824. (517) 353-7863. Leighton A. Price, Prof., Coord., Educational Systems Development Prog., Dept. of Counseling, Educational Psychology and Special Education. *Specializations:* Master's degree in Instructional Design, Educational Technology, and Instructional Computing Applications. *Minimum Degree Requirements:* 45 quarter hours; no thesis required. *Faculty:* 10 full-time. *Master's Degrees Awarded 1989-90:* 15. The school also offers a six-year Educational Specialist degree program in Instructional Technology.

*University of Michigan. Curriculum, Teaching and Psychological Studies, Ann Arbor, MI 48109. (313) 747-0612. Fax (313) 763-1229. Robert B. Kozma, Assoc. Prof., Chair, Instructional Technology Committee, Dept. of Curriculum, Teaching and Psychological Studies. *Specialization:* Master's degree. *Minimum Degree Requirements:* 30 credit hours (trimester), including project. *Faculty:* 5 full-time; 1 part-time. *Master's Degrees Awarded 1989-90:* 4.

*Wayne State University. College of Education, Detroit, MI 48202. (313) 577-1728. Fax (313) 577-3606. Instructional Technology Prog., Div. of Administrative and Organizational Studies. Rita Richey, Prof. and Prog. Coord. *Specialization:* Master's degree. *Minimum Degree Requirements:* 36 semester hours, including required project; internship recommended. *Faculty:* 3 full-time; 5 part-time. *Master's Degrees Awarded:* 43. The school also offers a six-year specialist degree program in Instructional Technology.

MINNESOTA

*Mankato State University. Library Media Education, Mankato, MN 56002. (507) 389-5210. Fax (507) 389-5751. Frank Birmingham, Prof., Chair, Library Media Education. *Specialization:* Master's degree. *Minimum Degree Requirements:* 51 quarter hours, including 27 in media. *Faculty:* 3 full-time. *Master's Degrees Awarded:* 20. The school also offers a six-year specialist degree program in the Instructional Technology/Media field.

St. Cloud State University. College of Education, St. Cloud, MN 56301-4498. (612) 255-2022. Fax (612) 255-4778. John G. Berling, Prof., Dir., Center for Information Media. *Specializations:* Master's degrees in Information Technologies, Educational Media, and Human Resources Development/Training. *Minimum Degree Requirements:* 51 quarter hours with thesis; 54 quarter hours, Plan B; 57 credits, portfolio; 200-hour practicum is required for media generalist licensure—coursework applies to Educational Media master's program. *Faculty:* 30 full- and part-time. *Students:* 75 full- and part-time. *Master's Degrees Awarded 1 July 1991-30 June 1992:* 13. The school also offers a 45-quarter-credit, six-year specialist degree.

University of Minnesota. Curriculum and Instructional Systems, 130 Peik Hall, 159 Pillsbury Dr. SE, Minneapolis, MN 55455. (612) 624-2034. Fax (612) 626-7496. Gregory C. Sales, Prof., Chair, Curriculum and Instructional Systems. *Specializations:* M.A., M.Ed. *Minimum Degree Requirements:* 44 quarter hours, including 22 in Instructional Systems. A thesis is required for the M.A., a practicum for the M.Ed. *Faculty:* 4, 4 associates. *Master's Degrees Awarded 1 July 1991-30 June 1992:* 2 M.A., 10 M.Ed.

MISSISSIPPI

*Jackson State University. School of Education, Jackson, MS 39217-0175. (601) 968-2351. William Rush, Prof., Chair, Dept. of Educational Foundations and Leadership, School of Education. *Specialization:* M.S.Ed. in Educational Technology. *Minimum Degree Requirements:* 36 semester hours, including 24 in media; thesis and field practicum optional. *Faculty:* 2 full-time; 1 part-time. *Master's Degrees Awarded 1989-90:* 2.

*University of Southern Mississippi. School of Library Science, Hattiesburg, MS 39406-5146. Jeannine Laughlin, Assoc. Prof., Dir., School of Library Science. *Specialization:* Master's degree. *Minimum Degree Requirements:* 41 semester hours, comprehensive required. *Faculty:* 9. *Master's Degrees Awarded 1989-90:* 41.

MISSOURI

Central Missouri State University. Department of Special Services and Instructional Technology, Warrensburg, MO 64093. (816) 543-8636. Fax (816) 543-4167. Kenneth Brookens, Prof., Instructional Technology. *Specialization:* Certification only; master's degree currently offered only in associated programs. *Minimum Degree Requirements:* 32 semester hours in master's degree programs in Administration and Supervision, Library Science, or Curriculum and Instruction; certification, 18 hours. *Faculty:* 2 full-time. *Financial Assistance:* Graduate assistantship. *Master's Degrees Awarded 1 July 1991-30 June 1992:* 0. The school also offers a certification program in learning resources through the Library Science program.

*University of Missouri-Columbia. College of Education, Columbia, MO 65211. John F. Wedman, Assoc. Prof., Coord., Educational Technology Prog., Curriculum and Instruction Dept., College of Education. *Specialization:* Master's degree. *Minimum Degree Requirements:* 32 semester hours, including 16 hours of upper-level graduate work. *Faculty:* 3. *Master's Degrees Awarded:* 7. The school also offers a six-year specialist degree program in Instructional Technology.

University of Missouri-St. Louis. School of Education, St. Louis, MO 63121. (314) 553-5944. Donald R. Greer, Assoc. Prof., Coord. of Educational Technology, Dept. of Educational Studies, School of Education. *Specialization:* Master's degree. *Minimum Degree Requirements:* 32 semester hours, including 18 in media. *Faculty:* 1 full-time; 1 part-time. *Master's Degrees Awarded 1989-90:* 5.

*Webster University. Instructional Technology, St. Louis, MO 63119. Fax (314) 968-7112. Paul Steinmann, Assoc. Dean and Dir., Graduate Studies and Instructional Technology. *Specialization:* Master's degree. *Minimum Degree Requirements:* 33 semester hours, including 24 in media; internship required. State Certification in Media Technology is a program option; six-year program not available. *Faculty:* 4. *Students:* 6 full-time; 24 part-time. *Master's Degrees Awarded:* 15.

MONTANA

University of Montana. School of Education, Missoula, MT 59812. (406) 243-2563. Fax (406) 243-4908. Geneva T. Van Horne, Prof. of Library/Media, School of Education. *Specializations:* Master's degree; K-12 School Library Media specialization. *Minimum Degree Requirements:* 36 semester credit hours, 28 in media; thesis optional. *Faculty:* 3.5 full-time. *Students:* 17 (School Library Media Certification). *Financial Assistance:* Contact the University of Montana Financial Aid Office. *Master's Degrees Awarded 1 July 1991-30 June 1992:* 5. The school has a School Library Media Certification endorsement program in addition to the master's program.

NEBRASKA

*University of Nebraska-Kearney. Department of Educational Administration, Kearney, NE 68849. (308) 236-8208. Daniel W. McPherson, Assoc. Prof., Supervisor of Educational Media, Dept. of Educational Administration. *Specialization:* Master's degree. *Minimum Degree Requirements:* 36 semester hours, including 15 in media; thesis optional. Since this is a cooperative program, Kansas State University provides the 15 hours required for media and computer coursework, and the supporting faculty. *Master's Degrees Awarded:* 2.

University of Nebraska-Lincoln. Instructional Technology, Teachers College, Lincoln, NE 68588. (402) 472-2018. Fax (402) 472-8317. David W. Brooks, Prof., Coord., Instructional Technology, Teachers College. *Specialization:* Master's degree. *Minimum Degree Requirements:* 36 semester hours, including 24 in media; thesis optional. *Faculty:* 4 full-time. *Master's Degrees Awarded 1 July 1991-30 June 1992:* 3. The school also offers an advanced certificate program.

University of Nebraska-Omaha. Department of Teacher Education, College of Education, Kayser Hall 414K, Omaha, NE 68182. (402) 554-2211. Fax (402) 554-3491. Verne Haselwood, Prof., Educational Media Prog. in Teacher Education. *Specializations:* M.S. in Education, M.A. in Education, both with Educational Media concentration. *Minimum Degree Requirements:* 36 semester hours, including 24 in media; practicum required; thesis optional. *Faculty:* 3 full-time; 2 part-time. *Students:* 10 full-time; 60 part-time. *Financial Assistance:* Contact Financial Aid Office. *Master's Degrees Awarded 1 July 1991-30 June 1992:* 15. The school also offers an advanced certificate program in Educational Administration and Supervision.

NEVADA

*University of Nevada-Reno. College of Education, Reno, NV 89557. (702) 784-4961. Fax (707) 784-4526. Thomas W. Sawyer, Dir. of the Learning and Resource Center, Curriculum and Instruction Dept., College of Education. *Specialization:* Master's degree. *Minimum Degree Requirements:* 36 semester hours, including 16 or more in (a) computer education-media or (b) library-media; thesis optional. *Faculty:* 2 full-time. *Master's Degrees Awarded 1989-90:* 2. The school also offers a six-year specialist degree program in curriculum and instruction with an emphasis in (a) or (b) above.

NEW JERSEY

*Glassboro State College. School and Public Librarianship, Glassboro, NJ 08028. (609) 863-6491. Regina Pauly, Graduate Advisor and Prog. Coord. for School and Public Librarianship. *Specialization:* Master's degree. *Minimum Degree Requirements:* 39 semester hours, including required thesis project. *Faculty:* 1 full-time; 4 part-time. *Master's Degrees Awarded:* 12.

*Montclair State College. Department of Reading and Educational Media, Upper Montclair, NJ 07043. Robert R. Ruezinsky, Dir. of Media and Technology. *Specializations:* No degree program exists. Two certification programs, A.M.S. and E.M.S, exist on the graduate level. *Minimum Degree Requirements:* 18-21 semester hours of media and technology are required for the A.M.S. program and 30-33 hours for the E.M.S. program. *Faculty:* Includes 5 administrators and 1 adjunct, teaching on an overload basis.

Rutgers-The State University of New Jersey. School of Communication, Information and Library Studies, New Brunswick, NJ 08903. (908) 932-8824. Fax (908) 932-6916. Dr. Betty J. Turock, Chair, Dept. of Library and Information Studies. *Specializations:* M.L.S. degree with specializations in Information Retrieval, Technical and Automated Services, Reference, School Media Services, Youth Services, Management and Policy Issues, Generalist Studies. A new course on Multimedia Structure, Organization, Access, and Production is being offered. *Minimum Degree Requirements:* 36 semester hours, in which the hours for media vary for individual students; practicum of 100 hours. *Faculty:* 18 full-time; 6 adjuncts. *Students:* 140 full-time; 210 part-time. *Financial Assistance:* Scholarships, fellowships, and graduate assistantships available. *Master's Degrees Awarded 1 July 1991-30 June 1992:* 138. The school also offers a six-year specialist certificate program.

Seton Hall University. Graduate Program in Educational Media, 22 Winding Way, Parsippany, NJ 07054. (201) 761-9392. Rosemary W. Skeele, Asst. Prof., Dir., Graduate Prog. in Educational Media, Div. of Educational Media, College of Education and Human Services. This program was discontinued in September 1992.

William Paterson College. School of Education, 300 Pompton Rd., Wayne, NJ 07470. (201) 595-2140. Fax (201) 595-2585. Dr. Amy G. Job, Librarian, Assoc. Prof., Coord., Prog. in Library/Media, Curriculum and Instruction Dept. *Specializations:* M.Ed. for Educational Media Specialist, Associate Media Specialist. *Minimum Degree Requirements:* 33 semester hours, including research projects and practicum. *Faculty:* 6 full-time; 2 part-time. *Students:* 30 part-time. *Financial Assistance:* Limited. *Master's Degrees Awarded 1 July 1991-30 June 1992:* 6.

NEW MEXICO

*University of New Mexico. College of Education, Albuquerque, NM 87131. (505) 277-0111. Dr. Frank Field, Chair; Guy A. Watson, Assoc. Prof., Training and Learning Technologies, College of Education. *Specialization:* Master's degree. *Minimum Degree Requirements:* 36 semester hours in Learning Technologies. *Faculty:* 8 full-time; 1 part-time. *Master's Degrees Awarded 1988-89:* 40.

NEW YORK

*Fordham University. Communications Department, Bronx, NY 10458. Donald C. Matthews, S.J., Chair; James A. Capo, Assoc. Prof., Dir. of Graduate Studies, Communications Dept. *Specialization:* Master's degree. *Minimum Degree Requirements:* 30 semester hours; internship or thesis required. *Faculty:* 9. *Master's Degrees Awarded 1990-91:* 9.

Ithaca College. School of Communications, Ithaca, NY 14850. (607) 274-3912. Diane M. Gayeski, Assoc. Prof., Chair, Graduate Corporate Communications; Roy H. Park, School of Communications. *Specialization:* M.S. in Corporate Communications. *Minimum Degree Requirements:* 36 semester hours; required seminar. *Faculty:* 8 full-time. *Students:* Approximately 25 full-time; 15 part-time. *Financial Assistance:* Full- and part-time research/lab assistantships. *Master's Degrees Awarded 1 July 1991-30 June 1992:* 18.

New School for Social Research. Media Studies Program, 2 W. 13th St., New York, NY 10011. (212) 229-8903. Fax (212) 645-0661. Mark Schulman, Chair, Communication Dept. *Specialization:* M.A. in Media Studies. *Minimum Degree Requirements:* 36 semester hours and thesis; 39 credit hours for non-thesis option. *Faculty:* 2 full-time; 30 part-time. *Students:* 40 full-time; 135 part-time. *Financial Assistance:* Assistantships, work-study, federal and state loans. *Master's Degrees Awarded 1 July 1991-30 June 1992:* 75.

*New York Institute of Technology. Graduate Communication Arts, Old Westbury, NY 11568. (Also in NYC.) (516) 686-7777. Fax (516) 626-7602. Josefa Cubina, Dean, School of Liberal Arts, Sciences and Communication. *Specializations:* Master's degree with specializations in Television, Film, Electronic Journalism, Advertising/Public Relations, Computer Graphics, Studio Arts, or Media Generalist. *Minimum Degree Requirements:* 32-34 semester hours with one specialization; thesis optional. *Faculty:* 3 full-time; 8 part-time. *Master's Degrees Awarded 1990-91:* 49.

New York University. School of Education, 239 Greene St., Suite 300, New York, NY 10003. (212) 998-5187. Fax (212) 995-4041. Francine Shuchat Shaw, Assoc. Prof. and Dir., Prog. in Educational Communication and Technology. *Specializations:* M.A. in Education with program emphasis on design and production, application and evaluation of materials and environments for all instructional technologies. *Minimum Degree Requirements:* 36 semester hours, including final master's project. *Faculty:* 2 full-time; 10 part-time. *Students:* 25 full-time; 30 part-time. *Financial Assistance:* Graduate and research assistantships from the university and the School of Education. *Master's Degrees Awarded 1 July 1991-30 June 1992:* 15. The school also offers a post-M.A. 30-point Certificate of Advanced Study in Education.

*New York University-Tisch School of the Arts. Interactive Telecommunications Program, 721 Broadway, New York, NY 10003. Red Burns, Prof., Chair, The Interactive Telecommunications Program/Institute of Film and Television. *Specialization:* Master's degree. *Minimum Degree Requirements:* 60 semester hours (15 courses at 4 credit hours each; program is 2 years for full-time students), including 5-6 required courses and thesis. *Faculty:* 3, 1, 4. *Master's Degrees Awarded 1989-90:* 40.

*Rochester Institute of Technology. Information Technology, Rochester, NY 14623-0887. (716) 475-2400. Clint Wallington, Prof., Dir., Dept. of Information Technology, College of Applied Science and Technology. *Specialization:* Master's degree. *Minimum Degree Requirements:* 48 quarter hours, including an instructional development project (noncredit). *Faculty:* 4, 3, 1. *Master's Degrees Awarded:* 19.

St. John's University. Division of Library and Information Science, Jamaica, NY 11439. Emmett Corry, O.S.F., Assoc. Prof., Dir., Div. of Library and Information Science. *Specializations:* M.L.S. with specializations in School Media, Public, Academic, Law, Health/Medicine, Business, Archives. Double degree programs: Pharmacy and M.L.S., Government and Politics and M.L.S. *Minimum Degree Requirements:* 36 semester hours; comprehensive; practicum (school media required). *Faculty:* 6 full-time; 14 part-time. *Students:* 21 full-time; 142 part-time. *Financial Assistance:* Assistantships and fellowships (10 for school media in 1992). *Master's Degrees Awarded 1 July 1992-30 June 1992:* 39. The school also offers a 24-credit Advanced Certificate program.

*State University College of Arts and Science. School of Professional Studies, Potsdam, NY 13676. (315) 267-2527. Norman Licht, Prof., Coord., Instructional Technology and Media Management, Center for Mathematics, Science and Technology. *Specializations:* Master's degree with emphasis in Instructional Technology, Media, and Computer Education. *Minimum Degree Requirements:* 33 semester hours; thesis optional. *Faculty:* 7 full-time; 3 part-time. *Master's Degrees Awarded 1989-90:* 37.

*State University of New York at Albany. Department of Program Development and Evaluation, Albany, NY 12222. (518) 442-3300. Instructional Design and Technology Prog. *Specialization:* Master's degree. *Minimum Degree Requirements:* 30 semester hours, including 15 in instructional design and technology; thesis optional. *Faculty:* 2, 3, 0. *Master's Degrees Awarded 1989-90:* 9.

State University of New York at Buffalo. Graduate School of Education, 480 Baldy Hall, Amherst, NY 14260. (716) 645-3164. Fax (716) 645-4281. Taher A. Razik, Prof., Instructional Design and Management, Dept. of Educational Organization, Administration, and Policy. *Specialization:* M.Ed. in Instructional Design and Management. *Minimum Degree Requirements:* 32 semester hours, including 21 hours in Instructional Design and Management; thesis or project required. *Faculty:* 3. *Students:* 12. *Financial Assistance:* Some graduate assistantships are available. *Master's Degrees Awarded 1 July 1991-30 June 1992:* 3.

State University of New York at Buffalo. School of Information and Library Studies, Buffalo, NY 14260. (716) 645-2411. Fax (716) 645-3775. George S. Bobinski, Dean. *Specialization:* Master's degree. *Minimum Degree Requirements:* 36 semester hours, including 15 in media; thesis optional. *Faculty:* 9 full-time; 6 part-time. *Students:* 102 full-time; 135 part-time. *Financial Assistance:* 12-18 assistantships available, plus fellowships and scholarships. *Master's Degrees Awarded 1 July 1991-30 June 1992:* 124. The school also offers a sixth-year, 30-credit-hour certificate program in Instructional Technology.

*State University of New York at Stony Brook. College of Engineering and Applied Sciences, Stony Brook, NY 11794-2250. (516) 632-8770. Fax (516) 632-8205. Thomas T. Liao, Prof., Chair, Dept. of Technology and Society, College of Engineering and Applied Sciences. *Specializations:* Master's degree with emphases in Technological Systems; Industrial, Management, Educational Computing; and Environmental and Waste Management. *Minimum Degree Requirements:* 30 semester hours. *Faculty:* 10 full-time. *Master's Degrees Awarded 1990-91:* 50.

Syracuse University. School of Education, Syracuse, NY 13244-2340. (315) 443-3703. Fax (315) 443-5732. Philip Doughty, Prof., Chair, Instructional Design, Development and Evaluation Prog. *Specializations:* M.S. degree programs for Instructional Design of programs and materials, Educational Evaluation, human issues in Instructional Development, Media Production (including computers and videodisc), and Educational Research and Theory (learning theory, application of theory, and educational and media research). Graduates are prepared to serve as curriculum developers, instructional developers, program and product evaluators, researchers, resource center administrators, communications coordinators, trainers in human resource development, and higher education instructors. *Features:* Field work and internships, special topics and special issues seminar, student- and faculty-initiated minicourses, seminars and guest lecturers, faculty-student formulation of department policies, and multiple international perspectives. *Minimum Degree Requirements:* 30 semester hours; comprehensive and intensive examinations required. *Faculty:* 5 full-time; 4 part-time. *Students:* 18 full-time; 22 part-time. *Financial Assistance:* Some fellowships, scholarships, and graduate assistantships entailing either research or administrative duties in instructional technology. *Master's Degrees Awarded 1 July 1991-30 June 1992:* 21. The school also offers an advanced certificate program.

Teachers College, Columbia University. Box 221, 525 W. 120th St., New York, NY 10027. (212) 678-3834. Fax (212) 678-4048. Robert P. Taylor, Chair, Dept. of Communication, Computing and Technology in Education. *Specializations:* M.A. in Computing in Education; M.A. or M.Ed. in Instructional Technology and Media; M.A., M.Ed. in Communication. *Minimum Degree Requirements:* M.A., 32 semester hours; graduate project. *Faculty:* 5. *Students:* 200. *Financial Assistance:* Direct scholarship, some assistantships, some work on grant projects. *Master's Degrees Awarded 1 July 1991-30 June 1992:* Approx. 50.

NORTH CAROLINA

*Appalachian State University. College of Education, Boone, NC 28608. (704) 262-2000. Ken McEwin, Prof., Coord., Dept. of Curriculum and Instruction, Library/Media Studies, College of Education. *Specialization:* Master's degree. *Minimum Degree Requirements:* 42 semester hours, including selected sources in media; thesis optional. *Faculty:* 6. *Master's Degrees Awarded 1989-90:* 25.

*Appalachian State University. Department of Library Science and Educational Foundations, Boone, NC 28608. John H. Tashner, Prof., Coord., Dept. of Library Science and Educational Foundations, College of Education. *Specialization:* Master's degree. *Minimum Degree Requirements:* 36 semester hours, including 15 in Computer Education; thesis optional. *Faculty:* 4, 1, 0. *Master's Degrees Awarded 1989-90:* 1 (new program).

East Carolina University. Department of Library Studies and Educational Technology, Greenville, NC 27858-4353. (919) 757-6621. Fax (919) 757-4368. Lawrence Auld, Assoc. Prof., Chair, Dept. of Library and Information Studies. *Specializations*: M.L.S.; areas of specialization include School Media, Community College Librarianship, and Public Librarianship. M.L.S. graduates are eligible for North Carolina School Media Coordinator certification and North Carolina Public Library certification. *Minimum Degree Requirements:* Minimum of 38 semester hours in Library Science and Media. *Faculty:* 10 full-time. *Students:* 6 full-time; 45 part-time. *Financial Assistance:* A limited number of assistantships are available. *Master's Degrees Awarded 1 July 1991-30 June 1992:* 19. A 14-hour post-master's program for School Media Supervisor certification is also offered.

*North Carolina A&T State University. School of Education, Greensboro, NC 27411. (919) 334-7848. James N. Colt, Dept. of Curriculum and Instruction. *Specializations:* Master's degree with emphases in Media Management, Telecommunications, Instructional Development, Materials Production, Information Systems, Librarianship. *Minimum Degree Requirements:* 30 semester hours; comprehensive examination; internship. *Faculty:* 3 full-time.

North Carolina Central University. School of Education, 238 Farrison-Newton Communications Bldg., Durham, NC 27707. (919) 560-6218. Dr. Marvin E. Duncan, Prof., Dir., Graduate Prog. in Educational Technology. *Specialization:* M.A. with special emphasis on Instructional Development/Design. *Minimum Degree Requirements:* 33 semester hours, including 21 in Educational Technology; thesis or project required unless student has already written a thesis or project for another master's program. *Features:* The master's program in educational technology is designed to prepare graduates to serve as information and communication technologists in a variety of professional ventures, among which are institutions of higher education (college resource centers); business; industry; and professional schools, such as medicine, law, dentistry, and nursing. The program is also designed to develop in students the theory, practical tools, and techniques necessary to analyze, design, and manage an instructional resources center. Many of our students teach in two- and four-year colleges. *Faculty:* 3 full-time; 1 part-time. *Students:* 22 full-time; 30 part-time. *Financial Assistance:* Assistantships and grants available. *Master's Degrees Awarded 1 July 1991-30 June 1992:* 12.

University of North Carolina. School of Education, Chapel Hill, NC 27514. (919) 962-3791. Fax (919) 966-4000. Ralph E. Wileman, Prof., Chair, Educational Media and Instructional Design, School of Education. *Specialization:* M.Ed. in Educational Media and Instructional Design. *Minimum Degree Requirements:* 36 semester hours, including a 3-hour practicum; comprehensive examination. *Faculty:* 2 full-time. *Students:* 20 full-time. *Financial Assistance:* Assistantships in many schools throughout the university. *Master's Degrees Awarded 1 July 1991-30 June 1992:* 5.

OHIO

*Kent State University. Instructional Technology Program, White Hall 405, KSU, Kent, OH 44242. (216) 672-2294. Dr. David Dalton, Prog. Coord. *Specialization:* Master's degree. *Features:* Two five-week summer sessions. *Minimum Degree Requirements:* 34 semester hours, including 14-20 hours of Instructional Technology coursework, depending upon certification sought. *Faculty:* 3 full-time; 4 part-time. *Master's Degrees Awarded:* Approx. 10-15 per year.

*Miami University. School of Education and Allied Professions, Oxford, OH 45056. (513) 529-3736. Joe Waggener, Assoc. Prof., Coord., Instructional Technology Program, School of Education and Allied Professions. *Specialization:* Master's degree. *Minimum Degree Requirements:* 30 semester hours; thesis optional. *Faculty:* 4 full-time; 1 part-time. *Graduates:* Data not available.

The Ohio State University. College of Education, 29 W. Woodruff Ave., 122 Ramseyer Hall, Columbus, OH 43221. (614) 292-4872. Fax (614) 292-7900. Marjorie Cambre, Assoc. Prof., prog. contact person, Instructional Design and Technology. *Specializations:* M.A. in Instructional Design and Technology with specialties in Educational Computing, Interactive Technologies, and Video; Library Media Certification. *Minimum Degree Requirements:* M.A. degree—50 quarter hours, including an individualized number of hours in media; thesis optional. *Faculty:* 6 full-time; 1 part-time. *Students:* 86 M.A. students—20 full-time; 66 part-time. *Financial Assistance:* Some assistantships available. *Master's Degrees Awarded 1 July 1991-30 June 1992:* Approx. 20.

The Ohio State University. College of the Arts, Department of Art Education, 340 Hopkins Hall, 128 North Oval Mall, Columbus, OH 43210. (614) 292-0259. Fax (614) 292-4401. Dr. Tony Scott, Prog. Coord., Prog. in Electronic Media in Art Education. *Specializations:* M.A. in Art Education with specialization in the teaching and learning of computer graphics and computer-mediated art; multimedia production and its curricular implications; electronic networking in the arts; multicultural aspects of computing; hypermedia applications for teaching and art education research; and the application of computing to arts administration, galleries, and museums. *Faculty:* 2 full-time in specialty; 14 in department. *Students:* 12 full-time in specialty. *Financial Assistance:* Graduate teaching associate positions that carry tuition and fee waivers and pay a monthly stipend; various fellowship programs for applicants with high GRE scores. *Master's Degrees Awarded 1991-92:* 0 (new program). For more details, see listing under Doctoral Programs.

Ohio University. College of Education, McCracken Hall, Athens, OH 45701-2979. (614) 593-4457. Fax (614) 593-0177. Dr. John W. McCutcheon, Asst. Prof., Coord., Educational Media Program. *Specialization:* M.Ed. in Educational Media Management. *Minimum Degree Requirements:* 52 quarter hours, including 26 in Educational Media. *Faculty:* 3 full-time; 2 part-time. *Students:* 24 full-time; 5 part-time. *Master's Degrees Awarded 1 July 1991-30 June 1992:* 3.

University of Cincinnati. College of Education, 608 Teachers College Bldg., Cincinnati, OH 45221-0002. (513) 556-3577. Randall Nichols, Dept. of Curriculum and Instruction. *Specialization:* M.A. in Curriculum and Instruction with an emphasis in Instructional Systems Technology. *Minimum Degree Requirements:* 54 quarter hours; written examination; thesis or research project. *Faculty:* 3 full-time; 10 part-time. *Students:* 20 full-time; 20 part-time. *Financial Assistance:* Scholarships and assistantships available. *Master's Degrees Awarded 1 July 1991-30 June 1992:* Approx. 9.

University of Toledo. College of Education and Allied Professions, Toledo, OH 43606-3390. (419) 537-3846. Fax (419) 537-3853. Amos C. Patterson, Prof., Dir. of Academic Programs. *Specialization:* M.Ed. in Educational Media. *Minimum Degree Requirements:* 48 quarter hours, including 36 in media; master's project. *Faculty:* 7 full-time; 2 part-time. *Students:* 13 full-time; 14 part-time (in graduate program). For more details, see the listing for Doctoral Programs. The school also offers a six-year specialist degree program in educational technology.

Wright State University. College of Education and Human Services, 244 Millett Hall, Dayton, OH 45435. (513) 873-2509 or (513) 873-2182. Fax (513) 873-3301. Dr. Bonnie K. Mathies, Chair, Dept. of Educational Technology, Vocational Education and Allied Programs. *Specializations:* M.Ed. in Educational Media or Computer Education, or for Media Supervisor or Computer Coordinator; M.A. in Educational Media or Computer Education. *Minimum Degree Requirements:* M.Ed. requires a comprehensive examination that, for this department, is the completion of a portfolio and videotaped presentation to the faculty; the M.A. incorporates a 9-hour thesis; students are eligible for Supervisor's certificate after completion of C&S; Computer Coordinator or C&S; Media Supervision programs. *Faculty:* 2 full-time; 13 part-time, adjuncts, and other university full-time faculty and staff. *Students:* 53 part-time (not including Computer Education students). *Financial Assistance:* Graduate assistantships available, including three positions in the College's Educational Resource Center; limited number of small graduate scholarships. *Master's Degrees Awarded 1 July 1991-30 June 1992:* 7.

*Xavier University. Department of Education, Cincinnati, OH 45207. (513) 745-3521. John Pohlman, Asst. Prof., Dir., Graduate Programs in Educational Media, Dept. of Education. *Specialization:* Master's degree. *Minimum Degree Requirements:* 30 semester hours, including 18 in media; no thesis, but field practicum required. *Faculty:* 1 full-time; 5 part-time. *Master's Degrees Awarded 1989-90:* 16.

OKLAHOMA

Central State University. See University of Central Oklahoma (name changed July 1991).

*Oklahoma State University. Curriculum and Instruction Department, Stillwater, OK 74078. (405) 744-7124. Douglas B. Aichele, Regents, Prof., Head, Curriculum and Instruction Dept. *Specialization:* Master's degree. *Minimum Degree Requirements:* 30 semester hours, including 18 in media; thesis optional. *Faculty:* 3; 8 teaching assistants. *Master's Degrees Awarded:* 9. The school also offers a Library/Media Specialist certificate program.

*Southwestern Oklahoma State University. School of Education, Weatherford, OK 73096. (405) 772-6611. Fax (405) 772-5447. Lessley Price, Asst. Prof., Coord. of Library/Media Prog., School of Education. *Specialization:* M.Ed. in Library/Media Education. *Minimum Degree Requirements:* 32 semester hours, including 24 in media; thesis optional. *Faculty:* 2 full-time, 2 part-time. *Master's Degrees Awarded:* 16.

University of Central Oklahoma. 100 N. University Dr., Edmond, OK 73034. (405) 341-2980, ext. 5886. Fax (405) 341-4964. Dr. Judith E. Wakefield, Assoc. Prof. *Specializations:* M.Ed. in Instructional Media; Library Media Specialist Certification. *Minimum Degree Requirements:* 32 graduate hours in Educational Research, Educational Media, Curriculum and Instruction, and electives. *Faculty:* 3 full-time; 1 part-time. *Students:* 4 full-time; 51 part-time. *Financial Assistance:* Yes. *Master's Degrees Awarded 1 July 1991-30 June 1992:* 12. The school also offers an advanced certificate program.

University of Oklahoma. Department of Educational Psychology, 820 Van Vleet Oval, Norman, OK 73019-0260. (405) 325-5974. Fax (405) 325-3242. Raymond B. Miller, Educational Technology Prog. Area Coord. *Specializations:* M.Ed. in Educational Technology as a Generalist or with emphasis on Computer Applications or Instructional Design; dual degree in Library Science and Educational Technology. *Minimum Degree Requirements:* 32 semester hours for the Generalist and Computer Applications options; 39 hours for the Instructional Design program; 60 hours for the dual degree; comprehensive examination required for all programs. *Faculty:* 10 full-time; 2 part-time. *Students:* 43 full- and part-time. *Financial Assistance:* Assistantships; out-of-state fee waivers; general and targeted minorities graduate scholarships. *Master's Degrees Awarded 1 July 1991-30 June 1992:* 6.

OREGON

*Portland State University. School of Education, P.O. Box 751, Portland, OR 97207. (503) 725-4678. Fax (503) 725-4882. Joyce Petrie, Prof., Coord., Educational Media, School of Education. *Specialization:* Master's degree in Educational Media. *Minimum Degree Requirements:* 45 quarter hours, including 42 in media; thesis optional. *Faculty:* 2 full-time; 4 part-time. *Master's Degrees Awarded 1990-91:* 37.

Western Oregon State College. Department of Secondary Education, Monmouth, OR 97361. Richard C. Forcier, Prof., Dir., Div. of Information Technology, Dept. of Secondary Education. *Specializations:* Master's degree in Computer Education or Instructional Systems. *Features:* Offers advanced courses in Media Management, Media Production, Instructional Systems, Instructional Development, and Computer Technology. Some specialization in distance delivery of instruction and computer-interactive video instruction. *Minimum Degree Requirements:* 45 quarter hours, including 36 in media; thesis optional. *Faculty:* 3 full-time; 4 part-time. *Students:* 5 full-time; 200 part-time. *Master's Degrees Awarded 1 July 1991-30 June 1992:* 15.

PENNSYLVANIA

*Clarion University of Pennsylvania. Department of Communication, Clarion, PA 16214. (814) 226-2541. William Lloyd, Chair, Dept. of Communication. *Specialization:* Master's degree with emphasis on training and development. *Minimum Degree Requirements:* 36 semester hours; courses in design, production, research; electives include interactive video, multi-image; thesis optional. *Faculty:* 9 full-time. *Master's Degrees Awarded 1989-90:* 28.

*Drexel University. College of Information Studies, Philadelphia, PA 19104. (215) 895-2474. Fax (215) 895-2494. Richard H. Lytle, Prof. and Dean, College of Information Studies. *Specialization:* M.S. degree. *Minimum Degree Requirements:* 48 quarter hours taken primarily from six functional groupings: Technology of Information Systems; Principles of Information Systems; Information Organizations; Collection Management; Information Resources and Services; and Research. *Faculty:* 18. *Masters Degrees Awarded 1990-91:* 108.

*Indiana University of Pennsylvania. Department of Communications, Indiana, PA 15701. Kurt P. Dudt, Assoc. Prof., Chair, Dept. of Communications Media. *Specialization:* Master's degree. *Minimum Degree Requirements:* 36 semester hours, including 21 in media; thesis optional. *Faculty:* 11. *Master's Degrees Awarded 1990-91:* 23.

*Lehigh University. Lehigh University School of Education, Bethlehem, PA 18015. (215) 758-3231. Fax (215) 758-5432. Leroy J. Tuscher, Prof., Dir. Educational Technology Center, Lehigh University School of Education. *Specialization:* Master's degree. *Minimum Degree Requirements:* 30 semester hours, including 15 in media; thesis optional. *Faculty:* 4 full-time; 8 part-time. *Master's Degrees Awarded 1989-90:* 14.

Pennsylvania State University. Division of Adult Education and Instructional Systems, 27D Chambers Bldg., University Park, PA 16802. (814) 865-0473. Fax (814) 865-3315. D. W. Johnson, Prof. in Charge, Instructional Systems Prog. *Specializations:* M. Ed., M.S. in Instructional Systems. *Minimum Degree Requirements:* 30 semester hours, including either a thesis or project paper. *Faculty:* 6 full-time; 2 affiliate; 2 part-time. *Students:* Approx. 260. *Financial Assistance:* Some assistantships, graduate fellowships, student aid loans. *Master's Degrees Awarded 1 July 1991-30 June 1992:* 23.

*Shippensburg University. Department of Communications and Journalism, Shippensburg, PA 17257. (717) 532-9121. Dr. Pat Waltermyer, Chair, Dept. of Communication, Journalism, College of Arts and Sciences. *Specialization:* Master's degree with emphasis on mass communications. *Minimum Degree Requirements:* 30 semester hours in media/communications studies; thesis optional.

*Temple University. Educational Media Program, Philadelphia, PA 19122. (215) 787-7000. Fax (215) 787-6926. Elton Robertson, Prof., Chair, Educational Media Prog. *Specialization:* Master's degree in Educational Media. *Minimum Degree Requirements:* 33 semester hours, including 24 in media; thesis optional. *Faculty:* 2 full-time. *Master's Degrees Awarded 1989-90:* 20.

*University of Pittsburgh. Instructional Design and Technology, School of Education, Pittsburgh, PA 15260. (412) 612-7254. Fax (412) 648-5911. Barbara Seels, Assoc. Prof., Prog. Coord., Instructional Design and Technology, Dept. of Instruction and Learning. *Specialization:* Master's degree in Instructional Technology. *Minimum Degree Requirements:* 36 trimester hours, including 18 in instructional technology, 9 in core courses, and 9 in electives; comprehensive examination. *Faculty:* 3. *Students:* 61. *Master's Degrees Awarded 1990-91:* 11. The school also offers a 45-credit specialist certification program.

*West Chester University. School of Education, West Chester, PA 19383. (215) 436-2447. Joseph Spiecker, Prof., Chair, Instructional Media Dept. *Specialization:* Master's degree in Instructional Media. *Minimum Degree Requirements:* 34 semester hours, including 28 in media; thesis optional. *Faculty:* 5 full-time. *Master's Degrees Awarded 1989-90:* 14.

RHODE ISLAND

Rhode Island College. 600 Mt. Pleasant Ave., Providence, RI 02908. (410) 456-8170. James E. Davis, Assoc. Prof., Chair, Dept. of Administration, Curriculum, and Instructional Technology. *Specialization:* M.S. in Instructional Technology. *Minimum Degree Requirements:* 30 semester hours, including 18 hours minimum in Instructional Technology, 6 hours in related disciplines, 3-6 hours in Humanistic and Behavioral Sciences; written comprehensive examination required. *Faculty:* 2 full-time; 3 part-time. *Students:* 4 full-time; 34 part-time. *Financial Assistance:* Contact college for options and details on available aid. *Master's Degrees Awarded 1 July 1991-30 June 1992:* 5. An individualized program at the sixth-year level is also offered.

*The University of Rhode Island. Graduate School of Library and Information Studies, Rodman Hall, Kingston, RI 02881-0815. (401) 792-2947. Fax (401) 792-4395. Elizabeth Futas, Prof. and Dir. *Specializations:* M.L.I.S. degree. Offers accredited master's degree with specialities in Archives, Law, Health Sciences, and Rare Books Librarianship. *Minimum Degree Requirements:* 42 semester-credit program offered in Rhode Island and regionally in Boston and Amherst, MA, and Durham, NH. *Faculty:* 9 full-time; 20 adjunct. *Students:* 300-plus. *Financial Assistance:* 6 half-time graduate assistantships, some scholarship aid. *Master's Degrees Awarded:* 57.

SOUTH CAROLINA

*University of South Carolina. Educational Psychology Department, Columbia, SC 29208. J. C. Rotter, Prof., Chair, Educational Psychology Dept. *Specialization:* Master's degree. *Minimum Degree Requirements:* 33 semester hours, including 3 each in administration, curriculum, and research, 9 in production, and 3 in instructional theory; no thesis required. *Faculty:* 3, 1, 2. *Master's Degrees Awarded 1989-90:* 4.

Winthrop University. Division of Leadership, Counseling and Media, Rock Hill, SC 29733. (803) 323-2151. George H. Robinson, Coord., Educational Media Prog., School of Education. *Specialization:* M.Ed. in Educational Media. *Features:* Students completing this program qualify for certification as a school library media specialist in South Carolina and most other states. *Minimum Degree Requirements:* 36-45 semester hours, including 15-33 in media, depending on media courses a student has had prior to this program; no thesis. *Faculty:* 2 full-time; 5 part-time. *Students:* 6 full-time; 32 part-time. *Financial Assistance:* Graduate assistantships of $1,500 per semester plus tuition. *Master's Degrees Awarded 1 July 1991-30 June 1992:* 11.

TENNESSEE

*East Tennessee State University. College of Education, Box 23020A, Johnson City, TN 37614. (615) 929-5848. Fax (615) 929-5770. Rudy Miller, Assoc. Prof., Dir. Media Services, Dept. of Curriculum and Instruction. *Specialization:* Master's degree. *Minimum Degree Requirements:* 36 semester hours, including 18 in instructional technology; thesis optional. *Faculty:* 2 full-time. *Master's Degrees Awarded:* 5.

*Memphis State University. College of Education, Memphis, TN 38152. (901) 678-3413. Fax (901) 678-4778. Thomas A. Rakes, Prof., Chair, Dept. of Curriculum and Instruction. *Specialization:* Master's degree. *Minimum Degree Requirements:* 36 semester hours, including 15 in instructional design and technology; thesis optional. *Faculty:* 4. *Master's Degrees Awarded:* 7. The school also offers a six-year specialist degree program in Instructional Technology.

Middle Tennessee State University. Department of Educational Leadership, Murfreesboro, TN 37132. (615) 898-2855. Ralph L. White, Prof. and Chair, Dept. of Educational Leadership. *Specialization:* Master's degree. *Minimum Degree Requirements:* 33 semester hours, including 15 in media; no thesis required. *Faculty:* 2 full-time. *Master's Degrees Awarded 1 July 1991-30 June 1992:* 29.

University of Tennessee-Knoxville. College of Education, Knoxville, TN 37906-3400. (615) 974-3165. Dr. Alfred D. Grant, Coord., Graduate Media Prog., Dept. of Curriculum and Instruction. *Specialization:* M.S. in Education, concentration in Instructional Media and Technology. *Minimum Degree Requirements:* 33 semester hours, thesis optional. *Faculty:* 1. *Master's Degrees Awarded 1 July 1991-30 June 1992:* 2. The Department of Curriculum and Instruction also offers a six-year specialist degree program in Curriculum and Instruction with a concentration in Instructional Media and Technology.

TEXAS

*East Texas State University. Department of Secondary and Higher Education, Commerce, TX 75428. (903) 886-5607. Fax (903) 886-5039. Robert S. Munday, Prof., Head, Dept. of Secondary and Higher Education. *Specialization:* Master's degree. *Minimum Degree Requirements:* 30 semester hours with thesis, 36 without thesis, including 18 in media. *Faculty:* 2 full-time; 2 part-time. *Master's Degrees Awarded 1989-90:* 27.

Prairie View A&M University. Department of School Services, Prairie View, TX 77446-0036. (409) 857-3018. Fax (409) 857-2911. Dr. Marion Henry, Dir., Educational Media and Technology Prog. *Specialization:* Master's degree in Educational Media and Technology. *Minimum Degree Requirements:* 36 semester hours in media; no thesis required. *Faculty:* 3 full-time; 1 part-time. *Students:* 22. *Financial Assistance:* None. *Master's Degrees Awarded 1 July 1991-30 June 1992:* 6.

Texas A&M University. College of Education, College Station, TX 77843-3256. (409) 845-7276. Fax (409) 845-9663. Ronald D. Zellner, Coord., Educational Technology Prog. *Specialization:* Master's degree, broad base with emphasis in Television or Computer Applications. *Minimum Degree Requirements:* 37 semester hours; no thesis; practicum or internship course. *Faculty:* 4 full-time; 1 part-time. *Students:* 15 full-time; 5 part-time. *Financial Assistance:* General teaching assistantships. *Master's Degrees Awarded 1 July 1991-30 June 1992:* 12.

*Texas Tech University. College of Education, Box 4560, Lubbock, TX 79409. (806) 742-2011. Robert Price, Assoc. Prof., Dir., Instructional Technology Prog. *Specialization:* Master's degree. *Minimum Degree Requirements:* 39 semester hours; no thesis. *Faculty:* 2 full-time; 2 part-time. *Master's Degrees Awarded 1990-91:* 17.

*University of North Texas. College of Education, Box 13857, Denton, TX 76203-3857. (817) 565-3790. Fax (817) 565-2185. Jan Young, Chair, Dept. of Computer Education and Cognitive Systems, College of Education. *Specialization:* Master's degree. *Minimum Degree Requirements:* 36 semester hours, including 27 hours in Instructional Technology and Computer Education; no thesis. *Faculty:* 8. *Master's Degrees Awarded 1992-93:* 35.

University of Texas-Austin. College of Education, Austin, TX 78712. (512) 471-5211. DeLayne Hudspeth, Assoc. Prof., Coord., Area of Instructional Technology, Dept. of Curriculum and Instruction, College of Education. *Specialization:* Master's degree. *Minimum Degree Requirements:* 30-36 semester hours minimum depending on selection of program; 18 in Instructional Technology plus research course; thesis optional. A sixhour minor is required outside the department. *Faculty:* 4 full-time; 1 part-time. *Master's Degrees Awarded 1 July 1991-30 June 1992:* 18.

The University of Texas-Southwestern Medical Center at Dallas. 5323 Harry Hines Blvd., MC8881, Dallas, TX 75235-8881. (214) 904-2360. Fax (214) 904-2522. Dr. Mary F. Whiteside, Dir., Media Development Graduate Prog., Biomedical Communications Dept. *Specializations:* M.A. in Biomedical Communications with an emphasis in Media Development. *Minimum Degree Requirements:* 36 semester hours; thesis required. *Faculty:* 4 (in media development). *Students:* Program limited to 6 full-time students each year. *Financial Assistance:* Student assistantships available when budget permits. *Master's Degrees Awarded 1 July 1991-30 June 1992:* 3.

UTAH

*Brigham Young University. Department of Educational Psychology, 201 MCKB, Provo, UT 84602. (801) 378-7072. Fax (801) 378-4017. Paul F. Merrill, Prof., Chair. *Minimum Degree Requirements:* 36 semester hours, including 13 in core; thesis required. *Faculty:* 7 full-time; 5 part-time. *Master's Degrees Awarded 1989-90:* 7.

Utah State University. Department of Instructional Technology, Logan, UT 84322-2830. (801) 750-2694. Fax (801) 750-2693. Dr. Don C. Smellie, Prof., Head, Dept. of Instructional Technology. *Specializations:* M.S. and Ed.S. with concentrations in the areas of Instructional Development, Interactive Learning, Educational Technology, and Information Technology/School Library Media Administration. *Features:* Programs in Information Technology/School Library Media Administration and Master Resource Teacher/Educational Technology are also delivered via an electronic distance education system. *Minimum Degree Requirements:* M.S.—60 quarter hours, including 45 in media; thesis or project option. Ed.S.—45 quarter hours if M.S. is in the field, 60 hours if it is not. *Faculty:* 9 full-time; 7 part-time. *Students:* 52 full-time; 68 part-time (in graduate program). *Financial Assistance:* Fellowships and assistantships. *Master's Degrees Awarded 1 July 1991-30 June 1992:* 36.

VIRGINIA

James Madison University. Department of Secondary Education, Library Science and Educational Leadership, Harrisonburg, VA 22807. (703) 568-6486. Fax (703) 568-6920. Alvin Pettus, Head, Dept. of Secondary Education, Library Science and Educational Leadership. *Specialization:* Master's degree. *Minimum Degree Requirements:* 33 semester hours, including 21 in media; thesis optional. *Faculty:* 3 full-time; 2 part-time. *Master's Degrees Awarded 1 July 1991-30 June 1992:* 1.

Radford University. Educational Studies Department, College of Education, P.O. Box 6959, Radford, VA 24142. (703) 831-5736. Richard A. Buck, Educational Media Dept. *Specialization:* Master's degree in Educational Media. *Minimum Degree Requirements:* 33 semester hours; thesis optional; practicum required. *Faculty:* 3 full-time; 2 part-time. *Students:* 2 full-time; 34 part-time. *Financial Assistance:* Graduate assistantship available. *Master's Degrees Awarded 1 July 1991-30 June 1992:* 5.

*University of Virginia. Curry School of Education, Ruffner Hall, Charlottesville, VA 22903. (804) 924-7471. Fax (804) 924-0747. John D. Bunch, Assoc. Prof., Coord., Instructional Technology Prog., Dept. of Educational Studies. *Specialization:* Master's degree. *Minimum Degree Requirements:* 36 semester hours, including 18 in media and computers. *Faculty:* 3 full-time. *Master's Degrees Awarded 1 July 1991-30 June 1992:* 5. The school also offers post-master's degree programs (Ed.S., Ed.D., and Ph.D.) in Instructional Technology.

Virginia Commonwealth University. Division of Teacher Education, Richmond, VA 23284. (804) 367-1324. Fax (804) 367-1323. Dr. Sheary Johnson, Asst. Prof., Core Coord. of Instructional Technology, Dept. of Teacher Education. *Specialization:* Master's Degree in Curriculum and Instruction with a specialization in Library Media. *Minimum Degree Requirements:* 36 semester hours; internship (field experience); externship (project or research study); comprehensive examination. *Faculty:* 2 full-time. *Students:* 40 part-time. *Financial Assistance:* Graduate assistantship in School of Education. *Master's Degrees Awarded 1 July 1991-30 July 1992:* 7.

Virginia Polytechnic Institute and State University (Virginia Tech). College of Education, Blacksburg, VA 24061-0313. (703) 231-5598. Fax (703) 231-3717. Thomas M. Sherman, Prof., Prog. Area Leader, Instructional Systems Development, Curriculum and Instruction. *Specializations:* M.S. in Instructional Technology, with emphasis on Training and Development, Educational Computing, Evaluation, and Media Management. *Features:* Facilities include 70-computer laboratory (IBM, Macintosh), interactive video, speech synthesis, telecommunications. *Minimum Degree Requirements:* 30 semester hours, including 15 in Instructional Technology; thesis optional. *Faculty:* 8 full-time; 5 part-time. *Students:* 8 full-time; 15 part-time. *Financial Assistance:* Assistantships are sometimes available, as well as opportunities with other agencies. *Master's Degrees Awarded 1 July 1991-30 July 1992:* 3. An advanced certificate program is available.

*Virginia State University. School of Education, Petersburg, VA 23803. (804) 524-5934. Vykuntapathi Thota, Prog. Dir., Dept. of Educational Leadership. *Specializations:* M.S., M.Ed. *Minimum Degree Requirements:* 30 semester hours plus thesis for M.S.; 33 semester hours plus project for M.Ed.; comprehensive examination. *Faculty:* 1 full-time.

WASHINGTON

*Eastern Washington University. Department of Education, Cheney, WA 99004. (509) 359-6200. Thomas Keith Midgley, Dept. of Education. *Specialization:* M.Ed. in Instructional Communications. *Minimum Degree Requirements:* 48-60 quarter hours; production thesis required. *Faculty:* 2 full-time.

*Saint Martin's College. Department of Education, Lacey, WA 98503. (206) 438-4333. Dan Windisch, Dir., Dept. of Education. *Specializations:* M.Ed. with emphasis on Instructional Design and Development, Hypertalk Programming, and Materials Production. *Minimum Degree Requirements:* 30 semester hours; thesis required. *Faculty:* 4 full-time.

*University of Washington. Department of Education, Seattle, WA 98195. (206) 543-1877. Fax (206) 543-8439. William D. Winn, Prof., Prog. in Educational Communication and Technology, School of Education. *Specialization:* Master's degree. *Minimum Degree Requirements:* 45 quarter hours, including 24 in media; thesis optional. *Faculty:* 2 full-time. *Master's Degrees Awarded 1989-90:* 3.

*Western Washington University. Woodring College of Education, Bellingham, WA 98225-9087. (206) 676-3381. Tony Jongejan, Assoc. Prof., Instructional Technology Prog., Dept. of Educational Administration and Foundations. *Specializations:* M.Ed. for Curriculum and Instruction, with emphasis in Computer Education, elementary and secondary programs; Adult Education, with emphasis on Instructional Technology and Design; Instructional Technology and Design, with emphasis on Multimedia Master's Program for education and industry persons; and Learning Resources (Library Science) for K-12 school librarians only. *Minimum Degree Requirements:* 52 quarter hours (15 hours in computers, 24 hours in education-related courses, 0 hours outside education); thesis required; internship and practicum possible. *Financial Assistance:* Standard financial assistance for graduate students, some special assistance for minority graduate students. *Faculty:* 3.5 full-time; 8 part-time. *Students:* 5 full-time; 15 part-time, 42 off-campus. *Master's Degrees Awarded 1990-91:* 17.

WEST VIRGINIA

Marshall University. Department of Instructional Technology and Library Science, Huntington, WV 25701. Virginia D. Plumley, Prof., Chair, Dept. of Instructional Technology and Library Science. This program has been discontinued.

West Virginia University. Technology Education, 706 Allen Hall, Morgantown, WV 26506. (304) 293-3803. Fax (304) 293-7300. David McCrory, Prof., Chair, Technology Education Prog., Communication and Information Systems, College of Human Resources and Education. *Specialization:* Master's degree. *Minimum Degree Requirements:* 37 semester hours, including 15 hours in communication technology; thesis or research project. *Faculty:* 4 full-time. *Master's Degrees Awarded in 1990-91:* 2.

WISCONSIN

*University of Wisconsin-La Crosse. Educational Media Program, Rm. 109, Morris Hall, La Crosse, WI 54601. (608) 785-8000. Fax (608) 785-8909. Russ Phillips, Dir., Educational Media Prog., College of Education. *Specialization:* Master's degree. *Minimum Degree Requirements:* 30 semester hours, including 15 in media; no thesis. *Faculty:* 2 full-time; 2 part-time. *Students:* 27. *Master's Degrees Awarded:* 15.

*University of Wisconsin-Madison. School of Education, Madison, WI 53706. (608) 263-4600. Fax (608) 263-9992. Ann DeVaney, Prof., Coord., Educational Communications and Technology, Dept. of Curriculum and Instruction, School of Education. *Specialization:* Master's degree. *Minimum Degree Requirements:* 30 semester hours, including 22 hours in media; thesis or project required. *Faculty:* 5. *Master's Degrees Awarded 1989-90:* 73.

University of Wisconsin-Oshkosh. College of Education and Human Services, 800 Algoma Blvd., Oshkosh, WI 54901-8666. (414) 424-1490. Richard R. Hammes, Prof., Coord., Dept. of Human Services and Professional Leadership, College of Education and Human Services. *Specialization:* M.S. in Curriculum and Supervision with special emphasis in Library/Media. *Minimum Degree Requirements:* 36 semester hours; thesis optional. *Faculty:* 3. *Students:* Approx. 30. *Financial Assistance:* Limited graduate assistantships. *Master's Degrees Awarded 1 July 1991-30 June 1992:* 3.

*University of Wisconsin-Stout. Menomonie, WI 54751. (715) 232-1202. Fax (715) 232-1274. Dr. Roger L. Hartz, Prog. Dir., Media Technology Prog. *Specializations:* M.S. in Media Curricular tracks may be developed in Instructional Development, Media Production, Media Management, and School Media. This is an Educational Media/Instructional Technology program, not a Mass Media or Media Arts program. *Minimum Degree Requirements:* 32 semester hours, including 15 in media; thesis optional. Coursework is drawn from many departments across the university; internship or field study strongly recommended. *Faculty:* 4 full-time. *Students:* 8 full-time; 6 part-time. *Financial Assistance:* Limited numbers of graduate and teaching assistantships available; on-campus employment available; out-of-state tuition waivers for some international students. *Master's Degrees Awarded 1990-91:* 9.

WYOMING

*University of Wyoming. College of Education, Box 3374, Laramie, WY 82071. (307) 766-3896. Fax (307) 766-6668. Dr. Patricia McClurg, Prog. Area Coord., Instructional Technology. *Specialization:* M.S. in Instructional Technology. *Minimum Degree Requirements:* 36 semester hours, including 32 in instructional technology and 4 in thesis option, or 36 hours of coursework including project option. Two tracks are available: Instructional Design and Library/Media Studies. *Faculty:* 6. *Master's Degrees Awarded 1990-91:* 15. For additional information, contact Dr. Patricia McClurg.

Graduate Programs in Educational Computing

When the directory of graduate programs in educational computing first appeared in the *1986 EMTY*, there were only 50 programs. This year's listing consists of 71 such programs in 31 states, the District of Columbia, and the U.S. Virgin Islands. The information in this section has been revised and updates the information assembled in *EMTY 1992*. Individuals who are considering graduate study in educational computing should contact the institution of their choice for current information. It should be noted that some programs that appear in this listing also appear in the listing of master's and six-year programs and doctoral programs.

Copies of the entries from the *1992 EMTY* were sent to the programs with a request for updated information and/or corrections, with the proviso that, if no response was received, the 1992 entry would be used again so that the program would be represented in the list. Programs from which no response was received are indicated with an asterisk (*). It should be noted that not all the information is necessarily correct for the current year.

We would like to express our appreciation to the 34 program administrators who complied with our request for the 1993 edition. Of the remaining programs, 13 were updated in the 1992 edition; for the remaining 26, information presented dates back to the 1991 edition. Two programs that have been discontinued—Southwest Baptist University and the University of Oregon—have been dropped from the listing. Our special thanks go to those who notified us of the status of these programs.

Data in this section include the name of the institution and the program, telephone and fax numbers, a contact person, the degree(s) offered and the year the program began, admission requirements and minimum requirements for each degree, the number of full- and part-time faculty, the number of students currently enrolled, information on financial assistance, and the number of degrees awarded.

This section is arranged alphabetically by state and name of institution.

ARIZONA

Arizona State University. Educational Media and Computers, FMC Payne 146, Tempe, AZ 85287-0111. Dr. Gary Bitter, Coord., Educational Media and Computers. (602) 965-7192. Fax (602) 965-8887. *Specializations:* M.A. and Ph.D. in Educational Media and Computers. Master's program started in 1971 and doctorate started in 1976. *Minimum Degree Requirements:* Master's—33 semester hours (21 hours in educational media and computers, 9 hours in education, 3 hours outside education); thesis not required; internship required; comprehensive exam and practicum required. Doctorate—93 semester hours (24 hours in educational media and computers, 57 hours in education, 12 hours outside education); thesis required; internship required; practicum required. *Admission Requirements:* MAT/TOEFL. *Faculty:* 7 full-time. *Students:* M.A., 87 full-time; 69 part-time. Ph.D., 11 full-time; 6 part-time. *Financial Assistance:* Assistantships are available. *Degrees Awarded 1 July 1991-30 June 1992:* M.A., 23; Ph.D., 1.

CALIFORNIA

San Diego State University. Department of Educational Technology, San Diego, CA 92182-0311. (619) 594-6718. Dr. Pat Harrison, Chair, Dept. of Educational Technology. *Specializations:* M.A. in Education with specializations in Educational Technology and Educational Computing. *Minimum Degree Requirements:* 36 semester hours (3 hours in education, hours in computers and outside education not specified); practicum required. *Admission Requirements:* GRE, 950 combined score; GPA 2.5 last 60 units of undergraduate work; evidence of writing competence. *Faculty:* 6 full-time. *Students:* 20 full-time; 80 part-time. *Financial Assistance:* Graduate assistantships, fellowships. *Degrees Awarded 1 July 1991-30 June 1992:* M.A., 40; Ph.D., 1.

*United States International University. School of Education, 10455 Pomerado Rd., San Diego, CA, 92131. (619) 6934721. Dr. Maria T. Fernandez, Prof. and Prog. Dir., Computer Education Programs. *Specializations:* M.A. in Computer Education and Ed.D. with specialization in Computer Education. Master's and doctoral programs started in 1983. *Minimum Degree Requirements:* Master's—45 quarter credit hours (30 hours in computers, 15 hours in education, 0 hours outside education); practicum required. Doctorate—95 quarter credit hours (60 hours in computers, 35 hours in education, 0 hours outside education); thesis, internship, and practicum required. *Faculty:* 4 full-time; 4 part-time. *Students:* M.A., 100; Ed.D., 50.

COLORADO

University of Colorado at Colorado Springs. School of Education, P.O. Box 7150, Colorado Springs, CO, 80933-7150. (719) 593-3266. Fax (719) 593-3554. Dr. Doris M. Carey, Dir., Educational Computing and Technology. *Specializations:* M.A. in Curriculum and Instruction with an emphasis in Educational Computing and Technology with emphasis on Educational Computing in K-College, Computer-Based Training, and Instructional Design. Master's program started in 1983. *Minimum Degree Requirements:* 33 semester hours (27 hours required in educational technology; 6 hours in education; 0 hours outside education); no thesis, internship, or practicum required. *Admission Requirements:* GRE or Miller Analogies Test; transcripts; four letters of recommendation; interview. *Faculty:* 1 full-time; 6 part-time. *Students:* 2 full-time; 51 part-time. *Degrees Awarded 1 July 1991-30 June 1992:* M.A., 14.

*University of Denver. School of Education, Denver, CO 80208. (303) 871-2508. Dr. Raymond Kluever, Coord., Graduate Study in Education. *Specializations:* M.A. in Curriculum and Instruction or in Educational Psychology. Master's program started in 1984. *Minimum Degree Requirements:* 45 quarter credit hours (20 hours in computers, 35 hours in education, 0-10 hours outside education); no thesis, internship, or practicum required. *Faculty:* 3 full-time; 3 part-time. *Students:* 4.

CONNECTICUT

Fairfield University. Graduate School of Education and Allied Professions, Fairfield, CT 06430. (203) 254-4000, ext. 2697. Fax (203) 254-4087. Dr. Ibrahim Hefzallah, Prof. of Educational Technology; Dr. John J. Schurdak, Assoc. Prof., Co-Directors, Computers in Education/Educational Technology Program. *Specializations:* M.A. in two tracks: (1) Computers in Education, or (2) Media/Educational Technology (for school media specialists, see listing of Master's Programs). *Minimum Degree Requirements:* 33 semester credits; comprehensive examination. *Admission Requirements:* Bachelor's degree and, for foreign students, TESOL Exam minimum score of 550. *Faculty:* 2 full-time; 9 part-time. *Students:* 60 part-time.

Financial Assistance: Work study, graduate assistantships. *Degrees Awarded 1 July 1991-30 June 1992:* 10. An advanced certificate program in Media/Educational Technology is also available.

University of Hartford. Educational Computing and Technology, 200 Bloomfield Ave., West Hartford, CT 06117. (203) 243-4277. Dr. Marilyn Schaffer, Assoc. Prof. of Educational Computing and Technology. *Specialization:* M.Ed. in Educational Computing. Master's program started in 1985. *Minimum Degree Requirements:* 30 semester hours (21 hours in computers, 9 hours in education); no thesis or practicum required; internships available. *Faculty:* 2 full-time; 24 part-time. *Students:* 35.

DISTRICT OF COLUMBIA

*The George Washington University. 2201 G St. NW, Washington, DC 20052. Mary Louise Ortenzo, Coord. of Admissions; (202) 994-6163. Dr. William Lynch; (202) 994-6862. *Specialization:* School offers M.A. in Educational Technology Leadership. Master's program started in 1988. *Minimum Degree Requirements:* 36 semester hours (15 hours in computers, 9 hours in education, 12 hours electives inside or outside education); thesis required; internship not required; practicum not required. *Features:* Beginning with the spring 1991 semester, this program will be offered nationally with the cooperation of Mind Extension University, the Education Network. Students can complete the entire degree via instructional television through cable or satellite delivery. *Faculty:* 5 full-time; 2 part-time. *Students:* 12.

FLORIDA

Florida Institute of Technology. Computer Education Department, 150 W. University Blvd., Melbourne, FL 32901-6988. (407) 768-8000, ext. 8126. Fax (407) 984-8461. Dr. Robert Fronk, Head of Computer Education Dept. *Specialization:* Master's Degree in Computer Education with emphasis on Hypermedia and Interactive Laserdisc Technology. *Admission Requirements:* GPA 3.0 for regular admission; 2.75 for provisional admission. *Minimum Degree Requirements:* 48 quarter hours (18 in computer, 18 in education, 12 outside education); no thesis or internship required; practicum required. *Faculty:* 6 full-time. *Students:* 10 full-time; 5 part-time. *Financial Assistance:* Graduate student assistantships available. *Degrees Awarded 1 July 1991-30 June 1992:* Master's, 6.

*Jacksonville University. Department of Education, 2800 University Blvd. N., Jacksonville, FL 32211. (904) 744-3950. Dr. Daryle C. May, Dir., Teacher Education and M.A.T. Prog. *Specialization:* M.A. in Teaching in Computer Education. Master's program started in 1983. *Minimum Degree Requirements:* 36 semester hours (21 hours in computer, 15 hours in education, 0 hours outside education); no thesis, internship, or practicum required; comprehensive exam required. *Faculty:* 5 full-time; 2 part-time. *Students:* 12.

*Nova University. Ed.D./CED Program, Ft. Lauderdale, FL 33314. (305) 475-7047; (800) 541-6682, ext. 7047. Dr. John Kingsbury, Dir. of Marketing. *Specializations:* M.S., Ed.D., and Ed.S. in Computer Education. Master's program started in 1985; specialist in 1984; doctoral in 1984. *Minimum Degree Requirements:* Master's—36 semester hours (24 hours in computer, 12 hours in education, 0 hours outside education); no thesis, internship, or practicum required. Doctorate—66 semester hours (33 hours in computer, 21 hours in education, 12 hours outside education); thesis and practicum required. *Faculty:* 2 full-time on master's level; 8 full-time on doctoral level. *Students:* M.S., 70; specialist, 5; Ed.D., 90.

*University of Florida. College of Education, G-518 Norman Hall, Gainesville, FL 32611. (904) 392-5049. Dr. Roy Bolduc, Prof. *Specializations:* Ed.S. and Ph.D. in Computers in Education. Specialist program started in 1984 and doctoral in 1984. *Minimum Degree Requirements:* Specialist—semester hours vary (dependent on student's background); a minor in Computer Science (not Computers in Education) is required; no thesis or internship is required; practicum required. Doctorate—semester hours vary (dependent on student's background); a minor in Computer Science is required; thesis required; no internship or practicum is required. *Faculty:* 2 full-time; 1 part-time. *Students:* Ed.S., 3; Ph.D., 5.

GEORGIA

*Georgia State University. Educational Foundations Department, Atlanta, GA 30303. (404) 651-2582. Dr. Dave O'Neil, Assoc. Prof. *Specializations:* Department offers M.A. and Ph.D. in Educational Psychology (emphasis option in Educational Computers). Master's and doctoral programs started in 1984. *Minimum Degree Requirements:* Master's—60 quarter hours (25 hours in computers, 35 hours in education); thesis required; no internship or practicum is required. Doctorate—90 quarter hours (35 hours in computers, 40 hours in education, 15 hours outside education); thesis required; no internship or practicum is required. *Faculty:* 2 full-time; 2 part-time. *Students:* M.A., 25; Ph.D., 10.

*University of Georgia. College of Education, Athens, GA 30602. (404) 542-3810. Dr. C. Hugh Gardner, Assoc. Prof. of Instructional Technology. *Specialization:* M.Ed. in Computer-Based Education. Master's program started in 1985. *Minimum Degree Requirements:* 60 quarter credit hours (25 hours in computers, 10 hours in education, 25 hours not specified [55 hours with applied project]); thesis not required; internship and practicum optional. *Faculty:* 3 full-time; 5 part-time. *Students:* 20.

HAWAII

University of Hawaii-Manoa. Educational Technology Department, 1776 University Ave., Honolulu, HI 96822. (808) 956-7671. Fax (808) 956-3905. Dr. Geoffrey Z. Kucera, Prof. and Chair, Educational Technology Dept. *Specializations:* M.Ed. in Educational Technology. Specialization in Computer Technology has three options: (a) Computer-Based Learning, (b) Courseware Development, and (c) Information Center Management. Program began in 1983. *Admission Requirements:* GPA 3.0, GRE min. 50th percentile standing. *Minimum Degree Requirements:* 39 semester credit hours (27 in computing, 6 in instructional design, 6 electives); thesis available; practicum and internship required. *Faculty:* 5 full-time; 2 part-time. *Students:* 5 full-time. *Master's Degrees Awarded 1 July 1991-30 June 1992:* 3.

ILLINOIS

Concordia University. 7400 Augusta, River Forest, IL 60305-1499. (708) 209-3023. Fax (708) 209-3176. Dr. Paul T. Kreiss, Assoc. Dean, School of Graduate Studies. *Specialization:* M.A. in Mathematics Education/Computer Science Education. Master's program started in 1987. *Admission Requirements:* GPA 2.85 or above, 2.25 to 2.85 provision status; bachelor's degree from regionally accredited institution; two letters of recommendation; GRE required in cases of inadequate evidence of academic proficiency. *Minimum Degree Requirements:* 48 quarter hours; no thesis, internship, or practicum required. *Faculty:* 5 full-time; 5 part-time. *Students:* 5 full-time; 44 part-time. *Financial Assistance:* A number of graduate assistantships;

Stafford Student loans and Supplement Loan for Students. *Degrees Awarded 1 July 1991-30 June 1992:* M.A., 0.

*Governors State University. College of Education, University Park, IL 60466. (312) 534-5000, ext. 2273. Dr. John Meyer, University Prof. *Specialization:* M.A. in Education (with Computer Education as specialization). Master's program started in 1986. *Minimum Degree Requirements:* 36-39 semester hours (15 hours in computer, 21-24 hours in education, 0 hours outside education); thesis/project and practicum required; internship not required. *Faculty:* 3 full-time; 5 part-time. *Students:* 46.

National-Louis University (formerly National College of Education). Department of Computer Education, 2840 Sheridan Rd., Evanston, IL 60201. (708) 475-1100, ext. 2355. Fax (708) 256-1057. Dr. Marianne G. Handler, Chair, Dept. of Computer Education. *Specializations:* M.Ed., M.S., C.A.S. (Certificate of Advanced Studies) in Computer Education, and Ed.D. in Instructional Leadership with minor concentration in computer education. Master's program started in 1983, specialist in 1983, and doctoral in 1984. *Admission Requirements:* GPA 3.0 of 4.0; Miller Analogies Test 3.3. *Minimum Degree Requirements:* Master's—34 semester hours (24 hours in computers, 10 hours in education, and 0 hours outside education); thesis optional; no internship or practicum is required. Specialist, C.A.S.—30 semester hours (26 hours in computers, 4 hours in education, 0 hours outside education); no thesis, internship, or practicum is required. Doctorate—63 semester hours (14 hours in computers, 37 hours in education, 0 hours outside education); thesis and internship required; practicum not required. *Faculty:* 3 full-time. *Students:* M.Ed. and M.S., 52; C.A.S., 13; Ed.D., 4. *Financial Assistance:* Fellowship program based on need. *Degrees Awarded 1 July 1992-30 June 1992:* M.S. and M.Ed., 16; Ph.D., 0.

Northern Illinois University. Instructional Technology Faculty, LEPS Department, DeKalb, IL 60115. (815) 753-0464. Fax (815) 753-9388. Dr. Gary L. McConeghy, Chair, Instructional Technology Faculty. *Specialization:* M.S.Ed. in Instructional Technology with a concentration in Microcomputers in School-Based Settings. Master's program started in 1968. *Admission Requirements:* GPA 2.75; GRE 800 combined scores; two references. *Minimum Degree Requirements:* 39 hours (27 hours in technology, 9 hours in education, 0 hours outside education); no thesis, internship, or practicum is required. *Faculty:* 5 full-time; 5 part-time. *Students:* 106 part-time. *Financial Assistance:* Some assistantships available at various departments on campus. *Degrees Awarded 1 July 1991-30 June 1992:* M.S.Ed., 23. See also the listing of Master's Programs.

*Southern Illinois University-Carbondale. Department of Curriculum and Instruction, Carbondale, IL 62901. (618) 536-2441. Dr. Pierre Barrette, Coord., Dept. of Curriculum and Instruction. *Specializations:* M.S. in Curriculum and Instruction with a specialization in Computer-Based Education and Ph.D. in Curriculum and Instruction with a specialization in Instructional Technology. Master's and doctoral programs started in 1983. *Minimum Degree Requirements:* Master's—32 semester hours (specialty in Computer-Based Education: 21 hours in computers, 9 hours in education, 2-6 outside education); thesis optional; no internship or practicum is required. Doctorate—64 semester hours (specialty in Instructional Technology: hours in computers vary, 17 hours in education, hours outside education vary); thesis required; no internship or practicum is required. *Faculty:* 5 full-time; 5 part-time. *Students:* M.S., 25; Ph.D., 9.

INDIANA

Purdue University. School of Education, Department of Curriculum and Instruction, West Lafayette, IN 47907-1442. (317) 494-5673. Fax (317) 494-0587. Dr. James Russell, Prof., Educational Computing and Instructional Development. *Specializations:* M.S., Ed.S., and Ph.D. in Educational Computing and Instructional Development. Master's program started in 1982 and specialist and doctoral in 1985. *Admission Requirements:* GPA of 3.0 or better; three letters of recommendation; statement of personal goals; total score of 1,000 or more on GRE for Ph.D. admission. *Minimum Degree Requirements:* Master's—36 semester hours (15 in computer or instructional development, 9 in education, 12 unspecified); thesis optional. Specialist—60-65 semester hours (15-18 in computer or instructional development, 30-35 in education); thesis, internship, and practicum required. Doctorate—90 semester hours (15-18 in computer or instructional development, 42-45 in education); thesis, internship, and practicum required. *Faculty:* 6 full-time. *Students:* 10 full-time; 12 part-time. *Financial Assistance:* Assistantships and fellowships. *Degrees Awarded 1 July 1991-30 June 1992:* Ph.D., 4; master's, 10.

IOWA

Dubuque Tri-College Department of Education (a consortium of Clarke College, The University of Dubuque, and Loras College). Graduate Studies, 1450 Alta Vista, Dubuque, IA 52001. (319) 588-7842. Fax (319) 588-7964. Judy Decker, Clarke College, (319) 588-6425. *Specializations:* M.A. in Education in Technology (a multimedia perspective for instructional development); M.A. in Education in Media (includes Iowa licensure for media specialists K-6 or 7-12). *Admission Requirements:* Minimum GPA 2.5 on 4.0 scale; GRE (verbal and quantitative) or Miller Analogies Test; application form and $25 application fee; and letters of recommendation. *Minimum Degree Requirements:* 22 semester hours in computer courses, 12 in education, 3 electives. Predominantly summer program. *Faculty:* Technology, 1 full-time; 1 part-time. Media, 3 part-time. *Students:* Technology, 8 part-time. Media, 23 part-time. *Financial Assistance:* Student loans. *Degrees Awarded 1 July 1991-30 June 1992:* 0 (program is new).

Iowa State University. College of Education, Ames, IA 50011. (515) 294-6840. Dr. Michael R. Simonson, Prof. *Specializations:* M.S., M.Ed., and Ph.D. in Curriculum and Instructional Technology with an emphasis in Instructional Computing. Master's and doctoral programs started in 1967. *Admission Requirements:* M.S. and M.Ed., three letters; top half of undergraduate class; autobiography. Ph.D., the same plus GRE. *Minimum Degree Requirements:* Master's—30 semester hours; thesis required; no internship or practicum is required. Doctorate— 78 semester hours, thesis required; no internship or practicum is required. *Faculty:* 3 full-time; 3 part-time. *Students:* 20 full-time; 20 part-time. *Financial Assistance:* 10 assistantships. *Degrees Awarded 1 July 1991-30 June 1992:* Ph.D., 3; M.S. and M.Ed., 5.

Teikyo Marycrest University. Department of Computer Science and Mathematics, 1607 W. 12th St., Davenport, IA 52804. (319) 326-9558. Fax (319) 326-9250. Dr. Gary Monnard, Dept. Head. *Specialization:* M.S. in Computer Science. *Admission Requirements:* Bachelor's degree in Computer Science from an accredited institution, or complete all preparatory courses *and* have a working knowledge of an assembly language, Pascal, and at least one other high-level programming language. *Minimum Degree Requirements:* 27 graduate semester hours plus 6 hours thesis; 36 graduate semester hours non-thesis. *Faculty:* 4. *Students:* Data not available. *Degrees Awarded 1 July 1991-30 June 1992:* Data not available.

KANSAS

*Kansas State University. Educational Technology and Computer Education, 253 Bluemont Hall, Manhattan, KS 66506. (913) 532-5556. Dr. Jackson A. Byars, Chair, Educational Technology and Computer Education. *Specializations:* M.S. in Elementary or Secondary Education with specialization in Computer-Based Education; Ed.D. in Computer Education; Ph.D. in Computer Education. Master's program started in 1982; doctoral in 1984. *Minimum Degree Requirements:* Master's—30 semester hours (minimum of 9 in computer education); thesis not required; internship not required; practicum not required (but these are possible). Doctorate—90 semester hours (minimum of 18 in Computer Education, 12 hours outside education); thesis required; internship and practicum not required but encouraged. *Faculty:* 4 full-time; 3 part-time on master's level; 4 full-time on doctoral level. *Students:* 20 on master's level; 9 on doctoral level.

KENTUCKY

*Spalding University. Education Technology Program, 851 S. Fourth Ave., Louisville, KY 40203. (502) 585-9911, ext. 237. Dr. Eileen Boyle Young, Dir., Education Technology Prog. *Specializations:* Ed.S. in Technology in Education; M.A. in Education Technology. Master's program started in 1983; Specialist in 1983. *Minimum Degree Requirements:* Master's—30-36 semester hours (21-27 in computers, 9 hours in education, 0 hours outside education); no thesis or internship is required; practicum required (directed study and position paper). Specialist— 30-36 semester hours (21-27 hours in computers, 9 hours in education, 0 hours outside education); no thesis or internship is required; practicum required (directed study and position paper). Students may obtain Kentucky certificate endorsements (K-12) as specialist in Computerized Instruction (36 graduate semester hours) and Indiana certificate endorsement (K-12) as Computer Educator (15 graduate semester hours). *Faculty:* 1 full-time; 1 part-time. *Students:* Master's, 11; specialist, 8.

*University of Kentucky. Department of Special Education, Lexington, KY 40506-0001. (606) 257-4713. Dr. A. Edward Blackhurst, Prof. *Specializations:* Ed.S. degree in Special Education Microcomputer Specialist program. Specialist program started in 1984. *Minimum Degree Requirements:* 35 semester hours (35 hours in education [all courses offered in Special Education Department and focus on computer applications], 0 hours outside education); thesis and practicum required; internship not required. *Faculty:* 5 part-time. *Students:* 13.

LOUISIANA

*Grambling State University. College of Education, Grambling, LA 71245. Dr. Vernon Farmer, Dept. Chair, (318) 274-2656; Dr. Ben Lowery, Assistant Prof., (318) 274-2238. *Specializations:* Ed.D. and M.A. in Developmental Education with an Instructional Systems and Technology specialization. Doctoral program started in 1986. *Minimum Degree Requirements:* 90-plus semester hours (6 hours CAI, 6 hours design, 6 hours educational psychology, 6 hours video, 6 hours theory, 36 hours minimum in education, 0 hours outside education [but encouraged as cognate]); dissertation required and internship required; practicum not required. *Faculty:* 9 full-time; 4-6 part-time. *Students:* (1990-91) 60 admitted, 120-plus taking classes and applying for admission.

MARYLAND

*Johns Hopkins University. Division of Education, Rm. 101, Whitehead Hall, Baltimore, MD 21218. (410) 516-8273. Fax (410) 516-8424. Dr. Dianne Tobin, Asst. Prof. *Specializations:* M.S. in Education, concentration in Technology for Educators, C.A.S.E. in Technology for Educators, and Ed.D. in Human Communication and Its Disorders—Technology and Special Education. Master's program started in 1980 and doctoral in 1984. *Minimum Degree Requirements:* Master's—33 semester hours (24 hours in computers, 9 hours in education [computer courses are all education-related]); thesis not required; internship and practicum required. Specialist—30 hours (30 hours in computers and education [computer courses are all educationrelated]); thesis not required; internship and practicum required. Doctorate—99 semester hours (hours in computers and education vary); thesis, internship, and practicum required. *Faculty:* 3 full-time; 25 part-time. *Students:* Not specified.

MASSACHUSETTS

*Fitchburg State College. Graduate Program in Educational Technology, 160 Pearl St., Fitchburg, MA 01420. (508) 345-2151, ext. 3308. Dr. Sandy Miller-Jacobs, Chair, Graduate Prog. *Specialization:* Program offers M.Ed. in Computers in Education. Master's program started in 1983. *Minimum Degree Requirements:* 39 semester hours (30 hours in educational computers, 9 hours outside education [electives]); no thesis, internship, or practicum is required. *Faculty:* 9 full-time; 5 part-time. *Students:* 85 (about 50 on campus and 35 off campus).

*Harvard University. Graduate School of Education, 111 Longfellow Hall, Cambridge, MA 02138. For more information contact the Office of Admissions at (617) 495-3414. *Specializations:* Ed.M. and C.A.S. with a concentration in Technology in Education. Master's program started in 1983. *Minimum Degree Requirements:* 32 semester hours (number of hours in computers, education, and outside education not specified); no thesis, internship, or practicum is required. *Faculty:* 8 part-time. *Students:* Data not available; students do not have to declare a concentration until the beginning of their last semester.

*Lesley College. 29 Everett St., Cambridge, MA 02138-2790. (617) 349-8419. Dr. Nancy Roberts, Prof. of Computer Education. *Specializations:* M.A. in Computers in Education; C.A.G.S. in Computers in Education; Ph.D in Education with a Computers in Education major. Master's program started in 1980. *Minimum Degree Requirements:* Master's—33 semester hours in computers (number of hours in education and outside education not specified); no thesis, internship, or practicum is required. Specialist—36 semester hours (hours in computers, education, and outside education not specified); thesis, internship, practicum not specified. Ph.D. requirements available on request. *Faculty:* 5 full-time; 12 part-time on the master's and specialist levels. *Students:* 37 on master's level; 5 on specialist level.

University of Massachusetts-Lowell. College of Education, One University Ave., Lowell, MA 01854. (508) 934-4621. Fax (508) 934-3005. Dr. John LeBaron, Assoc. Prof., College of Education. *Specializations:* M.Ed. in Curriculum and Instruction; C.A.G.S. in Curriculum and Instruction; Ed.D. in Leadership in Schooling. (Note: Technology and Learning Environments is a component of each of the programs.) Master's, specialist, and doctoral programs started in 1984. *Admission Requirements:* M.Ed.—undergraduate degree from accredited college or university with a minimum GPA of 2.75 on a 4.0 scale; Miller Analogies Test or GRE. C.A.G.S. and Ed.D.—master's degree from an accredited college or university with a minimum GPA of 3.00 on a 4.0 scale; Miller Analogies Test or GRE. *Minimum Degree Requirements:* Master's—33 semester hours (hours in computers, education, and outside education not specified); no thesis or internship is required; practicum required. Doctorate—60 semester hours beyond master's plus dissertation (hours in computers, education, and outside education not specified); thesis, residency, and comprehensive examination required. *Faculty:* 21 full-time; 26 part-time. *Students:* (professional education graduate programs) 134 full-time; 449 part-time. *Financial Assistance:* Limited assistantships available. *Degrees Awarded 1 September 1990-31 August 1991:* Doctoral, 9; master's, 162.

MICHIGAN

*Eastern Michigan University. College of Education, Boone Hall, Ypsilanti, MI 48197. (313) 487-3260. Dr. Bert Greene, Prof., Dept. of Teacher Education. *Specialization:* M.A. in Educational Psychology with an Educational Technology area of concentration. Master's program started in 1983. *Minimum Degree Requirements:* 30 semester hours (22 hours in computers, 8 hours in education); thesis optional. *Faculty:* 8 full-time. *Students 1989-90:* 192.

MINNESOTA

Mankato State University. Educational Technology Program, L.M.E., Mankato, MN 56002. (507) 389-1965. Fax (507) 389-5751. Kenneth C. Pengelly, Prof. and Coord. of Educational Technology M.S. Prog. *Specialization:* M.S. in Educational Technology, K-12 specialization. Master's program started in 1986. *Admission Requirements:* Miller Analogies Test. *Minimum Degree Requirements:* 51 quarter credit hours (6-15 hours in computers, 12-15 hours in education, 12-18 hours [optional] outside education); 60-hour internship required. *Faculty:* 4 full-time; 5 part-time. *Students:* 15-20 part-time. *Degrees Awarded 1 July 1991-30 June 1992:* M.S., 5.

University of Minnesota. Department of Curriculum and Instructional Systems, 130 Peik Hall, 159 Pillsbury Dr. SE, Minneapolis, MN 55455. (612) 624-2034. Dr. Gregory Sales, Curriculum and Instructional Systems. *Specializations:* M.Ed., M.A., Ph.D. in Instructional Design and Technology. Master's and doctoral programs started in 1972. *Minimum Degree Requirements:* Master's—45 quarter credit hours (18 hours in technology, 45 hours in education, 0 hours outside education); M.A. thesis (4 credits) required; practicum required for M.Ed. Doctorate—136 quarter credit hours; thesis (36 credits) required. *Faculty:* Not specified. *Students:* M.A. and M.Ed., 75; Ph.D., 40. *Financial Assistance:* Not specified. *Degrees Awarded 1 July 1991-30 June 1992:* Not specified.

MISSOURI

*Central Missouri State University. Lovinger 300, Warrensburg, MO 64093. (816) 429-4235. Dr. Max McCulloch, Prof. *Specialization:* M.S.E. Curriculum and Instruction with emphasis on Educational Computing. Master's program started in 1986. *Minimum Degree Requirements:* 32 semester hours (15 hours in computers, 10 hours in education, 7 hours outside education). *Faculty:* 15 full-time; 2 part-time. *Students 1989-90:* 7.

Fontbonne College. 6800 Wydown Blvd., St. Louis, MO 63105. (314) 862-3456. Dr. Mary K. Abkemeier, Master of Science in Computer Education. *Specializations:* M.S. in Computer Education. Master's program started in 1986. *Admission Requirements:* B.S. from accredited school; three letters of recommendation; GPA 2.5 or master's degree. *Minimum Degree Requirements:* 33 semester hours. *Faculty:* 3 full-time; 7 part-time. *Students:* 110 part-time. *Financial Assistance:* Title II funding for St. Louis City full-time school teachers. *Degrees Awarded 1 July 1991-30 June 1992:* M.S., 12.

*Northwest Missouri State University. Department of Computer Science, Maryville, MO 64468. (816) 562-1600. Fax (816) 562-1484. Phillip J. Heeler, Prof., Dir., School Computer Studies Prog., Dept. of Computer Science. *Specializations:* M.S. in School Computer Studies; M.S.Ed. in Educational Uses of Computers; M.S.Ed. in Using Computers in Specific Disciplines. *Minimum Degree Requirements:* 32 semester hours for each of the three master's degree programs. The first includes 26 credit hours of core computer courses; the second includes 14 credit hours of core computer courses and 12 hours of educational courses; and the third requires 7 hours of core computer courses, 12 hours of education courses, and 7 hours in technology-related areas. *Faculty:* 6. *Students:* 27 full-time; 8 part-time. *Degrees Awarded 1990-91:* 8.

NEBRASKA

*Kearney State College. Kearney, NE 68849. (308) 234-8513. Dr. Lynn Johnson, Chair, Professional Teacher Education. *Specializations:* M.S. in Educational Technology. Master's program started in 1984. *Minimum Degree Requirements:* 36 semester hours (18 hours in computers, 18 hours in education); no internship or practicum is required. *Faculty 1989-90:* 3 full-time; 5 part-time. *Students:* 32.

NEVADA

*University of Nevada-Reno. College of Education, Reno, NV 89557. (702) 784-4961. Fax (707) 784-4526. Dr. LaMont Johnson, Prof., Dept. of Curriculum and Instruction. *Specialization:* M.Ed. in Curriculum/Instruction. Master's program started in 1986. *Minimum Degree Requirements:* 36 semester hours (12 hours in computers, 24 in education); thesis optional; practicum required. *Faculty 1989-90:* 2 full-time; 2 part-time. *Students:* 35.

NEW JERSEY

*Saint Peter's College. Graduate Programs in Education, 2641 Kennedy Blvd., Jersey City, NJ 07306. (201) 915-9254. Dr. Henry F. Harty, Dir., Graduate Programs in Education. *Specializations:* M.A. in Education-Computer Science/Data Processing. Master's program started in 1979. *Minimum Degree Requirements:* 39 semester hours (27 hours in computers, 12 hours in education, 0 hours outside education). *Faculty 1989-90:* 9 full-time; 8 part-time. *Students:* 59.

NEW YORK

*Buffalo State College. 1300 Elmwood Ave., Buffalo, NY 14222-1095. (716) 878-4923. Mr. Anthony J. Nowakowski, Acting Coord. of M.S. in Education in Educational Computing. *Specializations:* M.S. in Ed. in Educational Computing. Master's program started in 1988. *Minimum Degree Requirements:* 33 semester hours (18 hours in computers, 12-15 hours in education, 0 hours outside education); thesis or project required; no internship or practicum is required. *Faculty 1989-90:* 10 part-time. *Students:* 68.

Iona College. 715 North Ave. NW, New Rochelle, NY 10801. (914) 633-2578. Robert Schiaffino, Asst. Prof. and Coord., Educational Computing Prog. *Specializations:* M.S. in Educational Computing. Master's program started in 1982. *Admission Requirements:* GPA 3.0 or better. *Minimum Degree Requirements:* 36 hours—trimester basis ("all hours listed in educational computing"). *Faculty:* 3 full-time; 5 part-time. *Students:* 50 part-time. *Financial Assistance:* None. *Degrees Awarded 1 July 1991-30 June 1992:* M.S., 9.

Long Island University. C. W. Post, Brookville, NY 11548; Brooklyn Campus, Brooklyn, NY 11201; Rockland Campus, Orangeburg, NY 10962. School of Education, Advisor of Educational Technology, (516) 299-2199. *Specialization:* M.S. in Education, concentration in Computers in Education. One of the oldest and most established programs on the East Coast. Master's program started in 1985. *Minimum Degree Requirements:* 36 semester hours for M.S.; technology project required; evening courses. Special programs available, some on weekends. *Faculty:* 5 full-time; 15 part-time. *Students:* Approx. 587 across three campuses. *Financial Assistance:* Assistance is available.

Pace University. Department of Educational Administration, 1 Martine Ave., White Plains, NY 10606. (914) 422-4198. Fax (914) 422-4311. Dr. Lawrence Roder, Chair. *Specialization:* M.S. in Curriculum and Instruction with a concentration in Computers and Education. Master's program started in 1986. *Admission Requirements:* GPA 3.0; interview; application. *Minimum Degree Requirements:* 33 semester hours (15 hours in computers, 18 hours in educational administration). *Faculty:* 2 full-time; 12 part-time. *Students:* 60. *Financial Assistance:* Assistance is available. *Degrees Awarded 1 July 1991-30 June 1992:* M.S., 20.

*State University College of Arts and Science at Potsdam. 204 Satterlee Hall, Potsdam, NY 13676. (315) 267-2527. Fax (315) 267-2771. Dr. Norman Licht, Prof. of Education. *Specializations:* M.S. in Education, Instructional Technology, and Media Management with Educational Computing concentration. Master's program started in 1981. *Minimum Degree Requirements:* 33 semester hours (15 hours in computers, 18 hours in education, 0 hours outside education); thesis not required; internship or practicum required. *Faculty 1990-91:* 6 full-time; 4 part-time. *Students:* 110.

*State University of New York. Department of Educational Theory and Practice, 1400 Washington Ave., Albany, NY 12222. (518) 443-5312. Dr. Audrey Champagne, Chair. *Specialization:* M.S. in Curriculum Development and Instructional Technology. *Minimum Degree Requirements:* Flexible curriculum designed by students with advisor; minimum requirement of 30 credit hours; thesis optional. *Faculty 1990-91:* 23. *Students:* 111 full- and part-time. *Degrees Awarded 1990-91:* M.S., 20.

State University of New York at Stony Brook. Department of Technology and Society, College of Engineering and Applied Sciences, Stony Brook, NY 11794. (516) 632-8767. Fax (516) 632-8205. Dr. Thomas T. Liao, Prof. and Chair. *Specializations:* M.S. in Technological Systems Management with concentration in Educational Computing. Master's program started in 1979. *Admission Requirements:* B.A. or B.S. in Sciences, Mathematics, or Social Sciences; GRE. *Minimum Degree Requirements:* 30 semester hours (hours in computer, education, and outside education not specified); thesis required; internship or practicum not specified. *Faculty:* 6 full-time; 4 part-time. *Students:* 5 full-time; 20 part-time. *Financial Assistance:* Teaching or research assistantships. *Degrees Awarded 1 July 1991-30 June 1992:* M.S., 12.

NORTH CAROLINA

*Appalachian State University. Department of Library Science and Educational Foundations, Boone, NC 28608. (704) 262-2243. Dr. John H. Tashner. *Specializations:* M.A. in Educational Media (Instructional Technology-Computers). Master's program started in 1986. *Minimum Degree Requirements:* 36 semester hours; thesis optional; internship required. *Admission Requirements:* Selective. *Faculty 1989-90:* 2 full-time; 1 part-time.

*North Carolina State University. Department of Curriculum and Instruction, P.O. Box 7801, Raleigh, NC 27695-7801. (919) 515-3221. Dr. Ellen Vasu, Assoc. Prof., Dept. of Curriculum and Instruction. *Specializations:* M.Ed. and M.S. in Instructional Technology-Computers (program track within one master's in Curriculum and Instruction). Master's program started in 1986. *Minimum Degree Requirements:* 36 semester hours; thesis optional; practicum required. *Faculty 1990-91:* 3 full-time. *Students:* 18.

*University of North Carolina-Charlotte. College of Education, Charlotte, NC 28223. (704) 547-4542. Dr. Clarence Smith, Prof. of Education. *Specializations:* M.Ed. in Curriculum and Instruction—Computer. Master's program started in 1987. *Minimum Degree Requirements:* 36 semester hours (12 hours in computers, 15 hours in education, 9 hours outside education); internship required. *Faculty 1989-90:* 6 part-time. *Students:* 20.

*Western Carolina University. Cullowhee, NC 28723. (704) 227-7415. Dr. Don Chalker, Head, Dept. of Administration, Curriculum and Instruction. *Specializations:* M.A.Ed. in Supervision, with concentration in Educational Technology-Computers. Master's program started in 1987. *Minimum Degree Requirements:* 41 semester hours (18 hours in computers, 20 hours in education, 3 hours outside education); internship required. *Faculty 1989-90:* 25-plus full-time. *Students:* 13.

NORTH DAKOTA

*Minot State University. 500 University Ave. W., Minot, ND 58701. (701) 857-3817. Dr. James Croonquist, Dean, Graduate School. *Specializations:* M.S. in Audiology, M.S. in Education of the Deaf, M.S. in Elementary Education, M.S. in Learning Disabilities, M.S. in Special Education, M.S. in Speech-Language Pathology, M.A.T. in Mathematics, M.S. in Criminal Justice, M.A.T. in Science, M.M.E. in Music. Master's program started in 1964. *Minimum Degree Requirements:* 45 quarter hours (hours in computers, education, and outside education vary according to program). *Faculty 1990-91:* 40 full-time; 9 part-time. *Students:* 80.

OHIO

*Kent State University. Educational Technology Program, 405 White Hall, KSU, Kent, OH 44242. (216) 672-2294. Dr. David Dalton, Prog. Coord. *Minimum Degree Requirements:* 34 semester hours, including 15-20 hours in computer studies, 12-17 in education. *Faculty 1990-91:* 4. *Students:* Data not specified. *Degrees Awarded:* Approx. 10 per year.

The Ohio State University. 236 Ramseyer Hall, 29 W. Woodruff Ave., Columbus, OH 43210-1177. (614) 292-4872. Dr. Marjorie A. Cambre, Assoc. Prof., The Ohio State University. *Specializations:* M.A. and Ph.D. in Computers in Education in the Program Area of Instructional Design and Technology. For additional information, see listings for Doctoral and Master's Programs.

Wright State University. College of Education and Human Services, 244 Millett Hall, Dayton, OH 45435. (513) 873-2509 or (513) 873-2182. Fax (513) 873-3301. Dr. Bonnie K. Mathies, Chair, Dept. of Educational Technology, Vocational Education, and Allied Programs. *Specializations:* M.Ed. in Computer Education; M.Ed. for Computer Coordinator; M.A. in Computer Education. Master's programs started in 1985. *Admission Requirements:* 2.7 GPA for regular admission; GRE or Miller Analogies Test. *Minimum Degree Requirements:* 48 quarter hours (hours in computers, education, and outside education not specified); thesis required for M.A. degree only; comprehensive examination in the form of the completion of a portfolio and a videotaped presentation to the faculty for M.Ed.; eligible for Supervisor's certificate after completion of C&S; Computer Coordinator program. *Faculty:* 2 full-time; 10 part-time adjuncts and other university full-time faculty and staff. *Students:* 39 part-time graduate students. *Financial Assistance:* Graduate assistantships available, including three positions in the College's Educational Resource Center; limited number of small graduate scholarships. *Degrees Awarded 1 July 1991-30 June 1992:* M.A. and M.Ed., 9.

*Xavier University. Department of Mathematics and Computer Science, 3800 Victory Parkway, Cincinnati, OH 45207. (513) 745-3462. Dr. David D. Berry, Dir., Computer Science. *Specialization:* M.Ed. with concentration in Computer Science. Master's program started in 1981. *Minimum Degree Requirements:* 30 semester hours (12 hours in computers, 12 hours in education, 6 hours either computers or education). *Faculty 1989-90:* 4 full-time in Computer Science; 24 part-time in Education. *Students:* 11.

OKLAHOMA

The University of Oklahoma. Department of Educational Psychology, 820 Van Vleet Oval, Norman, OK 73019. (405) 325-1521. Fax (405) 325-3242. Dr. Tillman J. Ragan, Prof. *Specialization:* M.Ed. in Educational Technology with Computer Applications emphasis. Master's program started in 1982. *Admission Requirements:* 3.0 GPA over last 60 hours of undergraduate work or at least 12 credit hours of graduate work with a 3.0 GPA from an accredited college or university. *Minimum Degree Requirements:* 32 semester hours (12 hours in computers, 21 hours in education [including computers 12]); internship required. *Faculty:* 10 full-time; 2 part-time. *Students:* 5 full-time; 24 part-time. *Financial Assistance:* Assistantships; out-of-state fee waivers; graduate scholarships (both general and targeted minorities). *Degrees Awarded 1 July 1991-30 June 1992:* M.Ed., 3.

PENNSYLVANIA

*The Pennsylvania State University. University Park, PA 16802. (814) 865-0473. Kyle L. Peck. *Specializations:* M.S., M.Ed., Ph.D., and D.Ed. in Instructional Systems. Master's program started in 1971. *Minimum Degree Requirements:* Master's—30 semester hours (15 hours in instructional design, 9 hours in education, 6 hours outside education); thesis or paper required; no internship or practicum is required. Doctorate—90 semester hours (27 hours in instructional design, 33 hours in education, 15 hours outside education); thesis required; no internship or practicum is required. *Faculty:* 7 full-time; 3 part-time. *Students:* M.S. and M.Ed., 44; Ph.D. and Ed.D., 75.

*Widener University. Center for Education, Chester, PA 19013. (215) 499-4497. Fax (215) 676-9715. Dr. James P. Randall, Asst. Prof. of Instructional Technology. *Specialization:* M.Ed. in Computer Science Education. Master's program started in 1986. *Minimum Degree Requirements:* 30 semester hours (18 hours in computers, 6-12 hours in education, up to 6 hours outside education); 3.0 GPA. *Faculty 1989-90:* 1 full-time; 2 part-time. *Students:* 53.

TEXAS

Texas A&M University. Department of Interdisciplinary Education, Educational Technology Program, College Station, TX 77843. (409) 845-7276. Fax (409) 845-9663. Dr. Ronald Zellner, Coord., Educational Technology. *Specializations:* M.Ed. in Educational Technology, emphasis in computer applications. Master's program started in 1984. *Admission Requirements:* GPA, 3.0; GRE 800. *Minimum Degree Requirements:* 37 semester hours (12 hours in computers, 6 hours in education); internship or practicum required. *Faculty:* 4 full-time; 1 part-time. *Students:* Data not available. *Financial Assistance:* Teaching assistantships available. *Degrees Awarded 1 July 1991-30 June 1992:* M.Ed., 12.

*Texas Christian University. P.O. Box 32925, Fort Worth, TX 76129. (817) 921-7660. Dr. Sherrie Reynolds, Asst. Prof. *Specialization:* Master of General Education with specialization in Computers in Education. Master's program started in 1984. *Minimum Degree Requirements:* 36 semester hours (18 hours in specialization, 6 hours in professional education, 6 hours thesis, 6 hours elective); thesis required; practicum required. *Faculty 1989-90:* 1 full-time; 1 part-time. *Students:* Not specified.

Texas Tech University. College of Education, Box 41071, TTU, Lubbock, TX 79409. (806) 742-2362. Fax (806) 742-2179. Dr. Robert Price, Dir., Instructional Technology. *Specializations:* M.Ed. in Instructional Technology (Educational Computing emphasis); Ed.D. in Instructional Technology (Educational Computing emphasis). Master's program started in 1981; doctoral in 1982. *Admission Requirements:* M.Ed., GRE score of 800+; GPA of 2.7 on last 30 hours of undergraduate program. Ed.D., GRE score of 1050; GPA of 2.7 on last 30 hours. *Minimum Degree Requirements:* Master's—39 hours (24 hours in computing, 15 hours in education or outside education); practicum required. Doctorate—87 hours (36 hours in computers, 27 hours in education, 24 hours in resource area or minor); practicum required. *Faculty:* 3 full-time; 3 part-time. *Students:* Approximately 25 FTE. *Financial Assistance:* Teaching and research assistantships available ($7,500/9 months). *Degrees Awarded 1 July 1991-30 June 1992:* Ed.D., 3; M.Ed., 7.

Texas Wesleyan University. School of Education, 1201 Wesleyan, Fort Worth, TX 76105. (817) 531-4952. Dr. R. J. Wilson, Coord., Information Processing Technology. *Specialization:* M.S.Ed. in Information Processing Technology. Master's program started in 1982. *Admission Requirements:* Undergraduate GPA 2.75 for conditional admission; 3.0 GAP for regular admission. *Minimum Degree Requirements:* 36 semester hours (18 hours directly related to Information Processing Technologies). Additional certification in IPT without a degree is also an option. *Faculty:* 1.5 full-time. *Students:* 18. *Financial Assistance:* Partial tuition waivers available to full-time teachers. *Degrees Awarded 1 July 1991-30 June 1992:* M.S.Ed., 14.

*Texas Woman's University. Denton, TX 76204. (817) 898-2256. Vera T. Gershner, Prof. *Specializations:* M.A. and M.Ed. major in Elementary Education. Master's program started in 1985. *Minimum Degree Requirements:* 36 semester hours (6 hours in computer science, 30 hours in education [6-9 hours in computers in education]); thesis, internship, practicum not specified. *Faculty 1989-90:* 3 full-time. *Students:* 4.

*University of Houston. University Park, College of Education, Houston, TX 77204-5872. (713) 749-1685. Department of Curriculum and Instruction. *Specializations:* M.Ed. and Ed.D. in Curriculum and Instruction with emphasis in Instructional Technology, specialization in Computer Education. Master's and doctoral programs started in 1981. *Minimum Degree Requirements:* Master's—36 semester hours without thesis. Doctorate—60 semester hours plus dissertation beyond master's. *Faculty 1989-90:* 3 full-time; 5 part-time. *Students:* M.Ed., approx. 50; Ed.D., approx. 12.

University of North Texas. Department of Computer Education and Cognitive Systems, Box 5155-UNT, Denton, TX 76203. (817) 565-3790. Fax (817) 565-2185. Dr. Jon Young, Chair. *Specializations:* M.S. in Computer Education and Cognitive Systems; Information Processing Technology Endorsement Levels I and II. Master's program started in 1987. *Admission Requirements:* Minimum GRE scores of 400 on verbal and 400 on quantitative with total score of 900; minimum of 18 undergraduate hours in education, personnel training and management, or the behavioral sciences. *Minimum Degree Requirements:* 36 semester hours (33 in computers, 6 in education); thesis, internship, practicum not specified. *Faculty:* 8 full-time tenure track; 4 non-tenure track lecturers. *Students:* M.S., 85; doctoral minors, 12. *Financial Assistance:* Teaching fellowships in spring and fall semesters; teaching assistantships available as computer laboratory consultants (contact is Dr. Kathlyn Y. Canaday, (817) 565-4436). *Degrees Awarded 1 July 1991-30 June 1992:* M.S., 33; doctoral, 0—program is still pending.

University of Texas-Austin. College of Education, Austin, TX 78712. (512) 471-5211. Dr. DeLayne Hudspeth, Assoc. Prof., Area Coord. *Specializations:* M.Ed. and M.A. in a specialization in Instructional Technology. Master's programs started in 1984. *Minimum Degree Requirements:* 12-18 semester hours in computers, 18-24 hours in education, 6 hours outside education; thesis and internship optional. *Faculty:* 4 full-time; 2 part-time. *Students:* Approx. 40. *Degrees Awarded 1 July 1991-30 June 1992:* M.Ed. and M.A., 11.

VIRGIN ISLANDS

*University of Virgin Islands. St. Thomas, VI 00802. (809) 776-9200. Dr. Dennis O. Harper, Assoc. Prof. of Computer Ed. *Specializations:* M.A. with emphasis in Computers and Technology in Education. Master's program started in 1989 (January). *Minimum Degree Requirements:* 36 semester credits (21 credits in computers and technology, 15 credits in education, 0 credits outside education); thesis optional; practicum required. *Faculty 1989-90:* 1 full-time. *Students:* Anticipated enrollment of 60.

VIRGINIA

George Mason University. Center for Interactive Educational Technology, 4400 University Dr., Fairfax, VA 22030-4444. (703) 993-2052. Fax (703) 993-2013. Dr. Charles S. White, Coord. of Instructional Technology Academic Programs. *Specializations:* M.Ed. in Instructional Technology with tracks in Instructional Design and Development, School-Based Technology Coordinator, Instructional Applications of Technology, Computer Science Educator; M.Ed. in Special Education Technology (S.E.T.); D.A.Ed. with specialization in Instructional Technology or Special Education Technology. Master's program started in 1983 and doctoral in 1984. *Admission Requirements:* Teaching or training experience; introductory programming course or equivalent; introductory course in educational technology or equivalent. *Minimum Degree Requirements:* M.Ed. in Instructional Technology, 36 hours; practicum/internship/project required. M.Ed. in Special Education Technology, 36-42 hours. D.A.Ed., 56-62 hours beyond master's degree for either specialization. *Faculty:* 4 full-time; 5 part-time. *Students:* M.Ed.-I.T.—4 full-time; 29 part-time. M.Ed.-S.E.T.—10 full-time; 8 part-time. D.A.Ed.—5 part-time. *Financial Assistance:* Assistantships and tuition waivers available for full-time (9 credits) graduate students. *Degrees Awarded 1 July 1991-30 June 1992:* M.Ed.-I.T., 12; M.Ed.-S.E.T., 7; D.A.Ed., 3.

Hampton University. School of Liberal Arts and Education, 301 A Phenix Hall, Hampton, VA 23668. (804) 727-5751. Fax (804) 727-5084. Dr. JoAnn W. Haysbert, Prof. and Coord. of Graduate Programs in Education. *Specialization:* M.A. in Computer Education. Master's program started in 1983. *Admission Requirements:* Completed application; B.A. from accredited college or university; acceptable GRE scores; two letters of recommendation from professional educators; undergraduate record of above-average scholarship. *Minimum Degree Requirements:* 36 semester hours (21 hours in computers, 15 in education, 0 hours outside education); practicum required. *Faculty:* 4 part-time. *Students:* 32 part-time. *Financial Assistance:* Limited number of teaching, research, laboratory, or resident hall assistantships are available to qualified graduate students, as well as fellowships. Also available are guaranteed student loans and college work-study and tuition assistance grant programs. *Degrees Awarded 1 July 1991-30 June 1992:* M.A., 4.

Virginia Polytechnic Institute and State University. Instructional Systems Development, College of Education, War Memorial Hall, Blacksburg, VA 24061-0313. (703) 231-5598. Fax (703) 231-3717. Thomas M. Sherman, Prof., Prog. Area Leader, Instructional Systems Development, Curriculum and Instruction. *Specializations:* Ed.D. and Ph.D. programs in Instructional Technology. *Features:* Areas of emphasis are Instructional Design, Educational Computing, Evaluation, Media Management, Speech Synthesis, and Telecommunications. *Admission Requirements:* 3.3 GPA for master's degree; three letters of recommendation; transcripts of previous academic work. *Faculty:* 8 full-time; 5 part-time. *Students:* 6 full-time; 6 part-time. *Financial Assistance:* 10 assistantships; tuition scholarships; contracts with other agencies. *Degrees Awarded 1 July 1991-30 June 1992:* Master's, 2; doctoral, 1.

WASHINGTON

Eastern Washington University. Department Computer Science, Cheney, WA 99004-2495. (509) 359-7092. Fax (509) 359-6927. Dr. Donald R. Horner, Prof. of Computer Science. *Specializations:* M.Ed. in Computer Education (elementary); M.Ed. in Computer Education (secondary); M.S. in Computer Education (Interdisciplinary). Master's program started in 1983. *Minimum Degree Requirements:* M.S., 52 quarter hours (30 hours in computers, 0 hours in education, 8 hours outside education—not specifically computer science; the hours do not total to 52 because of freedom to choose where Methods of Research is taken, where 12 credits of supporting courses are taken, and where additional electives are taken); thesis not required (a research project with formal report is required, although it need not be a thesis in format); internship and/or practicum not required. M.S., 52 quarter hours divided between computer science and another science or mathematics; one area is primary and includes a research project; the second area generally requires fewer hours than the primary. M.Ed., 48 quarter hours minimum (24 hours in computer science, 16 hours in education, 8 hours outside education). *Faculty:* 11 full-time; 2 part-time. *Students:* about 50, most active in summers only. *Financial Assistance:* Some research and teaching fellowships; financial assistance. *Degrees Awarded 1 July 1991-30 June 1992:* M.S. and M.Ed., 7.

*Western Washington University. Woodring College of Education, Bellingham, WA 98225. (206) 676-3090. Fax (206) 647-4856. Prof. Tony Jongejan, Asst. Prof. of Education. *Specializations:* M.Ed. in Computers in Education. Master's program started in 1981. *Minimum Degree Requirements:* 52 quarter hours (15 hours in computers, 24 hours in education, 0 hours outside education); thesis required; internship and practicum possible. *Faculty 1989-90:* 4 full-time; 2 part-time. *Students:* 25.

WISCONSIN

*Cardinal Stritch College. Department of Educational Computing, 6802 N. Yates Rd., Milwaukee, WI 53217. (414) 351-7516. Dr. Jim Kasum, Chair, Dept. of Educational Computing. *Specializations:* M.E. in Educational Computing and M.S. in Computer Science Education. Master's program started in 1984. *Minimum Degree Requirements:* M.E., 30-32 semester hours (15-21 hours in computers, 6-15 hours in education, 0 hours outside education). Degrees may be completed via coursework option or one of the culminating experiences: thesis, field experience, or software project. M.S., 30-32 semester hours (24-26 hours in computer, 3-6 in education, 0 hours outside education). *Faculty 1990-91:* 3 full-time; 3 part-time. *Students:* 104.

*Edgewood College. Department of Education, 855 Woodrow St., Madison, WI 53711. (608) 257-4861, ext. 2293. Dr. Joseph E. Schmiedicke, Chair, Dept. of Education. *Specializations:* M.A. in Education with emphasis on Computer-Based Education. Master's program started in 1987. *Minimum Degree Requirements:* 36 semester hours (18 hours in computers, 30 hours in education, 6 hours outside education). *Faculty 1990-91:* 2 full-time; 6 part-time. *Students:* 108.

Scholarships, Fellowships, and Awards

In the instructional technology/media-related fields, various scholarships, fellowships, and awards have been established. Many of these are available to those who either are or will be pursuing advanced degrees at the Master's, six-year specialist, or doctoral levels.

Because various colleges, universities, professional organizations, and governmental agencies offer scholarships, fellowships, and awards and may wish to have them included in this section, it would be greatly appreciated if those aware of such financial awards would contact either the editors or the publisher for inclusion of such entries in the next edition of *EMTY*.

We are greatly indebted to the staff members of the Association for Educational Communications and Technology (AECT) for assisting with this section.

Information is furnished in the following sequence:

- Overview of AECT and ECT Foundation Awards
- AECT Awards
- ECT Foundation Awards

AECT AND ECT FOUNDATION AWARDS

The Association for Educational Communications and Technology recognizes and rewards the outstanding achievement of its members and associates through a program that provides for three major annual awards—Achievement, Special Service, and Distinguished Service—and through the ECT Foundation, which provides awards in the areas of leadership, scholarship, and research.

AECT encourages members and associates to apply for these awards, and to disseminate information about the awards to professional colleagues. Specific information about each award is available from the AECT national office. The annual deadline for submitting most award applications is November 1.

All ECT Foundation and AECT awards are presented during the AECT National Convention and INFOCOMM International Exposition.

For additional information on all awards, please contact:

> AECT Awards Program
> 1025 Vermont Ave. NW
> Suite 820
> Washington, DC 20005
> (202) 347-7834

AECT Awards

The Association for Educational Communications and Technology (AECT) provides for three annual awards:

Special Service Award: Granted to a person who has shown notable service to AECT as a whole or to one of its programs or divisions (nominee must have been a member of AECT for at least 10 years and must not be currently an AECT officer, board member, or member of the Awards Committee).

Distinguished Service Award: Granted to a person who has shown outstanding leadership in advancing the theory and/or practice of educational communications and technology over a substantial period of time (nominee need not be an AECT member but must not have received this award previously).

Annual Achievement Award: Honors the individual who during the past year has made the most significant contribution to the advancement of educational communications and technology (nominee need not be a member of AECT, and the award can be given to the same person more than once).

ECT Foundation Awards

The ECT Foundation, a nonprofit organization that carries out the purposes of AECT that are charitable and educational in nature, coordinates the following awards:

AECT/SIRS Intellectual Freedom Award (in conjunction with the Social Issues Resources Services Inc.): Recognizes a media specialist at any level who has upheld the principles of intellectual freedom as set forth in AECT's publication "Media, the Learner, and Intellectual Freedom" and provides $1,000 for the individual and $1,000 for the media center of the recipient's choice (recipient must be a personal member of AECT).

AECT Annual Conference and Earl F. Strobehn Internship Award: Provides complimentary registration and housing at the annual conference plus a cash award for four full-time graduate students (applicants must be a member of AECT and enrolled in a recognized program in educational communications and technology).

Richard B. Lewis Memorial Award: Presented to the outstanding school district media utilization program along with a cash award (awarded to either a public or private school having media utilization programs in place).

AECT Leadership Development Grants: Supports innovative leadership development activities undertaken by affiliates, divisions, or regions with cash grants (special consideration will be given to proposals that demonstrate a commitment to leadership development, that propose programs unique to the applicant's organization, and that include activities of potential benefit to other AECT programs).

AECT Memorial Scholarship Award: Donations given in memory of specific past leaders of the field provide a scholarship fund that gives annual cash grants to AECT members enrolled in educational technology graduate studies (three letters of recommendation are required).

Dean and Sybil McClusky Research Award: Recognizes the year's outstanding doctoral thesis proposal that has been approved by the student's university and offers a cash reward to defray the research expenses (the winner must agree to complete the proposed study).

Carl F. and Viola V. Mahnke Film Production Award: Honors excellence in message design for film and video products created by undergraduate students who are members of AECT (products must have been completed within a two-year period prior to the competition).

Robert M. Gagné Instructional Development Research Award: Recognizes the most significant contribution by a graduate student to the body of knowledge on which instructional development is based with a plaque and a cash prize (the research must have been done in the past three years while the candidate was enrolled as a graduate student).

James W. Brown Publication Award: Recognizes the outstanding publication in the field of educational technology in any media format during the past year with a cash award (excluded from consideration are doctoral, master's, or other types of dissertations prepared in fulfillment of degree program requirements).

ETR&D Young Scholar Award: Recognizes a fresh, creative approach to research and theory in educational technology by a young scholar (applicant must be an individual who does not hold a doctorate degree or who has received a doctorate degree within the past three years.)

Young Researcher Award: Recognizes an outstanding unpublished report of research of an experimental, descriptive, or historical nature by a researcher who has not yet attained the doctorate or is less than three years beyond the degree (jointly published papers are not accepted).

Jerry R. Coltharp Award: Recognizes innovative media management practices which enhance the provision of instructional media services or advance media applications.

DOT-AECT Crystal Award: Recognizes the most innovative and outstanding instructional telecommunications project.

Mentor Endowment Scholarship: One scholarship of $3000 is awarded to a graduate student in Educational Communications and Technology to continue his or her studies in the field. The scholarship may be used to assist the recipients to further his or her education at the master's or doctoral level in a summer session or academic year of graduate study at any accredited college or university in the United States or Canada.

AECT Special Service Award

Qualifications

- Award is granted to a person who has shown notable service to AECT. This service may be to the organization as a whole, one of its programs, or one of its divisions.

- Nominee currently must be a member of AECT and have at least 10 years of service to AECT.

Disqualifications

- Recipient may not now be serving as an elected officer of AECT nor as a member of the board of directors.

- Nominee must not be currently serving as a member of the AECT Awards Committee.

Nomination

Nominations are judged and selected on the basis of an outstanding contribution to a division, committee, commission, or program of AECT but not to an affiliate organization. Please provide as much information as you can.

- Write in 100 words or less why you think nominee should receive this award. Include a description of nominee's contribution.

- What year did nominee join AECT?

AECT Distinguished Service Award

Qualifications

- Award is granted to a person who has shown outstanding leadership in advancing the theory and/or practice of educational communications and technology over a substantial period of time.

- The nominee need not be a member of AECT.

- Award may be given posthumously.

Disqualifications

- Nominee must not have received this award previously.

- Nominee must not be currently serving as a member of the AECT Awards Committee.

Nomination

Nominations are judged primarily on the distinction or magnitude of the nominee's leadership in advancing the field rather than the association.

Categories

- The following categories suggest areas in which the nominee may have rendered distinguished service to the field. The nominee may not be represented in these areas. Use those that apply or add others.
    - Leadership • Research/Theory • Development/Production • Writing
        - Major Contribution to Education Outside the United States

AECT Annual Achievement Award

Qualifications

- Recipient may be an individual or a group.
- The AAA honors the individual who during the past year has made the most significant contribution to the advancement of educational communications and technology.
- The nominee need not be a member of AECT.
- The contribution being honored should be publicly visible—a specific thing or event.
- It must be timely—taking place within approximately the past year.
- Award can be given to the same person more than once.

Nomination

The nature of this award precludes the use of a single checklist or set of categories for nomination. The nomination and selection are inherently subjective. You are asked simply to present a succinct argument in favor of your nominee. Your statement ought to answer the following questions:

- What is the specific achievement being honored?
- What impact has this achievement had, or is likely to have, on the field?
- How is the nominee connected with the achievement?

ECT Foundation
1993 AECT/SIRS Intellectual Freedom Award

Purpose: To recognize, annually, a media professional at any level who has upheld the principles of intellectual freedom as set forth in *Media, the Learner, and Intellectual Freedom: A Handbook*, published by AECT.

The Award: The award shall consist of:

1. a plaque and $1,000 for the winning media professional, to be presented at the AECT National Convention and INFOCOMM International Exposition;

2. a plaque plus $1,000 for the media center designated by the recipient;

3. the opportunity for the recipient to present a session on intellectual freedom at the AECT National convention and INFOCOMM International Exposition.

Selection: The following criteria will be used in the selection process:

1. the recipient will be a media specialist at any level.

2. the recipient will be a member of AECT.

3. the recipient shall not have received another intellectual freedom award in the same year if that award was sponsored by SIRS, Inc.

4. the recipient will meet at least one of the following criteria:

  • has developed and implemented an exemplary selection policy/challenge procedure for educational nonprint material.

  • has developed an innovative information program on intellectual freedom for nonprint media.

  • has upheld intellectual freedom principles in the face of a challenge to educational nonprint media.

  • has been active in the establishment and/or continuation of a coalition relating to intellectual freedom.

  • has been active in the development of a legal base for the continued enjoyment of intellectual freedom.

Selection
Committee: A subcommittee of the AECT Intellectual Freedom committee is responsible for the selection of the winner.

ECT Foundation
1993 AECT National Convention-
Earl F. Strobehn Internship Program

Awards: Six students will be chosen as convention interns. The winners will receive complimentary convention registration, complimentary housing, and $100 cash award. The interns will be expected to arrive at the convention on the day before the convention and to stay until the close of the convention. (Applicants are encouraged to request financial support for transportation and on-site expenses from their institutions or state affiliate organizations.)

Program
Activities: Each intern will be expected to participate fully in a coordinated program of activities. These activities include private seminars with selected association and professional leaders in the field, observation of the AECT governance and program committees, and behind-the-scenes views of the convention itself. Each intern will also be responsible for specific convention-related assignments, which will require approximately 15 hours of time during the convention. A former intern, who is now a member of the AECT Leadership Development Committee, will serve as the program coordinator.

Eligibility: To qualify for consideration, an applicant must be full-time student throughout the current academic year in a recognized graduate program in educational communications and technology, and must be a member of AECT. (Applicant may join AECT when applying for the award.)

Application
Process: To apply for the internship program, qualified graduate students must complete and return an application form and must submit two letters of recommendation.

ECT Foundation
1993 Richard B. Lewis Memorial Award

Award: $750, provided by the Richard B. Lewis Memorial Fund for "Outstanding School District Media Utilization," is awarded to the winner.

Selection
Process: The winner will be selected by a unified committee appointed from the divisions of Educational Media Management (DEMM) and School Media Specialists (DSMS) of the Association for Educational Communications and Technology, and the National Association of Regional Media Centers (NARMC).

Selection
Criteria: • Evidence of strong media utilization as gathered from:

                    1. special utilization studies conducted by or for the school district;

                    2. specific instances of good utilization as described in writing by school district or other personnel.

                  • Evidence of having provided in the school district budget means of implementing good utilization programs in its schools and of the degree to which AECT/ALA media standards are met for services, equipment, and personnel.

                  • Assessment of applicant's statements as to how the $750 (if awarded) would be spent, such as for:

                    1. attending national, regional, or state conferences or workshops related to media utilization;

                    2. selecting media specialist(s) to attend advanced training programs;

                    3. buying software or hardware needed to improve media utilization programs;

                    4. other purposes (indicating especially creative approaches).

                  • Recognition by an AECT state, regional, or national affiliate organization or representative, or from a National Association of Regional Media Centers state or regional representative:

                    1. through prior recognition or awards;

                    2. through a recommendation.

Eligibility: All school districts, public and private, having media utilization programs in place, and conforming to the preceding criteria, are eligible.

Other: The winning district will receive a plaque as part of this award.

ECT Foundation
1993 Leadership Development Grants

Grants: Grants of up to $500 are provided by the ECT Foundation and administered by the AECT Leadership Development Committee. The grants are awarded to assist AECT affiliates, AECT divisions, and AECT regional organizations to undertake leadership development activities that will improve participants' skills as leaders in the professional organization or in educational technology.

Selection: Grant awards will be recommended by the Leadership Committee's Subcommittee on Leadership Development Grants.

Criteria
for
Selection: All AECT state affiliates, divisions, and regional organizations are eligible for these competitive grants. An application from a previous grant recipient will not be considered unless a summary report has been submitted to the Leadership Development Committee and the AECT national office. Organizations that have not received a grant in the past are particularly invited to apply. Funds must be intended for some unique aspect or function not previously undertaken. Proposals that demonstrate a commitment to leadership development, that propose programs that are unique to the applicant's organization, and that include activities or products of potential benefit to other AECT programs will be given special consideration.

Awards: The awards will be presented during the AECT National Convention and INFOCOMM International Exposition.

ECT Foundation
1993 AECT Memorial Scholarships

Awards:　　　One scholarship of $1,000 and one scholarship of $750 are awarded to graduate students in educational communications/technology to carry out a research project in the field. The scholarships may be used to assist the recipients to further their education in a summer session or academic year of graduate study at any accredited college or university in the United States or Canada. Programs of study may be at the master's or doctoral level.

Eligibility:　　All recipients must be members of AECT and accepted in or enrolled in a graduate-level degree program as outlined above.

Selection
Criteria:　　　Selections will be based on the following:

1. scholarship;

2. experience related to the field of educational media, communications, or technology, such as employment, field experience, course work, assistantships, publications, etc.;

3. service to the field through AECT activities and membership in other related professional organizations;

4. three letters of recommendation from persons familiar with the candidate's professional qualifications and leadership potential;

5. the candidate's own knowledge of key issues and opportunities facing the educational communications/technology field today, with respect to the candidate's own goals.

ECT Foundation
1993 Dean and Sybil McClusky
Research Award

Award:

$1,000 is available to honor two outstanding doctoral research proposals in educational technology, as selected by a jury of researchers from AECT's Research and Theory Division. Each winner will be awarded $500.

Guidelines
for Preparing
and Submitting
Papers:

Submitted proposals may follow acceptable formats of individual schools but must include at least:

1. The definition of the problem including a statement of significance.

2. A review of pertinent literature.

3. Research hypothesis to be examined.

4. Research design and procedures including statistical techniques.

Applicants are encouraged to review pages 157-61 of Stephen Isaac and William B. Michaels, *Handbook in Research and Evaluation*, Robert R. Knapp, San Diego, CA, 1971.

Eligibility:

Applicants must be presently enrolled in a doctoral program in educational technology and have obtained committee acceptance of their proposal. The winner will be expected to sign a statement that the proposed doctoral study will be completed in accordance with the sponsoring university's graduate school policies (including any time limitations) or be required to return the funds received.

ECT Foundation
1993 Carl F. and Viola V. Mahnke
Film Production Award

Award: $500 will be awarded to honor a film or video product that demonstrates excellence in message design and production for educational purposes. In addition, certificates of merit will be awarded to entries with outstanding qualities worthy of recognition. In the event that no entry demonstrates excellence, in the opinion of the judges, no award will be given.

Eligibility: Eligibility is limited to film and video products that are educational in nature and produced by undergraduate or graduate students. The winners must be members of AECT. Only entries completed within a two-year period prior to the competition will qualify.

Formats: All entries must be either on film or videotape. Film entries are limited to 16mm. Video entries can either be 1/2-inch VHS or 3/4-inch U-matic.

Judging: All entries will be judged during the AECT National Convention by a panel of judges from the AECT Media Design and Production Division.

Entry Fee: Entrants must include an entry fee of $100 per program, made payable to MDPD-AECT. For programs consisting of more than one film or video-cassette, each must be submitted separately. An entry form must be completed for each entry. The entry form may be duplicated if necessary.

ECT Foundation
1993 Robert M. Gagné Award for Graduate Student
Research in Instructional Technology

Purpose: To provide recognition and financial assistance for outstanding research by a graduate student in the field of instructional development

Description: The Robert M. Gagné Award Fund is coordinated by the ECT Foundation, a nonprofit organization sponsored and controlled by the Association of Educational Communications and Technology (AECT). The Division of Instructional Development will solicit nominations for the Gagné Award and will select the winner. The ECT Foundation is responsible for the administration of the award fund and will issue the cash award to the recipient.

Award: $500 is awarded for the most significant contribution to the body of knowledge upon which instructional development is based. The Gagné Award competition is sponsored by the Association for Educational Communications and Technology (AECT) and its Division of Instructional Development. A jury of scholars will select the winning contribution. The award will be presented to the recipient during the AECT National Convention.

Eligibility: The work must have been completed after December 31, 1989, while the award candidate was enrolled as a graduate student.

Nomination
Procedure: You may nominate any individual (including yourself) for the Gagné Award.

ECT Foundation
1993 James W. Brown Publication Award

Award: $300 will be given to the author or authors of an outstanding publication in the field of educational technology.

Eligibility: Nominated items are not restricted to books or print; they may be in any media format (film, video, broadcast program, book, etc.). Any nonperiodic publication in the field of educational technology is eligible if it bears a publication date of 1990 or 1991.

Guidelines
for
Nominations: Nominations are solicited from all possible sources: AECT members, media-related publishers and producers, authors themselves, the AECT nonperiodic publications committee, and others.

Criteria: Nominated publications shall be judged on the basis of:

1. Significance of the item's content for the field of media/instructional technology, as defined in the *Definition of Educational Technology*, published by AECT in 1977, or in any subset of the publication.

2. Professional quality of the item.

3. Potential impact of the item's content on the field of media/instructional technology, as defined in the *Definition of Educational Technology*.

4. Technical quality of the item.

ECT Foundation
1993 ETR&D Young Scholar Award

Award:
$500 will be presented to the winner. Additionally, the winning paper will be published in *ETR&D*, the refereed scholarly research journal published by the Association for Educational Communications and Technology (AECT).

For:
The best paper discussing a theoretical construct that could guide research in educational technology, considered worthy by a panel of judges.

Eligibility:
An individual who does not hold a doctorate degree or who received a doctorate not more than three years ago as of September 1, 1992.

Guidelines
for Preparing
and Submitting
Papers:

1. Papers must deal with research and theory in educational technology and must include:

   • A problem area stated within a well-explicated theoretical construct;

   • Supporting citations and analyses of related research;

   • A concluding discussion centering on what directions future research might take, with specific regard to variables, subjects, settings, etc., and, if appropriate, suggestions concerning other theoretical constructs that should be taken into consideration;

2. The paper should not be a report of a specific study;

3. A fresh, imaginative approach—which may go beyond the data—is encouraged;

4. The paper must be an original unpublished work;

5. The paper should be a maximum of 35 double-spaced typewritten pages;

6. The paper must be submitted in publishable journal format and must conform to the *American Psychological Association Style Manual*, 3d ed.

Selection
of
Winner:
The selection of the winning paper will be the responsibility of the editor and editorial board of *ETR&D*. Only the best paper judged worthy of the award will win. (There may not be a recipient of this award every year.)

ECT Foundation
1993 Young Researcher Award

Award: $500 for the best report of an experimental, descriptive, or historical study in educational technology. The Young Researcher award competition is sponsored by the Research and Theory Division of the Association for Educational Communications and Technology (AECT). A jury of scholars will select the best contribution for presentation at the AECT National Convention and INFOCOMM International Exposition. The winner will receive the cash award plus a certificate suitable for framing.

Eligibility: Anyone who is not more than three years beyond a doctorate as of December 31, 1992. A doctorate is *not* required. Jointly published papers are not acceptable.

Guidelines
for Preparing
and Submitting
Papers: Papers must report an original, unpublished research effort of an experimental, descriptive, or historical nature and must include the following:

1. problem area stated within a well-explicated theoretical construct(s);

2. supporting citations and analyses of related research;

3. exemplary reporting of research design or procedures and full description of statistical procedures where applicable;

4. concluding discussion that centers on directions for future research and implications for future directions in the field.

Other: Manuscripts may be a maximum of 35 double-spaced typewritten pages. The manuscript must be submitted in publishable journal format and must conform to the *American Psychological Association Style Manual*, 3d ed. The author's name should be included *only* on the cover sheet. All manuscripts will be coded and reviewed "blind."

ECT Foundation
1993 Jerry R. Coltharp Memorial
Innovative Media Management Award

Award:
This award is funded and coordinated by DEMM. One $400 award is presented annually, in recognition of innovative media management practices that enhance the provision of instructional media services or advance media application.

Eligibility:
Media service programs in schools, school districts, colleges and universities, regional media centers, government/military, allied health, and business and industry are eligible for the award.

Submission:
Projects that demonstrate exemplary management practices and a potential for enhancing associated media services are to be described in an article format not to exceed 10 double-spaced typed pages. Supporting photographs and graphic materials are encouraged. Article organization may be determined by the author but must include a definition of the specific need to be addressed, a review of the management approach applied, and an evaluation of the effectiveness of the project. Project categories are unrestricted and may encompass such areas as staff development, client training, public relations, service assessment, facilities design, etc.

Selection:
Submissions are reviewed and the recipient is determined by a selection committee appointed by the president of the AECT Division of Educational Media Management.

Criteria:
Criteria for evaluating submissions are as follows:

> *Originality*: Did the project demonstrate a unique approach to addressing specific needs?

> *Need*: Did the need to be addressed relate to the enhancement of media services or the advancement of media utilization?

> *Design*: Was the structure of the project appropriate to the need?

> *Impact*: Was the project successful in meeting the defined needs?

Reporting:
Articles detailing project parameters shall be considered for publication in an AECT publication. Publication rights will be assumed by AECT.

Other:
Manuscripts may be a maximum of 35 double-spaced typewritten pages. The manuscript must be submitted in publishable journal format and must conform to the *American Psychological Association Style Manual*, 3d ed. The author's name should be included *only* on the cover sheet. All manuscripts will be coded and reviewed "blind."

1993 DOT-AECT Crystal Award

Purpose: To recognize the most innovative and outstanding instructional telecommunications project.

Sponsor: The Division of Telecommunications of the Association for Educational Communications and Technology (AECT).

Eligibility: Limited to telecommunications projects that include a video component, that are instructional in nature and are designed for any age level, and that have been completed since September 30, 1991. Awards will be presented to the producing agency.

Entry Fee: A $25 fee must accompany each entry. Make checks payable to DOT-AECT.

Judging: Entries will be judged by a "blue ribbon" panel chosen by the president of DOT.

Criteria: Entries will be judged using the following criteria:

- Instructional value and relevance
- Quality of production
- Evidence of successful utilization and implementation
- Evidence of achievement of goals and objectives

Entry
Information: The following information must be provided for each entry. Please provide the essential information only. This information may not exceed four pages.

1. Contact person's name, title, address, and telephone number
2. Official name of submitting agency
3. Name of individual to accept award for producing agency, if selected as winner
4. Intended audience(s)
5. Goals and objectives of project
6. Design and production process, including names of principal project staff
7. Time line for project
8. Budget and sources of funding
9. Evidence of successful utilization and implementation
10. Samples of all project components
11. Return address for all items sent.

ECT Foundation
1993 ECT Mentor Endowment Scholarship

Award:

One scholarship of $3,000, funded by the Mentor Fund of the ECT Foundation, is awarded to a graduate student in Educational Communications and Technology to continue his or her studies in the field. The scholarship may be used to assist the recipient to further his or her education in a summer session or academic year of graduate study at any accredited college or university in the United States or Canada. Programs may be at the master's or doctoral level.

Eligibility:

All recipients must be members of AECT and accepted in or enrolled in a graduate-level program, as outlined above.

Selection
Criteria:

Selections will be based upon:

- Scholarship;

- Leadership potential;

- Experience related to the field of educational communications and technology, such as employment, field experience, course work, assistantships, presentations, publications, etc.;

- Three letters of recommendation from persons familiar with the candidate's professional qualifications and leadership potential.

Part Eight
Mediagraphy
Print and Nonprint Resources

Nancy R. Preston
Assistant Director
ERIC Clearinghouse on Information Resources
Syracuse University
Syracuse, New York

Introduction

CONTENTS

This resource list includes media-related journals, books, ERIC documents, and journal articles of interest to practitioners, researchers, students, and others concerned with educational technology and educational media. Emphasis in this section is on *currency*; the vast majority of books, ERIC documents, and journal articles cited here were published in 1992. Media-related journals include those listed in past issues of *EMTY* and new entries in the field.

SELECTION

Items were selected for the Mediagraphy in several ways. The ERIC (Educational Resources Information Center) Database was the source for ERIC document and journal article citations. Most of these entries are from a subset of the database selected by the directors of the ERIC Clearinghouse on Information Resources as being the year's most important database entries for this field. Media-related journals were either retained on the list or added to the list when they met one or more of the following criteria: were from a reputable publisher; had a broad circulation; were covered by indexing services; were peer reviewed; filled a gap in the literature. Journal data were verified using *Ulrich's International Periodicals Directory 1992-93*. Finally, the complete contents of the Mediagraphy were reviewed by the editors of *EMTY 1993*.

OBTAINING RESOURCES

Media-Related Periodicals and Books: Publisher, price, and ordering/subscription address are listed wherever available.

ERIC Documents. ERIC documents can be read in microfiche at any library holding an ERIC microfiche collection. The identification number beginning with ED (for example, ED 332 677) is used to find the document in the collection. ERIC documents can also be ordered from the ERIC Document Reproduction Service. Prices charged depend upon format chosen (microfiche or paper copy), length of the document, and method of shipping. Online orders, fax orders, and expedited delivery are available.

To find the closest library with an ERIC microfiche collection, contact:

ACCESS ERIC
1600 Research Blvd.
Rockville, MD 20850-3172
1-800-LET-ERIC (538-3742)
Internet: ACCERIC@GWUVM.GWU.EDU

To order ERIC documents, contact:

ERIC Document Reproduction Service (EDRS)
7420 Fullerton Rd., Suite 110
Springfield, VA 22153-2852
voice: 1-800-443-ERIC (443-3742), 1-703-440-1400
fax: 703-440-1408
Internet: EDRS@GWUVM.GWU.EDU

Journal Articles. Journal articles can be obtained in one of the following ways: (1) from a library subscribing to the title; (2) through interlibrary loan; (3) through the purchase of a back issue from the journal publisher; or (4) from an article reprint service. Articles noted as being available from the UMI (University Microfilms International) reprint service can be ordered using their ERIC identification numbers (numbers beginning with EJ, such as EJ 421 772).

University Microfilms International (UMI)
Article Clearinghouse
300 North Zeeb Rd.
Ann Arbor, MI 48106
1-800-521-0600 ext. 2533, 2534 (toll-free in U.S.)
1-800-343-5299 ext. 2533, 2534 (toll-free in Canada)

ARRANGEMENT

Mediagraphy entries are classified according to major subject emphasis under the following headings:

- Artificial Intelligence and Robotics
- CD-ROM
- Computer-Assisted Instruction
- Databases and Online Searching
- Distance Education
- Educational Research
- Educational Technology
- Electronic Publishing
- Information Science and Technology
- Instructional Design and Training

- Libraries and Media Centers
- Media Technologies
- Simulation and Virtual Reality
- Telecommunications and Networking

Mediagraphy

ARTIFICIAL INTELLIGENCE AND ROBOTICS

Media-Related Periodicals

Artificial Intelligence Abstracts. Bowker A & I Publishing, 121 Chanlon Rd., New Providence, NJ 07974. mo.; $495. Primarily for the specialist; includes abstracts of journal articles, reports, research documents, and other sources about artificial intelligence.

Intelligent Tutoring Media. Learned Information, 143 Old Marlton Pike, Medford, NJ 08055. q.; $125. Concerned with the packaging and communication of knowledge using advanced information technologies. Studies the impact of artificial intelligence, hypertext, and interactive video.

International Journal of Robotics Research. MIT Press, 55 Hayward St., Cambridge, MA 02142. bi-mo.; $80 indiv., $170 inst., $50 students and retired. Interdisciplinary approach to the study of robotics for researchers, scientists, and students.

Knowledge-Based Systems. Butterworth-Heinemann Ltd., Turpin Tranactions, Ltd., Distribution Centre, Blackhorse Rd., Letchworth, Herts SG6 1HN, England. q.; £130. Interdisciplinary and applications-oriented journal on fifth-generation computing, expert systems, and knowledge-based methods in system design.

Mind and Machines. Kluwer Academic Publishers, Box 358, Accord Station, Hingham, MA 02018-0358. q.; $157. Discusses issues concerning machines and mentality, artificial intelligence, epistemology, simulation, and modeling.

Books

Sleeman, D., and Bernsen, N. O., eds. (1992). **Artificial intelligence**. Research directions in cognitive science, European perspectives, vol. 5. L. Erlbaum Associates, 365 Broadway, Hillsdale, NJ 07642. 276pp. $59.95. A collection of papers on programming, developments, and applications of expert and AI systems.

ERIC Documents

Spector, J. Michael, and others. (1992). **Intelligent frameworks for instructional design**. Paper presented at the Annual Conference of the American Educational Research Association, San Francisco, California, April 20-24, 1992. 22pp. ED 346 842. Presents a taxonomy describing various uses of artificial intelligence techniques in automated instructional development systems.

Journal Articles

Orwig, Gary, and Barron, Ann. (1992, February). Expert systems: An overview for teacher-librarians. **Emergency Librarian, 19**(3), 19-21. EJ 441 740. Covers the development of the MYCIN medical expert system; rule-based expert systems; the use of expert system shells to develop a specific system; and how to select an appropriate application for an expert system.

CD-ROM

Media-Related Periodicals

CD-ROM Databases. Worldwide Videotex, Box 138, Babson Park, Boston, MA 02157. mo.; $150 U.S., $190 elsewhere. Descriptive listing of all databases being marketed on CD-ROM, with vendor and system information.

CD-ROM Librarian. Meckler Publishing Corp., 11 Ferry Lane W., Westport, CT 06880-5808. 11/yr.; $82. Information about optical technologies relevant to libraries and information centers.

CD-ROM Professional. Pemberton Press, Inc., 11 Tannery Ln., Weston, CT 06883. bi-mo.; $86 U.S., $101 Canada and Mexico, $121 foreign airmail. Assists publishers, librarians, and other information professionals in the selection, evaluation, purchase, and operation of CD-ROM systems.

Books

Jacsó, Peter. (1992). **CD-ROM software, dataware, and hardware: Evaluation, selection, and installation**. Libraries Unlimited, P.O. Box 3988, Englewood, CO 80155. 256pp. $35. A comprehensive guide to CD-ROM information storage, including evaluations of hardware and software and a discussion of future developments.

Journal Articles

Geasler, Shelly. (1992, January-February). CD-ROM: A cost-effective alternative. **Instruction Delivery Systems, 6**(1), 21-23. EJ 446 204. Discusses CD-ROM as a multimedia hardware platform for office personal computers. Covers hardware requirements; CD-ROM capacity; mixed-mode CD-ROMs; audio-only CD-ROMs; and development costs.

COMPUTER-ASSISTED INSTRUCTION

Media-Related Periodicals

Apple Library Users Group Newsletter. Apple Computer, 10381 Bandley Dr., Cupertino, CA 95014. 4/yr.; free. For people interested in using Apple and Macintosh computers in libraries and information centers.

BYTE. Box 550, Hightstown, NJ 08520-9886. mo.; $29.95. Current articles on computer hardware, software, and applications, and reviews of computer products.

CALICO Journal. Computer Assisted Language and Instruction Consortium, 014 Language Building, Duke University, Durham, NC 27706. q.; $35 indiv., $65 inst. Provides information on the applications of technology in teaching and learning languages.

Collegiate Microcomputer. Rose-Hulman Institute of Technology, Department of Mathematics, Terre Haute, IN 47803. q.; $34. Features articles about instructional uses of microcomputers in college and university courses.

Compute. Compute Publications, Inc., Box 3244, Harlan, IA 51593-3244. mo.; $19.97. Specifically designed for users of IBM PC, Tandy, and compatible machines at home, at work, and in the school.

Computer Book Review. 735 Ekekela Pl., Honolulu, HI 96817. 6/yr.; $30. Reviews books on computers and computer-related subjects.

Computers and Education. Pergamon Press, 660 White Plains Rd., Tarrytown, NY 10591-5153. 8/yr.; $550. A theoretical refereed journal that emphasizes research project reports.

Computers and People. Berkeley Enterprises, Inc., 815 Washington St., Newtonville, MA 02160. bi-mo.; $24.50. Covers all aspects of information processing systems with articles, reviews, and games.

Computers and the Humanities. Kluwer Academic Publishers, Box 358, Accord Station, Hingham, MA 02018-0358. bi-mo.; $66 indiv., $189.50 inst. Contains scholarly articles on computer applications in the humanities.

Computers in Human Behavior. Pergamon Press, Inc., 660 White Plains Rd., Tarrytown, NY 10591-5153. q.; £180 ($342 U.S.). Addresses the psychological impact of computer use on individuals, groups, and society.

Computing Teacher. International Society for Technology in Education, University of Oregon, 1787 Agate St., Eugene, OR 97403-9905. 8/yr.; $47 nonmembers, $46 members, $23 student members. Focuses on teaching about computers, using computers in teaching and teacher education, and the computer's impact on curricula.

Digest of Software Reviews: Education. School & Home Courseware, Inc., 3999 N. Chestnut Diagonal, Suite 333, Fresno, CA 93726-4797. mo.; $147.50. Compiles software reviews from over 60 journals and magazines that emphasize critical features of the instructional software for grades K-12.

Dr. Dobb's Journal. M & T Publishing, Inc., 501 Galveston Dr., Redwood City, CA 94063-4728. mo.; $29.97. Articles on the latest in operating systems, programming languages, hardware design and architecture, data structures, and telecommunications; in-depth hardware and software reviews.

Education & Computing. Elsevier Science Publishers, 655 Avenue of the Americas, New York, NY 10010. q; $166. For educators, computer scientists, and decision makers in government, education, and industry, with emphasis on the technical developments in information technology.

Education Technology News. Business Publishers, Inc., 951 Pershing Dr., Silver Spring, MD 20910-4464. bi-w.; $267.54. For teachers and those interested in educational uses of computers in the classroom. Feature articles on applications and educational software.

Electronic Learning. P.O. Box 5397, Boulder, CO 80322-3797. 8/yr.; $23.95. Professional magazine for media specialists, teachers, and administrators that stresses nontechnical information about uses of computers, video equipment, and other electronic devices.

Home Office Computing. Scholastic, Inc., Box 53561, Boulder, CO 80321-1346. mo.; $19.97, foreign $27.97. For professionals who use computers and do business at home.

InCider-A Plus. IDG Communications, Box 58618, Boulder, CO 80322-8616. mo.; $27.97. A magazine for Apple computer users. Reviews new developments in software and hardware and provides how-to articles.

InfoWorld. InfoWorld Publishing, 155 Bovet Rd., Suite 800, San Mateo, CA 94402. w.; $110. News and reviews of PC hardware, software, peripherals, and networking.

Interactive Learning International. John Wiley & Sons, Baffins Lane, Chichester, Sussex PO19 1UD, England. q.; $250. Information about research and development of learning with the new information technologies for professional trainers and educators.

Journal of Computer Assisted Learning. Journal Subscription Department, Box 87, Blackwell Scientific Publications Ltd., Osney Mead, Oxford OX2 0DT, England. q.; $38 indiv., $155 inst. Articles and research on the use of computer-assisted learning.

Journal of Computer-Based Instruction. Association for the Development of Computer Based Instructional Systems, International Headquarters, 1601 W. Fifth Ave., Suite 111, Columbus, OH 43212. q.; $36 nonmembers, single copy $10. Contains both scholarly research and descriptions of practical CBI techniques.

Journal of Educational Computing Research. Baywood Publishing Co., 26 Austin Ave., Box 337, Amityville, NY 11701. q.; $75 indiv., $109 inst. Publishes new research in the theory and applications of educational computing in a variety of content areas and with various ages.

Journal of Research on Computing in Education. International Society for Technology in Education, University of Oregon, 1787 Agate St., Eugene, OR 97403-9905. q.; $55 nonmembers. A technical publication emphasizing current computer research and advances as they apply to all levels of education.

MacWorld. MacWorld Communications, Inc., Box 54515, Boulder, CO 80322-4515. mo.; $30. Describes software, tutorials, and applications for users of the Macintosh microcomputer.

Microcomputer Index. Learned Information, Inc., 143 Old Marlton Pike, Medford, NJ 08055-8750. bi-mo.; $159. Abstracts of literature on the use of microcomputers in business, education, and the home.

Microcomputer Industry Update. Industry Market Reports, Inc., Box 681, Los Altos, CA 94022. mo.; $295. Abstracts of product announcements and reviews of interest appearing in weekly trade press.

Nibble. Mindcraft Publishing Corp., Box 256, Lincoln, MA 01773-0002. mo.; $39.95. Type-in programs for Apple II owners, covering utilities, applications, software reviews, and more.

Observer. (Formerly **Office System Trends**.) Automated Office Resources, 812 Via Tornasol, Aptos, CA 95003-5624. 6/yr., $95. Contains information on office systems technology and educational computer use.

PC Magazine: The Independent Guide to IBM-Standard Personal Computing. Ziff-Davis Publishing Co., Box 54093, Boulder, CO 80322. bi-w.; $29.97. Comparative reviews of computer hardware and general business software programs.

PC Week. Ziff-Davis Publishing Co., 10 Presidents Landing, Medford, MA 02155-5146. w.; $160, free to qualified personnel. Provides current information on and analyses of hardware, software, and peripherals for the IBM PC, as well as buyers' guides and news of the industry.

PC World. PC World Communications, Inc., Box 55029, Boulder, CO 80322-5029. mo.; $29.90 U.S., $49.90 Canada and Mexico, $75.90 elsewhere. Contains new reports on hardware, software, and applications of the IBM PC.

School Tech News. Business Publishers, Inc., 951 Pershing Dr., Silver Spring, MD 20910-4464. mo.; $41. Reports on current developments in computer-based instruction that affect teachers directly.

Social Science Computer Review. Duke University Press, 6697 College Station, Durham, NC 27708. q.; indiv. $36, inst. $72. Features include software reviews, new product announcements, and tutorials for beginners.

Software Digest Ratings Report. National Software Testing Laboratories, Plymouth Corporate Center, Box 1000, Plymouth Meeting, PA 19462. 15/yr.; $445. For IBM personal computer users. Each issue reports the ratings for one category of IBM PC software, based on multiple-user tests.

Software Magazine. Sentry Publishing Co., 1900 W. Park Dr., Westborough, MA 01581. 17/yr.; $60 U.S., $72 Canada, $125 elsewhere (free to qualified personnel). Focuses on selecting and using business software. Gives addresses of vendors and features of new products.

Software Reviews on File. Facts on File, 460 Park Ave. S., New York, NY 10016. mo.; $210. Condensed software reviews from over 150 publications. Features software for all major microcomputer systems and programming languages.

Teaching and Computers. Scholastic, Inc., 730 Broadway, New York, NY 10003-9538. 6/yr.; $23.95. For the elementary school teacher, with articles on applications of computer-assisted instruction and integrating computers into the classroom environment.

T.H.E. Journal (Technological Horizons in Education). Ed Warnshius, Ltd., 150 El Camino Real, Suite 112, Tustin, CA 92680-3670. 11/yr.; free to administrators and trainers, $29 others. For educators of all levels. Focuses on a specific topic for each issue as well as technological innovations as they apply to education.

Books

Dijkstra, Sanne, Krammer, Hein P. M., and van Merrienboer, Jeroen J. G., eds. (1992). **Instructional models in computer-based learning environments**. NATO ASI Series F, No. 104. Springer-Verlag, 175 Fifth Ave., New York, NY 10010. 150pp. (Price not available.) Focuses on instructional models as explicit, potentially implementable representations of knowledge concerning one or more aspects of instruction.

Only the best: Annual guide to highest-rated education software/multimedia, preschool-grade 12. 1993 edition. (1992). Association for Supervision and Curriculum Development, Curriculum/Technology Resource Center, 1250 N. Pitt St., Alexandria, VA 22314-1453. 120pp. $25. (Also available in database form for IBM or Macintosh, $99.) More than 10,000 reviews of educational software are examined to identify the top courseware programs produced each year.

ERIC Documents

Doornekamp, B. Gerard. (1992). **The valuation by students of the use of computers in education**. Paper presented at the European Conference on Educational Research, Enschede, The Netherlands, June 22-25, 1992. ED 352 929. Discusses a study conducted at the Technology Enriched Schools Project examining students' perceptions, computer use in teaching-learning situations, students' backgrounds, and frequency of educational computer use.

Market Data Retrieval, Inc. (1992). **Report on the survey of microcomputers in schools (1992)**. Shelton, Connecticut: Author. ED 352 930. Reports on a survey of microcomputers in 85 percent of all public, private, and Catholic schools in the United States.

McLaughlin, Pamela. (1992, August). **Computer applications in education: The best of ERIC 1991**. Syracuse, New York: ERIC Clearinghouse on Information Resources. 100pp. ED 345 715. (Also available from Information Resources Publications, 030 Huntington Hall, Syracuse University, Syracuse NY 13244-2340; $10 plus $2 shipping and handling.) Provides an overview of literature entered into the ERIC database in 1991 on computer uses in elementary and secondary education, adult education, and special education.

Journal Articles

Austin, Mary B. (1992). CBT from scratch: Building a computer based training department. **TechTrends, 37**(1), 9-11. EJ 441 812. (Available UMI.) Provides a step-by-step reference for building a new development team in computer-assisted instruction and computer-based training. Covers staff development, computer-based training technology information, training methods, and teamwork.

Bailey, Jeff. (1992, Winter). Curriculum approaches in special education computing. **Journal of Computer-Based Instruction, 19**(1), 1-5. EJ 443 332. (Available UMI.) Focuses on five models of approaches to computer curriculum in special education: the role of the teacher; social and social-cognitive learning environments; improving cognitive capacities; expanding experiential horizons; and information management.

Becker, Henry Jay. (1992). Computer-based integrated learning systems in the elementary and middle grades: A critical review and synthesis of evaluation reports. **Journal of Educational Computing Research, 8**(1), 1-41. EJ 446 212. Discusses the use and advantages of integrated learning systems (ILSs) and reanalyzes 30 evaluations of ILSs by using effect size statistics.

Beishuizen, J. J. (1992, June). Studying a complex knowledge domain by exploration or explanation. **Journal of Computer Assisted Learning, 8**(2), 104-17. EJ 447 562. (Available UMI.) Highlights two experiments on the educational value of a Dutch computer simulation program that models the relationship between erosion and agriculture in a developing country.

Boland, Robert J. (1992, January-March). Computers from tools to tutors: An educational software evaluation construct for teachers of adults. **Interactive Learning International, 8**(1), 45-53. EJ 443 326. Discusses conceptual constructs that may be useful for inservice teacher education programs, evaluating the nature and educational use of instructional software for adult learners.

Chung, Jaesam, and Riegeluth, Charles M. (1992, October). Instructional prescriptions for learner control. **Educational Technology, 32**(10), 14-20. EJ 453 198. (Available UMI.) Describes six methods of learner control in instructional management: content control; sequence control; pace control; display or strategy control; internal processing control; and advisor strategies.

Dupagne, Michel, and Krendl, Kathy A. (1992, Spring). Teachers' attitudes toward computers: A review of the literature. **Journal of Research on Computing in Education, 24**(3), 420-29. EJ 447 483. (Available UMI.) Reviews the literature from the mid-1980s to the present on teachers' attitudes toward computers, including perceptions; impact of computer use on attitude; and impact of personal and learning environment.

Jackson, David F., and others. (1992). Computer-assisted thinking tools: Problem solving in graphical data analysis. **Journal of Educational Computing Research, 8**(1), 43-67. EJ 446 213. Describes a study of high school students that investigated the use of microcomputers to teach principles about the design and development of graphs.

Jensen, Eric. (1992, December-January). At-risk students online. **Computing Teacher, 19**(4), 10-11. EJ 438 043. (Available UMI.) Describes the Knowledge Gateway Project at Wenatchee (Washington) High School, which combines computer technology with a problem-solving approach to teach communication and information processing skills to at-risk students.

Kristiansen, Rolf. (1992, June). Evolution or revolution: Changes in teacher attitudes toward computers in education, 1970-1990. **Education and Computing, 8**(1-2), 71-78. EJ 448 864. Reports data from 1970, 1978, and 1990 surveys conducted in Norway to determine teacher attitudes toward new information and communication technolgies.

Liao, Yuen-Kuang. (1992, Spring). Effects of computer-assisted instruction on cognitive outcomes: A meta-analysis. **Journal of Research on Computing in Education, 24**(3), 367-80. EJ 447 478. (Available UMI.) Analysis of 31 studies indicated that CAI had moderately positive effects on student cognitive outcomes and that the outcomes of using CAI extend beyond the content of the specific software or subject area.

Maddux, Cleborne D., and Willis, Jerry W. (1992, September). Integrated learning systems and their alternatives: Problems and cautions. **Educational Technology, 32**(9), 51-57. EJ 451 921. (Available UMI.) Discusses computer networks and alternatives, theories of learning and teaching, turnkey systems, and the role of vendors.

McWeeney, Mark G. (1992, Winter). Computer-assisted instruction to teach DOS commands: A pilot study. **Research Strategies, 10**(1), 17-23. EJ 447 443. (Available UMI.) Describes a computer-assisted instruction program used to teach DOS commands to graduate students. Concludes that the CAI program significantly aided the students.

Milheim, William D., and Lavix, Carol. (1992, May-June). Screen design for computer-based training and interactive video: Practical suggestions and overall guidelines. **Performance and Instruction, 31**(5), 13-21. EJ 447 587. (Available UMI.) Covers general text and graphics design, screen layout, use of color, and effective design for program navigation.

Peled, Zimra, and others. (1992). A taxonomy for computer software adoption policy. **Journal of Educational Computing Research, 8**(1), 81-100. EJ 446 215. Proposes a taxonomy to aid decision makers in selecting computer software consistent with their educational values regarding the nature of instruction and the use of information technology.

Pelletier, Pierre. (1992). Word processing as a support to the writing process. **International Journal of Instructional Media, 19**(3), 249-57. EJ 457 838. (Available UMI.) Investigates the theoretical basis of the writing process and describes the possibilities of word processing as a tool to support it.

Pitsch, Barry, and Murphy, Vaughn. (1992, March). Using one computer for whole-class instruction. **Computing Teacher, 19**(6), 19-21. EJ 443 360. (Available UMI.) Discusses the development of teaching skills for delivering whole-class instruction, and the use of software to involve groups in collaborative learning and develop higher-order thinking skills.

Resta, Paul. (1992, June). Organizing education for minorities: Enhancing minority access and use of the new information technologies in higher education. **Education and Computing,** **8**(1-2), 119-27. EJ 448 867. Discusses the impact of current inequities in precollege access and use of computers by African-American, Hispanic, and American Indian students and ways to enhance the computer competence of minority students.

Sandals, Lauran H. (1992, Spring). An overview of the uses of computer-based assessment and diagnosis. **Canadian Journal of Educational Communication, 21**(1), 67-78. Presents an overview of the applications of microcomputer-based assessment and diagnosis for both educational and psychological placement and interventions.

Sawyer, W. D. M. (1992, January). The virtual computer: A new paradigm for educational computing. **Educational Technology, 32**(1), 7-14. EJ 441 707. (Available UMI.) Describes virtual personal computing, a computer-based educational infrastructure for all students, as a step toward meeting national education goals.

Schwartz, Ilsa, and Lewis, Molly. (1992, December-January). Selecting basic concept course-ware for preschools and early elementary grades. **Computing Teacher, 19**(4), 15-17. EJ 438 044. (Available UMI.) Discusses evaluation criteria for selecting courseware, including instructional quality, production quality, flexibility, and cost.

Shore, Ann, and Johnson, Marilyn F. (1992, September). Integrated learning systems: A vision for the future. **Educational Technology, 32**(9). 36-39. EJ 451 916. (Available UMI.) Discussion from the vendor's perspective covers the product development process, strengths and weaknesses, and future developments.

Stephenson, Stanley D. (1992, August). The role of the instructor in computer-based training. **Performance and Instruction, 31**(7), 23-26. EJ 451 800. (Available UMI.) Describes a study conducted to define what instructors should be doing while a student is engaged in computer-based training and to examine the effect of student-instructor interaction in CBT.

Van Dusen, Lani M., and Worthen, Blaine R. (1992, September). Factors that facilitate or impede implementation of integrated learning systems. **Educational Technology, 32**(9), 16-21. EJ 451 912. (Available UMI.) Discusses empirical studies of integrated learning systems, implementation models, and factors that determine level of success.

Yang, Yong-Chil. (1992). The effects of media on motivation and content recall: Comparison of computer- and print-based instruction. **Journal of Educational Technology Systems,** **20**(2), 95-105. EJ 441 671. Describes a study conducted with eleventh graders that compared the effects of computer-based instruction and print-based instruction on motivation, continuing motivation, and content recall.

Zane, Thomas, and Frazer, Connell G. (1992, Spring). The extent to which software developers validate their claims. **Journal of Research on Computing in Education, 24**(3), 410-19. EJ 447 482. (Available UMI.) Discusses the results of a survey of 15 educational software developers. Considers the importance of validating the effectiveness of educational software.

DATABASES AND ONLINE SEARCHING

Media-Related Periodicals

CompuServe (formerly **Online Today**). 5000 Arlington Centre Blvd., Columbus, OH 43220. mo.; $18. Gives current news about computer communication and information retrieval, in-depth articles on issues and techniques, and software and book reviews.

Data Sources. Ziff-Davis Publishing Co., One Park Ave., New York, NY 10016. 2/yr.; $440. A guide to the information processing industry. Covers equipment, software, services, and systems, and includes profiles of 10,000 companies.

Database. Online, Inc. 11 Tannery Ln., Weston, CT 06883. bi-mo.; $89 U.S. and Canada, $104 Mexico, $124 foreign airmail. Includes articles on new databases and techniques for searching online databases, as well as new products information and news updates.

Database Searcher. Meckler Publishing, 11 Ferry Ln. W., Westport, CT 06880-5808. mo.; $98. Includes techniques, new products, conferences, and tips and techniques for searching.

Directory of Online Databases. Gale Research Inc., 835 Penobscot Building, Detroit, MI 48226. q.; $190 U.S., $240 elsewhere. Identifies over 4,500 databases that are publicly available to online service users. Includes information on database selection and vendors.

Information Today. Learned Information, Inc., 143 Old Marlton Pike, Medford, NJ 08055. 11/yr.; $39.95. For users and producers of electronic information services. Articles and news about the industry, calendar of events, and product information.

Journal of Database Administration. Idea Group Publishing, 4811 Jonestown Rd., Suite 230, Harrisburg, PA 17109-9159. q.; $60 indiv., $105 inst. Provides state-of-the-art research to those who design, develop, and administer DBMS-based information systems.

Link-Up. Learned Information, Inc., 143 Old Marlton Pike, Medford, NJ 08055. bi-mo.; $25 U.S., $48 elsewhere. For individuals interested in small computer applications; covers hardware, software, communications services, and search methods.

Online. Online, Inc., 11 Tannery Ln., Weston, CT 06883. 6/yr.; $89 U.S. and Canada, $104 Mexico, $124 foreign airmail. For online information system users. Articles cover a variety of online applications for general and business use.

Online Review. Learned Information, Inc., 143 Old Marlton Pike, Medford, NJ 08055. bi-mo.; $95. An international journal of online information systems featuring articles on using and managing online systems, training and educating online users, developing search aids, and creating and marketing databases.

Resource Sharing and Information Networks. Haworth Press, 10 Alice St., Binghamton, NY 13904. semi-ann.; $32 indiv., $85 inst. A forum for ideas on the basic theoretical and practical problems faced by planners, practitioners, and users of network services.

Journal Articles

Agosti, M. and others. (1992). A hypertext environment for interacting with large textual databases. **Information Processing and Management, 28**(3), 371-87. EJ 447 508. (Available UMI.) Proposes a conceptual reference architecture for information retrieval systems and discusses functional capabilities of a hypertext environment.

Dyson, Mary C. (1992). How do you describe a symbol? The problems involved in retrieving symbols from a database. **Information Services and Use, 12**(1), 65-76. EJ 448 967. Analyzes attributes of symbols and identifies the need for a suitable management system for retrieving images from a database.

Sieverts, Eric G., and others. (1992, February). Software for information storage and retrieval tested, evaluated and compared. Part III—End-user software. **Electronic Library, 10**(1), 5-19. EJ 446 247. (Available UMI.) Lists and compares specifications, properties, and test results of eight microcomputer software programs for information storage and retrieval by end-users.

DISTANCE EDUCATION

Media-Related Periodicals

American Journal of Distance Education. Pennsylvania State University, School of Education, 403 South Allen St., Suite 206, University Park, PA 16801-5202. 3/yr.; $30. Focuses on the professional trainer, adult educator, college teacher, and others interested in the latest developments in methods and systems for delivering education to adults.

Appropriate Technology. Intermediate Technology Publications, Ltd., 103-105 Southampton Row, London WC1B 4HH, England. q.; $27 indiv., $33 inst. Articles on low-cost, small-scale technology, particularly for developing countries.

Development Communication Report. Clearinghouse on Development Communication, 1815 N. Ft. Myer Dr., Suite 600, Arlington, VA 22209. q.; $10 (free to readers in developing countries). Applications of communications technology to international development problems such as agriculture, health, and nutrition.

Distance Education. University College of Southern Queensland Press, Darling Heights, Toowoomba, Queensland 4350, Australia. semi-ann.; $55 (Australian currency). Papers on the history, politics, and administration of distance education.

International Council for Distance Education Bulletin. Open University, Regional Academic Services, Walton Hall, Milton Keynes MK7 6AA7, England. 3/yr.; $65. Reports on activities and programs of the ICDE.

Journal of Distance Education. Canadian Association for Distance Education, 151 Slater St., Ottawa, ON K1P 5N1, Canada. 2/yr.; $40. Aims to promote and encourage scholarly work of empirical and theoretical nature relating to distance education in Canada and throughout the world.

Research in Distance Education. Centre for Distance Education, Athabasca University, Box 10,000, Athabasca, AB T0G 2R0, Canada. q.; price not available. A forum for the discussion of issues surrounding the process of conducting research within the field of distance education.

Books

Collaborative learning through computer conferencing: The Najaden papers. (1992). NATO ASI Series F., No. 90. Springer-Verlag, 175 Fifth Ave., New York, NY 10010. 260pp. (Price not available.) Analyzes some of the main educational, social, and technological issues in the use of computer-mediated communication and computer networking for online collaborative learning in distance education and corporate environments.

Rossman, Parker. (1992). **The emerging worldwide electronic university: Information age global higher education**. Contributions to the Study of Education, No. 57. Greenwood Press, 88 Post Rd. W., Box 5007, Westport, CT 06881. 184pp. $42.95. Surveys and synthesizes the material currently available on the electronic globalization of higher education.

ERIC Documents

Hart, Russ A., and others. (1992, February). **Establishing rural ITFS distance education programs: The California State University, Fresno experience**. Paper presented at the Annual Conference of the Association for Educational Communications and Technology, Washington, DC, February 5-9, 1992. 19pp. ED 346 846. Identifies three important functions of establishing a distance education program and discusses the importance of communication between learner and teacher.

Hawkins, Jan. (1992, February). **Technology-mediated communities for learning: Designs and consequences. Technical report no. 21**. New York: Bank Street College of Education. ED 349 965. Presents five categories of issues that have arisen thus far in the development of distance learning, and describes four different exemplars of distance learning experiments and projects.

Schrum, Lynne. (1992, April). **Information age innovations: A case study of online professional development**. Paper presented at the Annual Conference of the American Educational Research Association, San Francisco, California, April 20-24, 1992. 19pp. ED 346 849. An independent study course designed to introduce educators to current classroom and personal uses of computer-mediated communication, databases, and distance learning.

Journal Articles

Barker, Bruce O., and Goodwin, Robert D. (1992, April). Audiographics: Linking remote classrooms. **Computing Teacher, 19**(7), 11-12, 14-15. EJ 446 197. (Available UMI.) Discusses use of audiographics for inservice courses to teachers in Hawaii, including appropriate telecommunications software, a model for teleteaching, strengths and weaknesses of audiographics, and suggestions for effective instruction.

Chacon, Fabio. (1992, February). A taxonomy of computer media in distance education. **Open Learning, 7**(1), 12-27. EJ 448 886. (Available UMI.) Identifies three major learning and behavioral processes that are extended by computers: information processing; interaction; and communication.

Dhanarajan, Gajaraj, and Timmers, Shannon. (1992, February). Transfer and adaptation of self-instructional materials. **Open Learning, 7**(1), 3-11. EJ 448 885. (Available UMI.) Discusses the collaborative use of learning materials in distance education. Covers curriculum issues, instructional design, academic standards, technical factors, and copyright regulations.

Doan, Michael. (1992, March-April). A primer on satellite equipment. **Media and Methods, 28**(4), 10, 12. EJ 443 363. (Available UMI.) Provides information for school districts planning distance education, including types of satellite dishes, satellite receivers, descramblers, copyright restrictions, other ancillary equipment, and selecting a dealer.

Hodgson, Vivien, and McConnell, David. (1992, September). IT-based open learning: A case study in management learning. **Journal of Computer Assisted Learning, 8**(3), 136-50. EJ 451 862. (Available UMI.) Focuses on Information Technology-based Open Learning (ITOL), a small-scale trial model of open learning developed at Lancaster University.

Holmberg, Robert G., and Bakshi, Trilochan S. (1992). Postmortem on a distance education course: Successes and failures. **Journal of Distance Education, 6**(1), 27-39. EJ 446 226. Considers the successes and failures associated with the design, production, delivery, and evaluation of a home study course through Athabasca University.

Jones, Ann, and others. (1992, January-April). Providing computing for distance learners: A strategy for home use. **Computers and Education, 18**(1-3), 183-93. EJ 441 702. (Available UMI.) Describes an experiment at the Open University in Great Britain that expanded the use of home-based microcomputers for distance education students enrolled in higher education courses.

Willis, Barry. (1992, June). Making distance education effective: Key roles and responsibilities. **Educational Technology, 32**(6), 35-37. EJ 447 500. (Available UMI.) Examines the roles and responsibilities of students, faculty, facilitators, support staff, and administration in distance education.

EDUCATIONAL RESEARCH

Media-Related Periodicals

American Educational Research Journal. American Educational Research Association, 1230 17th St. NW, Washington, DC 20036. q.; $33 indiv., $41 inst. Reports original research, both empirical and theoretical, and brief synopses of research.

Current Index to Journals in Education (CIJE). Oryx Press, 4041 N. Central at Indian School Rd., Phoenix, AZ 85012-3397. mo.; $225. A guide to articles published in some 780 education and education-related journals. Includes complete bibliographic information, annotations, and indexes. Semiannual cumulations available. Contents are produced by the ERIC (Educational Resources Information Center) system, Office of Educational Research and Improvement, U.S. Department of Education.

Education Index. H. W. Wilson, 950 University Ave., Bronx, NY 10452. mo. (except July and August); variable costs. Author-subject index to educational publications in the English language. Cumulated quarterly and annually.

Educational Research. NFER Publishing, Darville House, 2 Oxford Road E., Windsor, Berkshire SL2 1DF, England. 3/yr.; $90. Reports on current educational research, evaluation, and applications.

Educational Researcher. American Educational Research Association, 1230 17th St. NW, Washington, DC 20036. 9/yr.; $33 indiv., $41 inst. Contains news and features of general significance in educational research.

Research in Science and Technological Education. Carfax Publishing Co., P.O. Box 25, Abington, Oxfordshire OX14 3VE, England. 2/yr.; $99 indiv., $248 inst. Publication of original research in the science and technological fields. Includes articles on psychological, sociological, economic, and organizational aspects.

Resources in Education (RIE). Superintendent of Documents, U.S. Government Printing Office, Washington, DC 20402. mo.; $94 U.S, $117.50 elsewhere. Announcement of research reports and other documents in education, including abstracts and indexes by subject, author, and institution. Cumulative semiannual indexes available. Contents produced by the ERIC (Educational Resources Information Center) system, Office of Educational Research and Improvement, U.S. Department of Education.

Books

Borg, Walter R., Gall, Joyce P., and Gall, Meredith D. (1992). **Applying educational research: A practical guide for teachers** (3d ed.). Longman Publishing, 95 Church St., White Plains, NY 10601-1566. 443pp. $50.50. Comprehensive text designed to help students learn how to locate, read, and interpret research findings reported in the education literature.

Thompson, Ann D., Simonson, Michael R., and Hargrave, Constance P. (1992). **Educational technology: A review of the research**. Association for Educational Communications and Technology, 1025 Vermont Ave. NW, Suite 820, Washington, DC 20005. 96pp. $15 AECT members, $22 nonmembers. Presents an overview of the theories and research that support technology in teaching and learning activities including audio, still pictures, films, television, computer-based learning, and hypermedia.

Weller, Carolyn, and Houston, James E., eds. (1992). **ERIC identifier authority list (IAL) 1992**. Oryx Press, 4041 N. Central at Indian School Rd., Phoenix, AZ 85012-3397. 512pp. $55 prepaid. For use by ERIC database searchers, this guide lists over 44,000 Identifiers, semicontrolled retrieval terms used for emerging and infrequent education topics represented in ERIC.

ERIC Documents

Brown, William L., and Stevens, Betty L. (1992, April). **Using the microcomputer to equate ratings of student writing samples**. Paper presented at the American Educational Research Association, San Francisco, California, April 20-24, 1992. ED 352 926. Reports on a study to determine whether student writing portfolios could be rated reliably by trained judges, the effects on students ratings of the differential leniency of the judges, and the effects of writing-prompt difficulty and its interactions with rater leniency.

Field initiated studies program. Abstracts of funded projects 1990 and 1991. (1992, April). Washington, DC: Office of Educational Research and Improvement. 39pp. ED 343 584. Describes 29 projects funded to encourage promising and fresh ideas in education research.

Journal Articles

Ross, Steven M., and Morrison, Gary R. (1992). Getting started as a researcher: Designing and conducting research studies in instructional technology. **TechTrends, 37**(3), 19-22. EJ 447 492. (Available UMI.) Presents guidelines for research planning: select a topic; identify the research problem; conduct a literature search; state the research questions; determine the research design; determine methods; and identify data analysis procedures.

EDUCATIONAL TECHNOLOGY

Media-Related Periodicals

British Journal of Educational Technology. Council for Educational Technology, Sir Wm. Lyons Rd., University Science Park, Coventry CV4 7EZ, England. 3/yr.; $66.50. Published by the National Council for Educational Technology, this journal includes articles on education and training, especially theory, applications, and development of educational technology and communications.

Canadian Journal of Educational Communication. Association of Media and Technology in Education in Canada, AMTEC-CJEC Subscription, 3-1750 The Queensway, Suite 1318, Etobicoke, Ontario M9C 5H5, Canada. 3/yr.; $40. Articles, research reports, and literature reviews on all areas of educational communication and technology.

Education and Training Technology International. Kogan Page Ltd., Distribution Centre, Blackhorse Rd., Letchworth, Herts SG6 1HN, England. q.; £50 ($95 U.S.). Journal of the Association for Educational and Training Technology emphasizing developing trends in and the efficient employment of educational technology.

Educational Technology. Educational Technology Publications, Inc., 700 Palisade Ave., Englewood Cliffs, NJ 07632. mo.; $119, $139 foreign, $12 single copy. Covers telecommunications, computer-aided instruction, information retrieval, educational television, and electronic media in the classroom.

Educational Technology Abstracts. Carfax Publishing Co., P.O. Box 25, Abington, Oxfordshire OX14 3UE, England. 6/yr.; $159 indiv., $318 inst. An international publication of abstracts of recently published material in the field of educational and training technology.

Educational Technology Research and Development. Association for Educational Communications and Technology, 1025 Vermont Ave. NW, Suite 820, Washington, DC 20005-3516. q.; $45 U.S., $53 foreign, $12 single copy. Focuses on research and instructional development in the field of educational technology.

Journal of Instructional Delivery Systems. 50 Culpeper St., Warrenton, VA 22186. q.; $60 indiv., $75 inst., add $15 postage for foreign countries. Devoted to the issues and applications of technology to enhance productivity in education, training, and job performance.

Knowledge: Creation, Diffusion, Utilization. Sage Publications, Inc., 2455 Teller Rd., Newbury Park, CA 91320. q.; $45 indiv., $115 inst., $14 single copy. (In California, $48.26 indiv., $123.33 inst., $15.01 single copy.) An international, interdisciplinary journal examining the nature of expertise and the translation of knowledge into practice and policy.

TECHNOS. Agency for Instructional Technology, Box A, 1111 W. 17th St., Bloomington, IN 47402-0120. q.; $20. A forum for the discussion of ideas about the use of technology in education, with a focus on reform.

TechTrends. Association for Educational Communications and Technology, 1025 Vermont Ave. NW, Suite 820, Washington, DC 20005-3516. 6/yr.; $30 U.S., $35 elsewhere, $4 single copy. Features authoritative, practical articles about technology and its integration into the learning environment.

Books

Benathy, Bela H. (1992). **A systems view of education**. Educational Technology Publications, 700 Palisade Ave., Englewood Cliffs, NJ 07632. 224pp. $32.95 prepaid. A learning resource for those who wish to understand basic systems concepts and principles, to view and characterize education as a system, and to learn the basics of systems practice.

Fawson, E. Curtis, ed. (1992). **Focus on reform: State initiatives in educational technology**. Association for Educational Communications and Technology, 1025 Vermont Ave. NW, Suite 820, Washington, DC 20005. 44pp. $9 AECT members, $13.50 nonmembers. Supporting materials for a 1992 teleconference of the same name broadcast from the AECT National Convention in Washington, D.C.

Johnson, Jenny K. (1992). **Graduate curricula in educational communications and technology: A descriptive directory** (4th ed.). Association for Educational Communications and Technology, 1025 Vermont Ave. NW, Suite 820, Washington, DC 20005. 413pp. $24 AECT members, $36 nonmembers. Lists 192 U.S. and foreign schools, detailing courses, program concentrations, graduation requirements, and faculty research topics.

ERIC Documents

Brennan, Mary Alice. (1992). **Trends in educational technology 1991. ERIC digest**. Syracuse, New York: ERIC Clearinghouse on Information Resources. 4pp. ED 343 617. Derived from *Trends in Educational Technology 1991*, by Donald P. Ely, this digest reports the highlights of a content analysis of the educational technology literature published from October 1990 through September 1991.

Brunner, Cornelia. (1992, July). **Integrating technology into the curriculum: Teaching the teacher. Technical report no. 25**. New York: Center for Technology in Education. ED 350 980. Describes a technology integration curriculum created for teachers and administrators based on collaborative research in public schools.

Carey, Doris, and others, eds. (1992). **Technology and teacher education annual 1992. Proceedings of the Annual Conference on Technology and Teacher Education, Houston, Texas, March 12-15, 1992**. Charlottesville, Virginia: Association for the Advancement of Computing in Education. 668pp. ED 343 581. Contains 147 papers representing the cutting edge in the field of information technology for teacher education.

Ely, Donald P., and others. **Trends in educational technology 1991**. Syracuse, New York: ERIC Clearinghouse on Information Resources. 65pp. ED 346 850. Examines 10 trends identified through a content analysis of representative literature in the field of educational technology for October 1990 through September 1991.

Learning technologies essential for education change. (1992). Papers commissioned for the Council of Chief State School Officers' State Technology Leadership Conference, Dallas, Texas, October 31-November 3, 1992. Washington, DC: Council of Chief State School Officers. ED 349 967. Presents four papers intended to stimulate discussion and action among leading technology specialists at all levels of education, the private sector, and state agencies.

Mahmood, Mo Adam, and Hirt, Shirley A. (1992, May 21). **Evaluating a technology integration causal model for the K-12 public school curriculum: A LISREL analysis**. 36pp. ED 346 847. Reports on an empirical study that determined and defined seven factors involved in the process of integrating computer technology into the K-12 public school curriculum.

Journal Articles

Benathy, Bela H. (1992, June). The prime imperative: Building a design culture. **Educational Technology, 32**(6), 33-35. EJ 447 499. (Available UMI.) Explores the concepts of culture and design to characterize design culture, a pattern of behavior that integrates design thinking, language, principles, and methods.

Bruder, Isabelle. (1992, November-December). Can technology help? **Electronic Learning, 12**(3), 18-19. EJ 453 299. (Available UMI.) Examines the potentials of technology to help the cooperative learning process.

Bruder, Isabelle, and others. (1992, May-June). School reform: Why you need technology to get there. **Electronic Learning, 11**(8), 22-28. EJ 447 583. (Available UMI.) Reviews five goals currently on the national agenda and provides examples of how schools are using technology to address these goals.

Buchsbaum, Herbert. (1992, April). Portrait of a staff development program. **Electronic Learning, 11**(7), 18-23, 26-27. EJ 447 487. (Available UMI.) Describes the Center for Instructional Technology and Training, which was created by the Washington, DC, public schools to provide inservice technology training to teachers, administrators, and other school staff.

Buttolph, Diana. (1992, June). A new look at adaptation. **Knowledge: Creation, Diffusion, Utilization, 13**(4), 460-70. EJ 447 519. (Available UMI.) Examines terms used to describe the changing of an innovation by an adopter, and uses the theory of generative learning to explain internal motivating factors in the change phenomenon.

Campoy, Renee. (1992, August). The role of technology in the school reform movement. **Educational Technology, 32**(8), 17-22. EJ 450 458. (Available UMI.) Considers the role of educational technology in two views of the school reform movement: one that demands more from the existing educational system, and one that calls for restructuring of the existing system.

Harless, Joe. (1992, February). Whither performance technology? **Performance and Instruction, 31**(2), 4-8. EJ 443 282. (Available UMI.) Discusses a model for visualizing performance technology; needs assessment; front-end analysis; the design and development of relevant and cost-effective training/educational interventions; testing; implementation; evaluation; and job aids.

Hawkins, Jan, and Collins, Allan. (1992, September). Design-experiments for infusing technology into learning. **Educational Technology, 32**(9), 63-67. EJ 451 924. (Available UMI.) Discusses the role that technology must play in schools to be effective in changing the nature of students' learning.

Poirot, James L. (1992, August-September). Assessment and evaluation of technology in education—The teacher as researcher. **Computing Teacher, 20**(1), 9-10. EJ 451 823. Discusses appropriate research methodologies for use by elementary and secondary teachers.

Rossett, Allison. (1992, November-December). Performance technology for instructional technologists: Comparisons and possibilities. **Performance and Instruction, 31**(10), 6-10. EJ 457 826. (Available UMI.) Examines similarities between performance technology and instructional technology, including a systems approach, reliance upon analysis, theoretical antecedents, causes of performance problems, and anticipating obstacles to innovation.

Sleezer, Catherine M. (1992). Needs assessment: Perspectives from the literature. **Performance Improvement Quarterly, 5**(2), 34-46. EJ 446 268. The terms *need, needs assessment, needs analysis, front end analysis*, and *performance analysis* are examined, and different views about where the needs assessment process starts and ends are discussed.

Yeaman, Andrew R.J. (1992). Seven myths of computerism. **TechTrends, 37**(2), 22-26. EJ 446 142. (Available UMI.) Discussion of computerism, blind faith in the interent good of computers, focuses on myths about computer anxiety.

ELECTRONIC PUBLISHING

Media-Related Periodicals

Desktop Communications. International Desktop Communications, Ltd., 530 Fifth Ave., 4th Floor, New York, NY 10036. bi-mo.; $24. Helps small businesses, corporate, and individual computer users design and implement innovative and effective newsletters, reports, presentations, and other business communications.

Electronic Publishing: Origination, Dissemination, and Design. John Wiley & Sons, Ltd., Baffins Ln., Chichester, West Sussex PO19 1UD, England. q.; $185. Covers structured editors, authoring tools, hypermedia, document bases, electronic documents over networks, and text integration.

Publish. PC World Communications, Inc., Box 55415, Boulder, CO 80322-5415. mo.; $39.90. A how-to magazine for desktop publishing.

Books

Marcus, Aaron. (1992). **Graphic design for electronic documents and user interfaces**. ACM Press Tutorial Series, Addison-Wesley Publishing, Reading, MA 01867. 266pp. $33.50. Provides practical advice on how to use computer graphics to communicate information effectively.

Misanchuk, Earl R. (1992). **Preparing instructional text**. Educational Technology Publications, 700 Palisade Ave., Englewood Cliffs, NJ 07632. Holds that many text design practices in the publishing industry are ill-founded from a pedagogical point of view. Offers strategies for effective design of instructional materials.

Reynolds, Dennis J., ed. (1992). **Citizen rights and access to electronic information**. American Library Association Publishing Services, Order Department, 50 E. Huron St., Chicago, IL 60611. 199pp. $19.80 ALA members, $22 nonmembers. Collection of essays for the 1991 Library and Information Technology Association President's Program, "A Bill of Rights for an Electronic Society."

Journal Articles

Bailey, Charles W., Jr. (1992, March). Network-based electronic serials. **Information Technology and Libraries, 11**(1), 29-35. EJ 444 777. (Available UMI.) Discusses serials available through noncommercial networks such as BITNET and Internet. Issues affecting libraries and the future of electronic serials are considered.

Kahin, Brian. (1992, October). Scholarly communication in the network environment: Issues of principle, policy and practice. **Electronic Library, 10**(5), 275-86. EJ 454 680. (Available UMI.) Focuses on (1) communication, prepublication, and publication; and (2) the network as a distribution environment. Considers joint authorship, rights in computer conferencing, and derivative works.

Seiler, Lauren H. (1992, January-February). The concept of books in the age of the digital electronic medium. **Library Software Review, 11**(1), 19-29. EJ 443 386. (Available UMI.) Discusses the current and future status of printed books in light of rapidly progressing technology.

INFORMATION SCIENCE AND TECHNOLOGY

Media-Related Periodicals

Datamation. Reed Publishing, 44 Cook St., Denver, CO 80206. 24/yr.; $69 indiv., $47 libraries. Covers semi-technical news and views on hardware, software, and databases, for data and information processing professionals.

Information Processing and Management. Pergamon Press, Inc., 660 White Plains Rd., Tarrytown, NY 10591-5153. £255 ($465 U.S.). An international journal covering data processing, database building, and retrieval.

Information Retrieval and Library Automation. Lomond Publications, Inc., Box 88, Mt. Airy, MD 21771. mo.; $66 U.S., $79.50 foreign. News, articles, and announcements on new techniques, equipment, and software in information services.

Information Services & Use. Elsevier Science Publishers, Box 882, Madison Square Station, New York, NY 10159. bi-mo.; $188. An international journal for those in the information management field. Includes online and offline systems, library automation, micrographics, videotex, and telecommunications.

The Information Society. Taylor and Francis, 1900 Frost Rd., Suite 101, Bristol, PA 19007. q.; $40. Provides a forum for discussion of the world of information, including transborder data flow, regulatory issues, and the impact of the information industry.

Information Technology and Libraries. American Library Association, Library and Information Technology Association, 50 E. Huron St., Chicago, IL 60611-2795. q.; $45 U.S. nonmembers, $50 Canada and Mexico, $55 elsewhere. Articles on library automation, communication technology, cable systems, computerized information processing, and video technologies.

Journal of Documentation. Aslib, Association for Information Management, Publications Department, Information House, 20-24 Old St., London EC1V 9AP, England. q.; £60 members, £90 nonmembers. Describes how technical, scientific, and other specialized knowledge is recorded, organized, and disseminated.

Journal of the American Society for Information Science. Subscription Department, 605 3d Ave., New York, NY 10158-0012. bi-mo.; $375 U.S. nonmembers, $500 foreign. Publishes research articles in the area of information science.

Books

Glazier, Jack D., and Powell, Ronald J. (1992). **Qualitative research in information management**. Libraries Unlimited, P.O. Box 3988, Englewood, CO 80155. 238pp. $35. Fourteen essays cover various aspects of qualitative research methods and illustrate the value of such research to the library community.

Miller, R. Bruch, and Wolf, Milton T., eds. (1992). **Thinking robots, an aware Internet, and cyberpunk librarians**. American Library Association Publishing Services, Order Department, 50 E. Huron St., Chicago, IL 60611. 200pp. $19.80 ALA members, $22 nonmembers. Background essays collected for the 1992 Library and Information Technology Association President's Program, "Tools for Knowing, Environments for Growing: Visions of the Potential of Information Technology for Human Development."

Williams, Martha E. (1992). **Annual review of information science and technology, volume 27—1992 (ARIST)**. Learned Information, Inc., 143 Old Marlton Pike, Medford, NJ 08055. $71.20 members of American Society for Information Science, $89 nonmembers. A literary source of ideas, trends, and references that offers a comprehensive view of information science technology. Eight chapters cover planning information systems and services, basic techniques and technologies, applications, and the profession.

ERIC Documents

Brock, Dr. Jack L. (1992, February). **Information dissemination: Innovative ways agencies are using technology. Testimony before the Government Information, Justice, and Agriculture Subcommittee, Committee on Government Operations, House of Representatives**. Washington, DC: General Accounting Office, Information Management and Technology Division. 15pp. ED 346 837. Discusses ways in which some federal agencies use technology to provide the public with cheaper, faster access to a wider range of information, which can be searched and manipulated in ways never possible on the printed page.

Journal Articles

Chen, Ching-chih. (1992). Digital vs. analog video on microcomputers: Implications for information management. **Microcomputers for Information Management, 9**(1), 3-16. EJ 450 358. Discusses converting analog video to digital data; digital image compression technology; digital compression and digital video on Macintosh computers; and potential library and information-related applications.

Conference reports: EDUCOM '91: "Curricula, computing, and culture." (1992, January-February). **Library Hi Tech News, 88-89**, 1-16, 29. EJ 443 402. (Available UMI.) Overview of the 1991 EDUCOM meeting. Reviews and summarizes the general sessions; panel discussions on integrated library systems and computer networks; and sessions on information management, intellectual property, and other topics.

Frohmann, Bernd. (1992, December). The power of images: A discourse analysis of the cognitive viewpoint. **Journal of Documentation, 48**(4), 365-86. EJ 457 828. Identifies seven discursive strategies that constitute information as a commodity and persons as surveyable information consumers within a market economy.

Harman, Donna, and Lunin, Lois F. (1992, March). Perspectives on human-computer interface: Introduction and overview. **Journal of the American Society for Information Science, 43**(2), 153-55. EJ 443 291. (Available UMI.) Summarizes articles that provide librarians guidelines for selecting information-seeking systems; provide producers with directions for production or research; and show end users information-seeking techniques.

Laribee, J. (1992, March). Undergraduate and graduate courses in information resources management: Educational and managerial judgement about appropriate course content. **Education for Information, 10**(1), 17-33. EJ 447 536. Reports on a survey of 147 information science educators and managers.

Rezmierski, Virginia E. (1992, July-August). Ethical dilemmas in information technology use: Opportunity bumps on the road to civilization. **EDUCOM Review, 27**(4), 22-26. EJ 448 984. (Available UMI.) Discussion of how information technology affects higher education. Focuses on ethical dilemmas and creating appropriate policies and guidelines.

Tufte, Edward. (1992, June-July). The user interface: The point of competition. **Bulletin of the American Society for Information Science, 18**(5), 15-17. EJ 448 910. (Available UMI.) Provides guidelines for screen design in the areas of information resolution, interaction of design elements, color, and typography and icons.

VanWeert, Tom J. (1992, June). Informatics and the organization of education. **Education and Computing, 8**(1-2), 15-24. EJ 448 862. Defines *informatics* as both a pure and an applied science dealing with information technology and its uses, and examines the organization of education from two perspectives.

Woolliams, Peter, and Gee, David. (1992, October). Accounting for user diversity in configuring online systems. **Online Review, 16**(5), 303-11. EJ 456 120. (Available UMI.) Discusses cultural diversity in human-computer interactions and in the design of online systems.

INSTRUCTIONAL DESIGN AND TRAINING

Media-Related Periodicals

AVC Presentation Development & Delivery. PTN Publishing Co., 445 Broad Hollow Rd., Suite 21, Melville, NY 11747-4722. mo.; $25, $6 single copy. Industry news and applications for those who manage audiovisual, video, or computer presentation.

Data Training: The Monthly Newspaper for Information Trainers. Weingarten Publications, Inc., 38 Chauncy St., Boston, MA 02111. bi-mo.; $18 U.S., $30 Canada and Mexico, $45 elsewhere (free to qualified readers). Features training in information processing, office automation, and information maintenance.

Instructional Developments. School of Education, Syracuse University, 364 Huntington Hall, Syracuse, NY 13244-2340. 3/yr.; free. Features articles, research reviews, innovations, and job aids.

Instructional Science. Kluwer Academic Publishers, 101 Philip Dr., Norwell, MA 02061. bi-mo.; $50 indiv., $217 inst. Aimed to promote a deeper understanding of the nature, theory, and practice of the instructional process and the learning resulting from this process.

Journal of Educational Multimedia and Hypermedia. Association for the Advancement of Computing in Education, Box 2966, Charlottesville, VA 22902. q.; $55 indiv., $78 inst., Canada and Mexico add $10, other countries add $15. A multidisciplinary information source presenting research and applications on multimedia and hypermedia tools that allow the integration of images, sounds, text, and data in learning and teaching.

Journal of Educational Technology Systems. Baywood Publishing Co., 26 Austin Ave., Box 337, Amityville, NY 11701. q.; $102 plus $4.50 postage U.S. and Canada, $9.35 postage elsewhere. In-depth articles on completed and ongoing research in all phases of educational technology and its application and future within the teaching profession.

Journal of Interactive Instruction Development. Communicative Technology Corp., Society for Applied Learning Technology, 50 Culpeper St., Warrenton, VA 22186. q.; $30 members, $50 nonmembers. A showcase of successful programs to give awareness of innovative, creative, and effective approaches to courseware development for interactive technology.

Journal of Technical Writing and Communication. Baywood Publishing Co., 26 Austin Ave., Box 337, Amityville, NY 11701. q.; $36 indiv., $96 inst. Essays on oral and written communication, for purposes from pure research to needs of business and industry.

Journal of Visual Literacy. International Visual Literacy Association, 122 Ramseyer Hall, 29 W. Woodruff Ave., Ohio State University, Columbus, OH 43210. semi-ann.; $10 members, $25 nonmembers, $27.50 foreign. Interdisciplinary forum on all aspects of visual/verbal languaging.

Machine-Mediated Learning. Taylor and Francis, 1900 Frost Rd., Suite 101, Bristol, PA 19007. q.; $50 indiv., $98 inst. Focuses on the scientific, technological, and management aspects of the application of machines to instruction and training. Analyzes computer, telecommunication, videodisc, and other technological developments.

Multimedia Review. Meckler Publishing Corp., 11 Ferry Lane W., Westport, CT 06880. 4/yr.; $97. Dedicated to analysis of trends, paradigms, and strategies affecting the creation and production, design and development, and implementation and use of multimedia programs and configuration.

Performance and Instruction. National Society for Performance and Instruction, 1300 L St. NW, Suite 1250, Washington, DC 20005. 10/yr.; $50. Journal of NSPI, intended to promote the advantage of performance science and technology. Contains articles, research, and case studies relating to improving human performance.

Performance Improvement Quarterly. National Society for Performance and Instruction, 1300 L St. NW, Suite 1250, Washington, DC 20005. q.; $20 nonmembers. Represents the cutting edge in research and theory in performance technology.

Training. Lakewood Publications, Inc., 50 S. Ninth, Minneapolis, MN 55402. mo.; $54. News, how-to features, case studies, and opinions on managing training and human resources development activities.

Books

Gagné, Robert M., Briggs, Leslie J., and Wager, Walter W. (1992). **Principles of instructional design** (4th ed.). Harcourt Brace Jovanovich College Publishers, 7555 Caldwell Ave., Chicago, IL 60648. 384pp. (Price not available.) Describes a rationally consistent basis for instructional design that will prepare teachers to design and develop a course, unit, and module of instruction.

Greer, Michael. (1992). **ID project management**. Educational Technology Publications, 700 Palisade Ave., Englewood Cliffs, NJ 07632. 245pp. $34.95 prepaid. Provides a conceptual framework and presents 37 tools for finding answers to specific questions encountered in the project management process.

Leshin, Cynthia B., Pollock, Joellyn, and Reigeluth, Charles M. (1992). **Instructional design strategies and tactics**. Educational Technology Publications, 700 Palisade Ave., Englewood Cliffs, NJ 07632. 360pp. $34.95 prepaid. Addresses shortcomings of existing instructional systems development models and updates the ISD process to incorporate recent advances in the field.

Levell-Troy, Larry, and Eickmann, Paul. (1992). **Course design for college teachers**. Educational Technology Publications, 700 Palisade Ave., Englewood Cliffs, NJ 07632. 179pp. $21.95. Presents a process for designing college courses. Covers ways to expand content and learning resources and to design active-learning teaching strategies.

Lyons, Paul. (1992). **Thirty-five lesson formats: A sourcebook of instructional alternatives**. Educational Technology Publications, 700 Palisade Ave., Englewood Cliffs, NJ 07632. 160pp. $24.95. Prepared by instructors for instructors, this book presents lesson formats that may be employed across many disciplines and content areas for students in high school, college and university, and adult education settings.

McBeath, Ron J., ed. (1992). **Instructing and evaluating in higher education: A guidebook for planning learning outcomes**. Educational Technology Publications, 700 Palisade Ave., Englewood Cliffs, NJ 07632. 365pp. $34.95. Contents include preparing lectures, improving instructor-student relationships, constructing multiple choice and essay tests, and evaluating student performance.

Merrill, M. David, Tennyson, Robert D., and Posey, Larry O. (1992). **Teaching concepts: An instructional design guide**. Educational Technology Publications, 700 Palisade Ave., Englewood Cliffs, NJ 07632. 232pp. $34.95 prepaid. Covers procedures in concept lesson design, including analyzing subject matter content, designing learner guidance and instructional strategy, and presenting a concept lesson.

ERIC Documents

Reynolds, Lynne, and Erlich, Diane. (1992, June). **Multimedia in industry and education: A decision model for design**. Paper presented at European Conference on Educational Research, Enschede, The Netherlands, June 22-25, 1992. 5pp. ED 351 003. Presents a decision-making model that uses a systematic approach to design, is derived from traditional instructional system design models, and addresses the potential impact of multimedia as a delivery system.

Journal Articles

Campbell-Bonan, Katy, and Olson, Alton T. (1992, Summer). Collaborative instructional design as culture-building. **Canadian Journal of Educational Communication, 21**(2), 141-52. EJ 453 210. Examines paradigms in instructional design and the collaborative design process. A model of instructional design as art is proposed as an alternative to the generic characteristics of a systems approach.

Curtis, Ruth V. (1992, April). Taking AIM: Approaches to instructional motivation. **School Library Media Activities Monthly, 8**(8), 32-34. EJ 444 692. Presents an introduction to the ARCS Model of Motivational Design, which identifies four motivational factors required for increasing the appeal of instructional presentation.

Earle, Rodney S. (1992, April). Homework as an instructional event. **Educational Technology, 32**(4), 36-41. EJ 444 830. (Available UMI.) Instructional design theory is described and used as a theoretical base to suggest that homework can be a valid component of the learning process.

Earle, Rodney S. (1992, December). Talk about teaching: Fingers in the dike or bridge to reform? **Educational Technology, 32**(12), 32-35. EJ 456 189. (Available UMI.) Discusses instructional design and educational reform in public schools and describes teachers' use of instructional design in the planning process.

Macchia, Peter, Jr. (1992, July). Total quality education and instructional systems development. **Educational Technology, 32**(7), 17-21. EJ 448 993. (Available UMI.) Explains Total Quality Management and examines its relationship to instructional systems development as it is used for curriculum development.

McAlpine, Lynn. (1992, November-December). Highlighting formative evaluation: An instructional design model derived from practice. **Performance and Instruction, 31**(10), 16-18. EJ 457 827. (Available UMI.) Presents a model for instructional design that highlights formative evaluation as the central process.

Song, Xueshu. (1992). Computer-aided decision-making in choosing innovative education programs. **International Journal of Instructional Media, 19**(3), 235-42. EJ 457 836. (Available UMI.) Describes the development of a computer-aided decision-making system to assist educational practitioners in curriculum decision making about innovative program features and implementation requirements.

Yarusso, Lowell. (1992, April). Constructivism vs. objectivism. **Performance and Instruction, 31**(4), 7-9. EJ 447 488. (Available UMI.) Discusses constructivism and objectivism, how they lead to different understandings of human cognition, and how they affect both instructional design and outcome evaluations.

Yelon, Stephen, and Reznich, Christopher. (1992, July). Visible models of course organization. **Performance and Instruction, 31**(6), 7-11. EJ 448 902. (Available UMI.) Discussion of visible models covers uses for course designers, including clarifying course structure, planning lessons, communicating course requirements, and presenting a course overview.

LIBRARIES AND MEDIA CENTERS

Media-Related Periodicals

Collection Building. Neal-Schuman, 23 Leonard St., New York, NY 10013. q.; $55. Focuses on all aspects of collection building, ranging from microcomputers to business collections to popular topics and censorship.

Computers in Libraries. Meckler Publishing, 11 Ferry Ln. W., Westport, CT 06880-5808. 10/yr.; $72.50. Covers practical applications of microcomputers to library situations and recent news items.

Electronic Library. Learned Information, Inc., 143 Old Marlton Pike, Medford, NJ 08055. 6/yr.; $95. For librarians and information center managers interested in microcomputer and library automation. Features industry news and product announcements.

Emergency Librarian. Dyad Services, P.O. Box 46258, Station G, Vancouver, BC V6R 4G6. bi-mo. (except July-August); $45, $40 prepaid. Articles, review columns, and critical analyses of management and programming issues for children's and young adult librarians.

Government Publications Review. Pergamon Press, Inc., Journals Division, 660 White Plains Rd., Tarrytown, NY 10591-5153. 6/yr.; £180 ($342 U.S.). An international journal covering production, distribution, bibliographic control, accessibility, and use of government information in all formats and at all levels.

Journal of Academic Librarianship. Business Office, P.O. Box 8330, Ann Arbor, MI 48107. bi-mo.; $29 indiv., $52 inst. Results of significant research, issues and problems facing academic libraries, book reviews, and innovations in academic libraries.

Journal of Librarianship and Information Science. Bailey Bros. and Swinfen, Ltd., Warner House, Bowles Well Gardens, Folkestone, Kent CT19 6PH, England. q.; $115. Deals with all aspects of library and information work in the United Kingdom and reviews literature from international sources.

Library and Information Science Abstracts. Library Association Publishing, Bailey Bros. and Swinfen Ltd, Warner House, Bowles Well Gardens, Folkestone, Kent CT19 6PH, England. mo.; $498. Over 500 abstracts per issue from over 500 periodicals, reports, books, and conference proceedings.

Library and Information Science Research. Ablex Publishing Corp., 355 Chestnut St., Norwood, NJ 07648. q.; $39.50 indiv., $85 inst. Research articles, dissertation reviews, and book reviews on issues concerning information resources management.

Library Computer Systems & Equipment Review. Meckler Publishing, 11 Ferry Ln. W., Westport, CT 06880-5808. semi-ann.; $225. Features articles on automated systems for library and applications. Each issue focuses on one topic.

Library Hi Tech. Pierian Press, Box 1808, Ann Arbor, MI 48106. q.; $50. Concentrates on reporting on the selection, installation, maintenance, and integration of systems and hardware.

Library Hi Tech News. Pierian Press, Box 1808, Ann Arbor, MI 48106. 10/yr.; $70 indiv., $95 inst. News and ideas about technology related to library operations.

Library Journal. Box 1977, Marion, OH 43306-2077. 21/yr.; $74. A professional periodical for librarians, with current issues and news, professional reading, lengthy book review section, and classifieds.

Library Quarterly. University of Chicago Press, Box 37005, Chicago, IL 60637. q.; $23 indiv., $35 inst., $18 students. Scholarly articles of interest to librarians.

Library Software Review. Meckler Publishing Corp., 11 Ferry Ln. W., Westport, CT 06880. bi-mo.; $115 U.S., foreign add $10. Articles on software evaluation, procurement, applications, and installation decisions.

Library Trends. University of Illinois Press, Journals Department, 54 E. Gregory, Champaign, IL 61820. q.; $60, $18.50 single copy. Each issue is concerned with one aspect of library and information science, analyzing current thought and practice and examining ideas that hold the greatest potential for the field.

Microcomputers for Information Management. Ablex Publishing, 355 Chestnut St., Norwood, NJ 07648. q.; $34.50 indiv., $90 inst. Focuses on new developments with microcomputer technology in libraries and in information science in the United States and abroad.

The Public-Access Computer Systems Review. An electronic journal sent free of charge to participants of the Public-Access Computer Systems Forum (PACS-L), a computer conference on BITNET. Published on an irregular basis by the University Libraries, University of Houston. (To join -L, send an e-mail message to LISTSERV@UHUPVM1 (BITNET) or LISTSERV@UHUPVM1.UH.EDU (Internet) that says SUBSCRIBE PACS-L First Name Last Name.) Annual cumulated volume available in print from Order Department, American Library Association, 50 E. Huron St., Chicago, IL 60611. $20; $17 to members of the Library and Information Technology Association. Contains articles about all types of computer systems that libraries make available to their patrons and technologies to implement these systems.

Public Libraries. Public Library Association, American Library Association, 50 E. Huron St., Chicago, IL 60611. q.; $45 U.S. nonmembers, $55 elsewhere, $10 single copy. News and articles of interest to public librarians.

Public Library Quarterly. Haworth Press, 10 Alice St., Binghamton, NY 13904. q.; $36 indiv., $85 inst. Addresses the major administrative challenges and opportunities that face the nation's public libraries.

RQ. Reference and Adult Services Division, American Library Association, 50 E. Huron St., Chicago, IL 60611-2795. q.; nonmembers $42 U.S., $52 elsewhere, $12 single copy. Covers all aspects of library service to adults, and reference service and collection development at every level and for all types of libraries.

School Library Journal. Box 1978, Marion, OH 43305-1978. mo.; $63 U.S., $80 Canada, $104 elsewhere. For school and youth service librarians. Contains about 2,500 critical book reviews annually.

School Library Media Activities Monthly. LMS Associates, 17 E. Henrietta St., Baltimore, MD 21230. 10/yr.; $44 U.S., $54 elsewhere. A vehicle for distributing ideas for teaching library media skills and for the development and implementation of library media skills programs.

School Library Media Quarterly. American Association of School Librarians, American Library Association, 50 E. Huron St., Chicago, IL 60611. q.; $40 U.S. nonmembers, $50 elsewhere, $12 single copy. For library media specialists, district supervisors, and others concerned with the selection and purchase of print and nonprint media and with the development of programs and services for preschool through high school libraries.

The Unabashed Librarian. Box 2631, New York, NY 10116. q.; $30 U.S., $36 elsewhere. Down-to-earth library items: procedures, forms, programs, cataloging, booklists, software reviews.

Wilson Library Bulletin. H. W. Wilson Co., 950 University Ave., Bronx, NY 10452. 10/yr.; $50 U.S., $56 elsewhere. Significant articles on librarianship, news, and reviews of films, books, and professional literature.

Books

Dobrot, Nancy L., and McCawley, Rosemary. (1992). **Beyond flexible scheduling: A workshop guide**. Libraries Unlimited, P.O. Box 3988, Englewood, CO 80155. 75pp. $20. Step-by-step instructions for introducing flexible access to educators and school administrators. Covers concepts of flexible scheduling and planning issues.

Dukelow, Ruth. (1992). **Library copyright guide**. Association for Educational Communications and Technology, 1025 Vermont Ave. NW, Suite 820, Washington, DC 20005. 152pp. $29.95 AECT members, $39.95 nonmembers. Answers questions about the permissible levels of duplication of copyrighted materials for library patrons, interlibrary loan, and internal use. Covers fair use, performance rights for video, storytelling, recitals, and more.

Farley, Laine, ed. (1992). **Library resources on the Internet: Strategies for selection and use. RASD occasional paper No. 12**. American Library Association Publications, 50 E. Huron St., Chicago, IL 60611. $18 members, $20 others. (Available on the Internet, through anonymous FTP, from host dla.ucop.edu, directory pub/internet, filename libcat-guide.) Instructions for remote access to library catalogs through the Telnet protocol.

Foos, Donald D., and Pack, Nancy C., eds. (1992). **How libraries must comply with the Americans with Disabilities Act (ADA)**. Oryx Press, 4041 N. Central at Indian School Rd., Phoenix, AZ 85012-3397. 192pp. $29.95 prepaid. Includes procedures for seeking and evaluating community or client information and advice, listings of resource organizations and advocacy groups, and sections of the new law that apply directly to library operations.

Latrobe, Kathy Howard, and Laughlin, Mildred Knight, comps. (1992). **Multicultural aspects of library media programs**. Libraries Unlimited, P.O. Box 3988, Englewood, CO 80155. 250pp. $23.50. A collection of essays offering diverse, unique, and sometimes controversial perspectives on multicultural issues in the media program.

Shuman, Bruce A. (1992). **Foundations and issues in library and information science**. Libraries Unlimited, P.O. Box 3988, Englewood, CO 80155. 175pp. $28.50. A general introduction to the field of library science, covering the place of libraries and information in society, different types of libraries, and legal and ethical issues.

Smith, Jane Bandy, and Coleman, Gordon, Jr., eds. (1992). **School library media annual 1992**. Libraries Unlimited, P.O. Box 3988, Englewood, CO 80155. 290pp. $37.50. Part I of this tenth volume in the series contains articles by leading librarians and academicians. Part II is the year in review, including organizational activities, an almanac of information, and publications of note.

Strangelove, Michael, and Kovacs, Diane. (1992). **Directory of electronic journals, newsletters and academic discussion lists**. (2d ed.). Association of Research Libraries, Office of Scientific and Academic Publishing, 1527 New Hampshire Ave. NW, Washington, DC 20036. $25. (Available electronically, through the Internet, by sending e-mail to LISTSERV@KENTVM.BITNET. In the body of the message, type GET ACADLIST FILE1; GET ACADLIST FILE2; GET ACADLIST FILE3; GET ACADLIST FILE4; GET ACADLIST FILE5; GET ACADLIST FILE6.) A descriptive guide to over 900 resources available through BITNET or the Internet, with instructions for access.

ERIC Documents

Anderson, James A., and Cichocki, Ronald R. (1992, February 5). **Media equipped classrooms: Giving attention to the teaching station**. Paper presented at the Annual Conference of the Association for Educational Communications and Technology, Washington, DC, February 5-8, 1992. 56pp. ED 346 841. Provides an overview of the Media Equipped Classroom, a centrally scheduled or departmentally scheduled teaching space with permanently installed media and classroom support technology designed to enhance the quality of teaching.

Doyle, Christina S. (1992, June). **Summary of findings: Outcome measures for information literacy within the National Education Goals of 1990. Final report to the National Forum on Information Literacy**. ED 351 033. Summarizes a study conducted to create a comprehensive definition of information literacy and to develop outcome measures.

Humes, Barbara, and Lyons, Carol Cameron. (1992, March). **Library literacy program. Description of funded projects, 1990. Title VI, Library Services and Construction Act**. Washington, DC: Office of Educational Research and Improvement, Office of Library Programs. 50pp. ED 344 614. Provides a description of each of the 237 adult literacy projects funded in 1990 by Title VI of the Library Services and Construction Act.

Perkinson, Kathryn. (1992). **Como ayudar a sus hijos a usar la biblioteca (Helping your child use the library)**. Washington, DC: Office of Educational Research and Improvement. 34pp. ED 341 387. Focuses on the cooperative role of parents and public libraries in stimulating reading interests in children of all ages.

Stripling, Barbara K. (1992). **Libraries for the National Education Goals**. Syracuse, New York: ERIC Clearinghouse on Information Resources. 125pp. ED 345 752. (Also available from Information Resources Publications, 4-194 Center for Science and Technology, Syracuse University, Syracuse, NY 13244-4100; $10 plus $2 shipping and handling.) Reviews and summarizes information about the role of libraries in many different educational efforts designed to meet the National Education Goals.

Thrash, Blanche Carter. (1992). **Whole language and the media center**. Requirements for the Degree of Educational Specialist, Georgia State University. 43pp. ED 346 828. Describes a study to investigate the services provided by elementary and middle school media centers to support whole language instruction, and to determine how the media program contributes to the goals, resources, and teaching strategies of the whole language movement.

Journal Articles

Barron, Daniel D. (1992, February). School-based management and school library media specialists. **School Library Media Activities Monthly, 8**(6), 47-50. Discusses the impact of school-based management on standards of accreditation and performance-based guidelines and the role of teachers and administrators.

Bell, Michael, and Totten, Herman L. (1992, Winter). Cooperation in instruction between classroom teachers and school library media specialists. A look at teacher characteristics in Texas elementary schools. **School Library Media Quarterly, 20**(2), 79-85. EJ 441 729. (Available UMI.) Describes a study of the relationships between the number of times teachers voluntarily chose the library media specialist to cooperate with them on instructional problems and other teacher-related factors.

Eisenberg, Michael B., and Berkowitz, Robert E. (1992, January). Information problem solving: The Bix Six Skills approach. **School Library Media Activities Monthly, 8**(5), 27-29, 37, 42. EJ 438 023. Explains the components of a library and information skills curriculum and integrated instructional model that was developed to help students solve information problems.

Eisenberg, Michael B., and Brown, Michael K. (1992, Winter). Current themes regarding library and information skills instruction: Research supporting and research lacking. **School Library Media Quarterly, 20**(2), 103-10. EJ 441 731. (Available UMI.) Discusses the value of library and information skills instruction, the content of library and information skills, teaching library skills in the context of subject area curriculum, and alternative methods for teaching library media skills.

Everhart, Nancy. (1992, Winter). An analysis of the work activities of high school library media specialists in automated and nonautomated library media centers. **School Library Media Quarterly, 20**(2), 86-99. EJ 441 730. (Available UMI.) Describes results of a research study that used work sampling techniques to compare time spent by high school library media specialists using automated and nonautomated circulation systems.

Geraci, Diane, and Langschied, Linda. (1992, March). Mainstreaming data: Challenges to libraries. **Information Technology and Libraries, 11**(1), 10-18. EJ 444 775. (Available UMI.) Discusses the role of libraries in providing access to social, scientific, and humanities data in electronic form.

Johnson, Glenn. (1992, February). A process to help develop your "picture." **School Library Media Activities Monthly, 8**(6), 33-34. EJ 439 870. Discussion of the integration of information skills from a junior high school library media program into the curriculum focuses on the use of the Big Six Skills, a model for solving information problems.

Knirk, Frederick G. (1992, Summer). New technology considerations for media facilities: Video technologies and space requirements. **School Library Media Quarterly, 20**(4), 205-10. EJ 448 974. (Available UMI.) Presents guidelines for design of space for audiovisual media, including projection, distribution systems, viewing, and storage.

OCLC's linking strategy: Internet and NREN. (1992, December). **Electronic Library, 10**(6), 371-73. EJ 456 205. (Available UMI.) Describes the telecommunications environment for libraries and considers network links in terms of including governance, performance/support, economics, and future development.

Sapp, Gregg. (1992, January). Science literacy: A discussion and an information-based definition. **College and Research Libraries, 53**(1), 21-30. EJ 438 096. (Available UMI.) Discusses the role of the librarian in promoting science literacy.

Saunders, Laverna M. (1992, Spring). The virtual library today. **Library Administration and Management, 6**(2), 66-70. EJ 444 781. (Available UMI.) Discusses the concept of a virtual library, the work of the Coalition for Networked Information, and the National Research and Education Network.

Saunders, Laverna M. (1992, November). The virtual library revisited. **Computers in Libraries, 12**(10), 51-54. EJ 456 154. (Available UMI.) Discussion from the user perspective focuses on remote searching of library catalogs and databases and the availability of information through the Internet and other networks.

Smith, Eldred. (1992, February 1). The print prison. **Library Journal, 117**(2), 48-51. EJ 441 734. (Available UMI.) Discusses electronic information technology and possible effects on research libraries' transition from print-based collections to new configurations.

St. Clair, Gloriana. (1992, May). Intellectual property. **College and Research Libraries, 53**(3), 193-95. EJ 446 189. (Available UMI.) Discusses issues of copyright and the transfer or use of intellectual property as they relate to librarians. Covers cultural views of pirating, the fair use doctrine, and the impact of increasing library automation and networking.

Velho Lopes, Roseanne R. (1992, January). Reference services in developing countries. **Information Development, 8**(1), 35-40. EJ 444 766. Discusses meeting users' needs, criteria for the planning and organization of services, and technology.

Walling, Linda Lucas. (1992, Summer). Granting each equal access. **School Library Media Quarterly, 20**(4), 216-22. EJ 448 976. (Available UMI.) Summarizes federal legislation regarding equal access for students with disabilities and discusses environmental barriers to accessibility in the library media center.

MEDIA TECHNOLOGIES

Media-Related Periodicals

Broadcasting. Broadcasting Publications, 1705 DeSales St. NW, Washington, DC 20036. w.; $85 U.S., $125 elsewhere. All-inclusive news weekly for radio, television, cable, and allied business.

CableVision. Cable Publishing Group, 600 S. Cherry St., Suite 400, Denver, CO 80222. 26/yr.; $55. A news magazine for the cable television industry. Covers programming, marketing, advertising, business, and other topics.

Communication Abstracts. Sage Publications, Inc., 2455 Teller Rd., Newbury Park, CA 91320. bi-mo.; $105 indiv., $315 inst. Abstracts communication-related articles, reports, and books. Cumulated annually.

Communication Booknotes. Center for Advanced Study in Telecommunications (CAST), Graduate Telecommunications Program, George Washington University, 2020 K St. NW, Suite 240, Washington, DC 20006. bi-mo.; $45 indiv., $95 inst. Newsletter that reviews books and periodicals about mass media, telecommunications, and information policy.

Communications News. Nelson Publishing, 2504 N. Tamiami Trail, Nokomis, FL 34275. mo.; $27 (free to qualified personnel). Up-to-date information from around the world regarding voice, video, and data communications.

Document Image Automation (previously **Optical Information Systems Magazine**). Meckler Publishing, 11 Ferry Ln. W., Westport, CT 06880-5808. bi-mo.; $125. Features articles on the applications of videodisc, optical disc, and teletext systems; future implications; system and software compatibilities; and cost comparisons. Also tracks videodisc projects and covers world news.

Document Image Automation Update (previously **Optical Information Systems Update**). Meckler Publishing, 11 Ferry Ln. W., Westport, CT 06880-5808. 12/yr.; $297. News and facts about technology, software, courseware developments, calendar, conference reports, and job listings.

Educational Media International. Kogan Page, Ltd., Distribution Centre, Blackhorse Rd., Letchworth, Herts SG6 1HN, England. q.; £35 ($63 U.S.), plus £8 ($17 U.S.) airmail. The official journal of the International Council for Educational Media.

Federal Communications Commission Reports. Superintendent of Documents, Government Printing Office, Washington, DC 20402. w.; price varies. Decisions, public notices, and other documents pertaining to FCC activities.

Historical Journal of Film, Radio, and Television. Carfax Publishing Co., Box 2025, Dunnellon, FL 32630. 3/yr.; $113 indiv., $282 inst. Articles by international experts in the field, news and notices, and book reviews.

International Journal of Instructional Media. Westwood Press, Inc., 23 E. 22d St., New York, NY 10010. q.; $105 plus $5 postage U.S., $10 postage elsewhere. Articles discuss specific applications and techniques for bringing the advantages of a particular instructional medium to bear on a complete curriculum system or program.

Journal of Broadcasting and Electronic Media. Broadcast Education Association, 1771 N St. NW, Washington, DC 20036. q.; $40 U.S., $50 elsewhere, $25 students. Includes articles, book reviews, research reports, and analyses. Provides a forum for research relating to telecommunications and related fields.

Journal of Educational Television. Carfax Publishing Co., Box 2025, Dunnellon, FL 32630. 3/yr.; $112 indiv., $280 inst. This journal of the Educational Television Association serves as an international forum for discussions and reports on developments in the field of television and related media in teaching, learning, and training.

Journal of Popular Film and Television. Heldref Publications, 1319 18th St. NW, Washington, DC 20036-1802. q.; $27 indiv., $53 inst. Articles on film and television, book reviews, and theory.

Media International. Reed Publishing Services, 151 Wardour St., London W1V 4BN, England. mo.; $95. Contains features on the world's major media developments and regional news reports from the international media scene.

Multimedia and Videodisc Monitor (previously **Videodisc Monitor**). Future Systems, Inc., Box 26, Falls Church, VA 22040. mo.; $347 indiv., $150 educational inst. Describes current events in the videodisc marketplace and in training and development.

Telematics and Informatics. Pergamon Press, Inc., Journals Division, 660 White Plains Rd., Tarrytown, NY 10591-5153. q.; (price unavailable). Intended for the specialist in telecommunications and information science. Covers the merging of computer and telecommunications technologies worldwide.

Video Systems. Intertec Publishing Corp., 9221 Quivera Rd., Box 12901, Overland Park, KS 66212-9981. mo.; $45, free to qualified professionals. For video professionals. Contains state-of-the-art audio and video technology reports.

Videography. United Newspapers Publications, Inc., 2 Park Ave., 18th Floor, New York, NY 10016. mo.; $30. For the video professional; covers techniques, applications, equipment, technology, and video art.

Books

Gayeski, Diane M., ed. (1992). **Multimedia for learning**. Educational Technology Publications, 700 Palisade Ave., Englewood Cliffs, NJ 07632. Contents include skills required for effective multimedia, factors to consider in evaluating multimedia for widespread curricular adoption, the future of multimedia, and more.

Imke, Steven. (1992). **Interactive video management and production**. Educational Technology Publications, 700 Palisade Ave., Englewood Cliffs, NJ 07632. $19.95. Provides guidelines for decision makers on how production choices can affect the quality and cost of an interactive video presentation for training and personnel development.

ERIC Documents

Borsook, Terry K., and Higginbotham-Wheat, Nancy. (1992). **A psychology of hypermedia: A conceptual framework for R&D**. Paper presented at the Annual Meeting of the Association for Educational Communications and Technology, Washington, DC, February 5-8, 1992. 21pp. ED 345 697. Explores the insights that psychology can offer in understanding why hypermedia may work and in suggesting areas for future research.

Cates, Ward Mitchell. (1992, April). **Considerations in evaluating metacognition in interactive hypermedia/multimedia instruction**. Paper presented at the Annual Conference of the American Educational Research Association, San Francisco, CA, April 20-24, 1992. ED 349 966. Addresses ways in which interactive hypermedia/multimedia instructional programs might enhance the metacognitive abilities of the learners who use them.

Pina, Anthony A., and Savenye, Wilhelmina C. (1992, February). **Beyond computer literacy: How can teacher educators help teachers use interactive multimedia?** Paper presented at the Annual Conference of the Association for Educational Communications and Technology, Washington, DC, February 5-9, 1992. 12pp. ED 343 567. Provides a definition of interactive multimedia and explains why it is of interest to teachers and trainers, how it is produced and utilized, and how the role of teachers may be changed.

Turner, Sandra. (1992). Hypermedia, multimedia: What's going on in today's classrooms? In **National College of Education Quarterly**, Summer 1992. Evanston, Illinois: National Louis University. ED 350 990. Defines *hypermedia* and *multimedia* and discusses three different ways in which schools are using multimedia.

Yildiz, Rauf, and Atkins, Madeleine J. (1992, June). **How to evaluate multimedia simulations: Learning from the past**. Paper presented at the European Conference on Educational Research, Enschede, The Netherlands, June 22-25, 1992. ED 350 978. Identifies and discusses the main criticisms of media research, assesses the state of current interactive video simulation research, and identifies the most important points to be considered in future research.

Journal Articles

Berkman, Dave. (1992, December). The promise of early radio and television for education— As seen by the nation's periodical press. **Educational Technology, 32**(12), 26-31. EJ 456 188. (Available UMI.) A historical review of periodical literature published between 1919 and 1924 relating to the educational use of radio, and literature published between 1937 and 1974 relating to the educational use of television.

Caravello-Hibbert, Stephanie M. (1992, May). Teaching non-science majors: Science through interactive multi-media. **Collegiate Microcomputer, 10**(2), 97-102. EJ 447 582. (Available UMI.) Describes a linear, self-paced approach that uses interactive video to teach introductory science courses.

Elwell, Catherine Callow, and others. (1992, August). Captioning instructional video. **Educational Technology, 32**(8), 45-50. EJ 450 463. (Available UMI.) Addresses closed versus open captioning, captioning of prerecorded programs, external captioning sources, local captioning methods, and other topics.

Hofmeister, Alan M., and others. (1992, July). Learner diversity and instructional video: Implications for developers. **Educational Technology, 32**(7), 13-16. EJ 448 992. (Available UMI.) Discussion of the growing diversity in learners' language and communication skills and increasing use of video in instruction; focuses on the use of captioning in instructional video and the implications for educational and industrial training.

Hon, David. (1992, May). Butcher, baker, candlestick maker: Skills required for effective multimedia development. **Educational Technology, 32**(5), 14-19. EJ 446 157. (Available UMI.) Presents a matrix of skills for condensing time and materials, effecting rapid skills transfer, and managing feedback and evaluation.

The Jasper experiment: An exploration of issues in learning and instructional design. (1992). **Educational Technology, Research and Development, 40**(1), 65-80. EJ 446 172. (Available UMI.) Describes the Jasper Woodbury Problem Solving Series, a video-based instructional macrocontext for complex mathematics problem generation and solving.

Jones, Loretta L., and Smith, Stanley G. (1992, January-February). Can multimedia instruction meet our expectations? **EDUCOM Review, 27**(1), 39-43. EJ 441 738. (Available UMI.) Discusses differences in goals of multimedia and computer-assisted instruction and effective instructional uses of multimedia.

Lake, Daniel T. (1992, March). ART: Technologies in the curriculum. **Computing Teacher, 19**(6), 44-46. EJ 443 362. (Available UMI.) Describes the use of microcomputers and hypermedia with videodiscs and laser discs to teach art in three central New York schools.

Litchfield, Brenda C., and Dempsey, John V. (1992). A seven-stage quality control model for interactive videodisc projects. **Journal of Educational Technology Systems, 20**(2), 129-41. EJ 441 673. Discussion of videodisc instruction for education and training focuses on a seven-stage quality-control model for use with large development projects.

McMahon, Harry, and others. (1992, February). "Open" software design: A case study. **Educational Technology, 32**(2), 43-55. EJ 441 777. (Available UMI.) Discusses the use of *open software*, software that is essentially empty of content and can be customized by users to fit their own context.

Nelson, Wayne A., and Palumbo, David B. (1992). Learning, instruction, and hypermedia. **Journal of Educational Multimedia and Hypermedia, 1**(3), 287-99. EJ 448 904. Examines the psychological basis of hypermedia as a medium for learning, surveys the characteristics of current systems, and suggests ways to make hypermedia systems more valuable for instruction.

Park, Ok-choon. (1992). Instructional applications of hypermedia: Functional features, limitations, and research issues. **Computers in Human Behavior, 8**(2-3), 259-72. EJ 447 542. (Available UMI.) Discusses potentials of hypermedia for instructional delivery, idea generation and organization, file storage and organization, and development of computer-based instruction.

Reeves, Thomas C. (1992, May). Evaluating interactive multimedia. **Educational Technology, 32**(5), 47-53. EJ 446 164. (Available UMI.) Discusses the educational goals of interactive multimedia technology and methods of formative experimentation.

Shanahan, James, and Morgan, Michael. (1992). Adolescents, families and television in five countries: Implications for cross-cultural educational research. **Journal of Educational Television, 18**(1), 35-55. EJ 448 937. Examines results of a five-country study of television addressing broadcasting schedules, amount of viewing, social and family contexts in viewing, and parental attitudes.

Van Bergen, Marilyn A. (1992, July-August). Copyright law, fair use, and multimedia. **EDUCOM Review, 27**(4), 31-34. EJ 448 985. (Available UMI.) Examines issues related to copyright and how they affect the creation, protection, and distribution of multimedia materials.

Wohlers, Janet. (1992, January-February). The multimedia language lab. **Media and Methods, 28**(3), 38-40, 78. EJ 439 891. (Available UMI.) Describes the use of a multimedia language lab for teaching foreign languages and English as a Second Language, including hardware, visual databases, and vendors.

SIMULATION AND VIRTUAL REALITY

Media-Related Periodicals

Simulation and Gaming. Sage Publications, Inc., 2455 Teller Rd., Newbury Park, CA 91320. q.; $42 indiv., $125 inst. An international journal of theory, design, and research, published by the Association for Business Simulation and Experiential Learning.

Simulation/Games for Learning. Distribution Centre, Blackhorse Rd., Letchworth, Herts SG6 1HN, England. q.; £35. Main publication of the Society for the Advancement of Games and Simulations in Education and Training (SAGSET), which aims to encourage and develop the use of simulation and gaming techniques in applications in education and training.

Virtual Reality Report. Meckler Publishing, 11 Ferry Ln. W., Westport, CT 06880-5808. 9/yr.; $227. Covers developments in the field of virtual reality and cyberspace.

ERIC Documents

DeNardo, Anette, and Pyzdrowski, Anthony S. (1992, March). **The effects of teaching a hypothetical computer architecture with computer simulators**. Paper presented at the Annual Conference of the Eastern Educational Research Association, Hilton Head, South Carolina, March 5, 1992. ED 351 000. Reports on a study of the effects of using three simulators with 14 computer science majors enrolled in a computer architecture course.

Journal Articles

Ferrington, Gary, and Loge, Kenneth. (1992, April). Virtual reality: A new learning environment. **Computing Teacher, 19**(7), 16-19. EJ 446 198. (Available UMI.) Discusses virtual reality technology and its possible uses in military training, medical education, industrial design and development, the media industry, and education.

Helsel, Sandra. (1992, May). Virtual reality and education. **Educational Technology, 32**(5), 38-42. EJ 446 162. (Available UMI.) Describes the debate between conceptual and technological orientations to virtual reality and its impact on education.

Lanier, Jaron. (1992, October-December). Virtual reality: The promise of the future. **Interactive Learning International, 8**(4), 275-79. EJ 453 272. Defines *virtual reality* and discusses recent developments and applications, including experiential prototyping, telepresence, and educational applications.

Lederman, Linda Costigan. (1992, June). Debriefing: Toward a systematic assessment of theory and practice. **Simulation & Gaming, 23**(2), 145-60. EJ 447 569. (Available UMI.) Reviews the literature on debriefing and identifies the essential elements and phases of the debriefing process.

Middleton, Teresa. (1992, October-December). Applications of virtual reality to learning. **Interactive Learning International, 8**(4), 253-57. EJ 453 269. Describes the attributes of a virtual reality system and learning situations in which these attributes would play a key role.

Thiagarajan, Sivasailam. (1992, June). Using games for debriefing. **Simulation & Gaming, 23**(2), 161-73. EJ 447 570. (Available UMI.) Eight d-games (i.e., framegames that structure debriefing) related to the phases in the debriefing process are described, and applications of the d-games are illustrated with reference to a common base activity.

Wager, Walter W., and others. (1992). Simulations: Selection and development. **Performance Improvement Quarterly, 5**(2), 47-64. EJ 446 269. Examines factors affecting selection and development of computer simulations, including type of learner, simulation formats, instructional purposes, learning outcomes, fidelity, learning stages, and logistical issues.

TELECOMMUNICATIONS AND NETWORKING

Media-Related Periodicals

Canadian Journal of Educational Communication. Association for Media and Technology in Education in Canada, 3-1750 The Queensway, Suite 1318, Etobicoke, ON, M9C 5H5, Canada. q; $40 Canada, $50 U.S., $55 elsewhere. Concerned with all aspects of educational systems and technology.

Computer Communications. Butterworth-Heinemann, Ltd., Turpin Transactions, Ltd., Distribution Centre, Blackhorse Rd., Letchworth, Herts SG6 1HM, England. 10/yr.; £205 in UK and Europe, £225 elsewhere. Focuses on networking and distributed computing techniques, communications hardware and software, and standardization.

Data Communications. Box 473, Hightstown, NJ 08520. mo.; $95 U.S., $105 Canada. Provides users with news and analysis of changing technology for the networking of computers.

EDUCOM Review. EDUCOM, 1112 16th St. NW, Suite 600, Washington, DC 20036-4823. q.; $60 U.S., $70 elsewhere. Features articles on current issues and applications of computing and communications technology in higher education. Reports of EDUCOM consortium activities.

Electronic Networking: Research, Applications, and Policy. Meckler Corp., 11 Ferry Ln. W., Westport, CT 06880. q.; $95. A cross-disciplinary journal presenting research findings related to electronic networks, analyses of policy issues related to networking, and descriptions of current and potential applications of electronic networking for communication, computation, and provision of information services.

EMMS (Electronic Mail & Micro Systems). International Resource Development, Inc., Box 1716, New Canaan, CT 06840. semi-mo.; $535 U.S., $595 elsewhere. Covers technology, user, product, and legislative trends in graphic, record, and microcomputer applications.

Networking Management. Penn Well Publishing Co., Box 2417, Tulsa, OK 74101-2417. mo.; $42 (free to qualified individuals). Covers issues and applications for planning, support, and management of voice data networks.

Telecommunications. Horizon House Publications, Inc., 685 Canton St., Norwood, MA 02062. mo.; $60, free to qualified individuals. Features articles and news for the field of telecommunications.

T.I.E. News (Telecommunications in Education). International Society for Technology in Education, 1787 Agate St., Eugene, OR 97403-1923. q.; free to members of the SIG/Tel special interest group. Contains articles on all aspects of educational telecommunications.

Books

Kehoe, Brendan P. (1992). **Zen and the art of the Internet**. Available electronically on the Internet, through anonymous FTP, at host cd.widener.edu, directory pub/zen, filename zen-1.0.tar.z, zen-1.0.dvi, and zen-1.0.PS. An introductory reference work and foundation from which novice network users can explore the realm of Internet resources.

LaQuey, Tracy L. (1992). **The Internet companion: A beginner's guide to global networking**. Addison-Wesley Publishing, Route 128, Redding, MA 01867. 196pp. $10.95. Introduces the intricacies and workings of the Internet in clear, nontechnical language.

Waggoner, Michael D. (1992). **Empowering networks**. Educational Technology Publications, 700 Palisade Ave., Englewood Cliffs, NJ 07632. 263pp. $34.95. Highlights varied examples of computer-based telecommunications employed in education, including teacher training and professional development, distance learning, research collaborations, and more.

ERIC Documents

Newman, Denis, and others. (1992, May). **Local infrastructures for school networking: Current models and prospects. Technical report no. 22.** New York: Center for Technology in Education. ED 349 957. Discusses the need to retool schools with a local technical infrastructure that gives teachers and students immediate access to communication systems and information resources.

U.S. House of Representatives. Committee on Science, Space and Technology. (1992, July). **High definition information systems: Report prepared by the Subcommittee on Technology and Competitiveness transmitted to the Committee on Science, Space, and Technology**. Washington, DC: Government Printing Office. 31pp. ED 351 024. Describes the technical development of high-definition information systems and considers the far-reaching effects on international industrial competitiveness and on the American quality of life.

Journal Articles

Chapin, A. Lyman. (1992, September-October). The Internet Architecture Board and the future of the Internet. **EDUCOM Review, 27**(5), 42-45. EJ 453 218. (Available UMI.) Provides background on the Internet and describes the responsibilities of the Internet Architecture Board, Internet Engineering Task Force, and Internet Research Task Force.

Clement, John. (1992, September-October). Where we are in networking for K-12 education: A first annual review. **EDUCOM Review, 27**(5), 20-23. EJ 453 214. (Available UMI.) Examines developments including the High Performance Computing Act of 1991, national telecommunications proposals, participation in the National Research and Education Network, and the Consortium for School Networking.

Collis, Betty. (1992). Supporting educational uses of telecommunication in the secondary school: Part I. An overview of experiences. **International Journal of Instructional Media, 19**(1), 23-44. EJ 447 556. (Available UMI.) Uses a table to present brief descriptions, benefits, problems, and recommendations of 45 studies on the use of online databases and computer-mediated communication.

Deutsch, Peter. (1992, Spring). Resource discovery in an Internet environment—The Archie approach. **Electronic Networking: Research, Applications and Policy, 2**(1), 45-51. EJ 446 182. Describes the current scope and future development of Archie, an electronic indexing service for locating information on the Internet.

Duderstadt, James J. (1992, September-October). An information highway to the future. **EDUCOM Review, 27**(5), 36-41. EJ 453 217. (Available UMI.) Discussion of the evolution of a postindustrial, knowledge-based society addresses the importance of intellectual power and information technology as strategic resources, the development of the National Research and Education Network, and other topics.

Gore, Albert, Jr. (1992, September-October). The Information Infrastructure and Technology Act. **EDUCOM Review, 27**(5), 26-29. EJ 453 215. (Available UMI.) This statement highlights examples of applications of high-performance computing, the components of the Information Infrastructure Development Program, and participating agencies.

Polly, Jean Armour. (1992, June). Surfing the Internet. An introduction. **Wilson Library Bulletin, 66**(10), 38-42, 155. EJ 447 456. (Available UMI.) Describes resources of interest to librarians, including electronic newsletters and serials, online library catalogs, bulletin boards, software and text files, and others.

Roberts, Michael. (1992, May). A political perspective on the Internet and NREN. **Computers in Libraries, 12**(5), 58-61. EJ 446 261. (Available UMI.) Discusses the growth of computer information networks, the legislative process involved with creating the NREN, and future prospects for a National Information Infrastructure.

Roblyer, M. D. (1992, February). Electronic hands across the ocean: The Florida-England connection. **Computing Teacher, 19**(5), 16-19. EJ 439 910. (Available UMI.) Describes the development of a telecommunications network that links Florida schools with the United Kingdom's educational network, Campus 2000.

Index

This index gives page locations of names of associations and organizations, authors, titles, and subjects (bold entries indicate subjects). In addition, acronyms for all organizations and associations are cross-referenced to the full name. Please note that a classified list of U.S. organizations and associations appears on pages 164 to 170.

PCR: Films and Video in the Behavioral Sciences, 209
Pea, Roy D., 22, 26, 30
Pegasus Networks Communications Pty. Ltd., 110
Peled, Zimra, 316
Pelletier, Pierre, 316
Pennsylvania, professional education, 232, 263, 283
Pennsylvania State University, 4, 16, 232, 264, 283
Pepperdine University, 240
Perelman, Lewis J., 82
Performance & Instruction, 159, 160, 331
Performance Improvement Quarterly, 160, 332
"Performance Technology for Instructional Technologists: Comparisons and Possibilities," 326
Perkinson, Kathryn, 338
"Perspectives on Human-Computer Interface: Introduction and Overview," 330
PFA. *See* Pacific Film Archive
Photographic Society of America, 209
PIDT. *See* Professors of Instructional Design and Technology
Pinna, Anthony A., 342
Pitsch, Barry, 316
PLA. *See* Public Library Association
Planow, Mary, 55, 98
Plato, 99
Poirot, James L., 326
"Political Perspective on the Internet and NREN, A," 348
Pollock, Joellyn, 332
Polly, Jean Armour, 348
Portland State University, 263
"Portrait of a Staff Development Program," 326
Posey, Larry O., 332
"Postmortem on a Distance Education Course: Successes and Failures," 321
Potomac Company, 42
Powell, Ronald J., 329
"Power of Algebra, The," 88
"Power of Images: A Discourse Analysis of the Cognitive Viewpoint, The," 330
Power On!, 99
Prairie View A&M University, 266
Preparing Instructional Text, 327
"Prime Imperative: Building a Design Culture, The," 325
"Primer on Satellite Equipment, A," 321
Principles of Instruction, 332
"Print Prison, The," 339
"Process to Help Develop Your Picture, A," 339
Professors of Instructional Design and Technology, 209
Project CHOICE, 99-102
Project Gutenberg, 130
Project in Distance Education, 209
Project in Educational Technology, 210

"Promise of Early Radio and Television for Education—As Seen by the Nation's Periodical Press, The," 342
"Providing Computing for Distance Learners: A Strategy for Home Use," 321
PSA. *See* Photographic Society of America
Psychology of Hypermedia: A Conceptual Framework for R&D, A, 342
Public-Access Computer Systems Review, The, 335
Public Broadcasting Service, 210
Public Libraries, 335
Public Library Association, 174
Public Library Quarterly, 336
Public television, 87-90
Publish, 327
Puppeteers of America, 211
Purcell, James, 55, 78
Purdue University, 224, 248, 276
Purdue University-Calumet, 249
Pyzdrowski, Anthony S., 345

Qualitative Research in Information Management, 329

Radford University, 267
Radio Free Europe/Radio Liberty, 211
Rankin, Pauline M., 22, 44
RASD. *See* Reference and Adult Services Division
"Realism," 20, 56
Recording for the Blind, 211
Recording Industry Association of America, Inc., 211
Reeves, Thomas C., 344
Reference and Adult Services Division, 175
"Reference Services in Developing Countries," 340
Reiser, Brian J., 30
Rensselaer Polytechnic Institute, 80, 82
Report on the Survey of Microcomputers in Schools, 314
Research and Theory Division, 151, 180
Research in Distance Education, 320
Research in Science and Technological Education, 322
"Rescue at Boone's Meadow," 66
Resnick, L., 62
"Resource Discovery in an Internet Environment— The Archie Approach," 348
Resource Sharing and Information Networks, 318
Resources in Education (RIE), 322
Resta, Paul, 317
Review, 57
Reynolds, Dennis J., 327
Reynolds, Lynne, 333
Rezmierski, Virginia E., 330